IMISCOE Research Series

This series is the official book series of IMISCOE, the largest network of excellence on migration and diversity in the world. It comprises publications which present empirical and theoretical research on different aspects of international migration. The authors are all specialists, and the publications a rich source of information for researchers and others involved in international migration studies. The series is published under the editorial supervision of the IMISCOE Editorial Committee which includes leading scholars from all over Europe. The series, which contains more than eighty titles already, is internationally peer reviewed which ensures that the book published in this series continue to present excellent academic standards and scholarly quality. Most of the books are available open access.

More information about this series at http://www.springer.com/series/13502

Veronica Federico • Simone Baglioni

Editors

Migrants, Refugees and Asylum Seekers' Integration in European Labour Markets

A Comparative Approach on Legal Barriers and Enablers

 Springer

Editors
Veronica Federico
Department of Legal Sciences
University of Florence
Firenze, Italy

Simone Baglioni
Department of Economics and Management
University of Parma
Parma, Italy

ISSN 2364-4087   ISSN 2364-4095   (electronic)
IMISCOE Research Series
ISBN 978-3-030-67286-7   ISBN 978-3-030-67284-3   (eBook)
https://doi.org/10.1007/978-3-030-67284-3

This Springer imprint is published by the registered company Springer Nature Switzerland AG
The registered company address is: Gewerbestrasse 11, 6330 Cham, Switzerland

Introduction

'I want to work, I want to live. I am 20 years old. I sleep all day long. Today I got up at 11. This is not as it should be. My life is not as it should be'. (Asylum Seeker, Prato, 16 July 2019)

'Just let me work, please'. This is the persistent cry the authors of this volume recorded during the fieldwork that underlies the present publication. Working means earning a decent life for your family, making proper use of your knowledge and skills, expressing your individual self, climbing the social ladder, contributing to your community, and working to belong to a community and the wider society at large.

The research presented in this book investigates the legal *barriers* and *enablers* migrants, refugees and asylum seekers experience as they seek to enter and integrate into labour markets across seven European countries, six of which were EU member states at the time of research, and five after Brexit.

The Czech Republic, Denmark, Finland, Greece, Italy, Switzerland and the UK represent diversity under several aspects germane to our research: migration flows and migration governance regimes, labour market structure and economic parameters, rules on labour market access and working conditions, as well as Europeanisation processes.

Examining the legal barriers migrants, refugees and asylum seekers encounter and the enablers they make use of provides interesting insights that allow us to reflect on contemporary European societies' capacity to face the challenges and seize the opportunities of people moving across the planet – not only to escape from harsh living conditions due to wars, climate change, famines and persecutions, but also as they pursue better life chances and happiness for themselves and their families.

On the one hand, the book builds on the notion of *socio-spatial legal peripheries*, where discourses of inclusion and tolerance of diversity stand at odds with the real guarantee of fundamental rights in relation to democratic institutions and public administration services, and where basic human rights are systematically denied and become places where exclusion is widespread and intense.

On the other hand, the present volume draws on the understanding of social, economic, legal and personal factors as either *barriers* or *enablers*, elements that may facilitate or obstruct integration processes, and as such it contributes to developing integration theories. Interestingly, often the same factor may play both roles, depending on the group of people to whom it refers, the particular time or spatial dimension, providing evidence for an iterative dynamic understanding of integration factors.

Thus, the research presented in the volume focuses on the analysis of the hierarchy among migration statuses in terms of rights and entitlements related to the labour market. This entails scrutinising the two dimensions of integration. First, access to labour markets (translated into a rights-language: the right to work) with its corollaries (recognition of qualifications, vocational training, etc.). Second, non-discriminatory working conditions (translated into a rights-language: the right to both formal and substantial equality) and its corollaries of benefits and duties deriving from the fact of being part of the labour market. Overall, this gives us a more critical insight into the real working conditions of migrants, refugees and asylum seekers (MRAs) across European states.

Highlighting both specificities and common trends through combining the analytical tools of public comparative law research and a social science and policy-oriented analysis creates space for a critical discussion of the gap between the rhetoric of inclusion on the one hand, and the reality of legal status that hinders that very access to the labour market and its working conditions on the other. The identification of such 'legal peripheries' represents the *noyau dur* of the book, together with the identification of the barriers and enablers at both national and European levels.

Results presented in this volume were obtained through the research project *Skills and Integration of Migrants, Refugees and Asylum Applicants in European Labour Markets* (Sirius). This project was funded by the European Commission under the Horizon 2020 research and innovation programme (grant agreement 770515). The Sirius consortium was coordinated from January 2018 to March 2020 by the Glasgow Caledonian University (UK) and since then by the University of Parma (Italy). It included the University of Geneva (Switzerland), the European University Institute, the University of Florence (Italy), Charles University (Czech Republic), Roskilde University (Denmark), the University of Jyväskylä (Finland), the National Technical University of Athens (Greece), Solidar (Belgium), Solidarity Now (Greece) and the Multicultural Centre Prague (Czech Republic).

Data were collected through a combination of desk research of various sources (e.g. legal and policy documents, national and EU case law, research reports, and scientific literature), information requests to relevant institutions, and novel semi-structured interviews with legal and policy experts and academics held from March until May 2018 as part of the Horizon 2020 EU-funded project 'Sirius', and updated in December 2019 where they concern legal changes.

The first three chapters of the book begin by exploring the general frame that guided research at country level. Baglioni and Federico (Chap. 1) introduce a theoretical framework used for the individual chapter analysis, while Maggini (Chap. 2) discusses migration and asylum figures as well as and macro indicators of immigration and the labour market across the seven countries. Pannia (Chap. 3) discusses common trends and new developments of immigration law and asylum law, as well as their potential impact on MRAs labour market integration.

This contextualising opening part allows the subsequent nine chapters, based on a common research outline, to focus on the core business of the book: migrant, refugees and asylum seekers' integration in the labour markets in the Czech Republic (Čada and Hoření), Denmark (Bierre, Pace and Sen), Finland (Bontenbal and Lillie), Greece (Bagavos, Kourachanis, Lagoudakou and Chatzigiannakou), Italy (Chiaromonte and Federico), Switzerland (Mexi, Moreno Russi and Fernández Guzman) and the UK (Baglioni and Calò). Two chapters are devoted to the EU level: the first discusses the overarching legal framework related to migrants, refugees and asylum seekers' access to the labour markets and the anti-discrimination clauses (Gropas); the second focuses on the specific aspect of family reunification and labour market access in a gendered perspective (Isaakyan and Triandafyllidou).

This book appears at a time when an expected global pandemic has shown once more how important migrants' work is for our societies, and for our economies. In many European countries and beyond, the healthcare sector, which was on the frontline of the emergency due to its role in mitigating and contrasting the devastating effect of COVID-19, has heavily relied on migrant doctors, nurses and cleaners, and so have the agriculture and food production and supply chains, the waste collecting systems and the caregiving services. It will be wise for our societies and policy makers to learn from that experience and profit from what we unveil in this book about the too many barriers that still obstruct migrants and refugees' access to work and make a wise use of the enabling solutions we propose for a fairer, healthier and wealthier Europe.

Contents

About the Editors

Veronica Federico is Associate Professor of Public Comparative Law at the University of Florence. Her research interests include comparative migration law; African constitutional law; constitutional and democratic transitions; fundamental rights. She has participated in various multidisciplinary international research projects, among which the Sirius research.

Simone Baglioni is Professor of Sociology in the Department of Economics and Management at the University of Parma, Italy. His research interests include labour migration, forced migration, youth unemployment and the gig economy, civil society and social innovation. He is the PI and coordinator of the Sirius project.

Chapter 1
Europe's Legal Peripheries: Migration, Asylum and the European Labour Market

Veronica Federico and Simone Baglioni

1.1 Introduction

The participation of foreign nationals in European labour markets is an effective tool that facilitates those migrants enjoying a more fulfilling life, while at the same time contributing to Europe's wealth and economic and social development. However, many norms that regulate migration and labour migration undermine this spirit by limiting, both directly and indirectly, non-EU nationals' access to European labour markets.

From a legal perspective, the integration of non-EU migrants, refugees and asylum seekers (MRAs) depends on the country in which they settle and the legal status it affords them there. Entry and settlement into European countries is subject to strict limitations for non-EU nationals, but such limitations, far from promoting an integrated European legal space, take different shapes according to the European country and migrant status. Being a so-called 'economic migrant' with a long-term permit to stay entitles the beneficiary to a broader set of rights than is the case for a migrant with a short-term permit; similarly, a refugee is entitled to a much broader set of rights than an asylum seeker; while an asylum seeker is endowed with a smaller pattern of rights and benefits to a migrant benefiting from a complementary (compared to Geneva 1951) form of protection status. Furthermore, when labour market participation is at stake, as we discuss later in this chapter, an asylum seeker or beneficiary of a complementary form of protection is endowed with different rights and opportunities across Europe: he or she can work from the time of lodging

V. Federico (✉)
Department of Legal Sciences, University of Florence, Firenze, Italy
e-mail: veronica.federico@unifi.it

S. Baglioni
Department of Economics and Management, University of Parma, Parma, Italy
e-mail: simone.baglioni@unipr.it

© The Author(s) 2021
V. Federico, S. Baglioni (eds.), *Migrants, Refugees and Asylum Seekers' Integration in European Labour Markets*, IMISCOE Research Series,
https://doi.org/10.1007/978-3-030-67284-3_1

their application with different time-ban limits depending on the country they enter (ranging from 60 days in Italy to 1 year in the UK), while they are prevented from working at all in others.

This chapter discusses to what extent specific legal frameworks of migration and asylum work as either *enablers* or *barriers* to non-EU MRAs integration in European labour markets across seven countries: the Czech Republic, Denmark, Finland, Greece, Italy, Switzerland, and the United Kingdom. It argues that, in the last decade, a plethora of legal acts and the spirit of border closure and securisation that inspires them, have created a hierarchy among migration statuses in terms of the rights and entitlements related to the labour market. This hierarchy considerably influences the degree of transferability of newcomers' work-related capabilities when they move from their country of origin to the new country of settlement. At the top of the hierarchy in terms of rights are refugees and beneficiaries of subsidiary protection, along with long-term economic migrants, who are endowed with the stronger sets of rights, including those related to accessing the labour market and workers' rights and benefits. In other words, refugees, beneficiaries of subsidiary protection and long-term economic migrants are those who are closer to nationals in terms of fundamental rights and integration into labour markets (except political rights that fall beyond the remit of our research and, importantly, except the freedom of movement and settlement reserved to EU nationals). At the bottom of the hierarchy come asylum seekers, and below them irregular migrants who can count on a much stricter set of rights and entitlements. When rights and entitlements are mentioned here with reference to labour markets, we do not only refer to accessing work but also to those services conducive to employment such as skills and the recognition of educational attainment, but also access to vocational education and training.

However, it is worth noticing the size of the migrant population to which each status applies. In fact, among the countries we examine here – except in Denmark and Switzerland – only a minority of people applying for protection are recognised by a status conferring access to a broad set of rights, including those connected to labour market participation, and even a smaller number is recognised by the Geneva convention status (asylum and subsidiary protection). Hence, most non-EU migrants who *de facto* stay in a given host country remain at the bottom of the rights hierarchy.

We can visualise the hierarchy of rights as a pyramid (Fig. 1.1). The status conferred to the very few at the top would guarantee rights leading to an almost-equal to nationals' access and use of the labour market, while the more we move down the pyramid, the fewer these rights are, although far more individuals find themselves at those lower levels of the hierarchy. Finally, we need to clarify that in this introductory chapter and throughout the book as a whole we focus on the *de jure* aspect, and do not discuss the implementation of such rights in detail (we do that elsewhere, cfr. Lillie and Bontebal 2019).

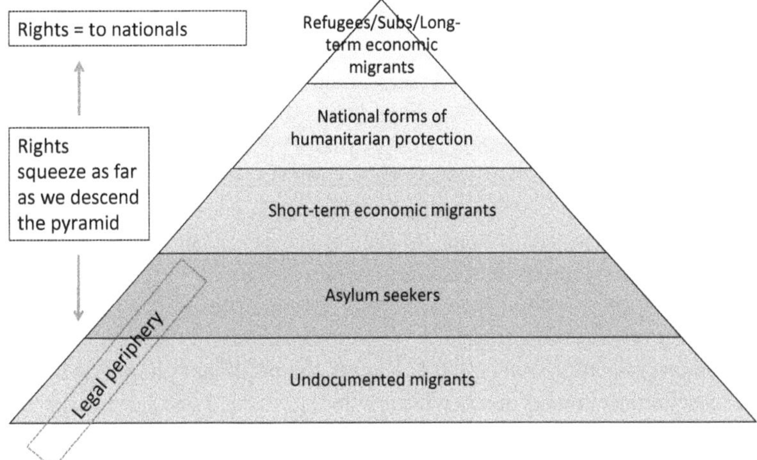

Fig. 1.1 Summarises the 'hierarchy of status and rights' model that the chapter discusses

A relevant consideration is the diversity of norms across states. As we discuss in Paola Pannia's chapter in this volume, the sole convergence we notice among European countries – and in particular among those studied here – is a convergence towards limiting access and long-term settlement for all categories of non-EU migrants, including those who used to be preserved from stricter limitations, such as asylum seekers and refugees. Despite the process of harmonization at EU level and regardless of the rhetorical claim of a more cogent Europeanisation of migration governance, nation states remain the dominant actor in this field, our research suggests that policy-makers are often more concerned with responding to public opinion than providing a coherent legal framework [as discussed in Pannia's and Maggini's chapters].

Overall, our book contributes to debating the existence in Europe of 'legal peripheries' (Chouinard 2001: 187), those spaces where a gap exists between narratives of inclusion and equality, and the legal provisions and their implementation supposed to support and justify such narratives, and we do that by discussing labour market-related rights for non-EU migrants, refugees and asylum seekers.

The chapter begins with a short introduction to the selection rationale for our countries under study. It turns to some reflections on MRAs' integration in European labour markets, distinguishing between legal provisions that grant access to those labour markets and provisions that ensure MRAs work as nationals do. Our concluding remarks point to four streams of consideration in terms of barriers and enablers to MRAs' integration into European labour markets.

1.1.1 Our Contexts

The seven countries examined here provide a variety of insights into MRAs' integration in European labour markets. Despite the harmonisation effort at EU level, variety across countries persists. This is partly due to countries being affected differently by migration flows, so that numbers of refugees, beneficiaries of subsidiary and humanitarian protection and of asylum seekers on the one hand, and of economic migrants, on the other, largely differ. However, states also have different legal and political systems that impact how authorities, citizens and organizations react to migration inflows. The countries we discuss in this chapter present a diverse constitutional organization of state. In fact, they have been explicitly selected to encompass a wide spectrum of variability, while remaining in the general frame of contemporary western liberal democracies. The countries under study mirror the diversity of European landscapes in terms of the structure of the state, the system of government, rights enforcement and litigation, the political system and the cultural and socio-economic background, while allowing at the same time for systematic comparison. The cleavage between the one country belonging to the common law system (the UK) and the others that are characterized by civil law systems is nuanced, and, at the same time, enriched by intertwining with other cleavages: centralized versus federal states; symmetric versus asymmetric decentralization (or devolution); constitutional monarchies versus republics; parliamentarian (in various typologies) versus semi-presidential and directorial systems of government; diffuse versus centralized (with the presence of a Constitutional Court) systems of judicial review. All countries except Switzerland and the United Kingdom are EU member states (and the UK was still part of the EU when we conducted our analyses), so they relate to the EU legal framework. Moreover, diverse mechanisms of rights enforcement and litigation among these countries add further texture to the analysis of the constitutional and legal framework.

Diversity is also the keyword in the discussion of the political systems, counting bi-party systems, pluri-party systems, even-multiparty systems, fragmented party systems; as well as in the discussion of the democratic model: majoritarian and consensus democracies, semi-direct and consociational democracies. The socio-economic background of the countries is no less so diverse, as the Czech Republic, Denmark, Finland, Greece, Italy, Switzerland, and the UK are characterized by the whole range of variation, with Greece representing the most deprived economic landscape and Denmark and Switzerland holding the most affluent positions. Diversity also describes the labour markets, *sufficit* here to recall that when the countries were chosen for our study, that is in 2016, the unemployment rate in the Czech Republic, United Kingdom and Switzerland was under 5% (and has remained so according to the last OECD available data up to December 2019), well below the EU28 average of 8.6% (which decreased to 6.1% by December 2019), while Finland had an unemployment level close to the EU28 average (as is still the case), whereas Italy and Greece were (and still are) above EU28 average: 11.7% in Italy and 23.6% in Greece (respectively 9.6% and 16.6% by December 2019).

1.2   Integration into the Labour Markets?

There is broad consensus that whether and how migrants, asylum seekers and refugees integrate into labour markets, and the time it takes for them to do so, determines not only their long-term impact on European economies but also their prospects for integrating socially and economically into European societies, and therefore their capacity to contribute to the overall wellbeing of the continent (Ruiz and Vargas-Silva 2017, 2018; Marbach et al. 2018; Zwysen 2019; Brell et al. 2020). The UNHCR experience reveals that early integration is desirable for at least three reasons: it is the most effective, efficient and meaningful method of facilitating this target group's integration into European societies; it can alleviate pressure on the public purse; it can help address current and future labour market shortages in the EU (UNHCR 2013).

We consider two main dimensions of the integration of refugees, asylum seekers and migrants into the labour markets: *(i)* access to the labour market (translated into a rights-language: the right to work) with its corollaries (recognition of qualifications, vocational training, etc.); and *(ii)* non-discriminatory working conditions (translated into a rights-language: the right to both formal and substantial equality) and its corollaries of benefits and duties deriving from being part of the labour market.

1.2.1   Accessing the Labour Market

Accessing the labour market means being entitled to work. In principle, allowing asylum seekers, refugees and migrants to work should be a win-win game: it empowers MRAs in both economic and socio-cultural terms, and it benefits the hosting societies that can profit from the skills, energy, competences and also taxes produced by MRAs' activities (Kahanec and Zimmermann 2009, 2016; Zimmermann 2014; Blau and Mackie 2016). However, due to either a real scarcity in jobs or a rhetorically constructed one, 'foreigners' (with no distinctions made between refugees and economic migrants) can often be perceived and portrayed in public discourses as 'job stealers' from native-born workers, regardless of labour market segmentation, which, in several countries, keep natives and migrants in separate labour market segments and therefore not competing for the same jobs (Ambrosini 2001; Allievi 2018).

Limits on the right to access national labour markets exist, and they are not necessarily connected with dire economic conditions since they pre-existed the last decade of economic crisis. For example, the Italian Constitution recognises the right to work for citizens only (art. 4), which means that Italian workers have preferential access to the labour market: before applying for the sponsorship of a third country national worker, employers must prove there is no relevant workforce available in the country. The same happens, for example, in Switzerland, where according to the "precedence provision" of the Federal Act on Foreign Nationals, third country workers can be admitted into the Swiss labour market only if no Swiss citizen or foreign national with a long-term residence permit or an EU/EFTA national can be recruited. Also in Finland, law No. 1218/2013 provides for the "availability test" to grant Finnish and EU/EEA citizens priority in entering employment.

There are different limitations on the right to access the labour market: limitations based on the nationality of the worker (as it is the case of the aforementioned limits in Italy, Switzerland and Finland); limitations based on the foreign legal status (as illustrated in Table 1.1 and discussed later in this chapter) and limitations based on workers' skills and qualifications, as is discussed later.

In principle, in none of the countries considered here are refugees, beneficiaries of subsidiary protection and of other forms of national protection limited in their access to the labour market. This means that *de jure* they can work, if they wish to do so, and they do not need further work permits. However, this does not mean that *de facto* they do access national labour markets, since they may experience other forms of constraint such as language barriers, spatial barriers (several countries adopt dispersal policies which compel refugees to live in areas where there are no available suitable vacancies, for example, and their effective mobility in the country may be more limited than nationals experience), and qualifications and skills barriers (their qualifications may not be recognised in the host countries and the skills required for specific tasks may be different from those they used to in their country of origin).

By contrast, asylum seekers experience time limitations in all our countries (Greece was the only exception until December 2019, when asylum seekers were allowed to work as soon as they lodged their application. But since January 2020 the new International Protection Act L.4636/2019 has introduced a 6-month employment ban for asylum seekers). Obviously, the same considerations on the *de facto* barriers persist in this case once asylum seekers are allowed to enter the labour market. It is interesting to have a graphical representation of the time barriers to asylum seekers' entry into national labour markets (Fig. 1.2), as this may be considered one good indicator of the country's openness to MRAs' integration, given that evidence suggests that the sooner an immigrant or asylum seeker/refugee enters the labour market, the quicker and smoother her/his integration path would be.

Moreover, Fig. 1.2 is clear concerning harmonisation at the EU level: seven jurisdictions present six different time-limits for asylum seekers to access domestic labour markets. Actually, in Finland there are two different options: asylum seekers can work after 3 months since lodging their application if they travel with valid identification documents, or after 5 months in the case they do not possess such documents. Hence, there is no consistency across these European countries in terms of rights for asylum seekers when entering the labour market. Some allow asylum seekers to work after a short period (Italy after 60 days), while others prevent them accessing the labour market for at least 1 year (the Czech Republic and the UK, in the latter, the 1 year ban from the labour market stretches even longer periods given that only those applicants who possess high skills can enter after 1 year, the rest have to wait until their claim is assessed, which can take also a couple of years).

Table 1.1 Right to work- Sirius project countries

	Asylum seekers	Refugees	Subsidiary protection	National form of temporary protection	Economic migrants- short term	Economic migrants – long term	Undocumented migrants
Czech Rep.	YES after 1 year stay	YES	YES	YES	YES if the worker has a contract prior to entering the country	YES	NO
Denmark	YES after 6 months stay	YES	YES	YES	YES but with a work permit	YES but with a work permit	NO
Finland	YES after 3 months stay if they have travel documents/5 months without them	YES	YES	–	YES but with a work permit	YES but with a work permit	NO
Greece	YES after 6 months stay	YES	YES	–	YES subject to the labour market's demand	YES	NO
Italy	YES after 60 days from application of refugee status	YES	YES	YES	YES subject to the labour market's demand	YES subject to the labour market's demand	NO – But if they work, they have certain labour rights
Switzerland	YES, after 3 months if the labour market allows	YES	YES	YES, after request for work permit	YES if allowed by the conditions for permit to stay	YES	NO – But if they work, they have certain labour rights
UK	YES, after 12 months but only in shortage occupation list	YES	YES	YES	NO	YES with specific visa	NO

Source: Sirius project

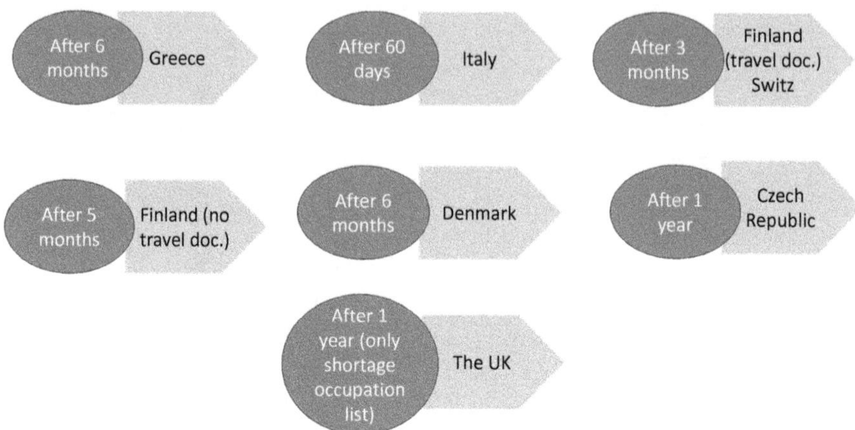

Fig. 1.2 Time limit to asylum seekers' access to national labour markets. (Source: Sirius project)

More complex is the position of so-called 'economic migrants', people who migrate to another country primarily to seek work and better life conditions, or for family reunification (as is discussed in detail in Isaakyan and Triandafyllidou in this volume). None of our countries opens its labour market unconditionally to third country nationals. Work permits are required in every country for extra EU citizens, and the possibility of working in such countries depends on the triangulation between the needs of national labour (determined on an annual basis by specific policy documents issued either by the Ministry of Interior or by the Ministry of Labour, as in Italy for example), or on a case-by case approach (as it is the case in Finland) and migrants' skills and qualifications. Curiously, but not surprisingly, limitations do not apply to highly specialised workers, who benefit from special conditions of entry, quite often beyond the implementation of the Blue Card directive 2009/50/EC. In Denmark, for example, a number of job schemes aim to attract high skilled labour and encourage quick and facilitated employment. In Finland, highly-skilled migrants receive their residence permits directly from the Finnish Immigration Service through an *ad hoc* procedure; in the UK 'Tier 1 visas' are reserved for people with exceptional talents in the fields of science, humanities, engineering, medicine, digital technology and art, or if they aim to invest at least £2 million in the country.

Finally, although irregular migrants' role in European labour markets is by definition left in the 'shadow' of policy consideration, in some jurisdictions the position of undocumented migrants is not fully overlooked. In Greece, for example, a 2016 circular opens access to the labour market in specific sectors (agriculture, domestic work, animal husbandry) to immigrants in the grey area between legality and illegality. In Italy, no formal access for undocumented migrants exists, but the law offers some forms of protection to undocumented migrants, even though a recent law (Law 199/2016) to contrast labour exploitation and exploitative labour intermediation could provide more instruments to fight against informal employment (for a further discussion of this law see: Chiaromonte et al. 2018).

1.2.2 Working as Nationals Do

The countries considered here enforce the joint principles of equality in working conditions and benefits and of non-discrimination for all workers once they have entered their labour markets, regardless of their citizenship or length of stay in the country. In the field of non-discrimination, a number of European directives (*Directive* 2000/43/EC *against discrimination* on grounds of race and ethnic origin; *Directive* 2006/54/EC on equal opportunities and equal treatment of women and men in employment and occupation; *Directive 2007/78/EC* against discrimination at work on grounds of religion or belief, disability, age or sexual orientation) have played a crucial role in harmonizing legislation in the different jurisdictions.

Yet, the formal absence of discriminations in the workplace and unequal working conditions does not naturally lead to MRAs working as nationals do, since they may encounter significant barriers that elude legal provisions focusing on formal equality (everyone is equal before the law) and on non-discrimination because they pertain to the sphere of substantial equality. However, we focus here on several aspects related to the concrete enforcement of the right to work, sometimes incorporated on framework immigration legislation, sometimes provided for in specific regulations, that contribute to overcoming substantial barriers.

Linguistic barriers are paramount; all our jurisdictions acknowledge the importance of language skills as a first step to integrating into the host society. Nonetheless, language courses are not offered for free everywhere, this is one field where space is left for collaboration with non-state entities, both non-profit and for profit companies. Moreover, attending language courses is rarely a duty imposed on MRAs. The duty exists solely in those countries where attending civic integration programs is compulsory: in Denmark for all MRAs except economic migrants, but as a requirement for those applying for permanent residency; in Finland for refugees, beneficiaries of subsidiary protection as well as for short and long stay economic migrants some welfare benefits, such as unemployment benefits are conditional on participation in integration programs that include language courses – and this *de facto* creates a duty, whereas it is not compulsory for asylum seekers; in Italy language proficiency is requested for both integration agreements (for refugees and beneficiaries of the former humanitarian protection regime) and integration programs (for long-staying economic migrants), whereas for asylum seekers some reception centres impose a duty on language course attendance. No duty exists in the Czech Republic, Greece, Switzerland (except for short-term economic migrants in those cantons where signing an integration convention is required to access social assistance), and in the UK.

The recognition of qualifications and competences is crucial for MRAs to work as nationals do, yet the majority of the countries examined here lag behind what substantial equality would entail in this field, as Table 1.2 clearly shows. Only Denmark, Switzerland and Italy (with the exception of asylum seekers) are open to the recognition of foreign titles and qualifications, even though in Italy the recognition process may be long and complex, substantially jeopardising the

Table 1.2 Recognition of qualifications/skills, Sirius project countries

	Asylum seekers	Refugees	Subsidiary protection	National form of temporary protection	Economic migrants, short term	Economic migrants – long term	Undocum migrants
Czech Rep.	YES upon evidence of formal qualifications	YES upon evidence of formal qualifications	YES upon evidence of formal qualifications	YES upon evidence of formal qualifications	YES upon evidence of formal qualifications	YES upon evidence of formal qualifications	NO
Denmark	NO	YES	YES	YES	YES	YES	NO
Finland	YES but with proof of citizenship	YES but with proof of citizenship	YES but with proof of citizenship	–	YES but with proof of citizenship	YES but with proof of citizenship	NO
Greece	YES upon evidence of formal qualifications	YES upon evidence of formal qualifications	YES upon evidence of formal qualifications	–	YES upon evidence of formal qualifications	YES upon evidence of formal qualifications	NO
Italy	YES upon evidence of formal qualifications	YES	YES	YES	YES	YES	NO
Switzerland	YES	YES	YES	YES	YES	YES	NOs
UK	Depending from country of origin and/or qualification	Depending from country of origin and/or qualification	Depending from country of origin and/or qualification	Depending from country of origin and/or qualification	Depending from country of origin and/or qualification	Depending from country of origin and/or qualifications	NO

Source: Sirius project

legitimate expectations of migrants. The UK recognises exclusively qualifications from selected countries of origin, on the basis of a common table of conversion. In the Czech Republic and in Greece, the formal equalisation of qualifications is substantially undermined by the requirement of the official certificates issued by competent authorities. Of course, this may be considered fair towards economic migrants, who, in principle, can plan their migration trajectory, whereas people fleeing from their country will hardly bring proofs of their diplomas, and requiring them to national authorities once in a host country sounds undoubtedly odd. In between lies Finland, where not diplomas but proof of citizenship is required to allow for fair conversions. Noticeably, in all countries where this is allowed, MRAs must apply for recognition, in the most favourable of cases, as in Finland, this is done during the application process.

Another relevant field to consider when discussing whether foreigners work as nationals do is vocational training. Vocational education and training is a relevant component of current active labour market policies, useful for easing young people's access to the labour market. It is equally a useful tool to facilitate migrants, refugees and asylum applicants' integration into their host societies (Flisi et al. 2016). Vocational qualifications can be particularly valuable for skilled refugees and economic migrants to find adequate employment, while for illiterate and poorly educated refugees and migrants, long-term vocational programmes could be a strategic target for investment. Does our pool of countries offer access to vocational training to third country nationals?

In Greece and Finland, all migrants except undocumented people can access vocational training on the same basis as Greek and Finnish citizens. In Italy and in Switzerland in addition to the undocumented migrant exception, asylum seekers may be restrained from vocational training either because there are no courses available in the reception centres (the Italian case), or because the courses length exceeds the asylum seeker's temporary permit to stay. In Denmark, only refugees, beneficiaries of subsidiary protection and of temporary protection status (the Danish national form of temporary protection) are entitled to vocational training, from which economic migrants are excluded, whereas in the UK, even though not formally entitled to by specific legal provisions, vocational training is open to refugees and beneficiaries of subsidiary protection (that in the UK is named humanitarian protection), by contrast, asylum seekers are excluded, but not in Scotland, where devolved legislation opens the door of vocational training also to them. Economic migrants may benefit from these measures, but with limits due to the type of visa they hold. Finally, in the Czech Republic neither asylum seekers nor short term economic migrants nor beneficiaries of national forms of temporary protection can access vocational training, that is open to refugees, beneficiaries of subsidiary protection and long-term economic migrants, who, in case of unemployment, can participate in the retraining schemes available to nationals.

Unemployment benefits are another important element for understanding legal barriers and enablers for MRAs' integration in the labour market. Switzerland and Italy are the countries that present fewer restrictions in accessing unemployment benefits: all are entitled as nationals are, except undocumented migrants and asylum seekers not allowed to work in Switzerland, and asylum seekers after 2 years of contributions – which is a tricky condition to impose on people with a temporary status. In Denmark, only refugees and long-term economic migrants holding a permanent residency permit can receive unemployment benefits. In Finland, unemployment benefits are made conditional upon permanent residency, which entails that neither asylum seekers nor short-time economic migrants are included. In Greece, refugees, beneficiaries of subsidiary protection and long-term economic migrants can access the unemployment register and receive all benefits and services as Greek citizens do, whereas asylum seekers can do so only after having completed the application procedure. The situation in the UK is not so different, since refugees and beneficiaries of subsidiary protections are equalised to British citizens, but long-term economic migrants must be granted the indefinite leave to remain in the UK to claim benefits. Similarly, in the Czech Republic, solely refugees, beneficiaries of subsidiary protection and long-term economic migrants are entitled to benefits.

Finally, we make a comparative assessment of the rights to self-employment and working in the public sector, as illustrated by Table 1.3.

Except in Greece, where the public sector is fully reserved to nationals only, in all jurisdictions refugees can both work as public officers (with exceptions of some crucial positions – high-ranking positions or extremely delicate jobs in terms of national security, for example – may be reserved for nationals) and as self-employed, and the same applies to long-term economic migrants. The strongest restrictions exist for asylum seekers and short-term economic migrants, which may be explained by the precariousness of the status for the former and by the time element for the latter.

Considering the variables described so far, not all foreign workers can enjoy the very same rights and benefits as national workers. They may be excluded from certain positions because they are reserved for nationals, or because their qualifications and skills are not recognised or not fully recognised, or because they do not speak the language fluently enough, or because they have limited access to vocational training. Lowering the barriers that prevent MRAs from working as nationals do would release important energies and capacities that could positively contribute to host societies' economic growth, social well-being and peaceful coexistence between populations.

1.3 More Barriers than Enablers? Concluding Remarks

Migrants, refugees and asylum applicants occupy a central position in public and political debates. The 'migration issue' has been the object of regular headlines in all the countries discussed in this chapter, and in the past 5 years much political tension at the EU level has stemmed from this topic. MRAs represent an asset for European ageing societies and their labour-demanding economies, as claimed by both academic and think tank literature (Benton et al. 2014; OECD 2016; IMF

Table 1.3 Right to self-employment and to work in the public sector, Sirius project countries

		Asylum applicants	Refugees	Subsidiary protection	National form of temporary protection	Economic migrants – short term	Economic migrants – long term	Undocumented migrants
CZ.	Self empl.	NO	YES	YES	NO	YES	YES	NO
	Public sector	YES (with exceptions)	YES (with exceptions)	YES (with exceptions)	YES (with exceptions)	YES (with exceptions)	YES (with exceptions)	NO
DK	Self empl.	NO	YES	NO	NO	NO	NO (unless permanent resident)	NO
	Public sector	NO	YES	YES	YES	YES	YES	NO
Fin	Self empl.	YES after 3 months and with valid documents	YES	YES	–	YES	YES	NO
	Public sector	YES (with exceptions)	YES (with exceptions)	YES (with exceptions)	–	YES (with exceptions)	YES (with exceptions)	NO
Gr	Self empl.	NO	YES	YES	–	NO	YES	NO
	Public sector	NO	NO	NO	NO	NO	NO	NO
It	Self empl.	YES	YES	YES	YES	NO	YES	NO
	Public sector	NO	YES (with exceptions)	YES (with exceptions)	YES (with exceptions)	NO	YES only EU (with exceptions)	NO

(continued)

Table 1.3 (continued)

		Asylum applicants	Refugees	Subsidiary protection	National form of temporary protection	Economic migrants – short term	Economic migrants – long term	Undocumented migrants
CH	Self empl	NO	YES (with exceptions)	YES (with exceptions)	YES (with exceptions)	YES (with exceptions)	YES	NO
	Public sector	YES (with exceptions)	YES (with exceptions)	YES (with exceptions)	YES (with exceptions)	YES (with exceptions)	YES (with exceptions)	NO
UK	Self empl.	NO	YES	YES	YES	YES (with limits)	YES (with specific visa	NO
	Public sector	NO (only if in Tier 2 shortage list)	YES	YES	YES	NO	YES	NO

Source: Sirius project

2016). Moreover, they have become central in the functioning of contemporary European societies, since without their contribution, for example in domestic work and care services, social structures would be very different (Ambrosini 2013). Yet, when we focus on their legal status, we realise that the central role migrants play in our societies does not reflect on their rights entitlements. On the contrary, most of them, in particular migrants with national temporary forms of protection, or awaiting an asylum decision, or living as undocumented people, hold a peripheral and often precarious position in terms of substantial rights and entitlements.

The comparative analysis of their right to be legally recognised the workers status (and subsequently a permit to stay and to work) in the European countries discussed in this chapter on the one hand, and to have a number of other rights stemming from this – first of all the rights to work as nationals do – on the other, demonstrates the legal marginalization of MRAs in European jurisdictions, despite narratives of inclusiveness. Scholars describe this phenomenon as the "production of legal peripheries or places in which law as discursively represented and law lived are fundamentally at odds" (Chouinard 2001: 187). Similarly to spatial and geographical peripheries, legal peripheries may have a detrimental effect on the wellbeing of both the people populating, physically and metaphorically, the peripheries, and also those populating the centres. Analysing how the frontiers between centres and peripheries are being built and consolidated is one of the *foci* of our research, to point out possible strategies to empower MRAs and to advance those rights aiming at social inclusion and participation in the same spaces of life as nationals do.

The first, already understood but nevertheless disturbing, finding emerging from the analysis of the status quo of MRA-related legislation and of their rights and entitlements in the policy-domain of labour in the selected jurisdictions analyses here is the deep unevenness existing among countries. On the one hand, regardless of the European competence on asylum policy, there is no proper 'Europeanization' of asylum policy and law; immigration remains one of those domains in which states are reluctant to devolve their authority to supranational jurisdictions. Despite the numerous limitations to national sovereignty brought in by EU membership, the crucial state prerogative of modern, post-Westphalian statehood, that is the decision about who should be admitted into the state territory and with which entitlements, still holds when non-EU nationals and asylum seekers are at stake.

More specifically, the EU fundamental principle of non-discrimination in labour markets is at odds with the reality of MRAs because of both their differentiated legal statuses (as not all legal statuses give access to the same rights) and the different approaches that countries adopt concerning each migrant status. On the other hand, this lack of homogeneity among countries makes it difficult for people, both foreign workers and employers, to understand who has the right to do what, when, how and where in Europe. Moreover, legal uncertainty favours secondary movements, i.e. refugees and beneficiaries of humanitarian or subsidiary forms of protection moving from one host country to another in search for better life and working conditions (Moret et al. 2006), which is one of the phenomena the Dublin Convention in 1990 and the Dublin Regulations II and III aim to avoid. In turn, this makes the overall migration management more complex and difficult and it can provide arguments for political and social entrepreneurs willing to capitalise on anti-migration attitudes. In sum, the lack of homogeneity among EU member states about the rights associated to specific categories of migrants constitutes a barrier for MRAs integration in labour markets and societies, even though sometimes it may create comparative advantages for determined people or categories of people in given situations.

The second observation pertains to the complexity of the legal frameworks. In all countries examined here, the legal framework on labour market integration is the result of a complex and rapidly changing legislation and of an institutional landscape scattered in a multiplicity of actors at different levels of government, from supranational to local. Legal statuses do not equalise in terms of rights and benefits, so that being recognised as a refugee makes a difference in terms of general fundamental rights and in terms of both accessing the labour market and working as nationals do. Complexity is definitely not an enabler of integration and equality.

Thirdly, despite the differences among countries, if we compare legal statuses across types of migrants, in all the countries examined here we can see the creation of a hierarchy in terms of access to rights and therefore in terms of capacity and opportunity of integration. Refugees and, to a smaller extent, beneficiaries of subsidiary protection and long-term economic migrants are at the top of the hierarchy, endowed with the broader and stronger sets of rights, including those related to accessing the labour market, workers' rights and benefits. In other words, refugees, beneficiaries of subsidiary protection and long-term economic migrants are those who move closer to nationals concerning fundamental labour-related rights. However, the very important differences are that (a) they do not benefit from the freedom of movement across Europe, and (b) political rights, that fall beyond the remit of our analysis. Moreover, the legal status may allow refugees, beneficiaries of subsidiary protection and long-term economic migrants to benefit from further important opportunities of integration (language courses, vocational training) neglected by other types of migrant, strengthening their chances to join the labour market. This means that legal statuses play a crucial role in enabling people to become full members of the host societies and to contribute to the overall well-being of those societies through, among others, a full participation in national labour markets. At the bottom of the hierarchy we find irregular migrants, and just above them, asylum seekers, both categories of migrants with the most restrictive access to rights and entitlements allowing them to enter an integration path.

Legal statuses may have a strong empowering effect, and may reconcile the centre-periphery conflicts inherent to the hierarchy legal statuses create. Widening the access to these statuses or enlarging rights and benefits connected with other statuses would multiply the enabling effect of a legal status easing integration of foreign workers. It would also avoid the creation of a migrant winner-looser divide, which would be at odds with any human rights, and a solidarity-based understanding of what a modern society should be.

References

Allievi, S. (2018). *Immigrazione: cambiare tutto*. Roma-Bari: Laterza.

Ambrosini, M. (2001). *La fatica di integrarsi*. Bologna: il Mulino.

Ambrosini, M. (2013). *Immigrazione irregolare e welfare invisibile*. Bologna: il Mulino.

Benton, M. et al. (2014). *Aiming higher: Policies to get immigrants into middle-skilled work in Europe*. Migration Policy Institute and International Labour Organization Publications. Available at: https://www.migrationpolicy.org/sites/default/files/publications/DG-OVR-EmplPolicy.pdf

Blau, F. D., & Mackie, C. (Eds.). (2016). *The economic and fiscal consequences of immigration*. Washington, DC: A Report of the National Academies.

Brell, C., Dustmann, C., & Preston, I. (2020). The labor market integration of refugee migrants in high-income countries. *The Journal of Economic Perspectives, 34*(1), 94–121.

Chiaromonte, W., Pannia, P., Federico, V., D'Amato, S., & Maggini, N. (Eds.). (2018). *Legal barriers and enablers to labour market integration of migrants, refugees and asylum applicants in European Labour Markets*. Research report submitted as a formal deliverable of the EU H2020 project Sirius. https://www.sirius-project.eu/publications/wp-reports-results

Chouinard, V. (2001). Legal peripheries: Struggles over disabled Canadians' places in law, society and space. *Canadian Geographer/Le Géographe Canadien, 45*(1), 187–192.

Flisi, S., Meroni, E. C., & Vera-Toscano, E. (2016). *Educational outcomes and immigrant background*. Available at: https://publications.jrc.ec.europa.eu/repository/handle/JRC102629

IMF (2016). *The refugee surge in Europe: Economic challenges*. Available at: https://www.imf.org/external/pubs/ft/sdn/2016/sdn1602.pdf

Kahanec, M., & Zimmermann, K. F. (Eds.). (2009). *EU labor markets after post-enlargement migration*. Berlin: Springer.

Kahanec, M., & Zimmermann, K. F. (Eds.). (2016). *Labor migration, EU enlargement, and the great recession*. Berlin: Springer.

Lillie, N., & Bontebal, I. (Eds.). (2019). *Policy barriers and enablers to labour market integration of migrants, refugees and asylum applicants in European Labour Markets*. Research report submitted as a formal deliverable of the EU H2020 project Sirius. https://www.sirius-project.eu/publications/wp-reports-results

Marbach, M., Hainmueller, J., & Hangartner, D. (2018). The long-term impact of employment bans on the economic integration of refugees. *Science Advances, 4*(9), EAAP9519.

Moret, J., Baglioni, S., & Efionayi-Maeder, D. (2006). *The path of Somali refugees into exile. A comparative analysis of secondary movements and policy responses thereto*. Neuchatel: Swiss Forum for Migration Studies.

OECD. (2016). *Making integration work: Refugees and others in need of protection*. Paris: OECD Publishing.

Ruiz, I., & Vargas-Silva, C. (2017). The consequences of forced migration for host communities in Africa. *Revue d'économie du développement, 25*(3), 135.

Ruiz, I., & Vargas-Silva, C. (2018). Differences in labour market outcomes between natives, refugees and other migrants in the UK. *Journal of Economic Geography, 18*(4), 855–885.

UNHCR. (2013). *A new beginning. Refugee Integration in Europe*. Available at: https://www.unhcr.org/protection/operations/52403d389/new-beginning-refugee-integration-europe.html

Zimmermann, K. F. (2014). Migration, jobs and integration in Europe. *Migration Policy Practice, 4*(4), 4–16.

Zwysen, W. (2019). Different patterns of labour market integration by migration motivation in Europe: The role of host country human capital. *International Migration Review, 53*(1), 59–89.

Chapter 2
Between Numbers and Political Drivers: What Matters in Policy-Making

Nicola Maggini

2.1 Introduction

Policy debate over immigration has intensified in a period characterised by global refugee crises and a wave of nationalist electoral victories. A body of literature has examined the reasons for the appeal of right-wing populist parties in Europe, highlighting the key role played by anti-immigrant attitudes and in general fears and concerns about immigration phenomena (Mudde 2011; Ivarsflaten 2008; Lucassen and Lubbers 2012). Indeed, migration is not a neutral issue from a political standpoint: scholars stress the importance of new cultural issues, such as migration, for the mobilisation of political conflicts (Flanagan and Lee 2003; Kriesi et al. 2006). Ivarsflaten (2008), using data collected in 2002–2003 to explain support for far-right parties in seven European countries, finds that anti-immigrant sentiment and a desire for tougher restrictions on immigration is the common and prevailing factor which has driven support for far-right parties, compared to other grievances such as dissatisfaction with the economy and distrust of politicians and/or the EU. Lucassen and Lubbers (2012) using the same data – this time across 11 countries – find that perceived cultural threat (i.e. the perception that immigration and cultural diversity pose a threat to the country's way of life) is a stronger predictor of support for far-right parties than perceived economic threat (i.e. the perception that immigration poses a threat to jobs and the economy). These findings are consistent with the idea that immigration issues are part of a new cultural cleavage emerging because of globalisation and integration processes: the integration-demarcation cleavage using Kriesi et al.'s terminology (2006) or the transnational cleavage according to Hooghe and Marks (2018).

N. Maggini (✉)
Department of Social and Political Sciences, University of Milan, Milan, Italy
e-mail: nicola.maggini@unimi.it

© The Author(s) 2021

V. Federico, S. Baglioni (eds.), *Migrants, Refugees and Asylum Seekers'
Integration in European Labour Markets*, IMISCOE Research Series,
https://doi.org/10.1007/978-3-030-67284-3_2

The interplay between a multiplicity of factors makes immigration a relevant issue on the public agenda. Scholars have focused mainly on three different factors: citizens' attitudes to immigration and issue salience (Gilligan 2015); issue entrepreneurship by radical right parties or moderate centre-right parties (Van Spanje 2010; Hobolt and De Vries 2015); and socio-economic factors such as the unemployment rate, migration patterns and models of integration (Green-Pedersen and Otjes 2017; Van der Brug et al. 2015). The increasing politicisation of immigration issues is relevant to explain not only citizens' voting behaviour and party competition, but also policy outcomes. Although the restrictiveness of migration policies is driven by factors such as economic growth, unemployment and recent immigration levels (de Haas and Natter 2015), political factors are noteworthy explanatory variables, too (Abou-Chadi 2016). In particular, the rise of populist right-wing parties in recent years has strongly influenced immigration policies in two ways: on the one hand, populist right-wing parties have come to power (for example in Italy, Austria, Poland), on the other their electoral rise has influenced the positions and policies of mainstream parties (Van Spanje 2010; Abou-Chadi and Krause 2018).

Therefore, the starting point of this chapter is the idea that the determinants of immigration policies and labour market integration policies concerning migrants, refugees and asylum seekers (MRAs) might include not only changes in economic conditions, but also shifts in power among political actors and the salience of issues on the political agenda (namely, perceptions about migration and immigrants).

This chapter aims to investigate whether policy measures on migration across seven European countries (the Czech Republic, Denmark, Finland, Greece, Italy, Switzerland and the UK) vary according to different political conditions at country level. It relies on the most recent data from both existing comparative datasets on public opinion (European Social Survey, Eurobarometer)[1] and a comparative database we built for the SIRIUS research,[2] which includes a systematic set of macro-level indicators spanning the time period 2010–2017. Thus, the chapter will compare and contrast the main features of the immigration and labour market integration policies for MRAs in the selected countries in light of both current data on MRAs stocks and flows in each national context, along with a number of indicators related to perceptions about migration and migrants and features of the political context (e.g. electoral strength of populist radical right parties, ideological configuration of political space).

As we will see in more detail in Chap. 3, in recent years the immigration policies of SIRIUS countries have been characterised by narrowing access to both international protection and legal entry for working reasons, although these countries are diverse in terms of socio-economic conditions, previous and current levels of MRAs and welfare state regimes. Hence, the hypothesis is that in recent years political

---

[1] For the analysis in this chapter, we relied on the last available data. The latter vary between 2017 and 2019 depending on the indicators.

[2] Horizon 2020 research project coordinated by the Glasgow Caledonian University on the topic "Skills and Integration of Migrants, Refugees and Asylum Applicants in European Labour Markets" (Grant Agreement n. 77051), https://www.sirius-project.eu/

factors are more relevant to explain the law and policy-making on immigration issues carried out in a similar fashion in such different European contexts, rather than the actual number of MRAs, their integration process or the effective European societies' demographic and economic needs, within each national context. More precisely, we hypothesise that if actual numbers of MRAs are still relatively low in the selected European countries despite the recent refugee crisis, then the adoption of restrictive policies on immigration can be better explained by political factors, listed as follows: prevalence of negative attitudes towards immigration among European citizens and salience of immigration issue; political relevance of populist radical-right parties who mostly mobilized on immigration issues and significant diffusion of their authoritarian/traditionalist/nationalist positions within each country's party system. The underlying idea is that vote-maximising parties are conditioned by public attitudes on immigration and issue salience, which in turn are shaped by the political entrepreneurship of radical right parties or, at least, by moderate centre-right parties (Van Spanje 2010; Hobolt and De Vries 2015). In particular, the (eventual) spreading in European party systems of authoritarian/traditionalist/ nationalist positions (Hooghe and Marks 2018), which are strictly linked to the aforementioned new cultural cleavage between supporters of cultural demarcation and international integration (Kriesi et al. 2006), can be seen as a signal of the previously mentioned influence of populist-radical parties on the positions and immigration policies of mainstream parties (Van Spanje 2010; Abou-Chadi and Krause 2018). This hypothesis is tested by contrasting legislative and policy measures on migration and integration issues with the numbers of MRAs in each national context, as well with the above-mentioned political features. Hence, the chapter is structured as follows: first, it provides a general picture of the legislative and policy measures on migration and integration issues carried out in the selected European countries. Secondly, it presents and discusses the numbers of MRAs in each national context. Thirdly, citizens' perceptions and attitudes towards immigration and salience of the immigration issue in each national context are analysed, along with the electoral strength of populist radical right parties and ideological configuration of the political space in terms of party positions on the cultural libertarian--authoritarian and economic left-right dimension. A concluding section follows.

2.2 Legislative and Policy Measures on Migration and Integration Issues

The results of integration policies should be seen in conjunction with the immigration policies that try to limit or encourage migration and manage migrants. Nevertheless, labour market integration policies and immigration policies are created with different goals in mind, and enforced by different sets of bureaucracies. Immigration policy is a widely used term, although often not clearly defined. Similar terms include migration regulation, control and restriction. A recent definition describes immigration policy as: "government's statements of what it intends to do or not do (including laws, regulations, decisions or orders) in regards to the selection, admission, settlement and deportation of foreign citizens residing in the country" (Bjerre et al. 2015: 559). Immigration policies therefore involve controlling borders, selecting new arrivals and maintaining national security, but cover also other areas including the labour market, integration, and humanitarian/asylum, family, co-ethnic, and irregular migration. Integration policies therefore are linked to immigration policies, but are more narrowly defined as "policies or programmes aimed at integrating immigrants into host society" (UN 2017). According to Goodman (2015: 12), integration policy is defined as *member-enabling*: "the state lowers itself to accommodate, promote, and alter the life changes of the immigrant". Integration policies include: anti-discrimination, access to labour market, family reunification, political participation, education rights (Migration Policy Group 2011). Likewise, integration policies are classified by Schibel et al. (2002) according to the related functional domain: education, employment, housing, health or community development. A series of OECD publications (OECD 2007, 2008, 2012) focuses on the labour market integration of immigrants. In this regard, integration policies are involved with training, advising and matching employees with jobs that ideally take under consideration the interests of both the MRAs themselves to find work and of employers to find the needed employees (and governments, in making the welfare system sustainable from the point of view of public finances).

Despite being different, immigration and integration policies can influence each other, with, for instance, employers being prevented from recruiting the employees they need, or with asylum-seekers forced into inactivity while awaiting their asylum requests. In other words, it is clear that a tightening of immigration policies can both reduce the scope of integration policies (for instance, by reducing the number of allowed foreign workers or refugees, restricting family reunification, and so forth) and make them more difficult (for instance, this occurs when the procedures for renewing the permit to stay are complicated or when certain categories of migrants such as asylum seekers are not allowed to work).

2.2.1 Immigration Policies: Narrowing the Access and Limiting Legal Rights

As we will see in more detail in Chap. 3, in recent years, the immigration policies of SIRIUS countries have been characterised by narrowing the access to both international protection and legal entry for working reasons. Raising physical and legal barriers to foreigners' entry went hand in hand with political discourses on migration, which tend to blend asylum seekers, economic migrants and irregular migrants. Reflecting narratives that question, for instance, the sincerity of asylum claims, restrictive asylum policies have been enacted. Furthermore, the restrictive trend is further aggravated in the field of the economic migration, where the state power to select and control who can entry and stay is affirmed even more resolutely.

The narrowing of access is pursued through physical restrictions (migrant push-backs –either at the borders as all SIRIUS countries experienced or at the sea – as it is the case in Italy and Greece; increasing border controls – best exemplified by the Swiss case-; physical conditions on application lodging –for example since 2002 asylum seekers can only lodge an application on Danish soil), and, through procedural restrictions concerning reforms of both international protection procedures (hotspots, 'safe third countries', admissibility test, accelerated asylum procedures, suppression of levels of guarantees) and the reduction of the quota for foreign workers.

The restrictive domestic asylum proceedings have found a legal basis in the EU asylum *acquis*, in particular implementing procedures provided by the recast Asylum Procedures Directive.[3] These legal and procedural devices, originally created with the goal of favouring greater efficiency in the management of migration and, particularly, in the refugee status determination process, in practice seem to also foster aims of containment and control of flows, resulting in curtailing access to the international procedure (Zetter 2007).

Moreover, as already discussed in Chap. 1, MRAs have also faced a legal marginalization in SIRIUS jurisdictions, namely as regards their right both to be legally recognised a status (and subsequently a permit to stay), and to have a number of other rights deriving from their status –*in primis* the right to work and the right to do it as nationals do.

2.2.2 Labour Market Integration Policies: More Barriers Than Enablers

Labour market integration policies in SIRIUS countries are characterised by more barriers than enablers (Bontenbal and Lillie 2019). Barriers to the labour market integration of migrants are similar across SIRIUS countries, and include ineffective administrative and legal structures, lack of recognition of skills and qualifications acquired in the home countries, lack of language skills, lack of needed skills and competences, lack of networks, labour exploitation, discrimination, a general atmosphere of xenophobia in society and (perceived) cultural barriers. The level of resources for integration programmes varies significantly across countries. This is due in part to the general level of resources dedicated to active labour market policies: if more resources are devoted to active labour market policy and social welfare generally, then there is more for MRAs as well. Hence, the national labour market

---

[3] Directive 2013/32/EU of the European Parliament and of the Council of 26 June 2013 on common procedures for granting and withdrawing international protection (recast), OJ 2013 L180/60. The Directive recast Council Directive 2005/85/EC.

structure and the model of welfare regime play a role (Banting 2000). In this regard, Nekby (2008) concludes that the same types of activation labour market policies work for immigrants as for the general population of unemployed workers. Conversely, other scholars (Rinne 2013) conclude that interventions such as work experience and wage subsidy programmes seem most effective: "programs that are relatively closely linked to the labor market (for example, work experience and wage subsidies) appear the comparatively most effective programs" (Rinne 2013: 548). In Nordic countries, Ho and Shirono (2015) find that the estimated effects of active labour market programme spending are much higher on foreign-born unemployment than on native-born unemployment (although the latter is also reduced), so that the foreign-native gap is narrowed as a result. Furthermore, Nagayoshi and Hjerm (2015) discover that labour market policies in the form of activation policies affect attitudes toward immigration. Pro-immigration attitudes are more widespread in welfare states that introduce activation of labour market policies with a robust safety net, compared to welfare states that spend a large amount of the budget on passive labour market policies.

However, political climate plays a role as well, with cuts to programmes fostered by anti-immigrant politics. The importance of political factors is well exemplified by the different policies pursued by two countries with similar and generous welfare state regimes: Sweden and Denmark. According to Schierup et al. (2006), Sweden provides a generous welfare state to both its natives and immigrants, partly via the accessible process to get Swedish citizenship. Conversely, in Denmark access to welfare benefits is harder for immigrants compared to natives, and the employment rate remains lower for migrants than natives. The explanation is that migration policy has become a much more salient issue to gain votes in Denmark than in Sweden (Green-Pedersen and Krogstrup 2008). This happened because "focusing on the immigration issue easily leads to a conflict with the centre-right, especially social liberal parties. In Sweden, such a conflict would undermine mainstream right-wing attempts at winning government power" (Green-Pedersen and Krogstrup 2008: 610). Conversely, the Danish People's Party has – in its role as an indispensable coalition partner for a non-socialist government – been able to carry out much of its anti-immigration agenda, including the introduction of dualist welfare policies (Bay et al. 2013). In other words, party competition determines this difference.

Cross-country differences regard both the entitlement of specific migrant groups to participate in labour integration programmes and the availability of specific services. In some countries, such as in Finland and in Greece, programmes are offered to all job-seeking migrants. Conversely, in other countries, such as the Czech Republic and Denmark, they are mainly offered to newly arrived refugees. In the UK, programmes are only offered for resettled refugees, which have been chosen in collaboration with the UNHCR. There is also huge variation in the duration of integration programmes, which range between 5 years in the UK to a few courses lasting a few days in Switzerland (Bontenbal and Lillie 2019). In countries with well-structured integration training programmes, there is a pressure to shorten these, and include rapidly migrants and refugees into labour market, as exemplified by the Denmark's relatively rigid 'job first'. This may lead well-qualified migrants and refugees to accept unqualified positions, with the risk of wasting human capital in the long term. Finally, the long processing time of the asylum applications and the enforced inactivity of the application period – in a number of jurisdictions asylum applicants do not have the right to work – is a problem, both for the integration into the labour market of asylum seekers with good chances of having their applications accepted, and from the perspective of public finances.

2.3 Migrants, Refugees and Asylum Applicants: The Numbers

So far, we have seen how policies are characterised by many barriers to the integration of MRAs into the labour market. Chapter 3 shows how immigration laws and policies in the analysed countries have had a restrictive turn in recent years. Is this restrictive legal and policy framework 'justified' by the real numbers related to the stock and flows of MRAs in European countries? On the one hand, it is true that during the 2000–2017 period, the international migrant stock grew worldwide by an average of 2.3%. In absolute values, it means that since 2000 the estimated number of international migrants has been constantly increasing in the whole planet, reaching 258 million in 2017. On the other hand, the share of international migrants in proportion to the world's population has remained relatively stable in the last four decades, fluctuating from 2.2 to 3.5% (UN 2017). International migrations show different patterns: the share of migrants residing in high-income countries increased from 9.6% in 2000 to 14% in 2017, and high-income countries host 64% of the total number of international migrants worldwide, but the picture reverses if we consider solely refugees and asylum seekers. They are about 26 million, representing slightly more than 10% of the total migrant population. Eighty-four per cent of them are hosted in low and middle-income countries (UN 2017). Therefore, high-income and low and middle-income countries face different challenges in migration management. In the present volume, the focus is on the first group, but keeping in mind that this is just a partial perspective on a broader, much more complex and diverse phenomenon.

The recent increase of the migrant population affected especially people of working age: in 2017, about 74% of all international migrants were between 20 and 64 years of age, compared to 57% of the global population falling in the same age group. This means that, in principle, a net inflow of migrants decreases the proportion of inactive population (children and elderly people), with positive effects for the host country's economy and welfare. In particular, scholars have highlighted how migrants in the working age, being net contributors to public finances, will be fundamental in sustaining fiscal revenues, needed to maintain publicly funded pension schemes in a context characterised by ageing population (Storesletten 2003). Relying on generational accounting approaches, several studies find net fiscal gains from immigrants in different European countries, for instance in Spain (Collado

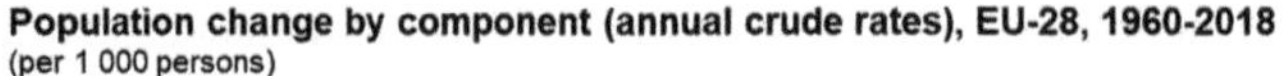

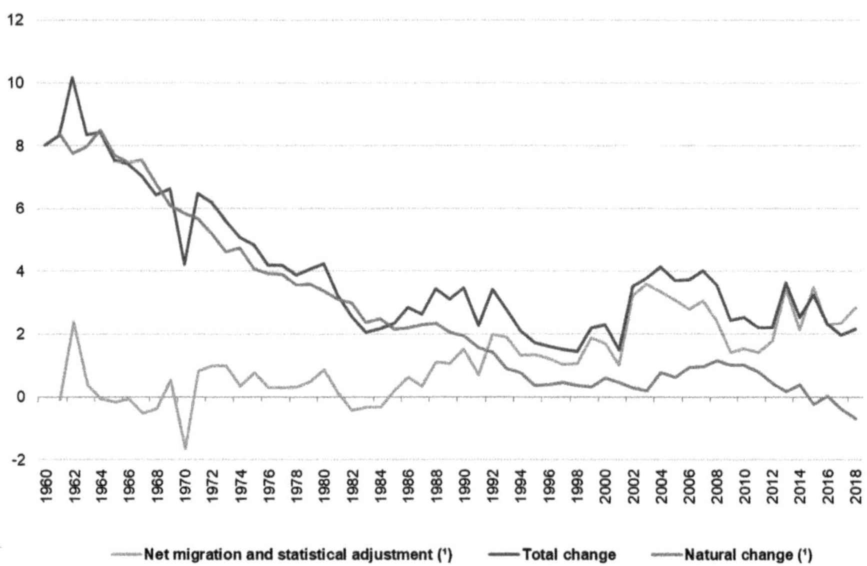

Fig. 2.1 Population change by component (annual crude rates) in the EU, 1960–2018 (per 1000 persons). (*Source*: Eurostat)

et al. 2004), in France (Chojnicki 2013), in Austria (Mayr 2005) and, especially as regards high-skilled immigrants, in the UK (Lee and Miller 2000) and in Sweden (Storesletten 2003).

Narrowing the analysis to Europe, we should highlight that there were 17.6 million persons living in one of the EU Member States on 1 January 2018 with the citizenship of another EU Member State, whereas third-country nationals residing in an EU Member State amounted to 22.4 million, equal to 4.4% of the population of the EU-28 (Eurostat 2019).[4] In terms of flows, 4.4 million people immigrated to one of the EU-28 Member States during 2017, including flows between EU Member States. Among these 4.4 million immigrants, people of non-EU countries amounted to 2.0 million, EU citizens amounted to 2.3 million and stateless people were around 11 thousand. These are not particularly high numbers, considering that the EU population is over 500 million people.

Moreover, in recent years, immigration has contributed to EU population change. This is indeed determined by two components: the natural population change – specifically the difference between the number of live births and deaths in a given year – and the net migration – precisely the difference between the number of immigrants and the number of emigrants. As reported by Fig. 2.1, since the mid-1980s

---

[4] For sake of comparability, it has been decided to use Eurostat data in this section.

Table 2.1 Total number of immigrants in SIRIUS countries, 2013–2017 (thousands)

	2013	2014	2015	2016	2017
Czech Republic	30,124	29,897	29,602	64,083	51,847
Denmark	60,312	68,388	78,492	74,383	68,579
Greece	57,946	59,013	64,446	116,867	112,247
Italy	307,454	277,631	280,078	300,823	343,440
Finland	31,941	31,507	28,746	34,905	31,797
United Kingdom	526,046	631,991	631,452	588,993	644,209
Switzerland	160,157	156,282	153,627	149,305	143,377

Source: Eurostat

net migration has increased, and from the beginning of the 1990s onwards the value of net migration and statistical adjustment has always been higher than that of natural change. Between 2016 and 2018, the net migration change (plus statistical adjustment) was even higher than the total change. Conversely, since the mid-1980s the natural change in the population decreased: the number of deaths increased, the number of live births decreased. The difference between live births and deaths narrowed significantly from 1961 onwards and deaths outnumbered live births in 2015, 2017 and 2018 resulting in a natural decrease in the population. The increase in population recorded between 2016 and 2018 was therefore due to net migration and statistical adjustment. Migration is thus fundamental to explain population change in the EU and during the past three decades population growth have been mainly driven by net migration. This trend is likely to persist in the future, given that the number of deaths is expected to increase because of the aging of the baby-boom generation.

If we look at immigration flows both from outside the EU and between EU countries, in 2017 a total of around 1.4 million people immigrated to one of the SIRIUS countries, with UK reporting the largest amount (644,209) and Finland the smallest (31,797) (Table 2.1).

Among the 1.4 million who migrated to one of the selected European countries in 2017, almost one million people (731,196) were from a non-EU country, with a constant increase over time. Again, the UK reports the largest number of non-EU immigrants (320,669), whereas Finland shows the smallest number (16,480) (Table 2.2). As regards migration stocks (Table 2.3), overall, more than eight million non-EU nationals live in one of the SIRIUS countries in 2018 (1.6% of total EU population), 221,911 more than in 2014. The largest number is recorded in Italy (3,581,561), whereas among SIRIUS countries Finland hosts the smallest number (148,491).

If we look at the share of non-nationals in the resident population of 1 January 2018 (see Fig. 2.2), Switzerland shows the highest share of non-nationals (25.1%), whereas Finland and the Czech Republic show the lowest shares (4.5% and 4.9%, respectively). The UK, Italy, Denmark and (to a lesser extent) Greece show very similar percentages (between 9% and 7.6%). However, if took into account only non-EU foreigners, the percentage in Switzerland drops, although it is still the highest among the SIRIUS countries (8.6%). Moreover, shares of non-EU foreigners in

Table 2.2 Number of non-EU arrivals in SIRIUS countries, 2013–2017 (migration flows in thousands)

	2013	2014	2015	2016	2017
Czech Republic	10,780	9386	10,619	29,902	30,725
Denmark	19,624	24,482	32,256	28,559	23,054
Greece	16,313	13,539	17,492	69,497	63,324
Italy	201,536	180,271	186,522	200,217	239,953
Finland	13,183	13,568	13,108	19,638	16,480
United Kingdom	248,464	287,136	278,587	265,390	320,669
Switzerland	37,247	35,713	37,382	37,585	36,991

Source: Eurostat

Table 2.3 Number of non-EU nationals living in SIRIUS countries, 2014–2018 (migration stocks in thousands)

	2014	2015	2016	2017	2018
Czech Republic	261,302	272,993	280,907	302,579	296,072
Denmark	233,023	244,380	267,192	274,990	284,537
Greece	662,335	623,246	591,693	604,813	604,904
Italy	3,479,566	3,521,825	3,508,429	3,509,089	3,581,561
Finland	121,882	127,792	133,136	143,757	148,491
United Kingdom	2,425,012	2,434,209	2,436,046	2,444,555	2,425,737
Switzerland	663,337	674,074	689,304	716,052	727,066

Source: Eurostat

Italy (5.9%) and Greece (5.6%) are higher than in UK (3.7%). Overall, however, non-EU nationals represents less than 10% of the resident population in each of the SIRIUS countries, contrary to the narrative about an 'invasion' of Europe. Many far-right parties in the last years have indeed campaigned showing ads like "stop the invasion!" or "secure our borders!".[5] However, as shown by the numbers we have presented so far and by previous empirical research (De Haas 2008), the reality is different.

Concerning the permits to stay – namely those authorisations issued by a country's authorities allowing non-EU nationals to legally stay on its territory – Table 2.4 clusters them by reason for issue. In 2017, slightly more than 3.1 million permits were released. The majority were issued for employment reasons (1.01 million; 32.2%) followed by family reasons (829,922; 26.5%), other reasons (766,798; 24.5%) – that include stays without the right to work or international protection – and education-related reasons (529,994; 16.9%). Therefore, Europe, despite the

---

[5] See https://www.euronews.com/2018/03/28/hungary-government-s-new-anti-immigration-ad-copies-ukip-s-controversial-anti-migrant-post; https://www.nytimes.com/interactive/2018/06/27/world/europe/europe-migrant-crisis-change.html; https://www.nytimes.com/2019/08/10/world/europe/sweden-immigration-nationalism.html

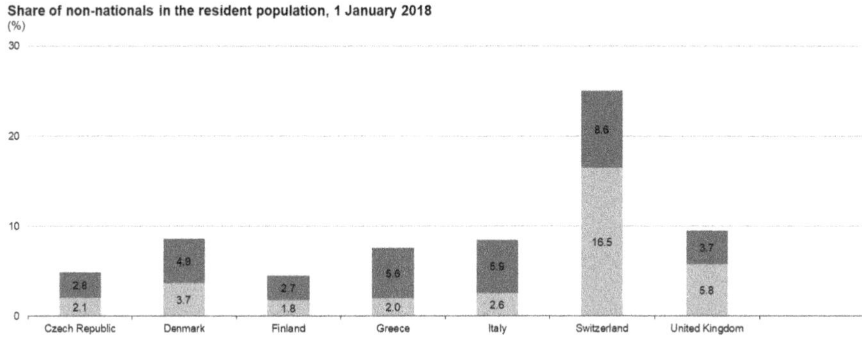

Fig. 2.2 Share of non-nationals in the resident population, 1 January 2018 (%). (*Source*: Eurostat)

Table 2.4 First residence permits issued by reason, 2013–2017 (thousands)

	Family	Education	Employment	Other	Total
2013	671,572	463,943	534,214	686,722	2,356,451
2014	680,388	476,845	573,321	595,423	2,325,977
2015	760,231	525,858	707,632	628,301	2,622,022
2016	780,429	499,775	854,715	889,622	3,024,541
2017	829,922	529,994	1,009,427	766,798	3,136,141

Source: Eurostat

recent economic crisis, continues to exercise a great pulling factor because of its ability to absorb work.

As far as statistics on asylum are concerned, the total number of asylum applications in the EU from non-EU nationals amounts to 638,240 in 2018, approximately half the number registered in 2015 and 2016, when applications amounted to 1,322,845 and 1,260,910 respectively (Fig. 2.3). Therefore, asylum applications reached their peaks in 2015 and 2016, when the EU witnessed an unprecedented influx of refugees and migrants, most of them fleeing from war in Syria. Considering the nationality of asylum applicants in 2018 (Eurostat 2019), most arrived from contexts affected by years of generalized violence, insecurity, authoritarian regimes, etc. (e.g., the first six countries of origin are, in descending order, Syria, Afghanistan, Iraq, Pakistan, Iran, Nigeria). This suggests that they will probably not come back soon. Therefore, it becomes appropriate to draw up strategies for their active integration into the labour market.

In the 2013–2018 period, the highest number of first instance decisions was issued in 2016 (1,106,395) (see Table 2.5). Out of the total number of decisions issued, 672,890 (61%) had a positive outcome. Furthermore, 366,470 (54%) positive decisions granted refugee status; 50,980 (8%) granted an authorisation to stay for humanitarian reasons; and 255,440 (38%) decided for subsidiary protection. It is worth mentioning that humanitarian status is specific to national legislations,

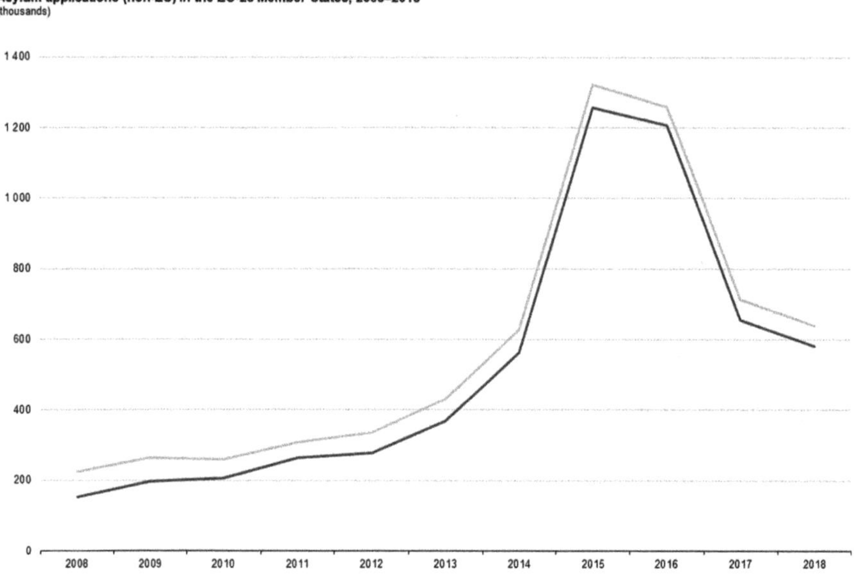

Fig. 2.3 Asylum applications (non-EU) in the EU, 2008–2018 (thousands). (*Source*: Eurostat)

Table 2.5 First instance decisions on (non-EU) asylum applications, 2013–2018 (thousands)

	Refugee status	Humanitarian status	Subsidiarity protection status	Total positive	Rejected	Total
2013	49,670	12,505	45,435	107,610	206,625	314,235
2014	95,380	15,710	56,295	167,385	199,470	366,850
2015	229,460	23,290	54,900	307,650	289,005	596,655
2016	366,470	50,980	255,440	672,890	433,505	1,106,395
2017	218,560	63,650	155,345	437,555	524,055	961,610
2018	122,070	33,435	61,900	217,405	364,325	581,735

Source: Eurostat

contrary to refugee status and subsidiary protection status which are defined by EU law. As for 2018, the total number of first instance decisions dropped to 581,735. Out of these decisions, 217,405 (37%) were positive, of which 122,070 (56%) granted refugee status.

As regards final decisions (i.e. those decisions taken by administrative or judicial bodies in appeal or in review and which are no longer subject to remedy), in 2018, 308,830 decisions were issued, of which 115,925 (38%) were positive (Table 2.6).

Table 2.6 Final decisions on (non-EU) asylum applications, 2013–2018 (thousands)

	Refugee status	Subsidiary protection status	Humanitarian status	Total positive	Rejected	Total
2013	14,845	5350	4480	24,675	109,965	134,640
2014	15,990	5415	4795	26,195	109,835	136,030
2015	18,110	4640	3650	26,400	152,900	179,300
2016	23,660	8275	10,700	42,630	188,355	230,985
2017	49,590	31,140	14,580	95,310	186,235	281,545
2018	41,720	38,410	35,800	115,925	192,905	308,830

Source: Eurostat

Table 2.7 International protections applications: success rate of all forms of international protection and success rate of refugee status in 2018 (first instance decisions)

	Number of applications	Decisions granting any form of international protection		Decisions granting the refugee status	
		Positive decisions	Success rate	Positive decisions	Success rate
Czech Republic	1385	155	11.2%	40	2.9%
Denmark	2625	1315	50.1%	825	31.4%
Finland	4440	2405	54.2%	1765	39.8%
Greece	32,340	15,210	47.0%	12,635	39.1%
Italy	95,210	30,670	32.2%	6490	6.8%
Switzerland	17,000	15,225	89.6%	6190	36.4%
UK	28,860	10,100	35.0%	7650	26.5%

Source: own calculations on Eurostat data

In particular, 41,720 (36%) resulted in grants of refugee status, 35,800 (31%) granted humanitarian status, and 38,410 (33%) granted subsidiary protection.

It is interesting to focus on 2018 data to highlight the success rate of international protection applications in SIRIUS countries, focusing on first instance decisions. Table 2.7 shows, on the left side, the total number of positive decisions about all international protection applications (including Geneva convention status, humanitarian status, subsidiary protection status) and their success rate; on the right side of the table positive decisions granting only the Geneva convention status (i.e. refugee status) and the related success rate are reported. As regards decisions granting any type of international protection, Switzerland is by far the country with the highest success rate (89.6%), followed by Finland (54.2%) and Denmark (50.1%). Conversely, the lowest success rate is definitely the Czech Republic (11.2%). Relatively lower rates also characterise Italy (32.2%) and the UK (35%). Greece lies in between (47%). People applying in Switzerland and in the Czech Republic might have different characteristics and different life paths, but such a wide gap in the success rate is likely to also depend on different legal provisions and the interpretation of protection standards (for more details on this, see Chap. 3).

Differences among SIRIUS countries become even wider when taking into account only the positive decisions granting refugee status and not considering other forms of protection, as shown by the right side of Table 2.7. Figures drop dramatically and vary from 39.8% in Finland and 39.1% in Greece to 2.9% in the Czech Republic. The country where the difference is minimal is Greece, whereas the maximum difference is in Switzerland. This means that in Greece the overwhelmingly majority of positive decisions granted refugee status, whereas in Switzerland other forms of international protection prevailed. Indeed, other Eurostat data[6] show that in Greece national forms of temporary protection are minimal, whereas in Switzerland refugee status is granted less than humanitarian protection (and even less considering also subsidiary protection). The second largest difference between success rate of any form of international protection and refugee status' success rate is shown by Italy, signalling that in 2018 other forms of international protection prevailed over refugee status. In particular, according to Eurostat data,[7] humanitarian protection status was by far the most granted form of protection.[8] In the other countries, there is a greater balance between decisions that guarantee refugee status and those that guarantee other forms of international protection, with a prevalence of the refugee status protection in UK, Finland and Denmark and a prevalence of the other forms of international protection (especially subsidiary protection)[9] in the Czech Republic. Clearly, not all statuses are entitled to the same rights and benefits, as shown by Chaps. 1 and 3. Differences may be significant, with a relevant impact on people's lives. In general, these data confirm the restrictive turn discussed in previous section.

The data we have presented so far denies once again the rhetoric of 'the invasion'. All the countries we analyzed are selective and rigid in granting international protection. Of course, a different discourse can be created about the fate of people who are denied status. Many of them, indeed, are ordered to leave the country, but few are actually repatriated and become illegal, with all the negative consequences that this fact can have for migrants themselves and host countries. This is the real problem that EU countries are not able to solve, and it has shown by statistics on the enforcement of immigration legislation presented in Table 2.8. On the one hand, the number of non-EU citizens who were refused entry into the EU, after a decline in 2014, increased between 2014 and 2018, reaching its peaks in 2017 and 2018 (439,505 and 471,155, respectively), confirming again the increasingly restrictive approach adopted by most EU governments. On the other, the highest number of non-EU citizens found to be illegally present was recorded in 2015 (2,154,675). In

---

[6] See   https://ec.europa.eu/eurostat/statistics-explained/images/f/f7/Asylum_statistics_YB19_10_05_2019.xlsx

[7] See   https://ec.europa.eu/eurostat/statistics-explained/images/f/f7/Asylum_statistics_YB19_10_05_2019.xlsx

[8] These data are clearly destined to change radically in the near future because the recent decree n. 113/2018 (the so-called Salvini decree) has abolished humanitarian protection.

[9] See   https://ec.europa.eu/eurostat/statistics-explained/images/f/f7/Asylum_statistics_YB19_10_05_2019.xlsx

Table 2.8 Non-EU citizens subject to the enforcement of immigration legislation, 2013–2018 (thousands)

	Refused entry	Illegally present	Ordered to leave	Returned to a non-EU country
2013	326,320	452,270	430,450	184,765
2014	286,805	672,215	470,080	170,415
2015	297,860	2,154,675	533,395	196,190
2016	388,280	983,860	493,790	228,995
2017	439,505	618,775	516,115	189,855
2018	471,155	601,500	478,155	157,895

Source: Eurostat

the same year, not surprisingly, it was registered the highest number of non-EU nationals who were ordered to leave the territory of one of the EU countries (533,395), but only slightly more than one fifth of them (196,190 third country nationals) were returned to their country of origin outside the EU. In 2016, this number increased to 228,995 non-EU citizens, whereas in the following years this number decreased, thus signalling how the increasingly restrictive immigration measures have not gone hand in hand with the capacity to effectively implement repatriations. Over time, indeed, those who are returned to a non-EU country are only a small share of those ordered to leave. This means that the tightening of immigration policies did not impede the presence of 'illegal' migrants within EU countries, despite 'fighting illegal immigration' being often the declared purpose of many governments. On the contrary, a restrictive approach can be seen as one of the causes of illegal entry: restricting legal entry may have prompted many immigrants to apply for asylum as the only legal access route, but many have been denied international protection, actually making them illegal. In this regard, scholars have talked about implementation gap and efficacy gap (Czaika and De Haas 2013). As regards the first, research has revealed that implementation gaps can be significant (e.g. Wunderlich 2010), especially when immigration policies on paper are unrealistic or not related to concrete migration experiences. The efficacy gap reflects the fact that efforts by states to regulate and restrict immigration have often failed (Bhagwati 2003; Castles 2004; Düvell 2005) because of unintended effects, for instance on other migration flows: rather than having an impact on the overall volume of inflows, immigration restrictions would mostly change the channel of access of immigrants, such as through an increased use of family migration or irregular means of entry. De Haas (2011) calls this reorientation toward other legal or illegal channels of immigration the *categorical substitution effect*. The low effectiveness of restrictive immigration policies is explained by structural determinants in origin and destination countries (such as labour market imbalances) as well as by the internal dynamics of migration networks and systems (Czaika and De Haas 2013). This explains why (illegal) migration often does not stop despite the tightening of borders control.

2.4 Citizens' Attitudes and Political Context

The demographic data presented so far show that MRAs stocks and flows are relatively low – apart from the 2015/16 refugee flow's peak (which in any case involved a few million people out of a European population of 550 million) – and do not justify the worsening of political discourse and the consequent exacerbation of the norms and of the policies. Against these numbers, therefore, it is worth looking at other data to analyse and comprehend the legislative and policy measures undertaken by public authorities of SIRIUS countries in recent years. In particular, in order to test our hypothesis that legislative and policy measures on immigration are mainly driven by political factors rather than by the numbers of immigration flows and stocks, it is important to investigate citizens' perceptions and attitudes towards immigration and the main features of the political context (electoral strength of the radical right, mean distribution of parties along the relevant dimensions of the political space) in which policy-makers have adopted their decisions. In recent years, in fact, immigration has been placed at the centre of the public agenda by political entrepreneurs who use it for electoral purposes: in this regard, scholars have stressed the relevance of new cultural issues such as migration for the mobilisation of political conflicts (Flanagan and Lee 2003; Kriesi et al. 2006) and for the success of right-wing populist parties (Mudde 2011). Before analysing the main indicators of the political context that may have influenced policy measures on immigration, it is important to look first at the configuration of public opinion relying on available survey data. These data deal with both perceptions concerning immigration and salience of the immigration issue. The idea, indeed, is that the magnitude of anti-immigration attitudes and the perceived salience of the issue are both elements that can lead political entrepreneurs to strategically emphasise this issue during the electoral campaigns with potentially rewarding results in electoral terms, as highlighted in previous studies (Emanuele et al. 2019). Furthermore, public opinion data are important not only to understand party competition and electoral results, but also public policy. Indeed, the effect of public opinion on public policy is contingent on public issue salience: salience enhances the impact of public opinion (Burstein 2003).

We start with European citizens' perceptions of inflows of foreign population as a positive or negative social factor. In particular, we have analysed the feelings of citizens from SIRIUS EU countries towards the immigration of non-EU people in the 2014–2019 time span according to Eurobarometer surveys (Switzerland data are unfortunately missing). If we look at the last available data (June 2019),[10] the most remarkable result is that positive attitudes prevail over negative ones only in the UK (57% vs. 32%, see Fig. 2.4), whereas in all other countries negative perceptions are more widespread, with the Czech Republic showing the most negative attitudes (82%, see Fig. 2.5). If we consider trends over time, we can notice that negative feelings about immigration are rather stable over recent years. In general, we

---

[10] See https://ec.europa.eu/commfrontoffice/publicopinion/index.cfm/Chart/getChart/themeKy/59/groupKy/279

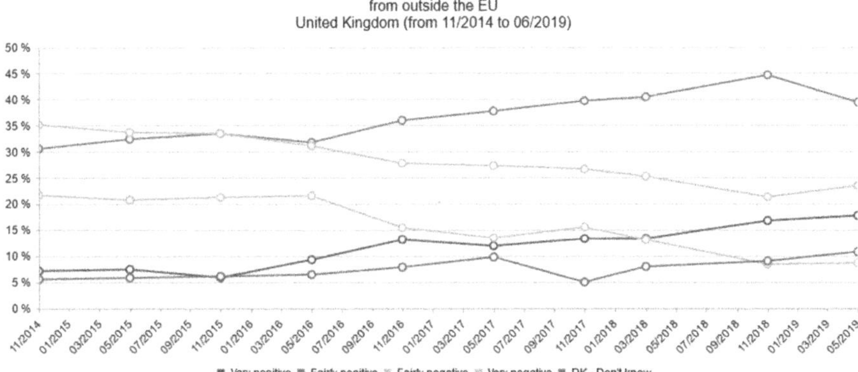

Fig. 2.4 Citizens' feelings about immigration of people outside the EU. (*Source*: Eurobarometer 87)

observe a common increase of very negative feelings in 2015, namely during the so-called refugee crisis. This pattern characterises (almost) all the analysed countries,[11] with some nuances: in Greece the highest increase occurred in 2018 (reaching the same high level of fairly negative attitudes), in Italy negative feelings are quite stable over time (with a decrease of very negative feelings after 2016 and especially after 2018, counterbalanced by an increase of fairly negative feelings). The UK, again, is the exception: since 2016, both kinds of negative attitudes have decreased (with a slight increase in 2019), whereas positive attitudes have increased, overcoming the previous ones (see Fig. 2.4).

These findings are confirmed if we analyse other attitudes towards immigrants/ immigration retrieved from the SIRIUS dataset, which includes data from Standard Eurobarometer and European Social Survey (see Table 2.9). Relevant shares of European citizens think that immigrants make their country a worse place to live[12]: in each country, at least around 20–25% of citizens share this opinion between 2010 and 2016, with a 75.2% peak in Greece in 2010. The Czech Republic and Italy are the countries that show the highest increase of such a negative perception of immigrants over time: in the latter, this negative attitude moved form 43.1% of 2012 to 59% of 2016, whereas in the former the percentage declined from 54.3% in 2010 to 50.4% in 2012 and then constantly increased reaching the peak of 60.6% in 2016. Conversely, the UK is the country facing the highest decrease in this negative perception, moving from 43.8% in 2010 to 29.2% in 2016. Similar results can be noticed if we examine the share of respondents who believe that own country's

---

[11] See   https://ec.europa.eu/commmfrontoffice/publicopinion/index.cfm/Chart/getChart/chartType/ lineChart//themeKy/59/groupKy/279/savFile/911

[12] "Immigrants make country worse or better place to live": percentage of respondents who take positions from 0 to 4 on a 0–10 scale where 0 means "worse place to live" and 10 "better place to live".

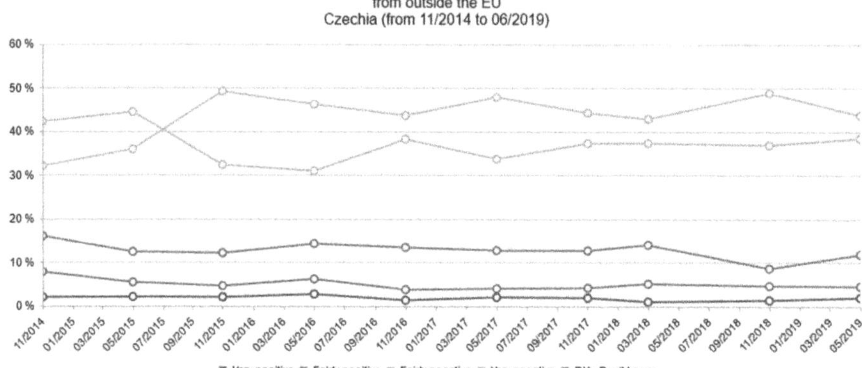

Fig. 2.5 Citizens' feelings about immigration of people outside the EU). (*Source*: Eurobarometer)

cultural life is undermined by immigrants[13] and that immigration is bad for the economy.[14] In Denmark and in Finland, concerns that the economy is being jeopardized by immigrants are higher than the perceived cultural damages that could come from incorporating more newcomers, while in the remaining countries culture-based fears prevail over economic ones. Probably, in the two Nordic countries, this result might be explained by citizens' fear that the traditional welfare state model which underpins their societies could be jeopardized by the arrival of foreigners. Already in the late 1980s, Freeman (1986) highlighted the difficult relationship between generous welfare policies and immigration. More recently, Alesina and Glaeser (2004) have argued that the increasing arrivals of ethnically distinct, poor immigrants within society characterised by high social spending and ethnic and racial homogeneity has favoured the rise of an anti-immigrant rhetoric with potential negative consequences also on redistributive policies. Conversely, Bay et al. (2013) have found that in Norway and Denmark the widespread perception that immigrants are less committed to work than the majority population is positively correlated with preferences for redistribution, although support is for welfare dualism. Other studies have shown how generous welfare spending tends to strengthen support for restrictive immigration policies (Faist 1996).

Despite the cross-country differences in terms of strength and trends of negative attitudes towards both immigration and immigrants, the salience, or 'perceived

---

[13] "Country's cultural life undermined or enriched by immigrants": percentage of respondents who take positions from 0 to 4 on a 0–10 scale where 0 means "cultural life is undermined" and 10 "cultural life enriched".

[14] "Immigration bad or good for country's economy": percentage of respondents who take positions from 0 to 4 on a 0–10 scale where 0 means "bad for the economy" and 10 "good for the economy".

Table 2.9 Citizens' attitudes toward immigration/immigrants by country over time

Country	Year	Immigration salience	Immigrants make country worse	Cultural life undermined by immigrants	Immigration bad for the economy
Czech Republic	2010	12.7	54.3	53.5	56.46
	2011	11.9	.	.	.
	2012	7.9	50.4	49.4	53.19
	2013	11.7	.	.	.
	2014	21.3	58.0	56.3	62.05
	2015	43.9	.	.	.
	2016	67.0	60.6	63.1	52.17
	2017	53.6	.	.	.
Denmark	2010	14.6	20.4	21.8	31.66
	2011	26.4	.	.	.
	2012	8.6	18.6	21.8	34.38
	2013	7.9	.	.	.
	2014	20.6	23.3	27.1	35.59
	2015	49.7	.	.	.
	2016	71.2	.	.	.
	2017	55.6	.	.	.
Finland	2010	12.8	25.8	10.1	32.35
	2011	12.7	.	.	.
	2012	9.9	21.9	7.1	28.39
	2013	7.2	.	.	.
	2014	14.9	24.1	11.6	32.05
	2015	24.1	.	.	.
	2016	47.7	23.7	10.6	28.65
	2017	33.3	.	.	.
Greece	2010	9.7	75.2	68.1	68.76
	2011	15.2	.	.	.
	2012	10.9	.	.	.
	2013	10.1	.	.	.
	2014	18.1	.	.	.
	2015	26.6	.	.	.
	2016	40.5	.	.	.
	2017	32.4	.	.	.
Italy	2010	14.8	.	.	.
	2011	27.2	.	.	.
	2012	5.3	43.1	29.4	33.65
	2013	6.6	.	.	.
	2014	24.8	.	.	.
	2015	43.3	.	.	.
	2016	43.8	59.0	46.4	48.57
	2017	40.4	.	.	.

(continued)

Table 2.9 (continued)

Country	Year	Immigration salience	Immigrants make country worse	Cultural life undermined by immigrants	Immigration bad for the economy
Switzerland	2010	.	22.2	23.3	16.86
	2011	.	.	.	.
	2012	.	24.5	21.9	18.36
	2013	.	.	.	.
	2014	.	24.4	23.9	18.23
	2015	.	.	.	.
	2016	.	21.8	22.8	19.92
	2017	.	.	.	.
United Kingdom	2010	18.6	43.8	40.9	44.35
	2011	23.8	.	.	.
	2012	11.5	42.8	37.9	45.5
	2013	19.4	.	.	.
	2014	29.2	41.3	40.3	38.58
	2015	36.0	.	.	.
	2016	51.3	29.2	28.5	24.7
	2017	36.8	.	.	.

Source: SIRIUS WP 2 Dataset (including Standard Eurobarometer, European Social Survey)

importance',[15] of immigration as a policy matter is a common feature in all SIRIUS countries (data for Switzerland in this case are not available). Indeed, Table 2.9 shows that the saliency of immigration has experienced a sharp uptick after 2013, reaching a peak in all countries in 2016, when it was the most important issue for 67% of Czechs, 71.2% of Danes, 47.7% of Finns, 40.5% of Greeks, 43.8% of Italians and 51.3% of Britons. In 2017, in all countries there has been a decline in the perceived importance of the immigration issue, albeit continuing to be salient for relevant shares of respondents (ranging from a minimum of 32.4% in Greece to a maximum of 55.6% in Denmark).

As previously mentioned, data about the salience of the issue are important because they can have a significant effect on electoral behaviour: when voters perceive immigration as highly prominent, those with pre-existing, latent, anti-immigration attitudes are more likely to switch their vote to populist radical right parties than when economic issues are considered more important (Dennison and Geddes 2018). To sum up, the data presented so far show that public opinion in SIRIUS countries represents a strong constraint for immigration policies: in fact, the immigration issue is very salient and negative attitudes towards immigration prevail over positive ones. Moreover, these are all aspects that favour the parties of the radical populist right (Ivarsflaten 2008; Lucassen and Lubbers 2012). Indeed, as

---

[15] Percentage of the population that picked immigration as the most important issue facing the EU at the moment ("don't know" answers included).

shown in Table 2.10, the electoral strength of populist radical right parties[16] (Mudde 2011) has increased over time, although with different trends and levels among SIRIUS countries. The maximum of electoral strength of such populist parties has been reached in some countries during the so-called refugee crisis, with a decline in the following years. This is the case in Denmark (26.6% of votes in the 2014 European Parliament elections and 21.1% in the 2015 national parliamentary elections) and Greece (20.5% and 16.0% in the two close national elections occurred in 2012 and 15.6% in the 2014 European Parliament elections). Other countries, conversely, show a trendless fluctuation: in Finland, the highest percentages of votes for populist parties were obtained in the national parliamentary elections of 2011 (19.1%), 2015 (17.7%) and 2019 (17.5%), whereas in UK the two peaks occurred in the 2014 and 2019 European Parliament elections (27.5% and 33.7%, respectively).[17] In Switzerland the share of the populist right has substantially remained stable around 30% over time, whereas in the Czech Republic, where populist radical right parties were irrelevant in 2010, they reached the 12.2% of votes in the 2017 national parliamentary elections. Finally, the most remarkable increase occurred in Italy, where the populist radical right moved from 6.1% of votes in the 2013 national election to 40.7% in the 2019 European Parliament elections.

Despite the above-mentioned cross-country differences in terms of right-wing populist electoral strength, it is a matter of fact that these parties are relevant political actors, which shape the public debate on immigration issues and influence decisions of policy makers and mainstream parties (Van Spanje 2010; Abou-Chadi and Krause 2018) or even adopt such decisions when in government, as best exemplified by the League of Matteo Salvini in Italy. Indeed, on the one hand such parties follow and represent opinions (and fears) about immigration that are widespread among European citizens over recent years. On the other hand, they actively contribute to form and spread such opinions: partisan mobilisation is fundamental for the politicisation of immigration issues (Green-Pedersen and Otjes 2017).

As previously mentioned, immigration issues are part of a new cultural cleavage opposing the winners and the losers of globalisation and integration processes: the so-called integration-demarcation cleavage according to Kriesi et al. (2006) or the transnational cleavage according to Hooghe and Marks (2018). This cleavage has not replaced the worker/employer cleavage, but cuts across the left-right divide (Hooghe and Marks 2018; Kriesi et al. 2006). Furthermore, concerns for group identity and diversity in an increasingly multicultural world are strictly connected to

---

[16] We calculated the electoral strength by summing the vote shares obtained in the elections for the national and European Parliament in the 2010–2019 time span by the parties that can be classified as populist radical right parties as defined by Mudde (2011). In Greece, Golden Dawn was also included for its electoral relevance, despite being a neo-fascist party rather than a populist party. We included only parties that obtained seats in at least one of the elections considered.

[17] The better performance of the populist radical right in European Parliament elections compared to national elections can be explained by the fact that a proportional representation electoral system is used for European Parliament elections, whereas in national elections a single-member district plurality electoral system is used.

Table 2.10 Political indicators by country over time

Country	Year	PRR electoral strength	GAL-TAN	Economic left-right
Czech Republic	2010	0.7%	5.0	5.1
	2013	9.3%	.	.
	2014	8.4%	5.4	5.5
	2017	12.2%	5.9	5.2
	2019	9.8%	.	.
Denmark	2010		4.5	5.1
	2011	12.3%	.	.
	2014	26.6%	4.3	4.8
	2015	21.1%	.	.
	2019	10.8% [b]	.	.
		11.1% [a]		
Finland	2010		5.1	4.9
	2011	19.1%	.	.
	2014	12.9%	4.7	5.0
	2015	17.7%	.	.
	2019	17.5% [a]	.	.
		13.8% [b]		
Greece	2010		5.0	3.4
	2012	20.5% [c]	.	.
		16.0% [d]		
	2014	15.6%	5.6	4.1
	2015	12.1% [e]	.	.
		10.7% [f]		
	2017		5.4	4.9
	2019	11.1% [a]	.	.
		6.6% [b]		
Italy	2010		4.2	3.9
	2013	6.1%	.	.
	2014	9.9%	5.6	4.8
	2017		5.6	4.6
	2018	21.8%	.	.
	2019	40.7%	.	.
Switzerland	2010		5.4	5.1
	2011	27.8%	.	.
	2014		5.7	5.2
	2015	30.7%	.	.

(continued)

Table 2.10 (continued)

Country	Year	PRR electoral strength	GAL-TAN	Economic left-right
United Kingdom	2010	3.7%	4.8	4.8
	2014	27.5%	4.5	4.9
	2015	13.2%	.	.
	2016		.	.
	2017	2.7%	4.4	4.4
	2019	33.7%	.	.

Note: *PRR* populist radical right
Source: SIRIUS WP 2 Dataset (including Comparative Political Dataset 1965–2015, ParlGov and own calculations based on Chapel Hill Expert Survey), own calculations based on official electoral results
[a]National parliamentary election
[b]European parliament election
[c]National parliamentary election of May 2012
[d]National parliamentary election of June 2012
[e]National parliamentary election of January 2015
[f]National parliamentary election of September 2015

a larger cultural conflict (Beramendi et al. 2015; Hooghe and Marks 2018) between libertarian and authoritarian values (Kitschelt 1994). Indeed, scholars analysing the ideological positions of public opinion detect a bi-dimensional structure of the political space (see Grasso and Giugni 2018). One dimension is linked to issues of economic equality, which separates pro-economic redistribution positions from positions in favour of laissez-faire economics (the traditional economic left–right distinction). The other dimension relates to issues of cultural diversity and social order, based on the opposition between authoritarian and libertarian positions (Kitschelt 1994). These two dimensions are relevant not only in terms of citizens' positions on policy issues, but also in terms of party positions. Restrictive positions on immigration are part of the so-called TAN (traditionalist/authoritarian/nationalist) pole of the cultural dimension, whereas pro-immigration positions are part of the GAL (green/alternative/libertarian) pole (Hooghe et al. 2002). Therefore, in order to capture the influence of the populist radical right on a given party system, it is not sufficient to consider only its electoral strength: it is necessary to investigate how culturally authoritarian/traditionalist/nationalist positions are widespread in that party system. Table 2.10 includes, indeed, indicators of the economic left-right dimension[18] and cultural libertarian-authoritarian dimension.[19] As shown by the

---

[18]It is the mean of the mean values of parties on a 0–10 economic left-right scale, where 0 means Extreme Left and 10 means Extreme Right. Parties have been classified in terms of their stance on economic issues. Parties on the economic left want government to play an active role in the economy. Parties on the economic right emphasize a reduced economic role for government: privatization, lower taxes, less regulation, less government spending, and a leaner welfare state.

[19]This is the so-called GAL-TAN index and it is the mean of the mean values of parties on a 0–10 'libertarian-authoritarian' scale, where 0 means Extreme Libertarian and 10 means Extreme Authoritarian. Parties have been classified in terms of their stance on democratic freedoms and

data, party systems of the SIRIUS countries are not particularly polarised. In general, however, socio-culturally TAN positions prevail, also in contexts in which economically left-wing positions prime. For instance, in Greece the cultural libertarian-authoritarian index (the so-called GAL-TAN index) ranges from 5.0 in 2010 to 5.6 in 2014, while the economic left-right index ranges from 3.4 to 4.1 in the same years (in 2017 the GAL-TAN index is still higher than the left-right one, 5.4 vs. 4.9). A very similar pattern is observed in Italy. In Switzerland and the Czech Republic, where both socio-culturally authoritarian and economically right-wing positions prevail, the former are more widespread than the latter. Czech Republic is the country that shows the highest level of the GAL-TAN index (5.9 in 2017), confirming to be a context not particularly favourable to pro-migrant positions. The UK is again an exception, being the context with an increasingly slight prevalence of both socio-culturally libertarian and economically left-wing positions over time.

The prevalence of TAN positions on the cultural dimension, even in contexts in which economically left-wing positions prime, confirm on the one hand that the cultural GAL-TAN and economic left-right divides are different dimensions of the political space, with some parties taking both TAN positions on the cultural dimension and left-wing positions on the economic dimension. On the other, these data show again that party positions in SIRIUS countries generally favour the adoption of restrictive policy measures on immigration.

To conclude, citizens' perceptions and political context are closely related phenomena that can explain the restrictive approach to immigration adopted by several European governments as mentioned in the first section, despite the factual reality which does not corroborate claims about an "invasion of immigrants in Europe" and regardless of evidence about immigration's positive effects in economic and demographic terms for European countries (Storesletten 2003; Lee and Miller 2000; Mayr 2005).

2.5   Conclusions

The European countries analysed in this study are characterised by very different socio-economic conditions, different stocks and flows of MRAs, and diverse welfare state regimes. Nevertheless, the law and policy-making on immigration issues in such different contexts has been characterised by a broadly restrictive approach, as shown more in detail in Chap. 3. Therefore, in the introduction we hypothesised that this policy approach is better explained by political factors, rather than the actual number of MRAs, their integration process, the effective European societies'

---

rights. "Libertarian" or "post-materialist" parties favour expanded personal freedoms, for example, access to abortion, active euthanasia, same sex marriage, or greater democratic participation. "Traditional" or "authoritarian" parties often reject these ideas; they value order, tradition, and stability, and believe that the government should be a firm moral authority on social and cultural issues.

demographic and economic needs, within each national context. More precisely, we hypothesised that if actual numbers of MRAs were still relatively low in the selected European countries despite the recent refugee crisis, then the adoption of restrictive policies on immigration could be better explained by the following political factors: prevalence of negative attitudes towards immigration among European citizens and salience of the immigration issue; political relevance of populist radical-right parties who mostly mobilized on immigration issues and significant diffusion of their authoritarian/traditionalist/nationalist positions within each country's party system. The underlying idea was that vote-maximising parties are conditioned by public attitudes on immigration and issue salience, which in turn are shaped by political entrepreneurship of radical right parties or moderate centre-right parties (Van Spanje 2010; Hobolt and De Vries 2015). In particular, populist-radical parties have become relevant political actors because on the one hand they have politicised immigration issues (Green-Pedersen and Otjes 2017) and have become more popular electorally by exploiting citizens' fears and concerns about immigration phenomena (Mudde 2011; Ivarsflaten 2008; Lucassen and Lubbers 2012); on the other, these parties have influenced the positions and immigration policies of mainstream parties (Abou-Chadi and Krause 2018) spreading in European party systems their authoritarian/traditionalist/nationalist positions (Hooghe and Marks 2018), which are strictly linked to the aforementioned new cultural cleavage between supporters of cultural demarcation and international integration (Kriesi et al. 2006). This hypothesis has been tested by contrasting legislative and policy measures on migration and integration issues with the numbers of MRAs in each national context, as well with the above-mentioned political features.

The analysis has shown that there is a certain inconsistency between legal and policy measures adopted by SIRIUS governments on immigration issues and the numbers of immigration. On the one hand, in fact, over time there has been both a narrowing of the legal access channels and a legal marginalization of MRAs as regards the access to social benefits and their right to work, thus making legal immigration more difficult and producing the phenomenon of the so-called legal peripheries (Chouinard 2001). In terms of labour market integration policies, there is a huge variation across countries in terms of duration of integration programmes, availability of services offered and migrant groups entitled to such programmes, with asylum seekers being usually the most disadvantaged. Despite national differences, which can be explained by the different welfare regimes and amount of resources dedicated in general to active labour market policies, several and similar barriers to labour market integration are a common feature of the analysed countries, which are not properly addressed by a usually short-term approach towards integration.

On the other hand, data on MRAs stocks and flows tell us that Europe is not facing an invasion: the amount of migrants and asylum seekers entering and living in Europe is perfectly manageable. It is true, indeed, that between 2014 and 2016 European countries faced a critical moment, with a clear rise of asylum seekers. However, in the following years there has a been a sharp decline in these figures and the number of first instance and final decisions granting a form of international protection have dropped. Moreover, it should be stressed that non-EU nationals represent less than 10% of the resident population in each of the analysed countries in 2018. Finally, the numbers of immigration tell us not only that the latter is not 'out of control', but also that it is somehow necessary from a demographic and economic standpoint: indeed, net migration has been the main driver of EU population growth during the last years and has reduced the proportion of inactive population given that most migrants are of working age (and the amount of work residence permits reflects this reality). Restrictive policy measures, therefore, seem to be not justified by the reality of immigration in the selected European countries. In addition, the claimed goal of fighting illegal immigration has not been achieved, given that the restriction of legal entry for non-EU migrants has not stopped illegal immigration and repatriations proved to be difficult: indeed, as shown by previous studies (De Haas 2011), restrictive immigration policies often result in being ineffective because they are unrealistic.

If policy-measures seem to be disconnected from data about immigration, they are totally connected with the political climate, with cuts to integration programmes and narrowing the access fostered by anti-immigrant politics. Anti-immigrant attitudes and in general fears and concerns about immigration phenomena, indeed, represent a constraint for decision-makers and are the main reason for right-wing populist parties' appeal in Europe (Mudde 2011; Ivarsflaten 2008; Lucassen and Lubbers 2012). In this regard, our data show that immigration issue is salient and in most countries negative attitudes towards immigration prevail. Such negative attitudes keep being widespread, albeit with different degrees according to national contexts, even after the so-called refugee crisis of 2014–2016. A clear example of this inconsistency between real data and perceptions is represented by the Czech Republic: among those discussed here it is the country with the lowest share of legally resident immigrants in 2018 (together with Finland) and it is the country showing the most negative attitudes towards immigration according to the Eurobarometer survey of 2018. These perceptions usually are disconnected from real data as shown by a recent study (Valbruzzi 2019), but they do count for both law and policy-making. Indeed, populist radical parties on the one hand follow and represent citizens' fears and negative perceptions of this phenomenon, on the other they shape the public debate on immigration issues, actively contributing to form and spread such negative attitudes and misperception about immigration numbers: hostility towards immigrants and misperception about the real presence of immigrants in one's own country are indeed very related phenomena (Valbruzzi 2019) and partisan mobilisation is fundamental for the politicisation of immigration issues (Green-Pedersen and Otjes 2017). As shown in this chapter, the electoral strength of populist radical right parties has increased over time, although with different trends and levels among SIRIUS countries. Despite these cross-country differences, the political relevance of populist right-wing parties in recent years is a matter of fact. These parties have strongly influenced immigration policies in two ways: on the one hand, populist right-wing parties have come to power in some countries (for example in Italy, Austria, Poland), on the other their electoral rise has influenced the positions and policies of mainstream parties (Abou-Chadi and Krause 2018).

The overall influence of populist radical right parties on European party systems is finally shown by the fact that socio-culturally authoritarian/traditionalist/nationalist positions prevail in SIRIUS countries, even in contexts where economically left-wing positions prime. These data confirm the increasing salience within the European political spaces of the cultural dimension related to issues of cultural demarcation vs. cultural integration (Kriesi et al. 2006). This new cleavage cuts across the economic left-right divide and is increasingly shaping party competition and voting behaviour (Hooghe and Marks 2018; Kriesi et al. 2006). To conclude, citizens' perceptions and party systems' features are closely related phenomena, which influence one another and are all key factors that need to be considered to explain the law and policy-making of recent years on immigration issues.

References

Abou-Chadi, T. (2016). Political and institutional determinants of immigration policies. *Journal of Ethnic and Migration Studies, 42*(13), 2087–2110.

Abou-Chadi, T., & Krause, W. (2018). The causal effect of radical right success on mainstream parties' policy positions: A regression discontinuity approach. *British Journal of Political Science, 50*, 1–19.

Alesina, A., & Glaeser, E. (2004). *Fighting poverty in the US and Europe: A world of difference.* New York: Oxford University Press.

Banting, K. (2000). Looking in three directions: migration and the European welfare state in comparative perspective. In M. Bommes & A. Geddes (Eds.), *Immigration and welfare: Challenging the borders of the welfare state* (pp. 13–33). London: Routledge.

Bay, A.-H., Finseraas, H., & Pedersen, A. W. (2013). Welfare Dualism in two Scandinavian welfare states: Public opinion and party politics. *West European Politics, 36*(1), 199–220.

Beramendi, P., Häusermann, S., Kitschelt, H., & Hanspeter Kriesi, H. (Eds.). (2015). *The politics of advanced capitalism.* Cambridge: Cambridge University Press.

Bhagwati, J. (2003). Borders beyond control. *Foreign affairs* (January/February), 98–104.

Bjerre, L., Helbling, M., Römer, F., & Zobel, M. (2015). Conceptualizing and measuring immigration policies: A comparative perspective. *International Migration Review, 49*(3), 555–600.

Bontenbal, I, & Lillie, N. (2019). *Policy Barriers and Enablers* (WP3 Report for the SIRIUS project). https://www.sirius-project.eu/sites/default/files/attachments/SIRIUS%20WP3%20-%20 D3.2_0.pdf

Burstein, P. (2003). The impact of public opinion on public policy: A review and an agenda. *Political Research Quarterly, 56*(1), 29–40.

Castles, S. (2004). Why migration policies fail. *Ethnic and Racial Studies, 27*, 205–227.

Chojnicki, X. (2013). The fiscal impact of immigration in France: A generational accounting approach. *The World Economy, 36*(8), 1065–1090.

Chouinard, V. (2001). Legal peripheries: Struggles over disabled Canadians' places in law, society and space. *Canadian Geographer/Le Géographe canadien, 45*(1), 187–192.

Collado, M. D., Iturbe-Ormaetxe, I., & Valera, G. (2004). Quantifying the impact of immigration on the Spanish welfare state. *International Tax and Public Finance, 11*(3), 335–353.

Czaika, M., & De Haas, H. (2013). The effectiveness of immigration policies. *Population and Development Review, 39*(3), 487–508.

De Haas, H. (2008). The myth of invasion: The inconvenient realities of African migration to Europe. *Third World Quarterly, 29*(7), 1305–1322.

De Haas, H. (2011). *The determinants of international migration* (DEMIG Working Paper 2). International Migration Institute. https://www.migrationinstitute.org/publications/wp-32-11

De Haas, H, & Natter, K. (2015). *The determinants of migration policies. Does the political orientation of governments matter?* (DEMIG project paper 29). International Migration Institute. https://www.migrationinstitute.org/publications/the-determinants-of-migration-policies-does-the-political-orientation-of-governments-matter.

Dennison, J., & Geddes, A. (2018). A rising tide? The salience of immigration and the rise of anti-immigration political parties in Western Europe. *The Political Quarterly, 90*(1), 107–116.

Düvell, F. (2005). *Illegal immigration in Europe: Beyond control?* Houndmills: Palgrave Macmillan.

Eurostat. (2019). *Key figures on Europe — Statistics illustrated* (2019th ed.). Luxembourg: Publications Office of the European Union. https://ec.europa.eu/eurostat/documents/3217494/10164469/KS-EI-19-001-EN-N.pdf/33ab6c0c-a0c6-5294-3948-b1fb9973d096?t=1574262443000.

Emanuele, V., Maggini, N., & Paparo, A. (2019). The times they are a-changin: Party campaign strategies in the 2018 Italian election. *West European Politics*. https://doi.org/10.1080/01402382.2019.1655966.

Faist, T. (1996). Immigration, integration and the welfare state: Germany and the USA in a comparative perspective. In R. Bauböck, A. Heller, & A. Zolberg (Eds.), *The challenge of diversity, integration and pluralism in societies of immigration* (pp. 227–258). Aldershot: Avebury.

Flanagan, S. C., & Lee, A.-R. (2003). The new politics, culture wars, and the authoritarian-libertarian value change in advanced industrial democracies. *Comparative Political Studies, 36*, 235–270.

Freeman, G. P. (1986). Migration and the political economy of the welfare state. *The Annals of the American Academy of Political and Social Science, 485*(1), 51–63.

Gilligan, C. (2015). The public and the politics of immigration controls. *Journal of Ethnic and Migration Studies, 41*(9), 1373–1390.

Goodman, S. W. (2015). Conceptualizing and measuring citizenship and integration policy: Past lessons and new approaches. *Comparative Political Studies, 48*(14), 1905–1941.

Grasso, M., & Giugni, M. (2018). Political values and extra-institutional political participation: The impact of economic redistributive and social libertarian preferences on protest behaviour. *International Political Science Review*. https://doi.org/10.1177/0192512118780425.

Green-Pedersen, C., & Krogstrup, J. (2008). Immigration as a political issue in Denmark and Sweden. *European Journal of Political Research, 47*(5), 610–634.

Green-Pedersen, C., & Otjes, S. (2017). A hot topic? Immigration on the agenda in Western Europe. *Party Politics, 25*(3), 424–434. https://doi.org/10.1177/1354068817728211.

Ho, G, & Shirono, K. (2015). *The Nordic Labor Market and Migration*. IMF Working Paper No. 15/254. https://ssrn.com/abstract=2733545

Hobolt, S. B., & de Vries, C. E. (2015). Issue entrepreneurship and multiparty competition. *Comparative Political Studies, 48*(9), 1159–1185.

Hooghe, L., & Marks, G. (2018). Cleavage theory meets Europe's crises: Lipset, Rokkan, and the transnational cleavage. *Journal of European Public Policy, 25*(1), 109–135.

Hooghe, L., Marks, G., & Wilson, C. J. (2002). Does left/right structure party positions on European integration? *Comparative Political Studies, 35*(8), 965–989.

Ivarsflaten, E. (2008). What unites right-wing populists in western Europe? Re-examining grievance mobilization models in seven successful cases. *Comparative Political Studies, 41*, 3–23.

Kitschelt, H. (1994). *The transformation of European social democracy*. Cambridge: Cambridge University Press.

Kriesi, H., Grande, E., Lachat, R., Dolezal, M., Bornschier, S., & Frey, T. (2006). Globalization and the transformation of the national political space: Six European countries compared. *European Journal of Political Research, 45*, 921–956.

Lee, R., & Miller, T. (2000). Immigration, social security and broader fiscal impacts. *American Economic Review, 90*(2), 350–354.

Lucassen, G., & Lubbers, M. (2012). Who fears what? Explaining far-right-wing preference in Europe by distinguishing perceived cultural and economic ethnic threats. *Comparative Political Studies, 45*, 547–574.

Mayr, K. (2005). The fiscal impact of immigrants in Austria: A generational accounting analysis. *Empirica, 32*(2), 181–216.

Migration Policy Group. (2011). *The Migrant Integration Policy Index (MIPEX)*. http://mipex.eu/

Mudde, C. (2011). Radical right parties in Europe: What, who, why? *Participation, 34*(3), 12–15.

Nagayoshi, K., & Hjerm, M. (2015). Anti-immigration attitudes in different welfare states: Do types of labor market policies matter? *International Journal of Comparative Sociology, 56*(2), 141–162.

Nekby, L. (2008). *Active labor market programs for the integration of youths and immigrants into the labor market: The Nordic experience*. Santiago: CEPAL.

OECD. (2007). *Jobs for immigrants. Volume 1. Labour market integration in Australia, Denmark, Germany and Sweden* (Vol. 1). Paris: OECD Publishing.

OECD. (2008). *Jobs for immigrants. Volume 2. Labour market integration in Belgium, France, the Netherlands and Portugal*. Paris: OECD Publishing.

OECD. (2012). *Jobs for immigrants. Volume 3. Labour market integration in Austria, Norway and Switzerland* (Vol. 3). Paris: OECD Publishing.

Rinne, U. (2013). The evaluation of immigration policies. In A. F. Constant & K. F. Zimmermann (Eds.), *International handbook on the economics of migration* (pp. 530–551). Cheltenham/ Northampton: Edward Elgar Publishing.

Schibel, Y., Fazel, M., Robb, R., & Garner, P. (2002). Refugee integration: Can research synthesis inform policy? Feasibility study report. *RDS On-line Report*, 13/02.

Schierup, C.-U., Hansen, P., & Castles, S. (2006). *Migration, citizenship, and the European welfare state: A European dilemma*. Oxford: Oxford University Press.

Storesletten, K. (2003). Fiscal implications of immigration – A net present value calculation. *Scandinavian Journal of Economics, 105*(3), 487–506.

United Nations, Department of Economic and Social Affairs, Population Division. (2017). *Trends in International Migrant Stock: The 2017 revision, United Nations database*. POP/DB/MIG/ Stock/Rev.2017.

Valbruzzi, M. (2019). *Immigrazione in Italia: tra realtà e percezione, research note of the Istituto Cattaneo, Bologna*.

van der Brug, Wouter, D'Amato, G., Berkhout, J., & Ruedin, D. (2015). A framework for studying the politicisation of immigration. In W. van der Brug, G. D'Amato, J. Berkhout, & D. Ruedin (Eds.), *The politicisation of migration* (pp. 17–34). London: Routledge.

van Spanje, J. (2010). Contagious parties: Anti-immigration parties and their impact on other parties immigration stances in contemporary Western Europe. *Party Politics, 16*(5), 563–586.

Wunderlich, D. (2010). Differentiation and policy convergence against long odds: Lessons from implementing EU migration policy in Morocco. *Mediterranean Politics, 15*, 249–272.

Zetter, R. (2007). More labels, fewer refugees: remaking the refugee label in an era of globalization. *Journal of Refugee Studies, 20*(2), 172–192.

Sources (Databases)

Chapel Hill Expert Survey (CHES) (https://www.chesdata.eu/)

Comparative Political Dataset (http://www.cpds-data.org/index.php/data)

Eurobarometers (http://ec.europa.eu/public_opinion/index_en.htm)

European Social Survey (http://www.europeansocialsurvey.org/)

Eurostat database (http://ec.europa.eu/eurostat/data/database)

SIRIUS database (https://www.sirius-project.eu/sites/default/files/attachments/WP2_D2.1.xlsx)

Chapter 3
Tightening Asylum and Migration Law and Narrowing the Access to European Countries: A Comparative Discussion

Paola Pannia

3.1 Detecting Patterns of Convergence on Immigration Policies Across EU Member States

Migration has not ceased to occupy a prominent role in the EU agenda over recent years, even if numbers of arrivals and asylum applications have considerably reduced. Indeed, in 2018, 141,472 arrivals were recorded, with a steady drop compared to the flows of foreigners approaching European coasts between 2014 and 2017.[1] The so-called 'refugee crisis',[2] or at least its most acute peaks, seems to belong to the past – and yet political discourses on migration show no sign of quieting down. Discussions about the entry and stay of foreigners continue to enflame public debate on both European and domestic levels, informing policies and triggering packages of legislative reform (Green-Pedersen and Otjes 2017; Meyer and Rosenberger 2015; Maggini in this volume).

What may appear as a kind of political schizophrenia, as yet another symbol of institutional detachment from reality, instead unfolds the tight and mutual

---

[1] See UNHCR, Mediterranean situation, available at https://data2.unhcr.org/en/situations/mediterranean. Data includes refugees and migrants arriving by sea to Italy, Greece, Spain, Cyprus and Malta and refugees and migrants arriving by land to Greece and Spain.

[2] The use of the expression should not be intended as an adherence to the emergency discourse spread both in the political and media spheres. Conversely, coherently with the theoretical frame presented below, in this contribution, the expression 'refugee crisis' aims to underline the complex web of relationships linking international migration and how it has been perceived and understood by the main actors of the management of migration (Triandafyllidou 2018).

P. Pannia (✉)
University of Florence, Florence, Italy
e-mail: paola.pannia@unifi.it

© The Author(s) 2021
V. Federico, S. Baglioni (eds.), *Migrants, Refugees and Asylum Seekers' Integration in European Labour Markets*, IMISCOE Research Series,
https://doi.org/10.1007/978-3-030-67284-3_3

relationships intertwining international migration debates and perceptions of policies that aim to regulate the entry and stay of foreigners.

People do not move in an empirical or legal vacuum. How international movements are perceived, comprehended and managed also depends on the intricate web of institutional, normative, social narratives and labels that are produced on migration by the 'hosting countries' (Geddes 2005). Against the understanding of international migration as an independent variable that challenges states, it is important to underline that migration "acquires meaning when it meets the borders (territorial, organisational and conceptual) of destination states" (Geddes and Scholten 2016: 4).[3] Policies, legislative acts and even case law attribute a specific quality, value and scope to international migration. Narratives generated by the policies and legislative acts on migration, but also case law, contribute to conditioning and shaping the identity, scope and character of international migration. Analysing these factors may help us to intercept some of the complex dynamics surrounding migration and its governance, while advancing our understanding of this complicated subject.

Against this heuristic backdrop, our contribution aims to analyse how selected EU states (namely the Czech Republic, Denmark, Finland, Greece, Italy, Switzerland, the UK, hereinafter also SIRIUS countries) respond to post-2014 migration flows. The purpose of the chapter is to compare and contrast how immigration laws are discussed and elaborated in these countries, through which tools and with what objectives.

The chapter thus departs from evidence provided by national reports within the SIRIUS research project. These data are adjourned, analysed and complemented by statistics, reports, research and specialist literature, in line with the multidisciplinary and socio-legal approach of this contribution. While acknowledging the peculiarities of each national context, discussed thoroughly in this book, the analysis here focuses on the main trends managing international migration.

The comparative analysis of migration governance presents multiple challenges. Amongst them are the dynamism and continuous changes that affect the institutional and normative framework over time (Menski 2006; Scarciglia 2015); the flexibility of categories used across national legislations (Zonca 2016); and the multiple levels of governance involved in the management of migration (Zincone and Caponio 2006). Being aware of these difficulties, the current contribution wants to avoid standard and definitive schemes to conceptually organize what is a complex reality. Instead, the research adopts an inductive strategy, departing from the observation of empirical data to identify tendencies and patterns of convergence across European countries. In using a flexible methodological approach, this comparative study attempts to grasp the main trends in legal and political responses to migration, while acknowledging the dynamism of the multifaceted processes that surround the phenomenon (Amico di Meane 2018).

---

[3] Further analysis should be conducted to better understand how migration governance affects migration, in particular the decision to integrate the perspective of third country nationals (Kraler 2006; Federico and Pannia 2018).

The chapter begins by giving an account of political representations and legal categorizations on migrants and asylum seekers produced by SIRIUS countries in the aftermath of the 'refugee crisis' and beyond. Relying on narratives that question the sincerity of asylum claims, and that criminalise migration and humanitarian assistance, restrictive measures are enacted in most SIRIUS countries. The legislative landscape of the countries under scrutiny is populated by symbolic laws that downgrade foreigners' rights and weaken standards, explicitly aiming to dissuade migrants from coming to the respective countries. The analysis then turns to look at international protection. The recourse to push-back operations, and/or, more blatantly, the construction of physical walls or fences, are not the only measures that prevent third country nationals from lodging an asylum claim. Indeed, restraining access to protection is also the consequence of a sophisticated procedural toolbox intended to streamline the refugee status determination procedure (i.e. hotspots and accelerated and fast-track procedures), often at the price of severe violations of fundamental guarantees, such as the right to defence. Final observations are devoted to the restraining tendency enacted by SIRIUS countries in the field of economic-related migration. Here, state power to select and control who can enter and stay in a country is exercised even more openly, in an attempt to respond to domestic electoral consensus-building while welcoming foreigners who cannot represent a burden to the national welfare system.

3.2 Gathering the Interplay Among Narratives on Migration and Asylum and the Restrictive Turn of Policies and Legislations

The right to asylum is explicitly entrenched in the Constitution of the Czech Republic, Italy and Finland, although to different degrees.[4] All countries discussed in the volume have signed the 1951 Geneva Convention and its additional protocols, they are bound by the EU *acquis* aimed at the creation of a Common European Asylum System, with the exception of Switzerland which is not a EU Member State,[5] of Denmark, which opted out,[6] and the UK, which only abides by the first

---

[4] The right to asylum is also entrenched in art. 18 of the EU Charter on Fundamental Rights. For a panorama of law references of this right on EU Member States' national constitutional law see the following web page: https://fra.europa.eu/en/charterpedia/article/18-right-asylum. The Switzerland Constitution also mentions the right to asylum. However, this right is not proclaimed, but only regulated in its main aspects. The Switzerland Constitution can be consulted here: https://www.admin.ch/opc/en/classified-compilation/19995395/201809230000/101.pdf

[5] Switzerland is bound by the Return Directive (Directive 2008/115/EC), the Dublin III Regulation (Regulation (EU) No 604/2013 of 26 June 2013) and Eurodac Regulation (Regulation (EU) No 603/2013 of 26 June 2013). Full titles of legislations are mentioned in the list of legislations below.

[6] Denmark only abides Dublin III Regulation and Eurodac Regulation.

phase of the Common European Asylum System[7] as a result of its opting out from the 'Asylum Recast Package'. Finally, most of the SIRIUS countries, such as Denmark, Finland and Italy, have incorporated the European Convention of Human Rights, together with its principle of protection against torture or inhuman or degrading treatments (art. 3 ECHR), in their Constitutions.

Despite these national, regional and international obligations, an overall restrictive approach can be observed among the surveyed countries, where the tightening of migration law conflates with both a discourse and normative categorizations that label migration and asylum as a threat.

3.2.1 Questioning the Authenticity of Asylum Claims

Throughout most of the SIRIUS countries, the regressive approach taken in the field of migration and refugee law seems to rely on a specific political construal of the 'bogus asylum seeker' or the 'illegal asylum seeker' (Lynn and Lea 2003; Zetter 2007; Squire 2009; Gabrielatos and Baker 2008).[8]

Illustrative of this tendency is the so-called 'deport first, appeal later' provision, introduced in the UK with the Immigration Act 2014. In the words of the Home Office, the new measure provides the power to deport foreigners pending their deportation appeal, and allows halting foreigners' "opportunity to launch spurious claims under the Human Rights Act or falsely claim asylum" (Home Office and the Rt Hon James Brokenshire MP 2015). In 2017, the Supreme Court declared that deportations issued under this scheme were unlawful, they contravene the right to family and private life entrenched in article 8 of the European Convention of Human Rights, and undermine the right to an effective appeal (R (on the application of Kiarie) (Appellant) v Secretary of State for the Home Department (Respondent) [2017] UKSC 42). Meanwhile, research shows that, in the UK media-based public sphere, migration is reduced to an issue of border controls or political management (Montgomery et al. 2018).

As the 'detention fast track procedure' exemplifies, discourses that surreptitiously associate asylum seekers with economic or illegal migrants instil doubts

---

[7] Namely the 'Refugee Qualification Directive' (2004/83/EC), the 'Asylum Procedure Directive' (2005/85/EC) and the 'Asylum Reception Conditions Directive' (2003/9/EC).

[8] The terms 'bogus asylum seeker' and 'illegal asylum seeker' are often used in the political and media discourse and carry varied connotations depending on the context. The term 'bogus asylum-seeker' is often used in opposition to the term 'genuine asylum seeker'. Instead, the term 'illegal asylum seeker' often refers to people who arrive by boat without documents and express the will to apply for protection. Nonetheless, as UNHCR (2018b) has pointed out, "There is no such thing as a bogus asylum seeker or an illegal asylum seeker. As an asylum seeker, a person has entered into a legal process of refugee status determination. Everybody has a right to seek asylum in another country. People who don't qualify for protection as refugees will not receive refugee status and may be deported, but just because someone doesn't receive refugee status doesn't mean they are a bogus asylum seeker".

about the truthfulness of asylum seekers' protection needs. In turn, this provides the theoretical framework to speed up and simplify the refugee status determination (hereinafter also RSD) procedures, sometimes in breach of procedural guarantees and the quality of assessment. Governments try to dispel doubts by immediately distinguishing the 'bogus asylum seeker' from the 'true' one. Therefore, when the authenticity of a foreigner's asylum claim is regarded as suspicious, his/her rights and guarantees are also questioned. Sometimes, legal presumptions and categorizations that inhabiting the refugee law of SIRIUS countries serve the same end. The concept of 'vulnerability' used in the frame of resettlement programs offers a good illustration of this trend (AIDA 2017; Peroni and Timmer 2013).

As a long-term, durable solution,[9] resettlement undoubtedly represents a fundamental tool to provide refugees with sound legal protection and guarantees. Although the number of people effectively resettled is much lower than pledges made by European states, in 2017 more than 26,400 refugees were resettled to Europe, the majority of whom were transferred to the UK. Although contributing to a lesser extent, Finland and Switzerland also provide active resettlement programs (UNHCR 2018a: 17), while Denmark declined to receive the UN refugees quota under the resettlement pact in 2016, and further extended the suspension to 2017 and 2018 (Wallis 2019).[10]

Nonetheless, it has been observed that the UK applies the label of 'vulnerable' to refugees in order to qualify those eligible for its resettlement programs. Among the resettlement programs put in place by the UK Government, three explicitly target the most vulnerable: the Syrian Vulnerable Persons Resettlement Scheme (VPRS), the Vulnerable Children Resettlement Scheme and children relocated under the 'Dubs amendments'. Whereas the latter programs address children specifically, the former scheme concerns vulnerable Syrian refugees, including the elderly, the disabled, persons who have experienced trauma, children, orphans and minorities (Home Office 2018). However, this may send the message that the general refugee population is either not vulnerable, or else not vulnerable 'enough' to deserve resettlement. Indeed, the approach favours the creation of two categories: the more deserving and the less deserving refugees. Only the former are protected and taken in charge by the state (Hirst and Atto 2018). Similarly, the EU relocation program,[11] which has realized the transferral of almost 22,000 asylum seekers from Greece and about 12,700 from Italy across Europe (EU Commission 2018), has reproduced the same rationale, considering as 'vulnerable' and therefore eligible only those asylum-seekers of nationalities with an average recognition rate of 75% or higher at EU level.

---

[9] A 'durable solution' is one that enables refugees to 'rebuild their life' (UNHCR 2003).

[10] In 2017, an amendment to the Aliens Act also left the decision on resettlement refugees to the Minister of Immigration and Integration alone, so potentially put an end to resettlement programs to Denmark. However, the new government, led by a different political party (social democratic) and in place since June 2019, might decide to again join the UN resettlement program.

[11] The relocation programme was a two year scheme provided by the 'Provisional measures in the area of international protection for the benefit of Italy and Greece' adopted by the European Council in 2015, aimed to reduce the migratory pressure on frontline states (Italy and Greece).

This 'fractioning' of the refugee label (Zetter 2007; Costello and Hancox 2015) creates a quasi-hierarchy among refugees. On the one hand, it reduces or slows access to international protection, while on the other, it regulates access according to reasons of social acceptance rather than the right to asylum.

3.2.2   The Criminalization of Migration and Humanitarian Assistance

Closely related to the narrative presented above, we can observe the tendency to merge the status of the 'protection seeker' with a condition of 'illegality' or 'irregularity', or to juxtapose migration to security concerns. Following this pattern, and increasingly frequently, governmental authorities deploy the punitive arsenal of the criminal law against migrants in an attempt to manage and control migration. Consequently, the distinction between criminal law and immigration law is progressively blurring. This may not only entail dangerous consequences for foreigners' human rights, but also contributes to throwing a negative light on social perception about them (Council of Europe, Commissioner for Human Rights 2010).

Evidence of the above scheme is analysed and theorized into what has been called the 'crimmigration law' (Stumpf 2006). Concrete manifestations of this understanding of migration are found in all the countries under scrutiny. Indeed, all SIRIUS countries consider unauthorised crossing of the border a criminal offence, punished with imprisonment and/or fines or with fines only (FRA 2014). Meanwhile, narratives that portray immigrants as a threat to national security and social welfare flourish across EU states. In both Greece (Bagavos et al. 2018) and Italy (Chiaromonte et al. 2018), the stereotypical correlation 'immigrant-criminal' is widely promoted by policymaking, and echoed by the media.

Similar criminalization processes may also affect people who enter Europe to seek protection. For instance, in the UK, according to section 2 of the Asylum and Immigration Act 2004, asylum applicants who cannot provide identification documents may be charged with a criminal offence, punishable by a prison sentence of up to 2 years. As Hirst and Atto report: "In the first 6 months since s2 of the Act came into force, at least 230 asylum seekers were arrested, and 134 convicted of this new offence. Multiple asylum seekers have received jail sentences" (2018: 854).

The 'criminalization trend' targets not only migrants, but also members of civil society who provide humanitarian assistance to foreigners' entry into Europe, including NGOs and volunteers involved in search and rescue (hereinafter also SAR) at sea. In 2018, more than 2000 people lost their lives crossing the Mediterranean, the death rate for numbers of arrivals almost triplicated compared to 2017 (UNHCR 2019). In this context, NGOs' intervention proved crucial in saving lives (Italian Coast Guard 2017), due also to the reduction of states-run SAR operations at sea (Council of Europe Commissioner for Human Rights 2019). Nonetheless, this did not prevent some policy-makers from running a delegitimization campaign focused on the media-based public sphere, and approving measures to restrict and criminalize NGO activities. In this regard, Italy is a quite paradigmatic case.

In 2017, the Italian Ministry of the Interior in consultation with the European Commission issued a 'code of conduct' for those NGOs operating in the rescue of migrants at sea, aiming to regulate the search and rescue operations in the Mediterranean conducted by non-governmental actors. Under the code, measures such as the presence of law enforcement officers on board, the prohibition from entering Libyan territorial waters and collaboration in the fight against smugglers were imposed on NGO vessels (ASGI 2017; MSF 2017). In 2018, since taking office as Minister of Interior, Mr. Salvini has restricted the entry of NGO vessels into Italian ports on several occasions, inaugurating a policy of 'closing ports' which significantly delayed migrants' disembarkation as well as their access to succour, reception and asylum procedures. In June 2019, an emergency decree was approved, establishing, among the other provisions, hefty fines (from 150,000 to 1,000,000 euro) on any boat entering the Italian sea without permission, with the possibility of suspending or revoking their licences in case of reiterated contraventions of the ban (arts. 1 and 2).[12]

Furthermore, as shown by the report released by the Fundamental Rights Agency of the European Union, since 2018, in both Italy and Greece, NGO ships have been seized and subjected to administrative and criminal proceedings. None of these procedures has resulted in conviction.[13] Meanwhile, numerous allegations that NGOs collaborate with smugglers are denied by the NGOs involved (del Valle, 2016) and dismissed by public institutions (Italian Senate, 2017). Empirical research also demonstrates that claims portraying NGOs as a 'pull factor', somehow encouraging people to migrate to Europe, are unsubstantiated (Cusumano 2017).

Despite concerns expressed by the UN and the Council of Europe in recommendations and official letters, this trend, which obstructs and criminalizes humanitarian acts, does not seem to stop. As a result, only a few NGOs currently operate in the Mediterranean, leading to a drastic reduction in the possibility of saving lives at sea.

---

[12] Law-Decree No. 53, 14 June 2019 'Urgent dispositions on order and public security', converted with amendments by Law No. 77, 8 August 2019.

[13] The list of current legal proceedings in the EU against private entities involved in SAR operations in the Mediterranean Sea is provided by the European Union Agency for Fundamental Rights. The list, up-to-date until 1 June 2019, is available here: https://fra.europa.eu/sites/default/files/fra_uploads/fra-2019-ngos-search-rescue-mediterranean-table-2_en.pdf

3.2.3 Law as Communication: Normative Provisions Aiming to Create a 'Hostile Environment'[14]

Over recent years, this restrictive trend in migration policies and legislations across Europe has is also expressed through progressive curtailment of foreigners' rights and guarantees. The explicit aim is to dissuade new arrivals, while at the same time catering to (some) natives' fears about migrants, thus making European states a 'less attractive' destination.

Denmark offers a paradigmatic example. In February 2019, the government passed a new immigration bill announcing a 'paradigm shift' from integration to repatriation. Indeed, Law L140 substantially amends residence rules, allowing permit renewals only when conditions in home countries are deemed unsafe, or else in the case of strong family attachment. Following the reform, the degree of integration into Danish society has ceased to have any relevance when it comes to allowing the stay of international protection holders. It is difficult to predict the concrete effects of this paradigm shift. However, the message conveyed by the law is clear: refugees' stay in Denmark should only be temporary. Even if a softer agenda on migration were adopted by the new government, the idea that refugees will *not* become permanent residents has been recently reiterated by the new Prime Minister, Mette Frederiksen: "When you are a refugee and come to Denmark, you can be granted our protection. But when there's peace, you must go home" she stated in June (Wallis 2019).

Although challenged by scholars who demonstrate that stricter rules do not stem migrant flows (Thielemanne 2004; Mayblin and James 2016), the proposition of stricter rules to staunch the flow of asylum seekers has found wide support among SIRIUS countries, where policies and legislation have led to the progressive downgrading of foreigners' fundamental rights and guarantees. Within these measures, the right to family reunification has been significantly eroded. This is again the case of Denmark. Here, over recent years, the steady reduction of integration benefits and the limited access to family reunification given to refugees serves the stated aim "to make sure that it is not attractive to come to Denmark", as declared by the previous immigration minister, Inger Støjberg (Walter-Franke 2019: 3). Coherent with this rationale, the new law L140 allows the minister to activate a limit over the number of family reunifications in the event "asylum applications 'increase significantly over a short period', – without specifying what a significant increase would mean" (FRA 2019a: 4). Meanwhile, complicated bureaucratic procedures and the caseload in immigration services cause waiting times of up to 2 years, which severely affects refugees' right to reunite with family members (Bendixen 2019).

Similarly, in Greece, due to persistent administrative shortcomings, in 2018 only a few refugees were able to trigger a procedure for family reunification (Council of

---

[14] The expression appears in the speech that Theresa May gave on 10th October 2013, accessible at:https://www.theguardian.com/politics/2013/oct/10/immigration-bill-theresamay-hostile-environment

Europe Commissioner of Human Rights 2018). Beyond this, in a highly symbolic way, the Labor and Social Affair Minister of the newly (August 2019) installed Greek government cancelled a circular concerning the issuing of social security numbers (AMKA) to migrants, refugees, asylum seekers, unaccompanied refugee children and non-EU nationals. As observed, the circular "actually codified a law passed under the New Democracy government in 2009" (Lefkofridi and Chatzopoulou 2019). Nevertheless, this measure makes it difficult for foreigners to access social rights, being the AMKA essential to access services in Health, Education and Labor. A very similar provision was approved by the Italian government in 2018, when 'Security Decree' No. 113/2018 stipulated that the asylum applicant status would not anymore allow enrolment on the Civil Registry or obtaining a residence card (art. 13). This has severe implications for the recognition of social rights and benefits, with foreigners increasingly turning to the Court to claim the right to be enrolled on the Civil Registry. Finally, in August, the Tribunal of Milan questioned the constitutional legitimacy of art. 13, referring the case to the Constitutional Court (referral order of 16.08.2019).

In Finland, since normative changes introduced in 2016, refugees and those beneficiaries of subsidiary protection who want to apply for family reunification must demonstrate they have sufficient means to cover family expenses (Law 43/2016). The purpose of the reform is "to make sure that the society does not have to pay for foreigners residing in Finland" (Bontenbal and Lillie 2018: 206). Under these measures, the requirements for family reunification became extremely difficult for many to meet.

Sometimes, messages are conveyed through symbolic legislation, such as the so-called 'jewellery law' approved in Denmark in 2016 (Bill No. L 87). According to this controversial normative provision, police officers have the power to search and confiscate asylum seekers' assets with a minimum value of 10,000 Dkk (€ 1.340), as a contribution to the expenses related to their stay in Denmark. Denmark is not an isolated case among SIRIUS countries. Indeed, similar provisions are currently also in place in Switzerland, where asylum seekers are required to declare all their valuables on arrival, and anything which is worth more than € 900 can be taken away by immigration authorities.[15]

The real impact of these laws seems, so far, modest. In Switzerland a total amount of € 200,000 has been collected from 112 individuals (Hartmann and Feith Tan 2016), whereas in Denmark, a car and about €24.000 have been confiscated (Barret 2019). Nonetheless, the anti-migrant signal sent by these manifesto-laws (laws adopted for their symbolic meaning rather than to effectively regulating the issue at stake) is powerful, and it can realise multiple aims. Indeed, these legislations, intended to discourage asylum seekers from coming to the country, may trigger a race to the bottom among SIRIUS countries and beyond insofar as they try to become the most 'unattractive destination'. Meanwhile, such measures

---

[15] Unlike the Danish case, the Swiss law provides the return of asylum seekers' confiscated assets, if they decide to leave the country (Hartmann and Feith Tan 2016).

symbolically construct asylum seekers as 'abusive individuals' who threaten the welfare state. Relying on these narratives, states may more easily neglect protection seekers' claims and weaken their legal status, in breach of international conventions.

The creation of a 'hostile environment', often the stated aim of legislative reforms, is mirrored by the complex and hypertrophic legal milieu featuring SIRIUS countries in the field of migration and asylum. Indeed, national legislations have been modified continuously, and not necessarily coherently, often in the aftermath of a change in government.[16] This is consistent with other evidence: over recent years, migration has become a salient argument that often dominates elections and referendum debates at both European and national level. In the UK, for instance, the 2016 EU referendum can be considered a paradigmatic case, since the Leave campaign mostly revolved around anti-migration discourses. The same can be said for arguments used by the UK Conservative Party in the last elections (Calò et al. 2018).

Overt manifestations of the labyrinthine landscape currently governing migration and asylum can be found in almost all the SIRIUS countries. For instance, in the UK, 12 Acts of Parliament regulating immigration issues have been approved in the last 20 years (Hirst and Atto 2018). In Italy, the Consolidated Law on Immigration is the result of multiple, fragmentary normative stratifications that jeopardise internal consistency and effectiveness. The same complexity and rapid evolution is seen in the legal frameworks of Greece, Switzerland and Denmark, too. With respect to Demark, it is noteworthy that from 2002 to 2011 the Aliens Act, one of the main laws regulating immigration, was changed 57 times – and since 2015, more than 85 times (Sen et al. 2018). The same also applies to the Czech Republic, where, due to the numerous amendments, Act No. 326/1999 regulating the residence of foreigners became a chaotic and confusing law (Čada et al. 2018). Paradigmatically, in 2018 and 2019 changes occurred in the legal framework of all the surveyed countries, whereas further legislative amendments have been announced in Denmark and Finland by those governments established in 2019.

To add further complexity, in most SIRIUS countries the acts of primary legislation only provide for the general framework, while specific immigration issues are *de facto* regulated in detail and implemented by a congeries of acts of secondary legislation (by-laws, regulations, ministerial circulars, administrative rules, etc). This trend is particularly relevant in the UK, where a number of secondary immigration laws had been rushed through Parliament once a month on average (Clayton 2016). Between 2014 and 2016, reportedly, "two primary provisions were enacted (Immigration Act 2014 and 2016), while 79 orders and rules were promulgated" (Calò et al. 2018: 465). This not only makes the legal framework difficult to access and navigate, but also divorces a significant part of immigration regulation from democratic control. Indeed, secondary acts are rarely subjected to Parliamentary

---

[16] Finland seems to constitute an exception to this trend. Indeed, according to research carried out so far and the opinion of some interviewed experts, since the peak of arrivals in 2015, Finland has not experienced changes in legislations, but a trend of more restrictive interpretation of the legal framework already in place (Bontenbal and Lillie 2018).

debate. Hence, away from any adequate parliamentary control, governments retain considerable spaces of discretion and room of manoeuvre in the regulation of migration issues.

3.3 Preventing or Restraining Access to International Protection

Focusing on the legislation governing international protection, this section discusses the tendency of most SIRIUS countries to narrow and sometimes even to obstruct access to the international protection process. SIRIUS countries have designed and deployed a sophisticated toolbox, including both physical and procedural barriers.

Concerning physical barriers, during the timeframe 2011–2017, all over Europe migrants were physically prevented from accessing territory and consequently submitting their asylum claim through the systematic recourse to push-back operations, and/or, in a more blatant way, by building actual walls or fences. Greece is maybe the most typical case of restricting analysis to a SIRIUS country. In 2012, in the Greek-Turkish border of the Evros area, a 12 km wall was built to impede access to the country by land. At Evros, multiple complaints about push-backs were reported in 2017, 2018 and 2019 by both NGOs and governmental institutions (Strik 2019; Greek Council for Refugees 2019). Meanwhile, extreme difficulties in lodging an application for international protection are observed in Greece, as a result of illegitimate practices. As recorded by the Greek Council for Refugees, in 2018, there were cases of people who, after several attempts to lodge an asylum application, were arrested due to being found "in the lack of legal documentations" and then detained, in view of removal (FRA 2019a: 12).

However, in the majority of cases, SIRIUS countries have not resorted to the aforementioned practices. Instead, restraining access to international protection has resulted from the implementation of tools and procedures already provided by the EU asylum *acquis*. Among them, the hotspots approach and procedures enacted in line with the recast Asylum Procedures Directive can be regarded as some of the main tools, making part of an overall European strategy of controlling access to the state, and more broadly, to Europe.

On this legal basis, extensive reforms involve the legal frameworks of SIRIUS countries, reshaping domestic asylum proceedings. However, as discussed later in this chapter, asylum policies and legislations intended to speed up the procedure are often oriented more towards deterrence than efficiency.

3.3.1   The Hotspots Approach

First presented in the European Agenda on Migration (EU Commission 2015), the 'hotspot approach' was intended to assist frontline Member States facing an exceptional migratory pressure at the EU external border. Hotspots identify a geographical space. At the same time, hotspots identify an approach where the European Asylum Support Office, Frontex and Europol "work on the ground with frontline Member States to swiftly identify, register and fingerprint incoming migrants" (EU Commission 2015: 6).

As pointed out by the EU Court of Auditors, hotspots have been found effective in improving operations of identification, registration and fingerprinting. Considering the whole of 2016, Italy could count for a 97% registration and fingerprinting rate (this was 60% in the first half of 2015). Greece witnessed a significant increase in the rate of registration of incoming migrants as well, with 78% of migrants registered and fingerprinted, compared to the 8% registration rate of September 2015. Thereby, "in this respect the hotspot approach contributed towards an improved management of the migration flows" (European Court of Auditors 2017: 38–39). However, as the EU Court of Auditors further observes, the effectiveness of the hotspot approach is strictly linked to the proper functioning of the follow-up process, namely asylum, relocation and return. But the "implementation of these follow-up procedures is often slow and subject to various bottlenecks, which can have repercussions on the functioning of the hotspots" (European Court of Auditors 2017: 7; 40–44).

More specifically, the state of play of hotspots in Greece has been dramatically affected by the EU-Turkey statement of 2016, which aims to curtail the migratory flow to the Aegean Sea. Indeed, initially intended to channel newly-arrived migrants into procedures of international protection or return, after March 2016, hotspots were substantially transformed into closed centres of detention to implement returns to Turkey (Guild et al. 2017). This reportedly led to collective expulsion and push-backs (ECRE 2016). Harshly criticized by national and international organizations (UNHCR 2017a), the detention of migrants has been substituted by an order of blanket geographical restriction imposed to newly arrivals, who are obliged to reside in the identification and reception centre for an indefinite period of time (AIDA Country Report: Greece 2018). Meanwhile, running short of staff, the Greek Asylum service experienced significant difficulties in handling the high number of asylum applications, which significantly raised after 20 March 2016. As a result, in September 2016, "the majority of migrants who arrived after 20 March had still not had the opportunity to lodge an asylum application" (European Court of Auditors 2017: 41).

In Italy, according to the Consolidated Law on Immigration, undocumented foreigners intercepted within Italian territory and helped during rescue operations at sea are conducted to hotspots, where they are fingerprinted and receive information on international protection, relocation and assisted voluntary return (art. 10 ter of the Consolidated law on Migration). However, in 2016, fewer than one third of incoming migrants were identified in hotspots, while others were registered in other ports of arrival. Undoubtedly, the crucial part of the identification procedure is pre-registration, a phase in which migrants are qualified as either 'undocumented' or 'asylum seekers'. In this regard, there have been allegations of migrants who have been delayed or denied access to international protection (UNHCR 2017b). In 2016, the Italian government put in place a comprehensive training program for police authorities responsible for receiving asylum applications. Nonetheless, several scholars have reported practices such as "profiling on grounds of nationality, treating arrivals from non-relocation countries directly as 'non-refugees', selectively (mis-)informing them about their options and swiftly expelling them" (Guild et al. 2017: 47).

Although numbers of arrivals significantly dropped, resulting in a general improvement of hotspot conditions,[17] some shortcomings persist. February 2019 saw allegations that 32 foreigners detained in the hotpots of Messina, Italy, had their access to the procedure of international protection unlawfully delayed while their legal status remained indefinite for long time, pending the negotiation of their resettlement to another EU state.[18]

3.3.2 The Proliferation of Asylum Procedures

Beyond hotspots and tightening borders, the narrowing and slowing down of access to international protection has also been the (secondary) effect of procedural tools intended to streamline the RSD process. The growing number of arrivals and asylum applications from 2011 to 2017 placed a strain on the asylum system of EU states, which responded, inter alia, with legislative reforms to boost the efficiency of RSD procedures.

Indeed, building on the set of rules and procedures provided by the recast Asylum Procedure Directive, all SIRIUS countries introduced procedural tools in their domestic asylum system to determine who should and should not have protection, without examining the merit of the asylum claim. Specifically, domestic legislations could rely on procedures provided by the recast Asylum Procedures Directive (hereinafter also APD) with the aim to streamline the RSD process, namely:

a) an 'admissibility procedure' which does not examine the merit of asylum claims protection needs, for asylum seekers who may be the responsibility of another country or have lodged repetitive claims (arts. 33 and 34); b) an 'accelerated procedure' to examine protection needs of ostensibly unfounded or security-related cases (art. 31(8)); and c) a 'border

---

[17] However, as FRA reports, "As the hotspots are underused, it is difficult to assess whether the system is equipped to handle future fundamental rights emergencies adequately, should arrivals increase again" (FRA 2019b: 7).

[18] The letter that a number of NGOs sent to the Ministry of the Interior, the Prefect of Messina and the Police Headquarters of Messina, urging them to clarify these foreigners' legal status can be consulted here https://www.asgi.it/allontamento-espulsione/immigrazione-hotspot-messina/

> procedure' to speedily conduct admissibility or examine the merits under an accelerated
> procedure at borders or in transit zones (art. 43). (AIDA 2016: 8)

Among the procedures mentioned above, the 'Accelerated Procedure' raises multiple concerns in reference to asylum applicants' rights and procedural guarantees. By way of example, the short time limits featuring this specific procedural regime end up with severely limiting the right to effective defence. Recital 20 of the recast APD states that,

> In well-defined circumstances where an application is likely to be unfounded or where there are serious national security or public order concerns, Member States should be able to accelerate the examination procedure, in particular by introducing shorter, but reasonable, time limits for certain procedural steps, without prejudice to an adequate and complete examination being carried out and to the applicant's effective access to basic principles and guarantees provided for in this Directive.

Although the recast APD does not offer a definition of the 'manifestly unfounded claim', art. 31(8) lays down the grounds upon which Member States may provide an accelerated procedure. Currently, following reforms mainly intervened in 2015, all SIRIUS countries apply the accelerated procedure. However, significant divergences can be observed concerning the various aspects of the accelerated procedure, such as the grounds on which the procedure is initiated, the time-frame within which the procedure should be conducted, the determining authorities.

Despite the difficulty in conducting a considered comparison, a convergence can be pointed out: all SIRIUS countries applying the accelerated procedure incorporate the notion of 'safe country of origin' in their domestic legislation. Based on this concept, asylum applications of migrants from a list of countries are presumed to be manifestly unfounded, unless applicants prove otherwise.

Among the accelerated procedures, the one approved in Switzerland has produced opposite reactions. Triggered by a referendum in 2016, after a 4-year testing phase in Zurich, the reform entered into force in 2019, mainly aiming to expedite the asylum procedure, with a strict timeline and defined steps. Indeed, according to the new law, asylum procedures are expected to be completed within 140 days, down to 100 days in case of accelerated procedures, intended to deal with the so-called 'easy cases'. From registration until the end of the first instance procedure, asylum applicants are provided with free legal assistance, including during the 21-days preparatory stage, when the applicant's file is prepared and channelled into the accelerated or the extended procedure. The accelerated procedure imposes a particularly pressing timeline: the decision is taken in eight working days, with an extra deadline of seven working days to lodge an appeal.

The new measures are enthusiastically supported by the Swiss Refugee Council, which highlights the many advantages stemming from: "the acceleration of procedures, along with fairness for asylum seekers, quality of decisions, suitable accommodation, efficient integration and return procedures" (Hruschka 2019). However, in contrast, some NGOs express concerns about the consequences of the contracted timescale on the quality of the refugee status determination. Hence, it has been contested that the very purpose of the reform was to speed up returns, as opposed to procedures (OSAR 2017).

3.4 Is Europe a Fortress or an Exclusive Club? Selecting Migration Legal Pathways

Although 'a new policy of legal migration' has been presented as the third pillar of the 2015 EU Agenda for Migration (EU Commission 2015), few steps have been taken so far to enhance the creation of legal channels for labour migration (EU Commission 2019a). However, these failures do not target all third country nationals in the same way. The Legal Migration Fitness Check, released by the EU Commission in March 2019, reveals a number of gaps between objectives and needs, which together undermine a comprehensive EU migration policy. This mainly results from the sectorial approach of the EU *acquis*, whose scope fails to cover some category of third country nationals, such as non-seasonal low- and medium-skilled workers (EU Commission 2019b).

Against the lack of EU legal labour migration policies, immigration for economic purposes remains an almost exclusive domain of national states. Indeed, the decision about who should be admitted in the state territory and with what entitlements is still one of the main prerogatives of modern, post-Westphalian, statehood. This prerogative is somewhat exacerbated for people who migrate for economic-related reasons, in respect to which fewer limitations to national sovereignty are brought in by EU membership and international obligations (Joppke 2005; Sohn 2014).

Hence, immigration on economic grounds can be considered a breeding ground for enacting restrictive policies to deliver government pledges to curtail overall net immigration. This was the case in the Czech Republic, where, in 2010, in the aftermath of the economic crisis, restrictive measures on migration were enacted, targeting mainly economic migrants and the issuance of employment permits. For instance, labour offices "were asked not to issue employment permits to foreigners for such job positions that can be filled by persons with free admission to the Czech labour market. The length of the stay or the level of integration of individual foreigners was completely disregarded." (Čižinský et al. 2014: 47).

However, more often, most of the SIRIUS countries have laid down policies to screen and accept potential migrants based on certain characteristics, such as sectors of labour shortage, short-term work, income and skills, so as to align immigration with the country's economic and political interests and needs. Following this trend, the traditional image of Europe as an impregnable fortress appears less fitting. Indeed, this fortress has some drawbridges, available only to those who are considered eligible due to their economic resources or talent.

In this regard, across the SIRIUS countries, several policies have been put in place to favour labour market access for two categories of economically suitable migrants: high-skilled foreign workers and international students. In Denmark, the immigration of third country nationals for work purpose is mostly limited to high-skilled professionals. In the UK, the 'Highly Skilled Migrants Programme', replaced by Tier 1, has allowed exceptionally talented foreigners to enter and settle in the UK, without the obligation to prove an offer of employment before arrival. Another programme (the 'International Graduate Student Scheme') was also launched to attract international students, allowing them to work in the UK for one year after completing their course of study. In recent years, the number of highly skilled workers has significantly increased, while international students' enrolment in UK universities grew by 92% between 2000 and 2014 (Hirst and Atto 2018). Beyond these specific programmes, the selectivity of the UK immigration policy is unveiled also by the so-called points-based system (PBS), a comprehensive system based on the accumulation of points across different categories (e.g. level of English language or amount of savings) which determines the success of foreign visa applications. As Hirst and Atto reports (2018), the PBS is complex and expensive and it "is also subject to rapid change, with work visa categories regularly being established and discontinued, reflecting the Government's attempts to both limit immigration, and be responsive to employer demands to have the skilled employees they need" (2018: 863).

In other countries, such as Italy and Switzerland, the control and selection process on economic-related migration has been enacted by introducing national numerical migration limits or other systems, which give priority to national job-seekers. Through these tools, states may easily cap the number of migrants allowed to enter the domestic labour market and target candidates for immigration according to economic necessities and social acceptance. Thus, in Switzerland, in July 2018, new measures entered into force aiming to support the domestic workforce in jobs and sectors with high rates of unemployment compared to the national average (art. 21a Foreign National Act). In these cases, job offers are announced, as a priority, to unemployed persons registered at the Regional Unemployed Office. This de facto entails giving precedence to Swiss nationals, who can more easily fulfil the requirement of registration (Moreno Russi and Nicole 2018). In Italy, since 2011, also due to the economic crisis, the government has decided to limit the entry quota only to few foreigners: mainly high-qualified workers, rich entrepreneurs and 'seasonal workers' in the field of agriculture and tourism (Chiaromonte et al. 2018). Following this trend, in Italy, Law No. 232 of 2016 (2017 Budget Law) modified the Italian Consolidated Law on Immigration, granting foreign investors entry and staying 'out of quota' (art. 26 bis of the Legislative Decree No. 286 of 1998). Beyond Italy, among SIRIUS countries, also Greece, the Czech Republic, Switzerland and the UK provide programmes that offer residence permits to investors (Dzankic 2019).

As this overview shows, access to national job markets is increasingly reserved for specific categories of third country nationals, with European states devoting their efforts to becoming more attractive to investors, entrepreneurs, talented students and professionals. After all, the promotion and development of a common space for research, scientific knowledge and technology was one of the main objective of the EU, as already stated in the 2009 Lisbon Treaty, (see in particular Title XIX). However, in countries where the domestic workforce has reached high levels of education and aspires employment in medium and high-skilled positions, many low-wage jobs such as the care of children and the elderly, construction and agriculture, remain performed by immigrants (Newland and Riestrer 2018). Nonetheless, given the almost complete unavailability of legal migration avenues, both employers and low-skilled migrants often turn to informal employment, as analysis of Italy's and Greece's labour market displays. Within the extra-legal pattern, migrants are exposed to various forms of exploitation, subjected to risks of sanctions, and/or detention and excluded from basic rights and legal guarantees.

3.5 Concluding Remarks

The entangled interplay of political discourses, policies and legislations in the field of asylum and immigration is a common thread running across all the SIRIUS countries.

As observed earlier, immigration, asylum and security concerns have become increasingly fused in the public discourse, triggering a number of measures that try to criminalize both migration and humanitarian assistance. The narrative of 'bogus asylum seekers', together with open discourses of deterrence, have underpinned reforms which curtail foreigners' guarantees, rights and social benefits, and also with the purpose of making European countries unattractive to certain types of migrant. The tightening of migration law, together with the increasing politicization of the 'refugee crisis', have contributed to creating a 'hostile environment' for migrants. Meanwhile, SIRIUS countries' legal and institutional frameworks on migration and asylum are extremely difficult to navigate. This is mainly the result of a complex and rapidly evolving legislation and of a fragmented legal framework, difficult to be correctly and consistently implemented and duly interpreted and applied.

Furthermore, an overall restriction of access to international procedure features in all SIRIUS countries. This is pursued through physical restrictions (i.e. pushbacks and the construction of fences), and procedural measures (including hotspots, acceleration procedures, the concept of 'safe countries of origin') to streamline the RSD procedure. However, procedural simplification is often realized at the expense of the principles of transparency and predictability, through the introduction of restrictions of rights and procedural guarantees, such as the right to effective defence. Meanwhile, access to Europe is narrowed for third country nationals who migrate for economic reasons, reserving permits to entry and stay to those who are deemed good for the economy, such as high-skilled workers, investors or rich entrepreneurs.

The restrictive approach that permeates narratives, policies and legislation risks becoming a 'logic trap' that effects not only on migrants but society as a whole. The anti-immigrant attitude of politicians, together with hostile public sentiment, mutually reinforcing each other, create a toxic environment. However, cultivating a culture of fear and defensiveness not only affects prospects of encounter and socialization for migrants who are already in the country, but also prevents governments from enacting reforms that would allow the country to benefit from migrants' presence and support their active engagement. The lack of legal migration pathways able to fill the demand for labour at all skills levels can be regarded as one of the most indicative implications of this blind and counterproductive 'policy of fear' which is taking over (and replacing) migration policies in Europe.

References

AIDA. (2017). *The concept of vulnerability in European asylum procedures.* http://www.asylumineurope.org/sites/default/files/shadow-reports/aida_vulnerability_in_asylum_procedures.pdf

AIDA. (2018). *Country Report: Greece.* https://www.asylumineurope.org/reports/country/greece

AIDA (Asylum Information Database). (2016). *Admissibility, responsibility and safety in European asylum procedures.* https://www.ecre.org/wp-content/uploads/2016/09/ECRE-AIDA-Admissibility-responsibility-and-safety-in-European-asylum-procedures.pdf

Amico di Meane, T. (2018). Beyond the pedagogical beauty of dichotomy. Comparative Law methodology in liquid times. In K. Topidi (Ed.), *Normative pluralism and human rights. Social normativities in Conflict* (pp. 9–60). New York.

ASGI. (2017). *Position paper on the proposed "Code of conduct for NGOs involved in migrants' rescue at sea".* https://www.asgi.it/wp-content/uploads/2017/07/Draft-ASGI-Position-Paper_Final_EN.pdf

Bagavos, C., Lagoudakou, K., & Xatzigiannakou, K. (2018). Greece. In V. Federico (ed.) *WP2 Report – Legal Barriers and Enablers* (pp. 243–303). https://www.sirius-project.eu/sites/default/files/attachments/WP2_D2.2.pdf

Barrett, M. (2019, January 24). Three years after Denmark's infamous 'jewellery law' hit world headlines, not a single piece has been confiscated. *The Local.* https://www.thelocal.dk/20190124/three-years-after-denmarks-infamous-jewellery-law-hit-world-headlines-not-a-single-piece-has-been-confiscated

Bendixen, M. C. (2019, January 29). New restrictions for refugees in the Finance Act. *Refugees Welcome.* http://refugees.dk/en/news/2018/december/new-restrictions-for-refugees-in-the-finance-act-2019/

Bontenbal, I., & Lillie, N. (2018). Finland. In V. Federico (Ed.), *WP2 report – Legal barriers and enablers* (pp. 193–242). https://www.sirius-project.eu/sites/default/files/attachments/WP2_D2.2.pdf

Čada, K., Hoření, K., & Numerato, D. (2018). Czech Republic. In V. Federico (Ed.), *WP2 report – Legal barriers and enablers* (pp. 98–128). https://www.sirius-project.eu/sites/default/files/attachments/WP2_D2.2.pdf

Calò, F., Montgomery, T, Baglioni, S., Biosca, O., & Bomark, D. (2018). United Kingdom. In V. Federico (Ed.), *WP2 report – Legal barriers and enablers* (pp. 439–497). https://www.sirius-project.eu/sites/default/files/attachments/WP2_D2.2.pdf

Chiaromonte, W., Pannia, P, Federico, V., D'Amato, S., & Maggini, N. (2018). Italy. In V. Federico (Ed.), *WP2 report – Legal barriers and enablers* (pp. 304–370). https://www.sirius-project.eu/sites/default/files/attachments/WP2_D2.2.pdf

Čižinský, P., Čech, V. E., Hradečná, P., Holíková, K., Jelínková, M., Rozumeka, M., & Rozumková, P. (2014). *Foreign workers in the labour market in the Czech Republic and in selected European countries.* Prague: Association for Integration and Migration, Organization for Aid to Refugees, Multicultural Center Prague. https://www.migrace.com/docs/141115_simi-zamestnanci-en-nahled.pdf

Clayton, G. (2016). *Textbook on immigration and asylum law.* Oxford: Oxford University Press.

Costello, C., & Hancox, E. (2015). The recast Asylum Procedures Directive 2013/32: Caught between the stereotypes of the abusive asylum seeker and the vulnerable refugee. In C. Vincent, P. De Bruycker, & F. Maiani (Eds.), *Reforming the common European Asylum system: The new European Refugee Law* (pp. 375–445). Leiden: Martinus Nijhoff.

Council of Europe Commissioner for Human Rights. (2010). *Criminalisation of migration in Europe: Human rights implications*. Issue paper, 4 February. https://www.refworld.org/docid/4b6a9fef2.html

Council of Europe Commissioner for Human Rights. (2018, November 6). *Report of the Commissioner for Human Rights of the Council of Europe Dunja Mijatović following her visit to Greece from 25 to 29 June 2018*. https://reliefweb.int/report/greece/report-commissioner-human-rights-council-europe-dunja-mijatovi-following-her-visit

Council of Europe Commissioner for Human Rights. (2019). *Lives saved. Rights protected. Bridging the protection gap for refugees and migrants in the Mediterranean*. https://rm.coe.int/lives-saved-rights-protected-bridging-the-protection-gap-for-refugees-/168094eb87

Cusumano, E. (2017). Emptying the sea with a spoon? Non-governmental providers of migrants search and rescue in the Mediterranean. *Marine Policy, 75*, 91–98.

Del Valle, H. (2016). Search and rescue in the Mediterranean Sea: Negotiating political differences. *Refugee Survey Quarterly, 35*, 22–40.

Dzankic, J. (2019). *The global market for investor citizenship*. London: Palgrave Macmillan.

ECRE (European Council on Refugees and Exiles). (2016). *The Implementation of the hotspots in Italy and Greece: A study*. www.refworld.org/docid/584ad1734.html

EU Commission. (2015, May 13). Communication from the commission to the European Parliament, the Council, the European Economic and Social Committee and the Committee of the Regions. *A European Agenda on Migration*. https://ec.europa.eu/home-affairs/sites/home-affairs/files/what-we-do/policies/european-agenda-migration/background-information/docs/communication_on_the_european_agenda_on_migration_en.pdf

EU Commission. (2018, 30 October). *Member states' support to emergency relocation mechanism*. https://goo.gl/HfbF8H

EU Commission. (2019a, March 6). Communication from the commission to the European Parliament, the European Council and the Council. *Progress report on the Implementation of the European Agenda on Migration*. https://ec.europa.eu/home-affairs/sites/homeaffairs/files/what-we-do/policies/european-agenda-migration/20190306_com-2019-126-report_en.pdf

EU Commission. (2019b, March 29). *Commission staff working document fitness check on EU legislation on legal migration*. https://ec.europa.eu/home-affairs/sites/homeaffairs/files/e-library/documents/policies/legal-migration/swd_2019-1055-staff-working-part1.pdf

European Court of Auditors. (2017). *Special report no. 06/2017: EU response to the refugee crisis: The 'hotspot' approach*. https://www.eca.europa.eu/en/Pages/DocItem.aspx?did=41222

Federico, V., & Pannia, P. (2018). Migrants' legal statuses in contemporary Italy. First attempts of conceptualization. *Percorsi costituzionali, 1*, 17–37.

FRA (Fundamental Rights Agency). (2014). *Criminalisation of migrants in an irregular situation and of persons engaging with them*. https://fra.europa.eu/en/publication/2014/criminalisation-migrants-irregular-situation-and-persons-engaging-them

FRA. (2019a). *Migration: Key fundamental rights concerns – Quarterly bulletin 2*. https://fra.europa.eu/en/publication/2019/migration-overviews-may-2019

FRA. (2019b). *Update of the 2016 opinion of the European Union Agency for fundamental rights on fundamental rights in the 'hotspots' set up in Greece and Italy*. March 4. https://fra.europa.eu/en/opinion/2019/migration-hotspots-update

Gabrielatos, C., & Baker, P. (2008). Fleeing, sneaking, flooding: A corpus analysis of discursive constructions of refugees and asylum seekers in the UK Press 1996–2005. *Journal of English Linguistics, 36*(1), 5–38.

Geddes, A. (2005). Europe's border relationships and international migration relations. *Journal of Common Market Studies, 43*(4), 787–806.

Geddes, A., & Scholten, P. (2016). Analysing the politics of migration and immigration in Europe. In A. Geddes & P. Scholten (Eds.), *The politics of migration and immigration in Europe* (pp. 1–21). Los Angeles: SAGE.

Greek Council for Refugees. (2019). *Complaint on push-back incidents in the region of Evros during the months of April–June 2019*. http://www.statewatch.org/news/2019/jul/greek-council-for-refugees-Push-backs%20April-June%202019.pdf

Green-Pedersen, C., & Otjes, S. (2017). A hot topic? Immigration on the agenda in Western Europe. *Party Politics, 25*, 1–11.

Guild, E., Costello, C., & Moreno-Lax, V. (2017). *Study on the implementation of the Council Decisions*. European Parliament. http://www.europarl.europa.eu/RegData/etudes/STUD/2017/583132/IPOL_STU%282017%29583132_EN.pdf

Hartmann, J., & Feith Tan, N. (2016, January 27). The Danish Law on seizing asylum seekers' assets. *EJIL: Talk!*, https://www.ejiltalk.org/the-danish-law-on-seizing-asylum-seekers-assets/

Hirst, C., & Atto, N. (2018, May 1). *United Kingdom – Country report: Legal and policy framework of migration governance*. https://www.respondmigration.com/wp-blog/2018/8/1/comparative-report-legal-and-policy-framework-of-migration-governance-pclyw-ydmzj-bzdbn-sc548-ncfcp-5a657

Home Office. (2018). *Resettlement: Policy statement*. https://assets.publishing.service.gov.uk/government/uploads/system/uploads/attachment_data/file/730643/Resettlement_Policy_document_pdf

Home Office and the Rt Hon James Brokenshire MP. (2015, January 6). *'Deport first, appeal later' measures start to bite*. https://www.gov.uk/government/news/deport-first-appeal-later-measures-start-to-bite

Hruschka, C. (2019, March). Op-ed: How to Design Fair and Efficient Asylum Procedures in Populist Times?. *ECRE Weekly Bulletin*. https://www.ecre.org/op-ed-how-to-design-fair-and-efficient-asylum-procedures-in-populist-times/

Italian Coast Guard. (2017). *Maritime Rescue Coordination Centre Roma, SAR operations in the Mediterranean sea*, https://www.guardiacostiera.gov.it/attivita/Documents/attivita-sar-immigrazione-2017/Rapporto_annuale_2017_ENG.pdf

Italian Senate. (2017). *Inquiry on the contribution of Italian military forces to control migratory flows in the Mediterranean and the impact of NGOs activity*. http://leg17.senato.it/service/PDF/PDFServer/BGT/1023441.pdf

Joppke, C. (2005). *Selecting by origin: Ethnic migration in the liberal state*. Cambridge: Harvard University Press.

Kraler, A. (2006). The legal status of immigrants and their access to nationality. In R. Baubock (Ed.), *Migration and citizenship, legal status, rights and political participation* (pp. 33–66). Amsterdam: Amsterdam University Press.

Lefkofridi, Z., & Chatzopoulou, S. (2019, August 5). The symbolism of the new Greek government. *LSE EUROPP Blog*. https://blogs.lse.ac.uk/europpblog/2019/08/05/the-symbolism-of-the-new-greek-government/

Lynn, N., & Lea, S. (2003). A phantom menace and the new Apartheid': The social construction of asylum-seekers in the United Kingdom. *Discourse & Society, 14*(4), 425–452.

Mayblin, L., & James, P. (2016). *Factors influencing asylum destination choice: A review of the evidence, University of Warwick*. https://asylumwelfarework.files.wordpress.com/2015/03/asylum-seeker-pull-factors-working-paper.pdf

Menski, W. (2006). *Comparative law in a global context*. Cambridge: The Legal Systems of Asia and Africa.

Meyer, S., & Rosenberger, S. (2015). Just a shadow? The role of radical right parties in the politicization of immigration, 1995–2009. *Politics and Governance, 3*(2), 1–17.

Montgomery, T., Calò, F., & Baglioni, S. (2018). Claims making and the construction of the refugee crisis in Brexit Britain (Research Report). In M. Cinalli (Ed.), *WP5 report – Integrated report on transnational solidarity in the public domain* (pp. 217–243). https://transsol.eu/files/2018/05/deliverable-5-1.pdf

Moreno Russi, P., & Nicole, O. (2018). Switzerland. In V. Federico (Ed.) *WP2 report – Legal barriers and enablers* (pp. 129–192). https://www.sirius-project.eu/sites/default/files/attachments/WP2_D2.2.pdf

MSF (Medici senza Frontiere). (2017). *Codice di condotta: la lettera di MSF al Ministro dell'Interno*. http://www.medicisenzafrontiere.it/notizie/news/codice-di-condotta-la-lettera-di-msf-al-ministro-dellinterno

Newland, K., & Riester, A. (2018). *Welcome to work? Legal migration pathways for low-skilled workers*. Washington, DC: Migration Policy Institute.

OSAR. (2017). *Restructuration du domaine de l'asile – modification de l'ordonnance 1 sur l'asile*. https://www.osar.ch/assets/asylrecht/stellungnahmen/171130-osar-stn-oa1-fr.pdf

Peroni, L., & Timmer, A. (2013). Vulnerable groups: The promise of an emerging concept in European human rights convention law. *International Journal of Constitutional Law, 11*(4), 1056–1085.

Scarciglia, R. (2015). Diritto globale e metodologia comparativa: verso un approccio verticale? *Diritto pubblico comparato ed europeo, 4*, 1012–1028.

Sen, S., Pace, M., & Bjerre, L. (2018). Denmark. In V. Federico (Ed.), *WP2 report – Legal barriers and enablers* (pp. 129–192). https://www.sirius-project.eu/sites/default/files/attachments/WP2_D2.2.pdf

Sohn, J. (2014). How legal status contributes to differential integration opportunities. *Migration Studies, 2*(3), 369–391.

Squire, V. (2009). *The exclusionary politics of asylum*. London: Palgrave Macmillan.

Strik, T. (2019, June 8). Committee on migration, refugees and displaced person. *The Pushback policies and practice in Council of Europe member States*. https://www.ecoi.net/en/file/local/2011497/pdf.aspx

Stumpf, J. (2006). The crimmigration crisis: Immigrants, crime, and sovereign power. *American University Law Review, 56*, 367–418.

Thielemanne, E. (2004). Why asylum policy harmonisation undermines refugee burden-sharing. *European Journal of Migration and Law, 6*, 47–65.

Triandafyllidou, A. (2018). A "refugee crisis" unfolding: "real" events and their interpretation in media and political debates. *Journal of Immigrant & Refugee Studies, 16*(1–2), 196–216.

UN High Commissioner for Refugees (UNHCR). (2003). *Framework for durable solutions for refugees and persons of concern*. http://www.refworld.org/docid/4124b6a04.html

UNHCR. (2017a). *Explanatory Memorandum to UNHCR's Submission to the Committee of Ministers of the Council of Europe on developments in the management of asylum and reception in Greece*. https://www.refworld.org/docid/595675554.html

UNHCR. (2017b). *Raccomandazioni dell'UNHCR per rafforzare la protezione e l'integrazione dei rifugiati in Italia* [UNCHR Recommendations to enhance refugees' protection and integration in Italy] https://www.unhcr.it/wp-content/uploads/2016/10/Italy-Recommendations-2017-ITA.pdf

UNHCR. (2018a). *Desperate journeys*. https://data2.unhcr.org/en/documents/download/63039

UNHCR. (2018b). *Asylum in the UK*. http://www.unhcr.org/asylum-in-the-uk.html

UNHCR. (2019). *Desperate Journeys: Refugees and migrants arriving in Europe and at Europe's borders: January–December 2018*. https://www.unhcr.org/desperatejourneys/

Wallis, E. (2019, July 8). Denmark's new government softens line on migration. *Infomigrants*. https://www.infomigrants.net/en/post/18031/denmark-s-new-government-softens-line-on-migration

Walter-Franke, M. (2019, March 14). Variable geometry risky for refugees: Example Denmark. *Jacques Delors Institute Berlin. Policy Brief*. https://www.delorsinstitut.de/2015/wp-content/uploads/2019/03/MWF-Denmarks-asylum-reform-final.pdf

Zetter, R. (2007). More labels, fewer refugees: Remaking the refugee label in an era of globalization. *Journal of Refugee Studies, 20*(2), 172–192.

Zincone, G., & Caponio, T. (2006). The multilevel governance of migration. In R. Penninx, M. Berger, & K. Kraal (Eds.), *The dynamics of migration and settlement in Europe. A state of the art* (pp. 270–304). Amsterdam: Amsterdam University Press, IMISCOE Joint Studies.

Zonca, E. V. (2016). *Cittadinanza sociale e diritti degli stranieri. Profili comparatistici*. Padova: Cedam.

List of Legislations and Cases

Council Decision (EU) 2015/1601 of 22 September 2015 establishing provisional measures in the area of international protection for the benefit of Italy and Greece. http://eur-lex.europa.eu/legal-content/EN/TXT/?uri=celex%3A32015D1601

Council Decision (EU) 2015/1523 of 14 September 2015 establishing provisional measures in the area of international protection for the benefit of Italy and of Greece.

Council Directive 2003/9/EC of 27 January 2003 laying down minimum standards for the reception of asylum seekers. https://eur-lex.europa.eu/LexUriServ/LexUriServ.do?uri=OJ:L:2003:031:0018:0025:EN:PDF

Council Directive 2004/83/EC of 29 April 2004 on minimum standards for the qualification and status of third country nationals or stateless persons as refugees or as persons who otherwise need international protection and the content of the protection granted. https://eur-lex.europa.eu/LexUriServ/LexUriServ.do?uri=OJ:L:2004:304:0012:0023:EN:PDF

Council Directive 2005/85/EC of 1 December 2005 on minimum standards on procedures in Member States for granting and withdrawing refugee status. https://eur-lex.europa.eu/LexUriServ/LexUriServ.do?uri=OJ:L:2005:326:0013:0034:EN:PDF

Denmark – Bill No. L87 amending the Aliens Act. https://www.ft.dk/RIpdf/samling/20151/lovforslag/L87/20151_L87_som_vedtaget.pdf

Denmark – Law No. L140. https://www.ft.dk/samling/20181/lovforslag/l140/index.htm

Directive 2008/115/EC of the European Parliament and of the Council of 16 December 2008 on common standards and procedures in Member States for returning illegally staying third-country nationals. https://eur-lex.europa.eu/LexUriServ/LexUriServ.do?uri=OJ:L:2008:348:0098:0107:EN:PDF

Directive 2011/95/EU of the European Parliament and of the Council of 13 December 2011 on standards for the qualification of third-country nationals or stateless persons as beneficiaries of international protection, for a uniform status for refugees or for persons eligible for subsidiary protection, and for the content of the protection granted. https://eur-lex.europa.eu/LexUriServ/LexUriServ.do?uri=OJ:L:2011:337:0009:0026:en:PDF

Directive 2013/32/EU of the European Parliament and of the Council of 26 June 2013 on common procedures for granting and withdrawing international protection. https://eur-lex.europa.eu/legal-content/EN/TXT/PDF/?uri=CELEX:32013L0032&from=en

Directive 2013/33/EU of the European Parliament and of the Council of 26 June 2013 laying down standards for the reception of applicants for international protection. https://eur-lex.europa.eu/legal-content/EN/TXT/PDF/?uri=CELEX:32013L0033&from=EN

Dublin III Regulation (Regulation (EU) No 604/2013 of the European Parliament and of the Council of 26 June 2013 establishing the criteria and mechanisms for determining the Member State responsible for examining an application for international protection lodged in one of the Member States by a third-country national or a stateless person). https://eur-lex.europa.eu/LexUriServ/LexUriServ.do?uri=OJ:L:2013:180:0031:0059:EN:PDF

Finland – Law No. 43/2016. Hallituksen esitys eduskunnalle laiksi ulkomaalaislain muuttamisesta. https://www.finlex.fi/fi/esitykset/he/2016/20160043

Italy – Law-Decree No. 113, 4 October 2018, converted with amendments by Law No. 281, 1 December 2018. https://www.normattiva.it/uri-res/N2Ls?urn:nir:stato:decreto.legge:2018-10-04;113!vig=

Italy – Law-Decree No. 53, 14 June 2019 "Urgent dispositions on order and public security", converted with amendments by Law No. 77, 8 August 2019. https://temi.camera.it/leg18/provvedimento/d-l-53-2019-disposizioni-urgenti-in-materia-di-ordine-e-sicurezza.html

Italy – Legislative Decree No. 286, 25 July 1998, "Consolidated Act on provisions concerning the Immigration regulations and foreign national conditions norms". https://www.altalex.com/documents/news/2014/04/08/testo-unico-sull-immigrazione-titolo-ii

R (on the application of Kiarie) (Appellant) v Secretary of State for the Home Department (Respondent) [2017] UKSC 42. https://www.supremecourt.uk/cases/docs/uksc-2016-0009-judgment.pdf

Switzerland – art. 21a Foreign National Act, inserted by No I of the FA of 16 Dec. 2016 (Controlling Immigration and Improving Implementation of the Free Movement Agreements), in force since 1 July 2018. https://www.admin.ch/opc/en/classified-compilation/20020232/201903010000/142.20.pdf

Chapter 4
Migrant Integration and the Role of the EU

Ruby Gropas

4.1 Introduction

Today there are around 22 million third-country nationals legally residing in the EU, constituting approximately 4.2% of the EU's total population. Almost half have lived in their host country for 10 years or longer. Among working-age third-country nationals (TCNs) residing in the EU, 64.5% are in employment (Eurostat 2019a). This is almost 10 percentage points lower than host-country nationals, and the gap is wider for migrant working age women and youths (OECD and European Commission 2018).

As the number of people migrating to Europe has steadily increased and migration pathways into the EU have diversified, migration management and integration have risen to the very top of the political agenda for all EU Member States. Given the wider context of regional instability and global power-shifts, and the deeply transformative demographic, technological and economic transitions that the EU is undergoing, migration has become an ever-pressing priority for the EU institutions. Indeed, since the end of the Cold War, but particularly over the course of the past two decades, the role of the EU level of governance in formulating migration policies to support the labour market and wider integration of migrants, refugees and asylum seekers has widened and deepened. The Union has developed a substantial framework to support Member States by establishing: (a) a legislative framework for integration, which includes common basic principles (CBPs); (b) specialised funding instruments to promote and support migrant inclusion; (c) a set of policy instruments that contribute to social cohesion, integration and anti-discrimination; and (d) a space for exchange of information, good practices, mutual learning and cooperation.

R. Gropas (✉)
European Commission, and College of Europe, Bruges, Belgium
e-mail: ruby.gropas@coleurope.eu

© The Author(s) 2021

V. Federico, S. Baglioni (eds.), *Migrants, Refugees and Asylum Seekers' Integration in European Labour Markets*, IMISCOE Research Series,
https://doi.org/10.1007/978-3-030-67284-3_4

This chapter first takes a look at the drivers that led to an EU framework for the integration of legally residing TCNs. It then traces the development of the most important instruments from the Treaty of Amsterdam to the Juncker Commission (2014–2019), which declared migration management and the need for effective migrant integration policies as being among the top political priorities for the EU (Juncker 2014; COM(2015) 240). It examines the Union's legislative framework in the field of migration, as well as its wider toolbox elaborated to contribute to immigrant integration. The chapter concludes with a discussion of some of the most important challenges that hinder fair and effective integration in the EU.

4.2   A Look Back at the Drivers and Motivations for a Common EU Framework

A European approach to migrant integration dates to long before the EU 'formally' acquired competence in this field in the late 1990s. An overview of various Commission communications and reports dating back to the 1970s–1980s indicates the attention accorded to ensuring equal treatment of individuals within the EEC/ EU as regards living and working conditions, social security provisions, vocational training, adult education and especially the education of migrant workers' children. Nationality acquisition, unemployment, education, housing and living conditions, as well as the participation of TCNs in local elections are all underlined as crucial elements for the social integration of third country migrants residing on a permanent and lawful basis in the Member States. Just as importantly, there is a consistent and clear invitation to Member States to guarantee the free movement of Community migrant workers, and to coordinate national policies on migrants from third countries (see Gilardoni et al. 2015). Beyond simply attempting to steer Member States towards a common approach to migration and integration, the Commission and the European Parliament have taken a prescriptive approach in terms of highlighting specific measures which would promote fair treatment and non-discrimination and effective integration of both male and female TCNs in the labour market.

Community competence for immigration and asylum was established in the Treaty of Amsterdam (1997), laying the ground for a common EU framework on integration for legally residing third-country nationals (TCNs) to gradually develop. Political impetus was subsequently provided by the 1999 Tampere European Council Presidency, which declared that:

> The European Union must ensure fair treatment of third country nationals who reside legally on the territory of its Member States. A more vigorous integration policy should aim at granting them rights and obligations comparable to those of EU citizens. It should also enhance non-discrimination in economic, social and cultural life and develop measures against racism and xenophobia.

By acknowledging the need for approximation of national legislations on the conditions for admission and residence of third country nationals across Member States, and the need for approximation of the legal status of third country nationals to that of Member States' nationals, the European Council provided the European Commission with the opportunity to develop a range of policies and instruments aimed at supporting the integration of migrants in the EU Member States. Tampere thus rendered comparable treatment of TCNs and EU citizens in terms of rights and obligation as a core objective of a common immigration policy.

The following articles have since served as the basis for common policies and instruments to be developed:

According to Article 79(1) of the Treaty on the functioning of the European Union (TFEU), the Union aims among others at 'fair treatment of third-country nationals residing legally in Member States.' On the basis of Article 79(2)(a) and (b) TFEU, the Union therefore has the power to legislate on 'the conditions of entry and residence, and standards on the issue by Member States of long-term visas and residence permits' as well as on 'the rights of third-country nationals residing legally in a Member State.' Article 79(5) TFEU lays out the rules on admission, stating that it is up to Member States to determine how many third-country nationals can be admitted to their territory in order to seek work, whether employed or self-employed. And, further on, Article 153(1)(g) TFEU stipulates that as part of its social policy support, the Union shall complement the activities of the Member States as regards the 'conditions of employment for third-country nationals legally residing in Union territory'. The competences to legislate on 'standards concerning the conditions for the reception of applicants for asylum' and 'a uniform status of asylum for nationals of third countries', along with the power to agree to rules on 'freedom of movement within Member States for workers from the countries and territories' in association agreements with third countries, are laid out in Articles 78(2)(a) and (f) and in 202 TFEU respectively.

Furthermore, Article 15(3) of the EU Charter of Fundamental Rights stipulates that 'Nationals of third countries who are authorised to work in the territories of the Member States are entitled to working conditions equivalent to those of citizens of the Union.' In other words, this right is granted solely to lawfully employed third-country nationals and guarantees 'equivalent' working conditions. The Charter is relevant for the rights of TCNs also in that Article 30 grants 'every worker (...) the right to protection against unjustified dismissal, in accordance with Union law and national laws and practises', and Article 31 grants 'every worker (...) the right to working conditions which respect his or her health, safety and dignity, and to limitation of maximum working hours, to daily and weekly rest periods and to an annual period of paid leave'. Article 31 does not have a restricting reference to Union law and national laws and practises and it explicitly refers to the dignity of the worker (drawing on Article 1 of the Charter which states that 'Human dignity is inviolable. It must be respected and protected.')

Before exploring the legislative framework that has been put in place over the course of the past two decades, it is useful to consider the motivations and arguments that have both encouraged and framed an inclusion agenda at EU level.

First, the EU's rights-and-responsibilities based approach to integration drew from the universal nature of the principles and values laid down in the Charter of

Fundamental Rights of the European Union (2001) and on Community law. In its 2000 Communication on Integration, the Commission introduced the concept of civic citizenship, based on civic coexistence and shared values within the transnational common space of the Union. Civic citizenship was seen as guaranteeing certain core rights and obligations to immigrants which they would acquire gradually over a period of years, so that they are treated in the same way as nationals of their host state, even if they are not naturalised (European Commission 2000). The Charter of Fundamental Rights established a basic framework for civic citizenship: some rights applying because of their universal nature, and others derived from those conferred on citizens of the Union. As mentioned above, these include the right to free movement and residence, the right to work, to establish oneself and to provide services, the right to vote and to stand as a candidate in elections to the European Parliament and in municipal elections, the right to diplomatic and consular protection, the right to petition, to access documents, and the right to non-discrimination on the basis of nationality. This also involved guaranteeing a degree of mobility for legally resident TCNs within the Union's area of freedom, security and justice, and the opportunity to obtain the nationality of the Member State in which they are resident (Tampere European Council Presidency 1999; COM(2000) 757; COM(2003) 336).

Second, calls for EU policies in the field of migrant inclusion have drawn on a market-related functionality perspective and on concerns of economic performance. Better integration of migrants contributes to higher long- term economic, social and fiscal gains for the country where they settle (Kancs and Lecca 2017; World Bank 2015). So, EU policies have been drawn up to primarily support Member States' efforts at improving migrant's labour market inclusion. Given that 40% of employers in the EU report difficulties in finding employees with the required skills (Cedefop 2014), the European Commission has argued that migration and successful integration of third-country nationals can mitigate these effects and positively contribute to the competitiveness of the EU economy (see Andor 2014; COM(2018) 635). At the same time, given the employment shortages in some Member States and the higher unemployment levels in other Member States, the mobility of long-term residents has long been seen as making economic sense and a positive contribution towards more flexible labour markets (Hansen 2005). Thus, migrant inclusion has come hand in hand with facilitating the free movement of persons in order to stimulate the rather limited overall levels of intra-EU labour mobility, contribute to strengthening the internal market, and improve the competitiveness of the EU economy (European Commission 2016a, b, c).

Third, measures to support migrant integration were boosted by the incorporation of Article 13 in the Amsterdam Treaty, which gave the Community the power to take legislative action to combat discrimination. The landmark Racial Equality Directive (Council of the EU 2000/43/EC) along with the Employment Framework Directive (Council of the EU 2000/78/EC) put into practice Article 13 thereby giving effect to the principle of equal treatment between persons irrespective of racial or ethnic origin or on grounds of religion, including in the labour market.

Fourth, after the Amsterdam and Lisbon Treaties, and again after the 2015–2016 polycrisis (Juncker 2016), EU institutions sought to define new roles for themselves and to expand their competences, tasks and functions. Already back in 1997, the Commission put forward proposals on temporary protection for refugees;[1] similarly, its efforts to guarantee certain common standards for the rights of third country nationals led to the EU Common Basic Principles for Immigrant Integration Policy which was adopted by the European Council in 2004 (European Council Conclusions 2004); in 1998 the action plan on free movement, immigration and asylum and the 2008 proposals to extend anti-discrimination competencies furthered the scope of EU actions. More recently, the 15 December 2015 proposal for a regulation on the European Border and Coast Guard Agency and the 4 May 2016 proposal to expand and strengthen the European Asylum Support Office (EASO)[2] further reflect an appetite to exceed support functions, and move towards monitoring-- like functions as well as functions which have the potential of steering policy implementation (Tsourdi 2019).

Finally, there exists a mutually reinforcing relationship at play between institutions and relevant interest groups. Empirical research has observed that once European policy commitments and networks are established in any field – migration and integration included – access-points and opportunities for influence for relevant (and most frequently pro-EU) interest groups multiply. This in turn feeds further institutionalisation whereby interest groups and networks pursue solutions which require 'more Europe' to the 'problems of Europe' and call for more powers and functions for the Commission, the Court and the European Parliament (Geddes 2000). In the case of migration and integration, widening the role of EU institutions has offered scope for more progressive policy outcomes to counterbalance lowest common denominator decision-making in the Council and the 'securitisation' of migration (Geddes 2013).

4.3   The EU Legislative Framework

Article 79 of the Treaty on the Functioning of the European Union (TFEU) stipulates that the Union shall develop a common immigration policy: 'The Union shall develop a common immigration policy aimed at ensuring, at all stages, the efficient management of migration flows, fair treatment of third-country nationals residing

---

[1] Already in 1997 the Commission submitted a proposal for Joint Action on Temporary protection. Eventually the Temporary Protection Directive was adopted in 2001 but to date it has not been implemented.

[2] For a detailed account see the European Parliament's legislative train schedule: at https://www.europarl.europa.eu/legislative-train/theme-towards-a-new-policy-on-migration/file-european-border-and-coast-guard-agency and https://www.europarl.europa.eu/legislative-train/theme-towards-a-new-policy-on-migration/file-jd-strengthening-the-european-asylum-support-office-(easo)

legally in Member States, and the prevention of, and enhanced measures to combat, illegal immigration and trafficking in human beings'.

It is important to underline that the 2009 Treaty of Lisbon (TFEU) expanded the Union's competences while also clarifying the division of competences between the Union and its Member States. For one, the EU level has shared competences with the Member States in the area of freedom, security and justice (Article 4(2)(j) TFEU), whereas in the field of integration, the EU has supporting competences. In other words, while national governments firmly retain the right to decide how many immigrants from outside the EU they admit, the European Parliament and the Council, acting in accordance with the ordinary legislative procedure (i.e. co-decision and Qualified Majority Voting (QMV) in the latter) can adopt measures in the following areas: (a) the conditions of entry and residence, and standards on the issue by Member States of long-term visas and residence permits, including those for the purpose of family reunification; (b) the definition of the rights of third-country nationals residing legally in a Member State, including the conditions governing freedom of movement and of residence in other Member States; (c) illegal immigration and unauthorised residence, including removal and repatriation of persons residing without authorisation; (d) combating trafficking in persons, in particular women and children.

As regards integration, supporting competences mean that the EU provides support in orientating national policy and promotes the exchange of information among stakeholders; it is able to intervene insofar as it does not aim to coordinate national policies. Thus, integration policies remain within the remit of States' competence and the objective of integration is not a competence conferred upon the Union (Neframi 2011).

Finally, as regards asylum issues, the Treaty of Lisbon broadened the competences of the EU. According to Art. 78 TFEU, a common policy on asylum is developed through the ordinary legislative procedure. There is no mentioning of minimum standards as before which sets the aim to convergence and it provides for the legal basis for the Common European Asylum System (CEAS).

The competences to legislate on immigration of TCNs granted by the Treaty of Amsterdam in the current Articles 78 and 79 of the Treaty on the functioning of the European Union (TFEU) led to a set of directives adopted between 2003 and 2016 (see Table 4.1). These directives cover various categories of third-country nationals and regulate admission and residence conditions, equal treatment rights and mobility within the EU.

The first set of directives lays out the rules on access to employment and employment related rights for the main categories of third-country nationals who are lawfully resident in the Member States. This includes the Family Reunification Directive (2003/86), the Long-Term Residents Directive (2003/109), the Students Directive (2004/114), the Reception Conditions Directive, originally 2003/9 now 2013/33, and the Qualification Directive on the status of refugees and beneficiaries of subsidiary protection, originally 2004/84 now 2011/95. These directives, and particularly the directive on family reunification, essentially cover the largest number of TCNs living in the EU (as an illustration, in 2018 alone, 915,000 first

Table 4.1 Directives under the European Legal Migration Policy and the Common European Asylum System (CEAS)

Directive	Purpose
Council Directive 2003/109/EC of 25 November 2003 as amended by Directive 2011/51/EU	Long-term residents – All migrants residing legally in the territory of an EU country for at least 5 years of continuous legal residence, are granted long-term resident status.
Council Directive 2003/86/EC of 22 September 2003	Family Reunification – Sets the rules and conditions under which migrants who are legally residing in the EU and bring their non-EU national spouse, under-age children and children of their spouse to the Member State in which they are residing.
Directive 2011/98/EU of 13 December 2011	Single Permit – Single application procedure for a single permit for migrants to reside and work in the territory of a Member State and on a common set of rights for migrant workers legally residing in a Member State.
Directive 2014/66/EU of 15 May 2014	Intra-corporate transferees – Conditions of entry and residence of migrants to facilitate intra-corporate transferees.
Directive 2014/36/EU of 26 February 2014	Seasonal workers – Minimum rules for the admission of low skills migrant workers.
Directive 2016/801 of 11 May 2016	Students and researchers – New rules for the entry and residence of migrant students and researchers as well as for school pupils, trainees, volunteers and au pairs.
Council Directive 2009/50/EC of 25 May 2009	EU Blue Card (revision currently on hold) – Conditions of entry and residence of third-country nationals for the purposes of highly qualified employment.
Directive 2013/32/EU of 26 June 2013 (recast)	Revised Asylum Procedures – Sets common procedures for granting and withdraw international protection. Currently under revision Commission Proposal COM(2016) 467
Directive 2013/33/EU of 26 June 2013 (recast)	Revised Reception Conditions – Sets standards for the reception of applicants for international protection Currently under revision Commission Proposal COM(2016) 465
Directive 2011/95/EU of 13 December 2011 (recast)	Revised Qualification directive – Standards for the qualification of third-country nationals as beneficiaries of international protection, for a uniform status for refugees or for persons eligible for subsidiary protection, and for the content of the protection granted. Currently under revision Commission Proposal COM(2016) 466
Council Directive 2001/55/EC of 20 July 2001	Temporary Protection - Minimum standards for giving temporary protection in the event of a mass inflow of displaced persons and on measures promoting a balance of efforts between Member States in receiving such persons and bearing the consequences thereof.

Note: Denmark does not apply EU-wide rules relating to migration, visa and asylum policies. Ireland and the United Kingdom (while it was an EU Member State) choose, on a case-by-case basis, whether to adopt them.
Source: European Court of Auditors; European Parliament legislative train schedule
See: https://www.europarl.europa.eu/legislative-train/theme-towards-a-new-policy-on-migration/file-jd-revision-of-the-blue-card-directive
See: https://www.europarl.europa.eu/legislative-train/theme-civil-liberties-justice-and-home--affairs-libe/file-jd-reform-of-the-asylum-procedures-directive/12-2019
See: https://www.europarl.europa.eu/legislative-train/theme-civil-liberties-justice-and-home--affairs-libe/file-jd-reform-of-the-reception-conditions-directive/12-2019
See: https://www.europarl.europa.eu/legislative-train/theme-civil-liberties-justice-and-home--affairs-libe/file-jd-reform-of-the-qualification-directive/12-2019

residence permits issued for family migration purposes were issued to third-country nationals across the EU28 (i.e. 28.4% of total) (Eurostat 2019b); for more see also Irina Isaakyan's chapter in this volume).

The second set of directives take a more 'sectoral' approach given that the efforts of the Commission to formulate a general directive on admission for employment were blocked by Member States in the mid-2000s. This set consists of the Blue Card Directive (2009/50), the Directive on admission for seasonal employment (2014/36) and the Directive on intra-corporate transferees (2014/66).

The third set of relevant EU instruments facilitates short-term employment and implicitly opens ways for third-country nationals to enter the Union and remain lawfully in a Member State for a short time and work or look for employment. These include the Visa Code (Regulation 810/2009), the EU Visa Regulation (539/2001) and the Regulation on local border traffic at external borders (1931/2006). In addition to these, the Single Permit Directive stipulates procedural rules to be applied by Member States and ensures equal treatment of third-country workers who have been issued the single permit with the nationals of the Member State where they reside (Groenendijk 2015).

A final set of directives falls under the Common European Asylum System (CEAS). The CEAS has consistently suffered from a lack of common implementation and substantial divergences between Member States as regards reception conditions, the procedures and qualifications for the examination of asylum applications, and the international protection offered to refugees. During the 2015–2016 crisis, CEAS' limitations became untenable, demonstrating the depth of the gridlock among EU Member States. The European Agenda on Migration which was launched in May 2015 aimed to replace the current directives on qualification and asylum procedures with regulations in an attempt to harmonise by decreasing the scope of Member States' discretion; recast the Dublin III Regulation No. 604/2013 and the Reception Conditions Directive 2013/33/EU extend the scope of the Eurodac Regulation No. 603/2013; and establish a permanent Union resettlement network, in order to address the secondary movement of asylum seekers and beneficiaries of international protection and improve the mechanism of responsibility-sharing (Jakulevičiene 2019). Efforts to render the CEAS more efficient, harmonised and responsive to the changing nature of migratory pressures and to future anticipated flows reached a deadlock in the period 2016–2019 as the political divisions between the Member States intensified, with a new round of initiatives launched by the von der Leyen Commission in the course of 2020.

As mentioned earlier, the fact that the EU level has shared competences with the Member States in the field of immigration and supporting competences regarding integration issues, has contributed to substantial discrepancies and a difficulty to adopt a holistic approach to migration and integration in spite of repeated declared intentions to do so. Thus, since the Lisbon Treaty (2009) it has been clarified that as regards integration policy, the EU is only able to adopt measures which aim to coordinate national policies, provide support in orientating national policy, and promote the exchange of information among stakeholders, as foreseen in the area of the supporting competences.

Having a shared EU legal framework for legal migration has led to a degree of harmonisation of conditions and rights, as well as a simplification of administrative procedures, helping to create a level(er) playing field across Member States. It has improved legal certainty and predictability for third-country nationals, employers, and administrations, and it has improved recognition of the rights of third-country nationals (namely the right to be treated on an equal basis with nationals in a number of important areas, such as working conditions, access to education and social security benefits, and procedural rights). In the case of specific categories of third-- country nationals (e.g. ICTs, researchers and students), it has facilitated intra-EU mobility (European Commission SWD(2019)1056). Additionally, through the use of its funding instruments, by establishing networks of experts, as well as events and conferences aimed at bringing together multiple stakeholders, it has created a community spanning across the EU Member States and far beyond of civil society organisations, migrant associations, experts, researchers and practitioners who have been actively engaged in working to find ways to improve policies and instruments aimed at promoting migrant integration and to tangibly advance immigrant integration on the ground.

Notwithstanding these advantages, the current legal migration framework falls short of achieving the Treaty objective of developing a common legal migration policy as a key element of a comprehensive policy on management of migratory flows.

For one, there is a set of gaps which essentially lead to a fragmented system. The directives that have been adopted do not cover various problems occurring in the course of the various 'migration phases', such as the procedures for obtaining an entry visa. Nor do they fully cover – at least as far as admission conditions are concerned – major categories of third- country nationals, such as non-seasonal low- and medium-skilled workers, job seekers, service providers covered by the EU's trade commitments except intra-corporate transferees, and self- employed people/ entrepreneurs that tend to be covered by national rules (European Commission SWD(2019a, b, c, 1056).

Furthermore, although EU directives on migration only provide a set of minimum entry and residence conditions as well as equal treatment rights, the discretion that Member States have in how they transpose these directives into national law means that rules applied to migrants are not identical in all Member States. This has been identified as one of the factors that might motivate migrants, including refugees and asylum seekers, to move from the country they first arrive in to another country (European Commission COM(2016)456). As an illustration, data from EURODAC, the EU's database that matches fingerprints to make it easier for EU states to determine responsibility for examining an asylum application by comparing fingerprint datasets, has shown that 30% of asylum applicants in 2016 had previously lodged an application in another Member State (European Parliament 2017). The significant increase in the number of persons seeking asylum in the EU particularly since 2015, raised awareness of the urgent need to ensure stronger enforcement of the directives, to improve their implementation and practical application – and therefore their overall effectiveness.

Similarly, different national implementation choices and the possibility for Member States to retain parallel national schemes have added to complexity and lack of coherence of the EU framework. For instance, the existence of national permits for permanent residents has limited the intended harmonisation of different types of long- term residence status provided for by the Long-Term Residents Directive. With 2.9 million EU long-term residents' permits issued at the end of 2018 vs. ten million national ones,[3] this Directive has been less successful than intended (European Commission COM(2019)161). The situation is similar for highly-skilled workers. The Blue Card Directive left Member States ample leeway on a variety of admission and residence criteria leading to the emergence of a confusing landscape of 25 distinct Blue Card systems (Denmark, Ireland, and the United Kingdom (when it was an EU Member State) have opted not to take part) often in parallel to already well-developed national channels for the highly skilled. This confusion has not contributed to the Blue Card's stated goal of facilitating the mobility of highly qualified professionals across Europe, nor has it served its intended purpose to be a magnet for international talent (Desiderio 2016). In addition, given the differences between Member States as regards the policies and resources devoted to integration issues, the outcomes of Europe's TCNs differ greatly across the Union. The impact of the EU framework on promoting the integration of third-country nationals and preventing labour exploitation, has been limited.

Moreover, one of the main objectives of the aforementioned directives is to contribute to the effective attainment of an internal market. The way that most Member States have implemented the intra-EU mobility provisions of the long-term residency directive has not really contributed to the attainment of the EU internal market. There is limited, and only partial data (survey data collected by the European Migration Network in 2013) on how many long-term residents have exercised their right to reside in another Member State, but what is clear is that intra-EU mobility rights provided under Directive 2003/109/EC seem to be consistently underused throughout the EU (European Commission COM(2019)161). A number of reasons could explain this. For one, in some cases, exercising this right is subject to as many conditions as the ones for a new application for a residence permit. In others, the competent national administrations do not have enough knowledge of the procedures, or they find it difficult to cooperate with their counterparts in other Member States. The Commission has declared its intention to monitor the implementation of the directive and encourage Member States to improve the implementation of the intra-EU mobility provisions, also by promoting the cooperation and exchange of information between national authorities (European Commission COM(2019)161).

Lastly, the structural deficiencies of the CEAS impact not only the reception and processing conditions of asylum seekers and refugees; they also impact the integration potential of would-be refugees. Delays in registration and lengthy

---

[3] Data on long-term residents on 31 December of each year [migr_reslong] provided by Eurostat: http://appsso.eurostat.ec.europa.eu/nui/show.do?dataset=migr_reslong&lang=en

asylum procedures hinder applicants' access to the labour market, while also increasing the reluctance of employers to recruit and hire asylum seekers due to the uncertainty of their legal status – including in situations when the person has a legal right to work (see the other relevant contributions in this volume). Moverover, the integration trajectory of asylum applicants is shaped by the economic conditions, the resources, networks and institutions that exist in the city or province where s/he is placed during the reception phase. This involves not only access to the labour market and the availability of employment opportunities; it also involves access to social services, health care, education and training, all of which impact integration. Beyond these tangible dimensions, the shortcomings of the CEAS have wider effects on the politics and social fabric of the receiving society which in turn impact deeply on the integration of TCNs. When asylum and migration policies appear deficient or unfair, then political polarisation, the rise of populist forces across almost all Member States, and public opinion affect the receiving society's overall commitment to integration of TCNs, and to integration as a 'two-way' process (Beirens 2018; European Social Survey and MPG 2017).

4.4 The EU's Integration Toolkit

In its 2003 Communication on Immigration, Integration and Employment, the Commission defined integration as a 'two-ways process' based on mutual rights and corresponding obligations of legally resident third country nationals and the host society (European Commission 2003). While recognising that priorities will vary between countries and regions, the Commission underlined the need for integration policies to be planned within a long-term, coherent overall framework, and to be responsive to the specific needs of particular groups and tailored to local conditions. Integration, it was argued, was to be addressed through a holistic approach taking into account 'not only the economic and social aspects of integration but also issues related to cultural and religious diversity, citizenship, participation and political rights.' (European Commission COM (2003) (Box 4.1).

The Common Basic Principles for Integration Policy adopted by the Council in 2004 and reaffirmed a decade later (Council Conclusions 2014), are the foundations for EU policy cooperation on the integration of migrants and comprise 11 non-binding principles against which Member States can assess their own efforts. These Common Basic Principles for Immigrant Integration Policy (CBPs), refer to access to the labour market and recognition of qualifications, education and language skills, housing and urban issues, health and social services, social and cultural environment, nationality and civic citizenship. Even though they are not binding, the CBPs have played a central role in defining and orienting integration policy and measures across EU Member States as they identify all issues involved in integration policy and have served to set future priorities.

Beyond the establishment of a legislative framework described above – and to compensate for the limitations of EU competences – the Commission has worked to

> **Box 4.1 A Shifting Definition of Integration**
>
> Over the course of these past 20 years, a number of shifts have occurred with regards to how integration is defined. When integration policy was first defined as a 'two-way process' the guiding thinking was that institutions, both at national and European level, had the main responsibility in regard to migrants' integration into the receiving society, and integration was a way to promote social inclusion, non- discrimination and access to rights. Integration was defined as a dynamic, long-term, and continuous two-way process of mutual accommodation, not a static outcome. The participation of immigrants and their descendants on the one hand to meet the rights and responsibilities in relation to their new country of residence was matched with the receiving society's efforts to create the opportunities for the immigrants' full economic, social, cultural, and political participation. Accordingly, Member States were encouraged to consider and involve both immigrants and national citizens in integration policy, and to communicate clearly their mutual rights and responsibilities (Carrera and Atger 2011).
>
> By the mid-2000s however, a number of Members States started to shift the burden to the TCNs in terms of their responsibility to learn the language and norms of the host country. For example, in the Netherlands and the UK (for specific target groups), immigrants have to pay for language instructions, thereby placing a burden particularly on low income TCNs (Gilardoni et al. 2015). For most Member States, integration increasingly became about TCNs demonstrating certain achievements and understandings in order to become socially included, to acquire a regular residence status and to have access to family reunion (Gilardoni et al. 2015). To the growing concern of migrant organisations, researchers and the EU institutions, integration was gradually transformed into a regulatory technique based on conditionality for the state to manage access by the foreigner to social inclusion and rights. As Member States began to add on obligations and requirements to TCNs, the Commission highlighted its concern with the shift from incentives to integrate to sanctions when requirements were not fulfilled and questioned the legal validity of these requirements under the Family and Long-term Residences Directives (European Commission 2006).

put these CBPs into practice by developing a wide-ranging toolkit aiming to stimulate Member States to assess their integration policies and practices, and, where necessary, to rethink them.

First of all, from the perspective of policy orientation and guidance, a number of documents underline core priorities and offer instruments in support of member States' integration policies. Already in 2011, the Commission's European agenda for the integration of third-country nationals (European Commission COM(2011) 455) highlighted the challenges of migrant integration and suggested areas for action by both the Commission and Member States to foster integration policies.

More recently, in 2016, the Action Plan on the Integration of Third-Country Nationals (excluding second and third generation migrants), was formulated to support Member States' efforts in developing and strengthening their integration policies following the 2015–2016 crisis. The Action Plan, together with over €5 billion of additional funding for migration up to 2021 mobilised from within the EU budget, encompasses a wide range of measures for the EU Member States and other organisations to focus their efforts on. These include pre-departure and pre-arrival measures aiming to support migrants at the earliest point of the migration process (for example: language and job-related training); education and training (particularly language learning), as well as the right to childcare and to quality education for children; measures aimed at increasing awareness of the laws, culture and values of the receiving society; employment and vocational training to support the timely and full integration of migrants in the labour market and help mitigate the need for specific skills in the EU; access to basic services such as housing and healthcare enabling migrants to start a life in a new country and to have a reasonable chance of employment; active participation of migrants in the receiving communities through social, cultural and sports activities. It should be reminded that these actions fall under the competence of the Member States, therefore, the Commission does not monitor them in terms of how these funds are disbursed or what their outcomes are. In 2018, the European Court of Auditors conducted a survey in the EU Member States to assess the support provided by the Commission for the development and implementation of their integration policy. Among those Member States who did respond, the Commission's support was considered as partially or fully relevant; nonetheless, the majority did not wish to see the current competences of the Commission in the field of migrant integration further increased (ECA 2018).

Second, through its funding tools, the EU has been able to influence national developments on the ground and a degree of European convergence. The European Integration Fund (EIF) (2007–2013) has directed its funding to integration projects conceived and implemented in line with the CBPs framework. EIF funding has been mainly directed towards Member States' public authorities and services, and used largely for implementing, developing and testing language skills, as well as civic courses and programmes in the context of immigration and citizenship legislation (Carrera and Atger 2011).

Articles 77–80 of the TFEU have served as the basis for specialised funding instruments covering projects on immigrant integration to be developed. The EIF was transformed into the Asylum, Migration and Integration Fund (AMIF) in the 2014–2020 financial cycle with a total of €3.137 billion[4] earmarked for the 27 Member States (excluding Denmark)[5] to be spent on: strengthening and developing the Common European Asylum System by ensuring that EU legislation in this field is efficiently and uniformly applied; supporting legal migration to EU Member

---

[4] See European Commission, DG Migration and Home Affairs: https://ec.europa.eu/home-affairs/financing/fundings/migration-asylum-borders/asylum-migration-integration-fund_en

[5] 88% of the AMIF is spent under shared management and 12% under direct management, to be divided between EU actions and emergency assistance.

States in line with the labour market needs and promoting the effective integration of non-EU nationals; enhancing fair and effective returns, which contribute to combating irregular migration with an emphasis on sustainability and effectiveness of the return process; and ensuring that EU States which are most affected by migration and asylum flows can count on solidarity from other EU States. In 2019, the European Parliament endorsed the renewed Asylum, Migration and Integration Fund (AMIF) for the 2021–2027 budget with an increase up to €9.2 billion (€10.41 billion in current prices). This will constitute 51% more than in the previous financial framework to contribute to these objectives (European Parliament 2019).

The AMIF regulation stipulates that at least 20% of the funds should be allocated to integration and at least another 20% to asylum. All Member States adhere to these requirements except Greece, which spends a share well below the 20% minimum on integration and legal migration, and Poland and Portugal, which fall marginally below the 20% threshold for spending on asylum (for further details and breakdown see Darvas et al. 2018). AMIF also provides financial resources for the activities of the European Migration Network (EMN) which has been set up to provide up-to-date, objective, reliable and comparable data on migration and asylum in order to support Member States' and EU institutions' policy-making. Special financial incentives for EU States have been built into the AMIF to support the Union Resettlement Programme through which, on the basis of Regulation EU No.516/2014, EU States voluntarily aim to provide international protection and effective integration in their territories to refugees and displaced persons identified as eligible for resettlement by UNHCR. Concrete actions funded through AMIF can include a wide range of initiatives, such as the improvement of accommodation and reception services for asylum seekers, information measures and campaigns in non-EU countries on legal migration channels, education and language training for non-EU nationals, assistance to vulnerable persons belonging to the target groups of AMIF, information exchange and cooperation between EU States and training for staff on relevant topics of AMIF.

Beyond this Fund, various dimensions of migrant integration are supported through a number of EU funds alongside other objectives (see Table 4.2) (ECA 2018). These include inter alia promoting labour market integration and addressing social exclusion; alleviating poverty and promoting social inclusion, including in rural areas; providing immediate support regarding food and other basic material assistance; or supporting medium and long- term measures regarding social, health, education, housing and childcare infrastructure. Moreover, EU funds implemented directly by the Commission or by delegated bodies such as Horizon 2020, Erasmus +, COSME, Europe for Citizens and the Employment and Social Innovation Programme, are also used to finance actions aiming at migrant integration.

Third, in order to help Member States assess, develop, monitor and evaluate their national frameworks on integration, the EU has encouraged the exchange of information and the sharing of best practices. For this, National Contact Points on Integration (NCPIs), i.e. national experts identified within the ministries responsible for integration policy in each of the member states, are brought together to exchange

Table 4.2 Overview of the most relevant EU funds to support migrant integration

Fund and purpose	Available funds (in million €)	Number of member states using the fund	Targeted migrants	Integration measures
Asylum, Migration and Integration Fund (AMIF) (contributes to efficient management of migration)	884	27	All legal residents	Counselling, education, training
European Social Fund/ Youth Employment Initiative (promotes employment, education and social inclusion)	85,455	20	Those who can legally participate in the labour market or who are minor	Education, training, actions to facilitate access to the labour market
European Regional and Development Fund (ERDF) (reinforces economic, social and territorial cohesion)	21,906	4	Not directly targeted	Education, social, health and housing infrastructures
European Agriculture Fund for Rural Development (EAFRD) (promotes sustainable rural development)	15,218	3	Not directly targeted	Assistance in housing, health care, education and employment
European Maritime and Fisheries Fund (EMMP) (promotes balanced development of fisheries and aquaculture areas)	581	0	Not directly targeted	Professional training and start-up support
Fund for European Aid to the Most Deprived (FEAD) (alleviates poverty)	3814	4	As defined by member states	Food, basic assistance and social inclusion activities outside active labour market measures

Notes: (1) As of March 2018; (2) Specific objective 2 (Integration/Legal migration). Specific objective 1 (Asylum) could also contain integration related actions, but the amount is not known and has not been included in the European Court of Auditors' (ECA) calculations; (3) Total available ESIF allocations for all target groups to thematic objectives 8 (Promoting sustainable and quality employment and supporting labour mobility), 9 (Promoting social inclusion, combating poverty and any discrimination) and 10 (Investing in education, training and vocational training for skills and lifelong learning); (4) Use of the fund for migrant integration measures as stated by Member States in the ECA's survey; (5) Regarding applicants for international protection, Member States may also grant access to vocational education and training prior to having access to the labour market

Source: European Court of Auditors (ECA), based on adopted amounts in the EU programmes as of January 2018, Commission's website https://cohesiondata.ec.europa.eu; ECA survey in the EU Member States; and European Commission's notes on synergies

insights, monitor progress and disseminate 'best practices' on integration policies at the national and EU levels.

These exchanges have been critical to the preparation of the European Commission's annual reports on immigration and integration and the elaboration of integration handbooks.[6] Similarly, the establishment of the European Integration Forum established in 2009 by the Commission and the European Economic and Social Committee was established to discuss on issues of migrant integration. In 2015, it was replaced by the European Migration Forum and has since served as a platform for dialogue where civil society and migrants' organisations are represented and which serves as a space for consultation, exchange of expertise (technical know-how and good practices) and identification of policy recommendations. The creation of a research-rich European website on integration,[7] along with other relevant policy and research networks have been among its outcomes. Networks such as the European Migration Network (EMN) or the European Integration Network (EIN) bring together representatives of national public authorities from all EU Member States and two EEA countries (Iceland and Norway) to consult with the European Commission on current developments and policy agenda in the field of integration. They also participate in targeted study visits, peer reviews, workshops and mutual assistance actions on specific integration aspects, with the main aim of exchanging knowledge.

As regards data availability and monitoring, since 2010 the Council agreed on a set of common EU core indicators (Zaragoza indicators) to measure migrant integration in the areas of employment, education, social inclusion and active citizenship. Although in principle these indicators are valuable in defining integration and identifying where the biggest challenges are, in practice their use is limited because data on the migrant population is not always harmonised, indicators are not always reliable, and the different groups of migrants cannot be identified. Indeed, a 2017 survey by the European Court of Auditors concluded that half of the Member States/national authorities do not use the Zaragoza indicators to monitor the outcomes of their integration policies and about a third do not use any indicator at all to monitor the outcome of their integration policies. None the less, monitoring is a fundamental tool for policy-makers and an area with significant EU added value. Monitoring enables the mapping of migrants' needs so that appropriate political responses are brought about, whether through integration policies or through more general social and economic policies. And, it allows policy-makers to watch over changes in the target groups' situation and to adjust policies accordingly, provided of course that monitoring is conducted regularly and comprises a set of relatively consistent and stable indicators (Gilardoni et al. 2015).

---

[6]The European Commission's Directorate-General Justice, Freedom and Security, has produced three editions of its *Handbook on Integration for policy-makers and practitioners* (2004, 2007 and 2010).

[7]European Website on Integration, Migrant Integration Information and good practices, https://ec.europa.eu/migrant-integration/home

To improve the availability of data, indicators of immigrant integration and research and strengthen the EU's ability to respond to prospective challenges posed by migration, the Commission set up a Knowledge Centre on Migration and Demography under the Commission's Joint Research Centre (JRC) in 2016[8] and deepened its collaboration with the OECD. The experience of the 2015–2016 crisis was a game changer as regards the importance of readily available, robust, reliable and timely data on migration flows, trends and integration outcomes. It also led the Commission to mainstream integration across all policy sectors and in 2015 set up an Inter-Service Group on the integration of TCNs to better coordinate policies under the 2016 EU Action Plan on the Integration of TCNs.

Finally, other EU measures beyond the area of freedom, security and justice have contributed to EU immigrant integration though in limited ways. As mentioned above, the Race Equality Directive 2000/43/EC allowed for anti-discrimination laws to be set up and/or extended across the EU Member States. The Equal Treatment Directive 2000/78/EC, which concerns different grounds of discrimination and is limited to employment, provided the grounds for important judgments on religion thereby contributing to immigrant integration beyond the legal scope of the Tampere conclusions and the area of freedom, security and justice (see Tsourdi 2019; Triandafyllidou and Martin 2009; Triandafyllidou and Gropas 2009). Nonetheless, the fact that EU competences are limited in the fields of social policy, education or political participation, restricts the effectiveness of EU integration policies (see inter alia Beirens et al. 2016; De Bruycker et al. 2019). Given Europe's increasingly diverse societies and given that integration in practice has very tangible dimensions and happens in the workplace, at school, in housing or in everyday civic and political life, it seems warranted for the EU to move to a more holistic approach of integration linking these diverse policy areas (OECD and European Commission 2018).

4.5 Looking Ahead to the EU's Integration Policies

Ensuring that migrants, asylum seekers and refugees can actively participate in the labour market and contribute to the receiving society is key to the well-being, prosperity and cohesion of European societies. Migrant integration is a dynamic process that is shaped both by the changing composition of the migrant flows and by the changes in the receiving country's economy and society. It also requires a series of reforms and new initiatives both in Member States and at the EU level, as well as coordinated measures to be pursued on three fronts. First, to work towards effective partnerships with third countries of origin or transit in order to be able to manage migration flows. Second, to work towards consolidating the CEAS and finding alternative solutions to unblock the Dublin deadlock. And third, to elaborate

---

[8] European Commission, Knowledge Centre on Migration and Demography (KCMD), https://ec.europa.eu/knowledge4policy/migration-demography_en

a robust framework for legal migration and integration which ensures TCNs with the fair treatment and opportunities they deserve so that they can contribute to Europe's prosperity, economic development and well-being.

In these times where discrimination, prejudice, racism and xenophobia are rising, and in spite of its weaknesses, the EU has a unique arsenal of legal, moral and economic tools and foundations on which to uphold the EU's fundamental rights, values and freedoms and contribute to more inclusive and cohesive societies. The commitment by the incoming President of the European Commission Ursula von der Leyen to develop a 'New Pact on Migration and Asylum' offered a much needed new impetus to address some of its important gaps and deficiencies.

References

Andor, L. (2014). *Labour mobility in the EU, speech at Ghent.* https://ec.europa.eu/commission/presscorner/detail/fr/SPEECH_14_622. Accessed 28 Jan 2020.

Beirens, H. (2018). *Cracked foundation, uncertain future: Structural weaknesses in the Common European Asylum System.* Brussels: MPI. https://www.migrationpolicy.org/research/structural-weaknesses-common-european-asylum-system. Accessed 7 Jan 2020.

Beirens, H., et al. (2016). *Study on the Temporary Protection Directive, Final Report for the European Commission (DG HOME).* https://ec.europa.eu/home-affairs/sites/homeaffairs/files/e-library/documents/policies/asylum/temporary-protection/docs/final_report_evaluation_tpd_en.pdf. Accessed 19 Jan 2020.

Carrera, S., & Atger, A. F. (2011). *Integration as a two-way process in the EU? Assessing the relationship between the European Integration Fund and the Common Basic Principles on Integration.* Brussels: CEPS. https://www.ceps.eu/wp-content/uploads/2011/07/Integration%20as%20a%20Two-way%20Process.pdf. Accessed14 Dec 2020.

Cedefop. (2014). *Skills Challenge in Europe, Skills Panorama.* Available at: https://skillspanorama.cedefop.europa.eu/sites/default/files/EUSP_AH_SkillsChallenges_0.pdf. Accessed 19 Jan 2020.

Commission of the European Communities. (2000). *On a community immigration policy, COM(2000) 757 final.* Brussels, 22. 11.2000, https://eur-lex.europa.eu/LexUriServ/LexUriServ.do?uri=COM:2000:0757:FIN:EN:PDF. Accessed 19 Jan 2020.

Commission of the European Communities. (2003). *On immigration, integration and employment, COM(2003) 336 final.* Brussels, 3.06.2003. https://eur-lex.europa.eu/legal-content/EN/ALL/?uri=CELEX%3A52003DC0336. Accessed 18 Dec 2019.

Council Directive 2000/43/EC of 29 June 2000 implementing the principle of equal treatment between persons irrespective of racial or ethnic origin.

Council Directive 2000/78/EC 27 November 2000 establishing a general framework for equal treatment in employment and occupation.

Council Conclusions, Immigrant integration policy in the EU. (2004). https://www.consilium.europa.eu/ueDocs/cms_Data/docs/pressData/en/jha/82745.pdf. 14615/04 (Presse 321), 19 November 2004. Accessed 15 Jan 2020.

Council Conclusions on the integration of third-country nationals legally residing in the EU. (2014, June 5–6). https://www.consilium.europa.eu/media/28071/143109.pdf. Accessed 15 Jan 2020.

Darvas, Z. et al. (2018). *EU funds for migration, asylum and integration policies, Study requested by BUDG Committee.* European Parliament. https://www.europarl.europa.eu/RegData/etudes/STUD/2018/603828/IPOL_STU(2018)603828_EN.pdf. Accessed 19 Jan 2020.

De Bruycker, P., et al. (Eds.). (2019). *From Tampere 20 to Tampere 2.0: Towards a new European consensus on migration.* Brussels: European Policy Centre.

Del Carpio X. V., & Wagner, M. (2015). The *Impact of Syrians Refugees on the Turkish Labor Market* (Policy Research Working Paper No 7402). World Bank. http://documents.worldbank. org/curated/en/505471468194980180/The-impact-of-Syrians-refugees-on-the-Turkish-labor-market. Accessed 30 Jan 2020.

Desiderio, M. V. (2016). Blue Card Redux: European Commission Plan to Recast Work Permit for Highly Skilled Holds Question Marks, MPI Commentaries. https://www.migrationpolicy.org/news/blue-card-redux-european-commission-plan-recast-work-permit-highly-skilled-holds-question-marks. Accessed 19 Jan 2020.

EU Charter of Fundamental Rights, see: https://eur-lex.europa.eu/legal-content/EN/TXT/?uri=CELEX:12012P/TXT. Accessed 19 Jan 2020.

European Commission. (2003). Communication on Immigration, Integration and Employment, COM(2003) 336, 03/06/2003. https://eur-lex.europa.eu/LexUriServ/LexUriServ.do?uri=COM:2003:0336:FIN:EN:PDF. Accessed 19 Dec 2019.

European Commission. (2006). Second Annual Report on Migration and Integration, (2006) 892, 30/06/2006. https://register.consilium.europa.eu/doc/srv?l=EN&f=ST%2011526%20 2006%20INIT

European Commission. (2011). European agenda for the integration of third-country nationals, COM(2011) 455 final, https://eur-lex.europa.eu/legal-content/EN/TXT/PDF/?uri=CELEX:52011DC0455&from=EN. Accessed 12 Jan 2020.

European Commission. (2015). A European Agenda On Migration, COM(2015) 240 final. Brussels, 15.05.2015. https://ec.europa.eu/anti-trafficking/sites/antitrafficking/files/communication_on_the_european_agenda_on_migration_en.pdf. Accessed 19 Dec 2019.

European Commission. (2016a). Proposal for a Directive laying down standards for the reception of applicants for international protection – COM(2016) 465 final of 13/07/2016. https://ec.europa.eu/home-affairs/sites/homeaffairs/files/what-we-do/policies/european-agenda-migration/proposal-implementation-package/docs/20160713/proposal_on_standards_for_the_reception_of_applicants_for_international_protection_en.pdf. Accessed 20 Jan 2020.

European Commission. (2016b). Single Market integration and competitiveness report 2016, DG GROW, https://ec.europa.eu/docsroom/documents/20210. Accessed 2 Feb 2020.

European Commission. (2016c). Action plan on the integration of third-country nationals. https://ec.europa.eu/home-affairs/what-we-do/policies/legal-migration/integration/action-plan-integration-third-country-nationals_en. Accessed 12 Jan 2020.

European Commission. (2018). Enhancing legal pathways to Europe: An indispensable part of a balanced and comprehensive migration policy, COM (2018) 635 final, Brussels, 12.09.2018. https://ec.europa.eu/commission/sites/beta-political/files/soteu2018-legal-pathways-europe-communication-635_en.pdf. Accessed 29 Jan 2020.

European Commission. (2019a). Report to the European Parliament and the Council on the implementation of Directive 2003/86/EC on the right to family reunification, COM(2019) 162, 29/03/2019. https://eur-lex.europa.eu/legal-content/EN/TXT/?qid=1567069070079&uri=CELEX:52019DC0162. Accessed 15 Jan 2020.

European Commission. (2019b). Executive Summary of the Fitness Check on EU Legislation on Legal Migration, SWD(2019) 1056 final, 29/03/2019. https://ec.europa.eu/home-affairs/sites/homeaffairs/files/e-library/documents/policies/legal-migration/swd_2019-1056-executive-summary_en.pdf. Accessed 15 Jan 2020.

European Commission. (2019c). Report to the European Parliament and the Council on the implementation of Directive 2003/109/EC concerning the status of third-country nationals who are long-term residents, COM(2019) 161, 29/03/2019. https://eur-lex.europa.eu/legal-content/EN/TXT/?qid=1567069007318&uri=CELEX:52019DC0161. Accessed 15 Jan 2020.

European Council Presidency Conclusions. (1999). Tampere, 15–16 October 1999. https://www.europarl.europa.eu/summits/tam_en.htm. Accessed 19 Jan 2020.

European Court of Auditors (ECA). (2018, May). The integration of migrants from outside the EU. *Briefing Note.* https://www.eca.europa.eu/Lists/ECADocuments/Briefing_paper_Integration_migrants/Briefing_paper_Integration_migrants_EN.pdf. Accessed 12 Jan 2020.

European Parliament. (2017). *Briefing paper on 'Secondary movements of asylum-seekers in the EU asylum system'*. https://www.europarl.europa.eu/RegData/etudes/BRIE/2017/608728/EPRS_BRI(2017)608728_EN.pdf. Accessed 19 Dec 2019.

European Parliament. (2019). *Migration and asylum: EU funds to promote integration and protect borders*. Press Release: 19/02/2019. https://www.europarl.europa.eu/news/en/press-room/20190218IPR26999/migration-and-asylum-eu-funds-to-promote-integration-and-protect-borders. Accessed 20 Jan 2020.

European Social Survey and Migration Policy Group (MPG). (2017). *Attitudes towards immigration in Europe: myths and realities*. https://www.europeansocialsurvey.org/docs/findings/IE_Handout_FINAL.pdf. Accessed 19 Jan 2020.

Eurostat. (2019a). *Migrant integration statistics – Labour market indicators*. https://ec.europa.eu/eurostat/statistics-explained/index.php?title=Migrant_integration_statistics_–_labour_market_indicators&oldid=436157#Labour_market_participation_.E2.80.94_activity_rates. Accessed 31 Jan 2020.

Eurostat. (2019b). *Residence permits – Statistics on first permits issued during the year*. https://ec.europa.eu/eurostat/statistics-explained/index.php?title=Residence_permits_-_statistics_on_first_permits_issued_during_the_year&oldid=456573#First_residence_permits_.E2.80.94_an_overview. Accessed 31 Jan 2020.

Geddes, A. (2000). Lobbying for migrant inclusion in the European Union: new opportunities for transnational advocacy? *Journal of European Public Policy, 7*(4), 632–649. https://doi.org/10.1080/13501760050165406. Accessed 17 Dec 2019.

Geddes, A. (2013). *The politics of migration and immigration in Europe*. London: Sage.

Gilardoni, G., et al. (Eds.). (2015). *KING Knowledge for INtegration Governance: Evidence on migrants' integration in Europe*. Milan: Fondazione ISMU. http://aei.pitt.edu/62271/1/pub_5379_king_report.pdf . Accessed 17 Dec 2019.

Groenendijk, K. (2015). Equal treatment of workers from third countries: The added value of the single permit directive, ERA forum (2015) 16: 547. https://doi.org/10.1007/s12027-015-0403-2. Accessed 15 Jan 2020.

Hansen, P. (2005). *A Superabundance of contradictions: The European Union's Post- Amsterdam Policies on Migrant 'Integration', Labour Immigration, Asylum, and Illegal Immigration* (ThemES Occasional Paper #28). Centre for Ethnic and Urban Studies, Linköping University. http://www.diva-portal.org/smash/get/diva2:235726/FULLTEXT01.pdf. Accessed 6 Jan 2020.

Jakulevičiene, L. (2019). The Common European Asylum System. In P. De Bruycker P. et al. (Eds.). (2019) *From Tampere 20 to Tampere 2.0: Towards a new European consensus on migration*. Brussels: European Policy Centre.

Juncker, J.-C. (2014). A New Start for Europe: My Agenda for Jobs, Growth, Fairness and Democratic Change, Political Guidelines for the next European Commission, Opening Statement in the European Parliament Plenary Session, 'Towards a new policy on Migration', 15 July 2014, https://ec.europa.eu/commission/presscorner/detail/en/SPEECH_14_546. Accessed 2 Dec 2019.

Juncker, J.-C. (2016). Speech at the EP Plenary session – Conclusions of the European Council meeting of 17 and 18 December 2015. https://ec.europa.eu/commission/presscorner/detail/en/SPEECH_16_112. Accessed 6 Jan 2020.

Kancs, D., & Lecca, P. (2017). Long-term Social, Economic and Fiscal Effects of Immigration into the EU: The Role of the Integration Policy, JRC Working Papers in Economics and Finance, 2017/4, doi:https://doi.org/10.2760/999095. Accessed 17 Jan 2020.

Neframi, E. (2011). Division of competences between the European Union and its Member States concerning immigration, Note for the DG for Internal Policies of the European Parliament, PE 453.178. https://www.europarl.europa.eu/RegData/etudes/note/join/2011/453178/IPOL-LIBE_NT(2011)453178_EN.pdf. Accessed 31 Jan 2020.

OECD and European Commission. (2018). *Settling in 2018: Indicators of immigrant integration*. http://www.oecd.org/publications/indicators-of-immigrant-integration-2018-97892643 07216-en.htm. Accessed 12 Jan 2020.
Triandafyllidou, A., & Gropas, R. (2009). *Education policies and the challenge of migration: Intercultural and multicultural concepts and policies*. Athens: EMILIE Policy Brief.
Triandafyllidou, A., & Martin, T. (2009). *The migration mix: Europe's multicultural challenge*. Athens: EMILIE European Policy Brief.
Tsourdi, E. (2019). EU Agencies. In De Bruycker P. et al (Eds.). (2019) From Tampere 20 to Tampere 2.0: *Towards a new European consensus on migration*. Brussels: European Policy Centre.

Chapter 5
"Enchanted with Europe": Family Migration and European Law on Labour-Market Integration

Irina Isaakyan and Anna Triandafyllidou

5.1   Introduction

During the last 15 years, the number of third-country nationals (TCNs) and mobile EU citizens living in the EU has increased from 34 million to 57 million, and EU Member States have experienced some common trends in what concerns integration of migrants, refugees and asylum seekers (MRAs). First of all, intra-EU mobility has grown, in terms of numbers and diversity (Kahanec and Zimmermann 2016; Lafleur and Stanek 2017). Second, the labour market integration of TCNs has come to the top of the EU agenda (ibid; Recchi 2015). However, Member States differ greatly in their policies on integration and citizenship acquisition as well as on reception and protection of refugees and asylum seekers. As noted by Geddes et al. (2020: 8), 'the EU does not have a comprehensive migration policy'. Finally, lengthy asylum procedures and low return rates of MRAs without appropriate permit to stay have led a considerable part of the MRA population to be in an irregular or insecure status (ibid; Kahance and Zimmermann 2016).

In this fluid milieu, scholars stop to view MRAs as holders of the fixed permit to work or stay but start to acknowledge the fragility – or 'fluidity' – of their status (Engbersen and Snel 2013). From this point of view, 'labour migrants' should not only be considered as those who enter the EU with the permit to work on pre-determined jobs but also a larger stream of refugees, asylum seekers and statistically dominating beneficiaries of family reunification (Geddes et al. 2020; Kahanec and Zimmermann 2016).

Family migrants, who actually make 40% of all TCNs in the EU (OECD 2019), represent a diverse MRA category with 'fluid boundaries' (Engbersen and Snel 2013). This group is comprised of a large range of people who enter the EU as

I. Isaakyan · A. Triandafyllidou (✉)
Ryerson University, Toronto, ON, Canada
e-mail: Anna.Triandafyllidou@ryerson.ca

© The Author(s) 2021
V. Federico, S. Baglioni (eds.), *Migrants, Refugees and Asylum Seekers'
Integration in European Labour Markets*, IMISCOE Research Series,
https://doi.org/10.1007/978-3-030-67284-3_5

dependent migrants to reunify with their EU-based family members, who may be either EU citizens or TCNs who migrated earlier (Castro et al. 2019; Geddes et al. 2020; Peña & Neufeld 2017; OECD 2017, 2019). This group includes skilled MRAs while marital ties and emerging social networks often provoke the 'fluidity' of their status: supported by their families, MRAs can get better access to jobs and employment-related educational resources, often benefiting from both the informal market and authorized work, and resuming or confirming the status of the skilled migrant (Castro et al. 2019; Costello 2016; Engbersen and Snel 2013; ETUC 2018; Isaakyan 2015). When discouraged by their families and diasporic communities, such MRAs may alternatively end up disqualified and unemployed (OECD 2019).

Studies note that TCNs, in general, and family migrants, in particular, encounter a number of legal barriers in their labour-market integration (LMI) across all EU 27 countries. The main LMI barriers for MRAs are insecure status (which also applies to legal economic migrants) and unrecognized qualifications. In this reference, the EU primary law represented by a number of directives: the *Family Reunification Directive* (2003/86/EC),[1] *Long-Term Residence Directive* (2003/109/EC),[2] *Free Movement Directive* (2004/38/EC),[3] *Blue Card Directive* (2009/50/EC),[4] and revised *Qualification Directive* (2011/95/EU).[5] These directives respectively concern the rights of family members of TCNs legally staying in the EU, long-term residents and their family members, family members of EU citizens, high-skill TCNs who come to the EU for qualified employment, and beneficiaries of international protection. However, these directives only provide guidelines to Member State. While the above mentioned barriers are mostly regulated on the national level and Member States differ significantly in their approaches (ETUC 2018). It is within this context that we may ask to what extent the European Court of Justice/ECJ (as the EU law enforcement organ) can help to foster harmonization.

This is not an easy question to answer because at the core of the EU constitutional basis lie two competing discourses: 'national security' versus 'free movement of people'. The EU is seen as a 'fortress' but also as a 'space without borders'. The theme of free movement becomes the red line in all EU documents and discourses on labour-market integration, stressing an unrestricted mobility throughout Europe for employment and a respective mobility of services such as recognition of professional qualifications. A deeper insight leads to see this enchanting project as limited mostly to intra-EU mobility (Recchi 2015).

It is within this context that the majority of studies argue that labour market integration on the EU level does not exist (ETUC 2018; Huddleston et al. 2015). Nevertheless, the EU has taken several steps in seeking to streamline, coordinate

---

[1] See Council (2003a).

[2] See Council (2003b).

[3] See Council (2004).

[4] See Council (2009).

[5] See European Parliament (2011).

and support the policies and practices of MRA integration across the continent (Kumric and Zupan 2016; Manko 2017; O'Cinneide 2012).

It is true that the ECJ does not support all MRA cases, and many of their claims are eventually refused. There are, however, a number of cases resolved by the ECJ in favour of the MRA-plaintiff (Jesse 2016; Leneartz 2015). And although their nuances are not precisely understood and are often interpreted differently by Member States, such ECJ decisions form the EU case-law platform for LMI. In this connection, legal studies scholars note on the 'intersectionality' of the ECJ's judgements, meaning that the ECJ considers a variety of EU Directives (or various sources of the EU primary law) while making a decision (Kortese 2016; Lenaertz 2012, 2015).

In the light of the discussion above, the chapter looks at barriers and enablers to skills recognition at the EU level by investigating the role of the ECJ in interpreting the rights of TCNs and their access to the labour market. We focus on the role of family reunification and EU citizen mobility provisions which tend to affect the court decisions in rather unexpected ways. We ask the following two research questions. Under what conditions are the permit to work for insecure TCNs and the recognition of TCNs' outside-the-EU qualifications supported by the ECJ? What role does the factor of family migration play in such decisions?

The following theoretical resources inform our work. First, we acknowledge the above-mentioned 'fluidity' of migration, which conveys the instability of the TCN's status. Given this, the ECJ often operates on the principle of 'intersectionality', taking into consideration various sources of EU primary law. In this connection, we finally assume that the 'free mobility' factor (which affects all EU discourses) and the 'family ties' factor (which is recognized in literatures as the most supportive of LMI) should presumably interact with the ECJ's decisions.

The discussion of our findings illuminates that the ECJ case-law on European LMI is affected by the overall EU atmosphere of 'positive contagion' by – or ideological attraction to - the idea of free movement (European Citizenship), which particularly crystalizes in the LMI of family migrants. This leads us to see family migration as a potential area of investment; whereas, at the same time, pointing to a complex interplay between intra-EU mobility, family reunification, gender bias and European case-law. While using the factor of family building in support of the TCN's claim, the ECJ in some cases reproduces gender bias in its reference to 'relational dependency' – a factor that often works to the detriment of even financially independent female MRAs and becomes a 'negative symbolic contagion' for European LMI.

The chapter has the following structure. Section 5.2 provides the background information on the family migration in the EU. It starts with an overview of family migration as a prevailing type of European immigration. In particular, it introduces the 'dependent migrant' (to be shown later as a specific group of ECJ plaintiffs). Then we briefly discuss the EU Family Reunification Strategy and the main LMI barriers that family migrants face when in the EU, posing the question about what the ECJ can practically do to assist such MRAs in confronting the LMI barriers.

In reference to this question, the *Professional Qualifications Directive (PQD)* and the *European Qualifications Framework (EQF)* are discussed in Sect. 5.3, which also analyzes ECJ cases that make precedent for evaluating foreign qualifications. This section argues that recognition of foreign qualifications stumbles over the MRA's permit to stay, the nuances of which are explored in Sect. 5.4. Looking at the ECJ case-law in relation to migrants who try to confirm on their permit to work, Sect. 5.4 points to the 'relational dependency' factor as the one that may not always act in favour of the (female) MRA when the case about her status transfer is assessed in court.

The chapter ends with the discussion of complex relations between qualifications, free mobility, law and gender (Sect. 5.5). It shows that some social forces (marriage to a EU national) may support the ECJ's decision in favour of the MRA, while others (dependency of the relationship) may actually work in the opposite direction, implying that the European space is not open for everyone.

5.2 Family Migration in the EU: Tendencies and Laws

5.2.1 'Dependent Migrants': Statistics and Basic Concepts

As observed by Eurostat (2019), 40% of the 37 million TCNs in the EU (that is, almost 15 million) are dependent migrants – or married adult MRAs who join their spouses abroad.[6] (Their incidence obviously wins the comparison with the 1.3 million MRAs who have entered the EU within the international protection scheme (European Parliament 2017a, 2017b).) Over the last 10 years, family migration associated with spouses' mobility has become the prevailing form of EU immigration (ibid). As noted by Geddes et al. (2020), 'family migration is a major component of immigration flows to the EU' (p. 29) and 'a key migration route' (p. 83).

According to the OECD Factsheet from 2018, such family migrants make 40% of all permanent migrations in the OECD countries (OECD 2018). This percentage has been relatively robust over the last 5 years (Chaloff 2013; OECD 2018), surpassing 30% of intra-EU mobility, 20% of refugees and asylum seekers, and 10% of economic (labour) migrants (ibid). Moreover, the inflows of family migrants to the EU become more and more dynamic with time. Thus almost 2 million family migrants have migrated to the OECD countries over the last 3 years, 1.6 of whom through the family reunification category (ibid).

Family migrants enter the country of destination (CoD) as 'dependent migrants' either simultaneously arriving with their principle migrant spouses (*accompanying*

---

[6] In this research, we do not include or refer to minors who are either biological children of principle migrants or international adoptees by EU citizens (although these two categories also fall under the overall umbrella of family migration.) By 'family migrants', we only mean married adults who are within the active working age and to whom the issue of LMI is at the moment related directly.

family migration), or later joining their long-term spouses who come to the CoD earlier as MRAs (*family reunification*), or migrating as newly-wedded spouses of residential foreigners and nationals (*family formation*).[7] In the EU, they all fall under the umbrella of Member States' national family reunification schemes, which are in theory informed by the European Family Reunification Strategy (Geddes et al. 2020).

Although marriage/family migration is an articulate migrant group, it conveys the characteristics and realities of other migrant types such as 'labour migration' and especially 'high-skill migration' (OECD 2018). In the EU, family migrants represent 40% of all MRAs. While their share specifically in the EU labour migration is also almost 40%, although a little lower than compared with 2000, mostly because of difficulties related to the recognition of their qualifications (Chaloff 2013).

5.2.2 EU Family Reunification Policy: Directives 2003/86 and 2004/38

The phenomenon of family reunification directly relates to the question of labour market integration since migrating spouses (dependent family migrants) should also have the right to work in the country of destination, thus adding to the EU workforce (Acosta Arcarazo 2009, 2010; Groenendijk 2007; Groenendijk et al. 2007; O'Cinneide 2015; Staiano 2017).

The multitude of cross-border marriage patterns in Europe leads toward a recognition of the overall EU Family Reunification Policy. The Family Reunification Policy consists of two Directives: the Family Reunification Directive 2003/86[8] and the European Citizens' Rights Directive (also known in press as the Free Movement- or EU Citizenship- Directive).[9] The reunification of family members of TCNs is covered by the provisions in the Family Reunification Directive 2003/86. As for TCNs who are overseas spouses of intra-EU mobile citizens, the EU Citizenship Directive 2003/38 comes into force.

Van den Broucke et al. (2016) explain that beneficiaries of the Family Reunification Strategy can be divided into two basic reunification categories, which have implications for their employment. The Family Reunification Directive entitles married spouses and unmarried under-age children of non-EU nationals who reside legally for at least 1 year in a Member State to reunite with them exactly in this Member State. Within this scheme, the reunifying family members (dependent migrants) have the right to work and access educational and vocational programmes immediately upon arrival, and also the right for the independent permit to stay after

---

[7] See Ibid.

[8] See: Council (2003a).

[9] See: Council (2004).

the 5 years of their legal residence. This directive does not cover the reunification of family members of refugees and EU nationals.[10]

The research conducted by Van den Broucke et al. (2016) shows that the reunification of overseas TNCs with their EU national spouses is covered by the European Citizenship Directive if the EU national sponsor has experience of intra-EU mobility. His/her family members can join him/her in the EU and live or travel with him/her all the time. In other words, if the EU national sponsor has worked, is now working or going to move to another Member State, his family members will be allowed to join him/her in the EU – given that they reside in a place of the sponsor's basement. Otherwise, the should apply under the national law.

Scholars argue that there is no European law on the harmonization of reunification procedures for TCNs who are family members of non-mobile EU nationals (Barbulescu 2017; Geddes et al. 2020; Van den Broucke et al. 2016). Such cases are often decided within the national law framework and are not resolved positively by the ECJ (Lanaertz 2015). There is, however, a special survival tool applied by such couples: to preserve the family integrity, the EU-national spouse finds a job in another EU Member State to where he/she can invite his/her TCN family for living and working.[11] Studies show that, although 'salient', the overall ides of Free Movement remains 'controversial' (Lafleur and Stanek 2017: 2015) because member states 'create hierarchies of family migrants by imposing conditions that define their eligibility, waiting periods and also integration measures (Geddes et al. (2020: 215).

Although the European Citizenship Directive remains fragmented and not applicable to all MRA categories, in those cases where it works it provides for the status that is equivalent to 'permit to work' – a strong factor that affects the rest of the labour market integration.

---

[10] The only entry condition is sponsorship, or the adequate financial support of the principle migrant of his/her incoming family. However, such nuances as the sponsor's financial threshold (for inviting his/her overseas-based family to the EU) and the composition of his/her immediate family are decided individually by national laws of Member States (Acosta Arcarazo 2009; Bonjour 2014; Block and Bonjour 2013; Bonjour and Vinck 2013; Van den Broucke et al. 2016). Moreover, the Directive grants Member States optional provisions to extend some parameters while restricting others. Member States differ a lot along this family reunification continuum, while the ECJ cannot force them to modify these additional parameters.

[11] This European Citizenship Directive makes the process of family reunification fast and effective– yet fragmented because some categories of MRA (such as long-term residents, specific visa holders and non-mobile EU nationals) are marginalized within this scheme as sponsors. Neither does this Directive clarify whether the EU-national sponsor's periods of study or vocational training in another EU country can count toward his/her intra-EU mobility experience.

5.3 Recognition of Professional Qualifications

As noted by a senior *DG Empl* officer, 'Everything starts from job search and skill match, where of vital importance are professional qualifications, which often remain unrecognized by the Member State'.[12] Within this pessimistic context, we may further ask if nothing at all can be done on the EU level, or if there are still any loopholes in EU law on LMI for TCNs. One such loophole is European citizenship and associated intra-EU mobility.

5.3.1 The European Space but for Whom?

In 1979, the Lebanon-issued medical degree of the Lebanese dental surgeon Dr. Tawil-Albertini was recognized in Belgium but later rejected in Ireland in 1986. In 1982, Hugo Fernando Hocsman, a Spanish doctor with all his degrees and professional qualifications from Argentina, was authorized to practice in Spain as part of the bi-lateral agreement between these two countries, but was later denied an opportunity to practice in France in 1992.

We may ask why the ECJ supported Hocsman's claim against France but opposed Tawil-Albertini's appeal against Ireland if they both had had their foreign degrees recognized in the EU. Why did the principle of mutual recognition work for Hocsman but not for Tawil-Albertini? The answer is: Hocsman was a EU national while Tawil-Albertini was not. Neither was the latter married to a EU national. Their ECJ cases, which have paved the platform for the 2005 Professional Qualifications Directive (PQD), point to the huge discrepancy between recognition services provided to EU citizens and those provided to TCNs.

Recognition refers to the 'free movement' rhetoric in the EU policy, which became an essential part of EU law after its endorsement in 1992 by the Amsterdam Treaty [TFEU Articles 4(2)(a), 20, 26 and 45–48]. The main freedom granted to EU citizens and their family members within this framework is the freedom of movement of professionals, which includes their fundamental right to move to and work in another Member State on the principle of Equal Treatment with nationals of that Member State (Papagianni 2014; Stetter 2008).[13] This freedom leads directly to a number of other freedoms such as establishment and service provision [TFEU Article(49)] – or the right to settle and to develop career so that the person would be able to provide professional services in a new Member State. This further conveys

---

[12] Interview held in Brussels on 12 December 2018 as part of the SIRIUS research. Available at: https://www.sirius-project.eu/sites/default/files/attachments/SIRIUS%20WP3%20-%20 D3.2_0.pdf

[13] The constitutional basis of the EU has been paved by the Treaties of Maastricht (1992) and Amsterdam (1999) have paid the, with the Maastricht Treaty focusing on human rights while the Amsterdam Treaty dealing with the EU employment and immigration policies.

the idea of the harmonization and mutual recognition of academic and professional qualifications by Member States, without which the freedom of establishment would not be possible (Maciejewski et al. 2019).

These ideas are further elaborated on in a number of EU Directives, including the EU Citizenship Directive 2004/38/EC on the free movement of EU nationals and their family members (which is also part of the European Family Reunification Strategy) and the Professional Qualifications Directives (PQD) 2005/36/EC and 2013/55/EU.

5.3.2   Professional Qualifications Directive and European Case-Law on Recognition

Evaluating the labour market situation in the EU, it is important to note that training standards for regulated professions actually differ across Member States. However, the Professional Qualifications Directive (PQD), which is the primary EU law on the recognition of professionals' qualifications, simplifies the recognition process.[14] The directive even makes the recognition automatic for some regulated professions including doctors, dentists, nurses, midwives, pharmacists, veterinary surgeons and architects. In other cases, the principle of mutual recognition is applied. The only problem is that the PQD provisions are applicable only to qualifications received in the EU.

To be more specific, the main rule of the PQD is the automatic assessment of EU-based qualifications in the absence of significant differences between educational systems and professional requirements in two Member States (Kortese 2016). The mutual recognition principle ensures that the qualifications obtained according to the laws and regulations in one Member State are to be recognized as such in another Member State. In such cases of mutual recognition, additional accreditation and minimum training period apply. As for the non-EU based qualifications of EU citizens, they are recognized automatically in the case of 'second recognition', meaning that it has been recognized by another Member State where the person has also practiced for at least 3 years (which is seen in the *Hocsman* case). The automatic mutual recognition thus often becomes synonymous to the automatic 'secondary recognition' (Ibid).

However, cases of significant discrepancies between Member States' educational systems and professional requirements may involve support from the *European Qualifications Framework (EQF)* for lifelong learning. The main EU reference framework for evaluating qualifications and credentials that enable education and employment within the EU, the EQF was established in 2008 and revised in 2017 to guide the Member States' National Qualifications Frameworks. As noted in the EQF Brochure (Thyssen 2018: 5), it is a European 'translation device between

---

[14] For more on the PQD provisions, see: European Parliament (2013).

different qualifications systems and their levels'. As stated by Devaux (2013: 3), 'the general objective of the EQF is to promote lifelong learning, increase employability, mobility and the social integration of workers and learners'. In Member States, formal credentials are assessed against the EU benchmarks from the EQF by either national or regional coordinating mechanisms. Informal credentials are usually assessed by employers through alternative methods such as job interview (CEDEFOP 2018).

Kahance and Zimmermann (2016: 440) point to a number of serious 'recognition problems'. In line with this, studies and policy reports agree that neither the PDF nor the EQF provides any imperatives – or even clear guidelines to Member States – on how to assess overseas qualifications of foreign nationals or the absence of such in refugees and asylum seekers (Devaux 2013; Kortese 2016; Thyssen 2018). In its latest bi-annual update on the *European Inventory of Formal and Informal Learning*, CEDEFOP (2018) notes that, in reference to overseas credentials, many EU Member States still have serious problems with their validation systems and coordinating mechanisms, which prove to be successful mostly on the level of intra-EU mobility.

For the recognition of outside-the-EU qualifications of EU citizens and their family members, there is abundant ECJ case-law, including the iconic precedents such as *Vlassipoulou v. Germany (1991)* and the above-mentioned *Hocsman v. France (2000)* and *Tawil- Albertini v. Ireland* (1986), among many other cases that were considered by the ECJ before the adoption of the first PQD. Although they mostly refer to the recognition of cases that fall under the mutual recognition, they provide the case-law guidance for the recognition of TCN degrees. For example, the case of Irene Vlassipoulou v. Germany (about a Greek lawyer who held degrees and professional experience from both Greece and Germany and who tried to practice in Germany)[15] gives the precedent on evaluating all circumstances of the person's career in the EU – thus supporting the idea of a multi-faceted evaluation with emphasis on prior professional experience in any part of the EU for the EU citizen or for a person with derivative (equal treatment) status.

This rule applies to the evaluation of TCN qualifications of EU citizens, which is further illuminated by the earlier discussed case of Hugo Fernando Hocsman v. France.[16] According to TFEU Article 49 and the *Vlassipoulou* precedent, the ECJ confirmed, in *Hocsman*, on the rule of the second within-EU recognition for the EU citizen or a person with the derivative (equal treatment) status specifically in relation to TCN qualifications. However, the ECJ-rejected case of *Tawil Albertini* shows that the second within-EU recognition does not apply to un-naturalized TCNs who are not family members of EU citizens.[17]

These cases had enabled the consequent PQF 2005 and its modernized 2013 version, whose Article 3(3) provides that 'qualifications obtained by EU nationals and issued by a third country shall be regarded as evidence of formal qualifications by

---

[15] See: Case C-340/89 Vlassipoulou [1991] ECR I-2357.
[16] See: Case C-238/98 (2000) Hocsman ECR I-6623.
[17] See: Case C-154/93 Tawil-Albertini [1991'ECR I-451.

the Directive, if the holder has three years' professional experience in the profession concerned on the territory of the MS which initially recognized this qualification' (Kortese 2016; European Parliament 2013). This means that the EU-national would only benefit from this second-recognition procedure if he/she moves to a different MS.

While TCNs (with EU qualifications) definitely fall under the PDF, they become excluded from its beneficiary list when they aim at the recognition of qualifications received outside the EU. In this case, they become subjected to national laws and may be placed under strict conditions of evaluation (Kortese 2016; Maciejewski et al. 2019). As professionals, they may in some cases be recognized under the EU law, subjected, however, to 'a patchwork of secondary legislation [Directives]' that determines their EU status (Jesse 2016: 146). Among the Directives that grant the equal treatment in the recognition of professional qualifications to TCNs are the Long-term Residence Directive[18] and the European Citizenship Directive, which apply to TCNs who are family members (spouses). In such cases of family reunification, TCNs must undergo the above mentioned second within-EU recognition (as supported by the EU primary law in the face of the PQD and TFEU, and also by the EU case-law in the face of the *Vlassipoulou* and *Hocsman* cases). Marriage thus becomes an important factor of recognition because it changes the status.

5.4 The 'Relationship of Dependency': A Loophole for a Fluid Status?

5.4.1 *Looking at the* Zambrano *Case*

The recognition procedures show that, for TCNs, everything stumbles over their status in the country of destination. MSs have different entry bans on MRAs and different citizenship and immigration approaches. Because of the existing contradictions within their immigration policies, one and the same TCN may appear both as an irregular and regular migrant, who is both prohibited and allowed to work.

For example, the Columbian national Ruiz Zambrano came to the EU as an asylum seeker and soon married a Belgian citizen of the Colombian origin. His application for asylum in Belgium was soon refused, and in spite of his non-refoulment due to dangerous political situation in his country of origin, he had no permission to work in Belgium. He had still managed to work in that MS for 6 years (2001–2006), during which he had regularly and officially paid all taxes, and his Belgian-national son and daughter were born (Hailbronner and Thym 2011). However, the *Belgian*

---

[18] Directive 2003/109 gives the long-resident status to TCNs who have been legally residing, without an interruption, in an EU MS for at least 5 years. The acquisition of this status is subject to evidence of the applicant's financial resources and integration exams established in the MS. See: https://eur-lex.europa.eu/legal-content/EN/TXT/?uri=celex:32003L0109

Office National de L'Emploi rejected his claim for unemployment benefits and created a strong case for his expulsion from the country. Zambrano's consequent appeal to the ECJ was based on 'a derived right of residence as the ascendant of minor children who are nationals of a Member State' and was supported by the Court (ibid).

The revolutionary Zambrano case, which took place in 2011,[19] illuminates the ECJ's acknowledgement of factor of relational dependency between the plaintiff and his/her EU family. If Ruiz Zambrano had left the country, he should have taken his children with him because they were his dependents. This would mean that they would not be able to exercise their right of free movement around the EU. With emphasis on the 'citizenship of the Union as intended to be the fundamental status of nationals of the Member States' (Case C-34/09, EU:C:2011:124, para 41), the ECJ concluded its judgment with the recognition that 'Article 20 TFEU precludes national measures that have the effect of depriving citizens of the Union of the genuine enjoyment of the substance of the rights conferred by virtue of their status as citizens of the Union' (Case C-34/09, EU:C:2011:124, para 42).

The 'relationship of dependency' between the TCN and his/her EU-national minor children, which had become the key factor influencing the ECJ's decision in favour of the plaintiff, should be assessed both in financial (or care-providing) terms as well as from the point of view of European citizenship (which is in itself rather restrictive as applied not to anyone) (Hailbronner and Thym 2011). Thus in order to fit the requirements of Article 20, the minor children should be first of all directly dependent on the plaintiff in physical and emotional terms. At the same time, they should be EU citizens (or Member States' nationals) either by birth or through naturalization. If any of these two conditions is missing, the relational dependency becomes no more than a 'hypothetical' factor, and it would support more the idea of expulsion (in lines with the 'national security' rhetoric) rather than the idea of free movement (in favour of the 'one-Europe-for-all') (Lenaerts 2015).

5.4.2 Broken Relational Dependency

An example of the broken relational dependency is the Lida case (2012), which was rejected by the ECJ as 'falling outside the scope' of the TFEU provisions on EU citizenship (Adam and Van Elsuwege 2012: 176–183; Lida Case 2012, *para 56*). In that case, Mr. Iida, a Turkish national and a legal migrant in Germany, whose permit to work was expiring, applied for a permit to stay as the husband and father of EU citizens. However, both German authorities and the ECJ denied his claim on the basis of separation. This meant that his German-national wife and daughter were not dependent on him either in financial- or EU-mobility terms as living in Austria (another MS) and already exercising their Article 20 right (Lenearts 2015).

---

[19] See: Case C-34/09, EU:C:2011:124 (Ruiz Zambrano). For case analysis, see also: Lenaertz (2012, 2013, 2015).

There have been recently many cases (including the K.A. et al. Case C-82/16), where the ECJ confirms on the relational dependency as a way to avoid violation of the fundamental EU citizenship right, and successfully advises Member States on considering all circumstances around this complex LMI factor that work in favour of the TCN and his/her labour market participation (Progin-Theukauf 2018).

However, the gender bias illuminated by the 2017 Chavez-Vilchez et al. case[20] adds to the 'big puzzle' around both the European citizenship and the TCN status (Progin-Theukauf 2018). Although the Venezuelan national Mrs. Chavez-Vilchez completely fitted the relationship of dependency as the other of a EU national daughter and her main care-provider, the ECJ had rejected her claim. In fact, Mrs. Chavez-Vilchez and seven other TCN women whose claims were simultaneously considered and rejected had been lawfully living with their Dutch families in the Netherlands for years. As (former) asylum seekers, they were balancing between regular and irregular status for years. All eight women had, in their full custody and maintenance, minor Dutch-national children from Dutch-national men (Khan 2017). However, their claims were rejected by both the Dutch authorities and by the ECJ on the grounds of inadequate dependency factor: by the decision of the ECJ, the care provider is always the man unless he is imprisoned or institutionalized (placed in a mental institution) (Lenearts 2015).

The comparison of the *Zambrano* and *Chavez-Vilchez* cases shows that the EU citizenship- and family provisions create a non-playing field for women, where the father is considered indispensable as a career and provider for the children while the mother is not, even in spite of her financial eligibility.

5.5 Case-Buffers: Law and Gender

5.5.1 The Contagious Attraction of European Citizenship

The Chavez-Vilchez case adds to the overall rather pessimistic situation for dependent female MRAs in the EU, who reunite with their husband-sponsors. Even though independent financially (as the Chavez-Vilchez case demonstrates), female MRAs continue to experience various kinds of socio-economic barriers in their integration, including the 'double labour market disadvantage'. Because of their frequently unrecognized credentials and insecure status, they are sidelined in the job market against local women, while the lack of specific professional experience and impeded access to additional training fosters their marginalization also in relation to foreign men (Castro et al. 2019; Dumont 2007; Rubin 2008; OECD 2017). Such women are, in fact, among the 'most vulnerable populations for labour market integration' (Kahanec and Zimmermann 2016: 4). Often having restricted access to job postings, they also suffer from various forms of indirect discrimination in relation

---

[20] C-133/15 ECLI:EU:C:2017:354 (10 May 2017).

to employment (ENAR 2013; UNHCR 2016), which is illuminated by a number of ECJ-rejected claims (Groenendiijk 2007; Romic 2010; Rubinstein 2015).[21]

Yet in spite of all this fragmentation of European integration and free movement, there is still a powerful unionization tool for recognition and labour market accession. Thus the exception to laws that create barriers and hierarchies for family migrants (and other TNCs) is the segment of the EU free movement framework that 'guarantees rights of family reunion for all mobile EU citizens' (Geddes et al. 2020: 83).

The 'EU legitimacy tools' of free movement and intra-EU mobility 'go together in the legitimization of the integration process' (Recchi 2015: 47). From this angle, the free movement regime has become 'the single piece of EU legislation that most explicitly alludes to a federalization of the Union' (ibid: 43).

When some attractive potential facilitates choices of people, including court judges, its effect is akin to moral (or symbolic) contagion, about which sociologists of post-modern consumption often write (Argo et al. 2008; Nemeroff and Rozin 1994). According to their approach, the moral contagion (or moral contamination) takes place when symbols that are attached to the subject [such as a piece of law or a directive] make very strong influence upon human action – the influence that, by its strength, resembles contagion (ibid). For example, we can see from the discussion above and also from literatures on integration that the idea of European citizenship (with accent on free movement) becomes both attracting attention and positively contagious (as affecting EU law in favour of the TCN). Argo et al. (2008: 692) explain that positive contagion occurs because people want to be close to something for which they have strong positive feeling and attitudes'.

From this point of view, the work of the ECJ in respect to TCNs' obviously becomes positively contaminated by the European Citizenship Directive, as many of the ECJ's pro-MRA decisions demonstrate. When ECJ considers cases of MRAs, the decision is, in fact, often taken as a result of *intersectionality,* meaning that the issue can be interpreted by more than one directive (Kortese 2016; Romic 2010). This produces the effect of *legislative contamination,* which means that the Court's decision can be influenced by an article from an additional directive. *Positive contamination* means that the decision is in favour of the plaintiff, which is due to the additional application of the European Citizenship Directive in our case. Among the examples of such positive legislative contamination is the *Zambrano* and *Hocsman* cases.

These two cases show that the legislative positive contagion with the EU may work for TCNs through the principles of 'relational dependency' and 'second recognition'. This can be illuminated by the functioning of recognition loopholes.

---

[21] The European Anti-Discrimination Policy is actually represented through the two Directives – the *Racial Equality Directive 2000/43* and the *Employment Equality Directives 2000/78* – which identify three main forms of discrimination: direct discrimination, indirect discrimination and harassment. And there is a huge divergence in national cultures of the EU MSs on criteria for classifying something as indirect discrimination (Niessen et al. 2016; Tymowski 2016). As a result, indirect discrimination is often justified by exceptional cases (ENAR 2015).

5.5.2 Thoughts on LMI, Marriage and Gender

These loopholes take place as supported by various bi-lateral agreements and historical alliances that can make the first EU recognition easier for TCNs. For example, the Baltic States automatically accept foreign papers issued in Russia, Ukraine, Uzbekistan, Belarus, Kyrgyzstan and Moldova. Qualifications from these countries are, in many cases, also accepted in such former socialist states as Bulgaria and Romania (which belong to the EU periphery).

TCNs from India, Pakistan and a large number of African countries, which constitute the British Commonwealth, may benefit from the *Commonwealth Professional Qualifications Comparability Programmes*, also known as *Commonwealth Recruitment Protocols* (Keevy and Jansen 2006). Commonwealth countries promote harmonization in the recognition of professional qualifications, as based on established common standards. To some extent, 'education and training routes and qualifications in a number of professions are standardized and transferrable with cross-recognition among Commonwealth countries' (Commonwealth 2019).[22] This applies to professional qualifications for a number of both regulated and unregulated professions (financial, legal, health and technological qualifications) as well as general certificates of secondary education.[23]

Such harmonization may work together with the principles of 'intra-EU mobility' and 'second recognition' for a large number of skilled TCNs. For example, a Russian or Ukrainian woman can easily receive the first EU recognition in such a state as Lithuania or Estonia, and then marry a EU national living anywhere in Europe. This means that, as the spouse of a EU-national, she will be automatically granted the right for the EU second recognition. A similar example could be a Pakistani woman who holds a university degree or a professional qualification from Pakistan, marries a diasporic Pakistani man who is also a British citizen, reunites with him in the UK and easily receives the UK recognition of her qualifications as her first EU recognition. This would mean that, she could then find a job anywhere in Europe as a beneficiary of mutual recognition. The EU family migration patterns are, in fact, dominated by female spouses of EU nationals or of TCN permanent residents (Chaloff 2013). Making 60–80% across Europe, such women hold high levels of education from their countries of origin (Ibid; OECD 2018), and many of them could definitely benefit from the herein emerging complex patterns of skill- and family migrations.

In reality, there are not, however, many cases of female MRAs challenging the PQD because they remain marginalized within their families and ethnic communities and lack motivation as well as financial and informational resources in order to make an appeal (ENAR 2013; ETUC 2018; FRA 2013, 2017). The gender bias that penetrates all layers of European societies (ENAR 2013; FRA 2013) may also affect the ECJ's decisions [as the *Chavez-Vilchez* case shows].

---

[22] See: http://www.commonwealthofnations.org/sectors/business/human_resources/
[23] See Ibid.

5.5.3   Conclusive Remarks

As Geddes et al. (2020: 92) conclude in reference to the intersections between free movement and family migration, 'the development of the EU capacity in the area of family integration fits with an understanding of the EU as sovereignty-enhancing rather than sovereignty-denuding (Geddes et al. 2020: 92).

Having examined some of the ECJ cases - both in direct and indirect relation to insecure status and recognition of qualifications of TCNs – we argue that, in spite of the overall implementation of LMI by MSs, the ECJ can still do something tangible to help TCNS overcome the main LMI barriers. The legislative loophole that clearly crystallizes in its rulings is the factor of free mobility and family building. Marriage becomes supportive in the process of recognition while having minor children may help the TCN to transfer his 'fluid' status into a stable permit to work.

Using this loophole, the Court operates on the principle of intersectionality of EU Directives, which creates the effect of positive contagion, or enchantment, with intra-EU mobility. This enchantment works in favour of the married TCN such as the dependent family migrant. Marriage thus becomes an important area to invest under certain conditions.

However, the intersectionality and symbolic contagion do not work in the same way in the recognition of professional qualifications and in the status transfer. Here we can observe two different forms of legislative intersectionality and symbolic contagion. In the Recognition of TNC qualifications of TCNs, a number of Directives (on Long-Term Residence, Family Reunification and PQD) work together to support free movement from various angles – and produce the effect of multi-vector positive contagion with Europe. On the contrary, in the 'status' cases, the Long-Term Directive becomes surpassed by the MSs immigration policies. This creates the effect of negative legislative contamination, which is reflected in the ECJ's decisions.

Summing up, the work of the ECJ illuminates a complex interplay between European law, marriage migration, free movement and gender. The complexity is added by the gendered asymmetry in the above mentioned EU citizenship- and family provisions. These provisions end up, inadvertently, creating LMI barriers for some TCNs while facilitating the LMI of others.

References

Acosta Arcarazo, D. (2009). Immigration in the European Union: Family reunification after the Metock case. *UCD Law Review, 9*, 64–89.

Acosta Arcarazo, D. (2010). A belief in the purity of the nation: The possible dangers of its influence on migration legislation in Europe. *Studies in Ethnicity and Nationalism, 10*(2), 235–254.

Adam, S., & Van Elsuwege, P. (2012). Citizenship rights and the federal balance between the European Union and its member states. *European Law Review, 37*, 176–190.

Argo, J., Dahl, D., & Morales, A. (2008). Positive consumer contamination: Responses to attractive others in a retail context. *Advances in Consumer Research, 35*, 181–184.

Barbulescu, R. (2017) From international migration to freedom of movement and Back? In J. M. Lafleur & M. Stanek (Eds.), Southern Europeans moving North in the era of retrenchment of freedom of movement rights. In *South-North Migration of EU citizens in times of crisis* (pp. 15–32). Berlin: Springer.

Block, L., & Bonjour, S. (2013). Fortress Europe or Europe of rights? The Europeanisation of family migration policies in France, Germany and the Netherlands. *European Journal of Migration and Law, 15*, 203–224.

Bonjour, S. (2014). The transfer of pre-departure integration requirements for family migrants of the European Union (2004). Directive 2004/38/EC of the among member states of the European Union. *Comparative Migration Studies, 2*(2), 203–226.

Bonjour, S., & Vinck, M. (2013). When Europeanization backfires: The normalization of European migration politics. *Acta Politica, 48*(4), 389–407.

Case C- 34/09, EU:C:2011:124 (Ruiz Zambrano).

Castro, M., Koops, J., & Vono de Vilhena, D. (2019). *Migrant families in Europe*. Population Europe discussion paper # 11. Available at: https://population-europe.eu/discussion-paper/discussion-paper-no-11-migrant-families-europe.

CEDEFOP. (2018). *Analysis and overview of NQF level descriptors in European countries*. CEDEFOP research papers 26/06/2018. https://doi.org/10.2801/566217. Available at: http://www.cedefop.europa.eu/en/publications-and-resources/publications/5566.

Chaloff, J. (2013). *Global trends in family migration in the OECD*. Presentation held at the Conference 'Adapting to changes in Family migration: The experience of OECD countries', 18/11/2013, Washington D.C. Available at: http://www.oecd.org/els/mig/Chaloff.pdf.

Commonwealth. (2019). *The Commonwealth factor in human resources*. Commonwealth Education Online. Available at: http://www.commonwealthofnations.org/sectors/business/human_resources/.

Costello, C. (2016). *The human rights of migrants and refugees in European law*. Oxford: Oxford University Press.

Council of European Union. (2003a). Council Directive 2003/86/EC of 22 September 2003 on the right to family reunification. EC. *Official Journal of the European Union*. Available at: http://eur-lex.europa.eu/legal-content/EN/TXT/PDF/?uri=CELEX:32003L0086&from=en.

Council of European Union. (2003b). Council Directive 2003/109/EC of 25 November 2003 concerning the status of third-country nationals who are long-term residents. *Official Journal of the European Union*. Available at: https://eur-lex.europa.eu/legal-content/EN/ALL/?uri=CELEX:32003L0109.

Council of European Union. (2004). Directive 2004/38/EC of the European Parliament and of the Council of 29 April 2004 on the right of citizens of the union and their family members to move and reside freely within the territory of the member states. *Official Journal of the European Union*. Available at: https://eur-lex.europa.eu/legal-content/EN/TXT/?uri=CELEX:32004L0038.

Council of European Union. (2009). Council directive 2009/50/EC of 25 may 2009 on the conditions of entry and residence of third-country nationals for the purposes of highly qualified employment. *Official Journal of the European Union*. Available at: https://eur-lex.europa.eu/legal-content/EN/TXT/PDF/?uri=CELEX:32009L0050&from=EN.

Devaux, A. (2013). *Evaluation of the implementation of the European qualifications framework recommendation*. Final report. Available at: https://ec.europa.eu/ploteus/sites/eac-eqf/files/DG%20EAC%20-%20Evaluation%20EQF%20-%20Final%20Report%20-%20Final%20Version.pdf.

Dumont, J. (2007). *Women on the move*. Paris: OECD.

ENAR. (2013). *Shadow report on racism and discrimination in employment in Europe*. ENAR shadow reports 2013/17. Available at: https://www.enar-eu.org/IMG/pdf/shadowreport_2016x2017_long_final_lowres.pdf.

ENAR. (2015). *Shadow report on racism and migration in Europe*. ENAR shadow reports 2015/16. Available at: https://www.enar-eu.org/IMG/pdf/shadowreport_2015x2016_long_low_res.pdf.

Engbersen, G., & Snel, E. (2013). Liquid migration. Dynamic and fluid patterns of post-accession migration flows. In B. Glorius, I. Grabowska-Lusinka, & A. Kuvik (Eds.), *Mobility in transition. Migration patterns after EU enlargement* (pp. 21–40). Amsterdam: Amsterdam University Press.

ETUC. (2018). *ETUC statement on the European refugees and asylum seekers emergency, and on integration of migrants in European labour markets and societies.* ETUC position papers 25/06/2018. Available at: https://www.etuc.org/en/document/etuc-statement-european-refugees-and-asylum-seekers-emergency-and-integration-migrants.

European Parliament. (2011). Directive 2011/95/EU of the European Parliament and of the Council of 13 December 2011 on standards for the qualification of third-country nationals or stateless persons as beneficiaries of international protection, for a uniform status for refugees or for persons eligible for subsidiary protection, and for the content of the protection granted. Available at: https://eur-lex.europa.eu/legal-content/EN/TXT/PDF/?uri=CELEX:32011L0095&from=EN.

European Parliament. (2013). Directive 2013/55/EU of the European Parliament and of the Council of the European Union 20 November 2013 amending Directive 2005/36/EC on the recognition of professional qualifications and Regulation (EU) No 1024/2012 on administrative cooperation through the Internal Market Information System ('the IMI Regulation'). Available at: https://eur-lex.europa.eu/LexUriServ/LexUriServ.do?uri=OJ:L:2013:354:0132:0170:en:PDF.

European Parliament. (2017a). EU migrant crisis: Facts and figures. *News European Parliament* 30/06/2017. Available at: http://www.europarl.europa.eu/news/en/headlines/society/20170629STO78630/eu-migrant-crisis-facts-and-figures.

European Parliament. (2017b). *Infographics*. Available at: http://www.europarl.europa.eu/external/html/welcomingeurope/default_en.htm.

Eurostat. (2019). *Migration and migrant population statistics*. Available at: https://ec.europa.eu/eurostat/statistics-explained/index.php/Migration_and_migrant_population_statistics.

FRA. (2013). *FRA Strategic Plan 2013–2017*. Available at: fra.europa.eu/sites/default/files/fra_strategic_plan_en.pdf.

FRA. (2017). Recommendations regarding changes in the Agency, its working practices and the scope of its mission. *MB Decisions* 2017/05. Available at: ec.europa.eu/newsroom/just/document.cfm?doc_id=49323.

Geddes, A., Hadj Abdou, L., & Brumat, L. (2020). *Migration and mobility in the European Union*. London: Red Globe Press.

Groenendijk, K. (2007). *Integration tests abroad as a condition for family reunification in the EU*. Immigration Law Practitioners Association European Update 06/2007.

Groenendijk, K., Fernhount, R., van Dam, D., Van Oers, R., & Strik, T. (2007). *The family reunification directive in EU member states: The first year of implementation*. Nijmegen: CMR/Centre for Migration Law Press.

Hailbronner, K., & Thym, D. (2011). Case C-34/09, *Gerardo Ruiz Zambrano* v. *Office national de l'emploi*. *Common Market Law Review, 48*, 1253–1270.

Huddleston, T., Bilgili, O., Joki, A.-L., & Vankova, Z. (2015). *Migrant Integration Policy Index 2015*. Available at: www.ismu.org/en/2016/04/the-publicatio-mipex-2015-is-available-online/.

Isaakyan, I. (2015). American women in Southern Europe: A new source of high-skill workforce for the Euro-crisis zone. In A. Triandafyllidou & I. Isaakyan (Eds.), *High-skill migration and recession: Gendered perspective* (pp. 265–292). Basingstoke: Palgrave Macmillan.

Jesse, M. (2016). *The civic citizens of Europe*. Leiden: Brill.

Kahanec, M., & Zimmermann, K. (2016). *Labor migration, EU enlargement, and the great recession*. Berlin: Springer.

Keevy, J., & Jansen, J. (2006). *Teacher qualifications compatibility table*. Available at: https://www.thecommonwealth-educationhub.net/wp-content/uploads/2016/07/Teachers_Comparibility_Table.pdf.

Khan, A. (2017). *Reflections on Zambrano: The judgment in Chavez-Vilchez.* UK Immigration Law Blog 30/06/2017. Available at: https://asadakhan.wordpress.com/2017/06/30/reflections-on-zambrano-the-judgment-in-chavez-vilchez/.

Kortese, L. (2016). Exploring professional qualification in the EU: A legal perspective. *Journal of International Mobility, 1*(4), 43–58.

Kumrić, N., & Župan, M. (2016). European case law on asylum matters: Interrelation and interdependence of the European court of human rights and the court of justice of the European Union. In N. Bodiroga-Vukobrat, S. Rodin, & G. Sander (Eds.), *New Europe – Old values?* (Europeanization and globalization) (Vol. 1). Cham: Springer.

Lafleur, J. M., & Stanek, M. (2017) Lesson from the South-North migration of EU citizens in time of crisis. In J. M. Lafleur & M. Stanek (Eds.), Southern Europeans moving North in the era of retrenchment of freedom of movement rights. In *South-North migration of EU Citizens in times of crisis* (pp. 215–224). Berlin: Springer.

Lenaertz, K. (2012). The concept of EU citizenship in the case law of the European Court of Justice. *ERA Forum, 13*(4), 569–583.

Lenaertz, K. (2015). 'EU citizenship and the European court of Justice's 'stone-by-stone' approach. *International Comparative Jurisdiction, 1*, 1–10.

Maciejewski, M., Ratcliff, C., & Dobrita, A. (2019). *The mutual recognition of diplomas.* European Parliament Factsheets on the European Union 05/2019. Available at: https://www.europarl.europa.eu/factsheets/en/sheet/42/the-mutual-recognition-of-diplomas.

Manko, R. (2017). *EU accession to the European Convention on Human Rights.* EPRS briefings PE 607.298. Available at: http://www.europarl.europa.eu/RegData/etudes/BRIE/2017/607298/EPRS_BRI(2017)607298_EN.pdf.

Nemeroff, C., & Rozin, P. (1994). The contagion concept in adult thinking in the United States. *Ethos, 22*(2), 158–186.

Niessen, C., Weseler, D., & Kostova, P. (2016). When and why do individuals craft their jobs? The role of individual motivation and work characteristics for job crafting. *Human Relations, 69*(6), 1289–1300.

O'Cinneide, C. (2012). *The Evolution and Impact of the Case-Law of the Court of Justice of the European Union on Directives 2000/43/EC and 2000/78/EC.* European Commission: Directorate-General for Justice. Available at: https://www.ehu.eus/documents/2007376/2226923/The+evolution+and+impact+of+the+case-law+of+the+Court+of+Justice+of+the+European+Union.

O'Cinneide, C. (2015). The constitutionalization of equality within the EU legal order: Sexual orientation as a testing ground. *Maastricht Journal of European and Comparative Law, 22*(3), 370–395.

OECD. (2017). *Making integration work: Family migration.* Paris: OECD.

OECD (2018). *Family migration.* OECD Factsheets 2018. Available at: https://migrationdataportal.org/sites/default/files/2019-01/FAMILY%20migrants-def-infographic-03.png.

OECD. (2019). *International migration outlook.* Paris: OECD.

Papagianni, G. (2014). EU migration policy. In A. Triandafyllidou & R. Gropas (Eds.), *European Immigration – A source book* (pp. 377–388). London: Ashgate Publishing.

Peña, K., & Neufeld, J. (2017). *Overview of family-based immigration and the effects of limiting chain migration.* Niskanen Centre reports 11/2017. Available at: https://www.niskanencenter.org/wp-content/uploads/old_uploads/2017/11/Overview-of-Family-Migration-Report.pdf.

Progin-Theukauf, S. (2018). *K.A and others – The Zambrano Story Continues.* European Law Blog. 22/05/2018. Available at: https://europeanlawblog.eu/2018/05/22/k-a-and-others-the-zambrano-story-continues/.

Recchi, E. (2015). *Mobile Europe: The theory and practice of free movement in the EU.* Basingstoke: Palgrave Macmillan.

Romić, M. (2010). Obtaining long-term resident status in the European Union. *Croatian Yearbook of European Law and Policy, 6*, 153–166.

Rubin, J. (2008). *Migrant women in the European labour force: Technical report prepared for the European Commission*. Santa Monica, CA: RAND Corporation.

Rubinstein, M. (2015). Recent and current employment discrimination cases in the court of justice of the European Union. *The Equal Rights Review, 15*, 57–74.

Staiano, F. (2017). *The human rights of migrant women in international and European Law*. Hague: Eleven International Publishing.

Stetter, S. (2008). Regulating migration: Authority delegation in justice and home affairs. *Journal of European Public Policy, 7*(1), 80–103.

Thyssen, M. (2018). *The European qualifications framework*. Available at: https://webcache.googleusercontent.com/search?q=cache:WK0VHSXUviUJ:https://ec.europa.eu/social/BlobServlet%3FdocId%3D19190%26langId%3Den+&cd=3&hl=it&ct=clnk&gl=it.

Tymowski, J. (2016). *The Employment equality directive – European Implementation Assessment*. Available at: http://www.europal.europa.eu/thinktank.

UNHCR. (2016). *This is our home*. UNHCR Reports 3/11/2016. Available at: https://www.unhcr.org/ibelong/wp-content/uploads/UNHCR_EN2_2017IBELONG_Report_ePub.pdf.

Van den Broucke, S., Vanduynslager, L., & De Cuyper, P. (2016). *The EU Family Reunification Directive revisited: An analysis of admission policies for family reunification of Third Country Nationals in EU Member States*. KU Leuven Factsheets. Available at: https://lirias.kuleuven.be/bitstream/123456789/547583/1/Fact+sheet+family+reunification.pdf.

Chapter 6
Governing Through Rituals: Regulatory Ritualism in Czech Migration and Integration Policy

Karel Čada and Karina Hoření

6.1 Introduction

With low unemployment levels and a large industrial sector, over the last decade the Czech Republic has faced a significant shortage in the workforce that migrants have been able to fill, and migration has begun to feature in economic debates. Despite the pressing need for foreign employees, migrants still face complicated administration, precarious working conditions and a lack of support from public bodies. Migration policy is primarily driven by the vision of short-term labour migration that is regulated according to economic needs. This does not take into account the perspective of migrants or any need for them to integrate into broader Czech society.

This chapter summarizes the current situation of labour migration in the Czech Republic, focusing on migrants from non-EU countries. We here give an overview of the policies and legal framework that govern migration based on an analysis of the governmental Strategy of Migration and the Act on Residence of Foreign Nationals in the Czech Republic. The development of these official documents is explained together with the broader social and historical context of the Czech Republic. Our overview is accompanied by a description of the integration tools established over the last decade, which represent important milestone in dealing with migration.

K. Čada (✉)
Institute of Managerial Psychology and Sociology, Facility of Business Administration, Prague University of Economics and Business, Prague, Czech Republic
e-mail: karel.cada.kmps@vse.cz

K. Hoření (✉)
Institute of Sociological Studies, Faculty of Social Science, Charles University (CUNI), Prague, Czech Republic
e-mail: karina.horeni@fsv.cuni.cz

© The Author(s) 2021
V. Federico, S. Baglioni (eds.), *Migrants, Refugees and Asylum Seekers' Integration in European Labour Markets*, IMISCOE Research Series,
https://doi.org/10.1007/978-3-030-67284-3_6

This evidence is based on analysis of existing documents and statements produced on a long-term basis by various actors in the field of migration: non-governmental organisations, labour unions and employers' organisations, alongside interviews with twenty-five experts and practitioners (representatives of non-governmental organisations and public bodies).

We employ the concept of *regulatory ritualism* to grasp the distinctive features of the Czech system. Regulatory theorists (Braithwaite et al. 2007; Braithwaite 2008; Braithwaite 2009; Adcock 2012; Heimer and Gazley 2012; Ford 2016) use this term to describe a way of adapting to a normative order. The authors build on sociologist Robert Merton's typology of five modes of individual adaptation to cultural values: conformity, innovation, ritualism, retreatism and rebellion (Merton 1968) and on 'new institutionalism' that conceives institutions as myths or ceremonies (Meyer and Rowan 1977).

Merton (1968) argues that following the rules becomes an end in itself rather than a means to an end. Following Merton, Braithwaite (2008: 141) defines regulatory ritualism as the "acceptance of institutionalised means for securing regulatory goals while losing focus on achieving the goals or outcomes themselves". Policies, as organizations, might be conceived along a continuum with, at one end, production policies under "strong output controls" and, at the other, policies "whose success depends on the confidence and stability achieved by isomorphism with institutional rules" (Meyer and Rowan 1977: 346). Institutional means that have lost focus on their outcomes play a more ceremonial or ritual function in relation to gaining external legitimacy (Charlesworth 2017), or in relation to comforting the public and cementing the dominant normative order (Power 1997). In particular, there might be a ritual or ceremonial function to the introduction or implementation of new rules. The mechanism for introducing rules usually results from a history of institutional layering (Mahoney and Thalen 2009), in which new rules have been introduced on top of or alongside existing ones. This creates a complicated and complex regulatory framework that migrants will struggle to navigate. In relation to rules implementation, we also face classical 'bureaucratic rituals' (Cicourel 2005) or 'administrative rituals' (Samier 1997) that construct the social roles of clients and personnel.

This chapter sheds light on the causes of such institutional settings and the consequences of complex, centralized and rigid systems for migrants and their integration. What kind of normative order is produced by this institutional setting, and how is migration governed through administrative practice and institutional work? We introduce the historical and political context of migration policy, its institutional design, the Act on Residence of Foreign Nationals in the Czech Republic, the position of foreigners in Czech labour law, and at the end of the chapter we describe the contours of Czech integration policy and the consequences of such a status quo.

6.2 Historical and Political Context

The Czech Republic has the lowest unemployment rate in the EU, i.e. 1.9% in August 2019 (Czech Statistical Office 2019). It is the only EU country where the unemployment rate of third country nationals is very close to that of the overall population (European Migration Network 2019). The labour market is segmented, as in other European countries. As Drbohlav (2003) argues, one of the characteristic features of the Czech labour market is that individual ethnic immigrant groups have found specific economic niches in mostly manual, low paying, low quality positions that are unattractive to the domestic labour force: Ukrainians in construction, Vietnamese in retail trade and Mongolians in manufacturing. Generally speaking, foreigners represent 13% of the workforce in construction, 6% in the manufacturing sector, and 5% in commerce (see Consortium of Non-Governmental Organisations Working with Migrants in the Czech Republic 2015). Consequently, immigrant labour plays more of a complementary than a competitive role.

During the communist regime (1948–1989), Czechoslovakia was a sending country – an estimated 200,000 citizens left – and the important migration flows were domestic. Slovaks and minorities from the Slovak part of the federation (Roma, Hungarians) moved into Czech industrial cities. Nowadays, Slovaks are the second biggest group of foreign nationals, but their status is special both in the several aspects of the legal system and the perceptions of the wider society (there is no major language or cultural difference). In terms of international migration, Czechoslovakia is historically an industrial country with a need for a workforce, and therefore, migration from other socialist countries (Yugoslavia, Cuba, Vietnam) was organised in the 1970s and 1980s. There were no specific integration efforts from the state and those workers left after the fall of communism in 1989. However, a strong current of migration from Vietnam is a legacy of networks that were established in this period. Currently, the strongest migrant flows are also from other post-socialist countries because of close cultural, language and personal bonds. These migration flows started in the early 1990s.

The number of foreigners has been growing since 1990 with a short break during the financial crisis. Especially between 2004 and 2008, the country saw a significant increase in the number of immigrants due to a favourable economic situation and labour shortages. In 2018, the total number of foreign nationals living in the Czech Republic was 552,000, approximately 4.5% of the population. The national structure of incoming migrants is stable: the main routes are from post-socialist countries (the Ukraine, Slovakia, Russian Federation or Moldova) and from Vietnam. The biggest groups by nationality are consistently Ukrainians, Slovaks, Vietnamese and nationals of the Russian Federation, who altogether constitute around 75% of non-EU migrants in 2018 (Czech Statistical Office). There are important streams of labour migration from other EU countries: Romania, Bulgaria and Poland. However, there is also a significant number of expats from the UK or Germany who occupy white collar jobs in big cities.

The highest share of foreigners lives in the capital of Prague (14.5%). Prague's migrant population is also the most diverse. The three largest non-EU migrant communities (Ukrainians, Vietnamese, Russians) comprise only half of the foreigners in Prague. The second highest share of foreigners in the population is in the Karlovy Vary region (6.5%) and the third highest share is seen in the Plzeň region (5.1%) in the west of the Czech Republic, close to the border with Germany. Migration flows to these regions have deeper historical roots. Migrant communities from Vietnam developed their businesses through cross-border trade in the 1990s. A sizable population of foreigners, mostly males, can be found in the city of Mladá Boleslav, the seat of the Škoda car factory (Czech Statistical Office 2018a, b).

Because of relatively low numbers of migrants[1] and the export-oriented economy, the domestic workforce is becoming dependent on foreign labour. The main characteristic of public debate and migration policy is the current clash between the insufficient labour force and the needs of employers on the one hand, and a general reluctance towards migrants on the other. Generally, a reluctant attitude[2] could be observed in Czech society during and after the recent refugee crisis, although the number of actual refugees was very low at the time in the country (Čada, Frantová 2019).

Until the so-called refugee crisis of 2015, migration was not significantly present in political discourse, but since then anti-migration rhetoric has been shared on different scales by both far-right political parties (Dawn of Direct Democracy, later Freedom and Direct Democracy), and mainstream parties on both the left and the right proposing the securitization of migration policies. However, the Czech Republic is not an exception. The general refusal to redistribute refugees, along with a wave of anti-Muslim sentiment, are common features in all the post-socialist countries of the EU (Pachocka 2016). This demand for securitization and tighter control of migration is a significant driver for regulatory rituals. In 2018 and 2019, when the Act on The Residence of Foreign Nationals in the Czech Republic was changed for the last time and discussed in the Czech Parliament, the Members of Parliament repeatedly emphasized the need to protect Czech citizens.[3]

The securitization trend can be seen as a version of penal populism, "a punishment policy developed primarily for its anticipated popularity" (Roberts et al. 2003: 6) or "a political style that builds on collective sentiments of fear and demands for punitive politics" (Curato 2016: 93) which is driven by increasing popularity of

---

[1] Even though, in 2017, the number of third-country nationals holding a valid permit was the highest among post-socialist Central European states. In the Czech Republic, there were 26 valid permits per 1000 people in the total population. There were nine in Slovakia, six in Hungary and 16 in Poland. However, in Germany, there were 56 valid permits per 1000 inhabitants (see European Migration Network 2019).

[2] According to a poll organised by the Public Opinion Research Center in April 2019, 53% of the Czech population thinks that 'incoming foreigners' represent a problem for the Czech Republic (Public Opinion Research Center 2019).

[3] Parliamentary Discussions in 19the September 2018, 7th December 2018 and 13th March 2019 (see http://www.psp.cz/sqw/historie.sqw?T=203&O=8 – Accessed 7the November 2019).

populist radical right-wing parties and the tabloid media (see Boda and his colleagues 2015). The extension of rules intended for tight control over migration might be seen as a response to fear discourses that portray migrants as a danger for domestic societies.

6.3 Migration Policy

The Czech migration policy is highly centralized with the Ministry of Interior being a crucial actor. The Ministry is responsible for both migration regulation and integration policy. This is a result of a change in 2008 that moved the responsibility for integration policy from the Ministry of Labour and Social Affairs to the Ministry of the Interior. In the economic boom between 2004 and 2008, the Ministry of the Interior was responsible for asylum policy, visa and residence permits, and the Ministry of Labour and Social affair for integrating foreigners. However, in the aftermath of economic crisis, both streams of policy were integrated into the Ministry of the Interior.

This high level of centralization is not only typical for migration policy in the Czech Republic. The proportional electoral system tends towards a coalition government with strong ministries but a weak prime ministerial cabinet, so cross-section issues like migration, social inclusion or drug policy are seized by one ministry at expense of the others. The position of the Ministry of the Interior in the Czech migration policy partly stems from the restrictive tendencies towards migration in the Czech policy discourse but also from the Czech governmental tradition, which is marked by strong departmentalization and a lack of coordination in government.

Switching between liberal and restrictive tendencies has been symptomatic of the development of the Czech migration policy framework since 1989. Bauerová (2018), with a reference to Baršová and Barša (2005), distinguishes six periods of the Czech integration policy: (1) the laissez faire period (1990–1995) with relatively liberal conditions of entry, but an absence of tools for the integration of immigrants; (2) the restrictive period (1996–1999): the conditions of entry were tightening due to the economic crisis and fears of increasing numbers of immigrants from western Balkan and post-Soviet states; (3) the EU accession period (1999–2004), in which a complex migration policy was formulated[4]; (4) the neoliberal period (2005–2008), in which the state formulated a long-term framework for the integration of foreigners, however, this contained only a vague call for cooperation to be developed at the local level; (5) the neo-restrictive period (2008–2014), in which the Czech Republic introduced a more restrictive policy to reduce the numbers of foreigners because of the economic crisis and to deal with corruption problems at embassies in Ukraine or

---

[4]This was reflected in two documents: (1) Principles of Integration of Foreigners in the Czech Republic and (2) The Conception of Integration of Foreigners in the CR, which "promotes the integration of foreigners as individuals" (Baršová and Barša 2005, pp. 233–236).

Vietnam[5]; (6) the migration crisis period (since 2015), when the Czech Republic actively negotiated with the European Commission and the Czech Republic refused to accept a quota system.

Different migration policies are also reflected in the numbers of foreigners. These numbers culminated during the neo-liberal period, so more than 45,000 incoming MRAs in 2008 (Czech Statistical Office 2019), and they later stagnated during the restrictive phase after the economic crisis (8177 in 2010). In the last period, the numbers have increased again (more than 30,000 incoming MRAs in 2018), despite the restrictive frame of migration regulation that has prevailed. The increase can be assigned to the labour shortage and the economic boom.

Czech migration policy is marked by the coexistence of national and European levels, which has created somewhat schizophrenic conditions. On one hand, efforts have been made to introduce more restrictive conditions of entry and stay, while on the other, Czech migration policy must comply with EU regulation that strengthens civil rights and supports permanent settlement (Kušniráková 2014).

In the most recent period, the main document that states the goals of the government is the Strategy of Migration Policy (Czech Government 2015). The Strategy, proposed by the Ministry of the Interior, strengthens the security aspects and emphasizes that migration should be regulated or even prevented with development aid. The particular situation of economic migrants is reflected only in the final goal, while labour migration is treated pragmatically and only from the perspective of the needs of the labour market.

6.4 Legislation Governing Migration

The Constitution of the Czech Republic should ensure basic rights to all citizens and migrants with regular status, and it incorporates the Charter of Fundamental Rights and Freedoms as a component of the constitutional order.[6] The main document that guides regulation of stay for different groups of foreigners is Act No. 326/1999

---

[5] The Government Resolution No. 1205/2009 of 16 September 2009 limited foreigners' options to apply for a long-term visa (in excess of 90 days), the amendment to Act No. 326/1999 Coll., on the Stay of Foreigners in the Czech Republic tightened conditions for foreigners, who had to indicate the purpose of their business as the reason for their stay, there was a change in the conditions of travel health insurance for foreigners and the introduction of biometric ID cards for foreigners (see Bauerová 2018).

[6] The Charter includes, among other important rights, guarantees of citizens' economic, social and cultural rights. Among these are the right to the free choice of occupation (Article 26/1), the right to acquire the means of one's livelihood by work (Article 26/3), the right of employees to fair remuneration for work and satisfactory working conditions (Article 28/3), the right of women, young persons and persons with disabilities to increased safety and health at work, including special working conditions and assistance in vocational training (Article 29), the right to freely associate with others with a view to protecting economic and social interests (Article 27/1), or the right to strike (Article 27/4).

Coll., the Act on Residence of Foreign Nationals in the Czech Republic, and by Act No. 325/1999 Coll., on Asylum.

In the context of the Act on Residence of Foreign Nationals in the Czech Republic, one can distinguish four categories of permit: (1) short-term visas (for stays of up to 90 days); (2) long-term visas (for stays of over 90 days); (3) long-term residence (for the purpose of doing business, an employee card, for the purpose of a family living together in the Czech Republic); and (4) permanent residence. Short-term visas are valid for one or more entries, they give the right to stay in the Schengen area for the period indicated in them. The length of continuous residence or the total length of successive stays in the Schengen area must not exceed 90 days within any 180-day period. In terms of a long-term visa, the Czech law distinguishes long-term visas for the purposes of a business, family reunification, studies, exceptional leave to remain and other (Section 42 of Act 326). The foreigner must apply for a long-term visa 14 days before his or her visa expires, at the latest. The Ministry is very restrictive and, with the exception of serious health problems or a proven impossibility of contacting the public administration, the Ministry does not accept applications lodged after the deadline (Koldinská et al. 2015).

Long-term residence for business purposes can be applied for if a foreigner is a self-employed person in the Czech Republic, a statutory authority (executive director, manager) or a member of the statutory bodies of a company or cooperative. With respect to long-term residence for the purpose of family reunification, MRAs face a number of obstacles to the realization of their right to family life, such as unreasonably long deadlines for processing their application and poor information about processing their applications (Organization for Aid to Refugees 2016).

A renewal application for a long-term residence permit (over 90 days) can be submitted only between the 120th and the 14th day before the expiry of such a permit. The Ministry is also highly restrictive in this issue. The recent practice is criticized by Czech NGOs: "The current arrangement is an unnecessary impediment in terms of the costs of such procedures" the NGOs wrote in their manifesto (Consortium of Non-Governmental Organisations Working with Migrants in the Czech Republic 2015).

Permanent residence (Section 63 Act 326) can be applied for after five years of uninterrupted temporary stay in the territory of the Czech Republic. Without compliance with the condition of five years of uninterrupted temporary stay, permanent residence can still be applied for under certain exceptions, e.g. for humanitarian reasons, for reasons deserving special consideration, in some cases following the conclusion of proceedings on international protection, etc. The application can be submitted at a branch of the Ministry of the Interior, or in some cases at a Czech embassy. The foreigner must pass Czech language exams (A1 level). Foreigners with permanent residence have very limited legal possibilities for political participation. They cannot vote in local elections. They cannot establish political parties and cannot be members of established parties.

In terms of refugees and asylum seekers, administrative proceedings for granting international protection are held by the Ministry of the Interior (Act No 325/1999 Coll., on Asylum). These proceedings are launched by the foreigner's declaration that he or she is willing to apply for international protection. The asylum seeker is obligated to appear at a reception centre within twenty-four hours after the declaration, and there he or she files an application for international protection and the Foreign Police performs identification processes. The asylum seeker is also required to undergo a medical examination. The Ministry may detain the applicant at the reception centre for up to 120 days if his or her identity has not been verified (he or she does not have a valid travel document, or the identity document is falsified) or there is a danger to state security, public health or public order.

During the application for international protection, the reasons that led refugees to depart from the country where he or she was staying are determined. When the required tasks are completed, the applicant is transferred to a reception centre, where he or she awaits the first instance decision. The Ministry grants asylum according to the Geneva convention to the applicant, if it is proved that the foreigner was persecuted for the exercise of political rights and freedoms or has a justified fear of persecution on the basis of race, gender, religion, nationality, membership in a particular social group or certain political views in the state of which he or she is a national or, if he/she is a stateless person, in the state of his/her last permanent residence. Over the course of this period, an interview is conducted with the applicant, which is intended to verify the reasons for international protection that were stated in the application.

The Ministry issues a decision within six months. If a decision cannot be made within this timeframe due to the specific nature of the matter, the Ministry can extend it appropriately, up to 18 months, the maximum allowed by EU regulation. As the Consortium of Migrants Assisting Non-Governmental Organizations (2015) points out, undocumented refugees routinely wait up to 120 days in special detention facilities, which house families with children, traumatised people, and torture victims. In addition to detention, undocumented refugees are added to a database to prevent them from applying for any form of visa in the Czech Republic or the EU.

The Act on Residence of Foreign Nationals in the Czech Republic has been incrementally changed many times. As Čižinský and his colleagues (2014) note, due to numerous amendments, the Act on Residence of Foreign Nationals in the Czech Republic has become an unclear and chaotic piece of legislation. For example, between 2017 and 2019, the Parliament passed two extensive amendments and the Constitutional Court cancelled a number of provisions of the first one.[7] Layering new rules on top of old rules seems to be common practice in the Czech policy. In the Czech system, Members of Parliament have rights to legislative initiative – they are allowed both to propose amendments to government bills and to propose their own bills. The legislative process combined with the multiple party proportional system and fragile government coalitions create a chaotic and unpredictable legislative environment.

---

[7] See the Judgment 41/17 in which the Constitutional Court cancelled the number of provisions of the act because they do not comply with the EU law or Czech constitutional principles.

These problems can be illustrated by the story of the last two amendments of the Act on Residence of Foreign Nationals. Both amendments were justified by the need to adapt the EU directives into Czech law. The first concerned Directive 2014/66/EU and the second Directive 2016/801/EU. However, in both cases the transposition of European law was used to tighten residency rules beyond the scope of the original directives. In the first case, the transposition of the EU directive introduced a special type of permit for foreign investors and seasonal workers; however, the amendment also limited possibilities for transition to a business residence, it made it more difficult to change employer or request permanent residence. In the second amendment, which passed in 2019, the transposition of the EU directive should significantly improve the situation of university students and scientific personnel who, after they finish their studies or scientific work, will be allowed to stay in the Czech Republic for a period of up to nine months to search for employment or commence business activities.

Besides this transposition, the amendment introduces the duty of non-EU foreigners to attend an eight-hour adaptation and integration course within one year of the date they receive their permanent or long-term residency permit, and the possibility for government to introduce quotas of permits for specific countries of origin, sectors of the Czech economy and types of work. The amendment also introduces into Czech law a model of temporary labour migration (*Gastarbeiter*), in which foreigners are able to come to the country for only one year, then leave and arrange a new visa again abroad. This model thus reduces foreigners to a mere labour force, explicitly excluding foreigners from integrating into the Czech Republic. As critics of the amendment point out (Consortium of Non-Governmental Organisations Working with Migrants in the Czech Republic 2018), experiences of countries such as Germany (which applied the model in 50s and 60s) prove that a significant portion of seasonal workers settled down in the new country and lived there, but without sufficient integrational support.

Instead of comprehensive change based on dialogue among governmental actors, public authorities, employers, NGOs and representatives of migrants, The Act on Residence of Foreign Nationals in the Czech Republic has been being changed piecemeal without any clear implementation plan. The compulsory adaptation and integration courses can easily illustrate this feature of Czech policy-making. There is no guarantee the state will be able to build the necessary infrastructure to run the adaptation and integration courses compulsory from 2020. The amendment lists selected groups of foreigners who are exempted from this duty. However, it does not deal with individuals who cannot complete the course because of language, physical disability or, indeed, lack of available courses.

With respect to the anti-migration discourse, the tightening of rules driven by the need to protect domestic citizens might be interpreted as a 'ritual of comfort' (Power 1997) in a situation where Czech public and political elites are aware of the negative consequences of migration. Tightening rules serves a ceremonial function by claiming boundaries between Czech citizens and migrants. Through the implementation of new rules, politicians and policymakers prove they act in the name of citizens. However, such a ritualistic character is mostly rooted in the idea that migration can be governed by the rules alone, without complex policies of rule enforcement, implementation and institution-building. There are rules proposed without clear evidence, such as in the case of the model of temporary labour migration, or without a clear implementation plan, such as in the case of compulsory integration courses. The large number and complexity of rules does not improve migrant selection, however, it does drive inconsistency in how standards are enforced. Moreover, a proliferation of more specific laws is a resource that expands discretion, rather than limits it (Baldwin and Hawkins 1984).

The experiences of migrants can substantiate such uncertainty and arbitrariness in administrative decisions. Elena Tulupova, a Russian scientist living in the Czech Republic, summarizes her experience with the Czech system in this way: "Public officers do not manage to deal with requests in a timely manner and cases last for several years and decisions are questionable" (Rahimi 2017).

Czech migration policy seems locked in a mutual circle of suspicion. The administrative bodies look at migrants through lenses of suspicion, while migrants through lenses of suspicion interpret administrative decisions. These circles of suspicion broaden barriers between migrants and the state. They significantly decrease the level of trust between migrants, administrative bodies and, in the end, the rest of the society. But institutional trust is key currency in integrational policies.

6.5 Labour Market Integration

The access of third-country nationals to the labour market is regulated both by the Labor Office of the Czech Republic and the Ministry of the Interior of the Czech Republic. Work permits may be issued in various forms, such as: (1) an Employee Card (dual or non-dual); (2) a Blue Card (for highly qualified professions); or a (3) permit to work issued for a previously authorized stay (usually for other purposes such as business, family reunion, study, etc.) or to seasonal work up to six months.

The Employee Card works as a permit for a long-term residence, granting the foreigner temporary residence in the territory for a period exceeding three months and allowing work performance in the position for which the Employee Card was issued. The Employee Card can be either dual (combining a work-permit and a residence permit) or single-purpose (it grants the foreigner only residence in the territory). The dual Employee Card is issued by the Ministry of the Interior for a specific job position, which is listed by the Ministry of Labour and Social Affairs in the central register of vacancies occupied by employee cardholders (a job that has not been filled within 30 days of its notification to the regional branch of the Labour Office). If the job position is listed and cannot be filled by the domestic labour force, the labour office is obliged to issue a work permit. Then, the foreigner must demonstrate his or her professional competence. In justified cases, especially when there is reasonable doubt whether the foreigner has the required education or whether this education corresponds to the character of the job, the foreigner is obliged to prove – upon request of the Ministry of the Interior – that his/her education was recognized as equivalent by a competent authority of the Czech Republic.

A non-EU migrant may apply for the single-purpose Employee Card if he or she wants to stay in the territory of the Czech Republic for more than three months for the purpose of employment and he or she is: (1) a foreign national who is obliged to apply for an employment permit; or (2) a foreign national with free access to the labour market. In such cases, the job position in question is not listed in the Central Register of Job Vacancies and the Ministry of the Interior does not look into the professional competence of the applicant: it is monitored either by the labour office as a part of the procedure for granting an employment permit, or it is up to the employer to decide whether or not it is required.

For both types of card, it is required that a form of labour-law relationship exists between the foreigner and the employer, which the applicant must prove by submitting an employment contract, an agreement to perform work or a letter of intent. In all cases, the weekly working hours must amount to at least 15 hours and the monthly wage, salary or remuneration may not be lower than the basic monthly rate of the minimum wage.

A job vacancy, which can be filled under the Blue Card regime, means such vacancy that has not been filled within 30 days since it was reported to the regional labour office and for performance of which a high qualification is required – i.e. regularly completed higher education or higher professional education provided that the study lasted for at least three years.

An employment permit has to be applied for at the regional branch of the Labour Office within whose remit one plans to work. The employer must announce the intention to employ a migrant to the regional office of the labour office. The office will carry out the so-called labour market test to assess the demand of employers for the given profession in the given region and the probability of its satisfaction by Czech workers or EU citizens.

An employment permit is valid only for a specific employer (who is mentioned in the decision) and for a specific type and place of employment (if one plans to work for one employer on two job positions, then one needs an individual employment permit for each job; if one wants to perform the same job position for another employer, then one must obtain a new employment permit as well). An employment permit is non-transferable (another person cannot make use of it) and it is issued for a fixed period of time, two years maximum. An employment permit can be applied for repeatedly.

A work permit, Employee Card or Blue Card is not required for the employment of a foreigner with a permanent residence permit, a foreigner who has been granted asylum, a foreigner whose work in the Czech Republic does not exceed seven calendar days or a total of 30 days in a calendar year or a foreigner who is a performer, scientist, student under 26 years of age, an athlete or a person who supplies goods or services in the Czech Republic on the basis of a commercial contract, or performs warranty and repair work. Foreigners can also do business in the Czech Republic in the same way as Czech citizens without any limits. The number of foreigners holding a trade licence has been gradually increasing year by year. At the end of 2017, there were 472,354 registered with the Employee Cards, Blue Cards or permits to work and 87,228 holding a valid trade licence. Among those registered at labour office, there were 142,200 third-country nationals. Among them, 101,48 did not need a work permit, 15,162 holding a valid work permit, 24,753 Employee Cards and 413 Blue Cards. A total of 55,439 third-countries nationals had a valid trade licence. The vast majority comes from Vietnam (21,773) and the Ukraine (21,746) (Czech Statistical Office 2018b).

The rules governing the issuing work permits have changed in different periods of migration policies. In 2010 as a part of restrictive migration policy after the financial crisis, for example, labour offices were asked to act more strictly in issuing employment permits to foreigners:

> They were asked not to issue employment permits to foreigners for such job positions that can be filled by persons with free admission to the Czech labour market. The length of the stay or the level of integration of individual foreigners was completely disregarded. (Čižinský et al. 2014:47)

The attempts to make work permits more restrictive continued in 2012 when granting employment permits to low-qualified positions was heavily discussed among politicians and employer organisations. A fundamental change came into effect in June 2014. The reason for the amendment was to implement Directive 2011/98/EU of the European Parliament and of the Council of 13 December 2011 on a single application procedure for a single permit for third-country nationals to reside and work in the territory of a Member State and on a common set of rights for third-country workers legally residing in a Member State.

In the last decade, labour migration was influenced by the establishment of several nation-specific migration programmes. These were promoted mainly by the Ministry of Trade and supported by employers' associations, such as the Czech Chamber of Business. Due to these programmes, registered employers can more easily hire workers from countries such as the Ukraine, Mongolia, the Philippines and Serbia. Specific programmes to hire highly skilled workers were also established, such as The Programme India, but its quotas were never filled and the programmes to hire workers for unskilled positions were always more successful.

In the last amendment of the Act on Residence of Foreign Nationals in the Czech Republic, these specific programmers were re-formed into three main programmes. The programmes 'Highly-qualified employer' and 'Key and Research Personnel' are open to all countries. The Programme 'Middle or Low Qualified Employer' is open to nine countries (Belarus, Montenegro, the Philippines, India, Kazakhstan, Mongolia, Moldavia, Serbia, the Ukraine). The government will settle migration quotas for these countries. Other than these, the 'Extraordinary Labour Visa' was introduced, which can be activated in the case of a lack of workforce in a certain segment of the economy. Visa programmes for low-skilled professions are short--term, there are limits if the holder wants to bring their family to the country and limits to its prolongation. These recent changes are in accordance with the Strategy of Migration, with its vision of circular and short-term labour migration.

In practice, the quotas in programmes for specific countries have been quickly filled quickly. Especially Ukrainian embassies are notoriously well known for long waiting periods, and in the past also for illegal practices for obtaining a slot to apply for the visa.

A time-consuming, rigid and unreliable system of hiring third-country nationals has led to an increasing number of irregular workers. The year 2017 saw a total of 2151 foreign citizens performing irregular work (1530 in 2016), of whom 234 were EU nationals (193 EU nationals in 2016) and 1917 third-country nationals (1337 third-country nationals in 2016) (Czech Statistical Office 2018b). Milena Jabůrková, vice president of the Confederation of Industry of the Czech Republic, comments: "The lack of workers is critical. Some companies opt for the employment of foreigners without the necessary documents" in Czech media (Zelenka and Štěpánek 2018).

Companies also avoid this dilemma by subcontracting a workforce from employment agencies. Subcontracting represents a significant factor that contributes to the labour exploitation of migrants (see Čaněk et al. 2016). Agency employees are often disadvantaged compared to other employees regarding fixed-term contracts. Many of the workers work without a contract, sign a contract they do not understand, or are given an *Agreement to Complete a Job*, which legally allows them to work for only 300 hours per year per employer and forces them to pay medical insurance on their own.

Labour unions characterise the current situation:

> For the Czech-Moravian Confederation of Labour Unions, the employment of foreigners who are lured to the Czech Republic and have wages that are on the poverty level is unacceptable. The Czech Republic can't work against social dumping and support it at the same time. (Czech-Moravian Confederation of Trade Unions 2017)

However, this position is mostly supported by economic arguments rather than paying attention to the situation of migrants:

> Unregulated labour migration is a dangerous factor leading to destabilisation of the labour market, social dumping and the end of rising wages. (Ibid.)

Labour unions do not support the change in the situation of foreign workers but use critical descriptions of the situation to oppose the growth of migration: The Czech Confederation of Labour Unions will oppose attempts to broaden the influx of cheap work labour from the third-party countries to the Czech Republic. We will support maximal usage of the inner workforce (Svoboda 2015).

Widespread praxis is to use agency employment workers. These workers are recruited by private agencies rather than by employers themselves and their working contracts often do not cover overtime hours or secure their wages. A strict set of regulations on these agencies is recommended by the Confederation of Labour Unions. On the other side are employers organisations who prefer flexible conditions in labour contracts.

The precarity of foreign workers is further multiplied by the limited social rights foreign workers enjoy compared to Czech citizens. Third-country migrants living and working in the Czech Republic but without permanent residence are obligated, in the same way as Czech citizens, to contribute to the social security system and the state employment policy, however, they cannot use unemployment benefits and they have only limited amount of social benefits. Furthermore, if they lose their job, they will be at risk of having their permanent residency revoked. Non-EU migrants who are not employed by a Czech company are excluded from the public health insurance system, and therefore must opt for commercial insurance which does not guarantee the same level of coverage as public health insurance (see The Consortium of Non-Governmental Organisations Working with Migrants in the Czech Republic 2015).

It seems that the regulatory ritualism of Czech migration law is creating a situation that is not favourable either for employers or for employees because it slows down the process of issuing of work permits and makes the process more insecure. Both by foreigners and by employers, the administrative process is perceived as very difficult. Especially the whole length of issuing of work permit and strict process of extending those permits. (Multicultural Centre Prague 2013).

If the focus of regulation is supposed to be the protection and stabilization of the labour market, the recent regulation framework does not work well.

> Instead of clear, well-founded and lawful conditions, the migration is regulated rather by processual obstructions and administrative barriers. (Consortium of Migrants Assisting Organisations in the Czech Republic 2015)

Public authorities often provide unreliable and incomprehensible information. Information provided by different staff members from the same institution can differ, while foreigners are forced to deliver new documents and repeatedly visit these offices. According to interviews conducted with members of the two largest migrant communities (Vietnamese and Ukrainian communities) in the framework of SIRIUS research, this lack of support creates a space for commercial companies to offer their guidance services, which are sometimes connected with semi-legal practices (such as re-selling time slots for visa applications or selling bank account statements) and which could lead to the exploitation of foreign workers.

With actual labour shortage, when Czech companies need to fulfil more than half-million vacant jobs (Czech Chamber of Commerce 2018), the labour market tests carried by the Labour Offices seem to be another example of regulatory rituals. However, through these rituals, the dominant normative framework of securitization and protection of domestic workforce is reinforced. In contrast to the strict administrative scrutiny of work permits, the conditions in which foreign workers are employed is loosely monitored and protection of foreign workers is significantly weaker than their Czech counterparts.

6.6   Integration Policy and Barriers to Integration

The main vehicle of integration policy in the Czech Republic is the network of regional Centres to Support the Integration of Foreigners. These centres, initiated by the Ministry of the Interior, are operated on the basis of projects and partially funded from the European Fund for the Integration of Third-country Nationals (EIF) from 2009 to 2015, and the European Asylum, Migration and Integration Fund (AMIF) starting from 2015. From July 2016 to June 2019, such centres have been operating in all of the Czech regions under individual projects. Nine are funded by the Asylum, Migration and Integration Fund (AMIF), whereas four are operated by NGOs or regional governments and only co-financed from this fund. The task of each centre is to ensure the formation of regional counselling platforms to address the current problems of foreign nationals.

In each region, the Centre mainly cooperates with the regional government and municipalities, the Foreign Police, state and municipal police, labour offices, tax authorities, trade licence offices and other entities. The goal is to create opportunities for improved information exchange and to stimulate measures to respond to the current demand of issues related to the integration of foreign nationals. All services are free of charge. They are not limited to the city where each centre is established and should cover the entire region. The centres offer: (1) social counselling; (2) legal advice (by external providers); (3) Czech language courses; (4) translation and interpreting services (mostly by Vietnamese, Mongolian, Ukrainian and Russian interpreters); (5) socio-cultural courses (fostering orientation mainly in the social security, health and educational systems); (6) an internet point and library; and (7) community outreach.

The Ministry of the Interior has also initiated the implementation of municipality projects. Funded predominantly from its subsidies, these projects are implemented by local governments, particularly in municipalities with significant numbers of foreign nationals in direct collaboration with those foreign nationals living in the municipality, with non-governmental organisations, schools and other local integration actors. The projects aim to provide comprehensive support for integration at the local level, to prevent the potential risk of – or to mitigate the tension between – foreign nationals and other inhabitants of the municipalities as well as to prevent the risk of residential segregation. The Ministry has supported municipal projects in Pilsen, Pardubice, Havlíčkův Brod (where extremist actions had occurred, such as burning the Mongolian flag and the dissemination of hate leaflets), or in Prague's district of Libuš (where the biggest Vietnamese open market, 'SAPA', is located).

The Ministry of the Interior also finances NGOs that focus on integrating foreigners through specific programmes. The non-governmental sector is an important and vocal player in the field of integration because, until the establishment of integration centres, all services were provided by non-governmental organisations. Until now, regional integration centres were unable fulfil the demand for services. Other than financing from the Ministry of Interior, NGOs are also dominantly financed by the Ministry of Social Affairs or municipalities. Therefore, NGOs are fulfilling governmental or local strategies of integration.

Even though Centres to Support the Integration of Foreigners represent an important hub for integration policies, these policies face numerous obstacles as the local level. Local authorities are active only when there are serious problems that require a change in the situation between the majority society and foreigners. The absence of local integration strategies means local authorities are unprepared for such situations and they cannot effectively prevent them. Local municipalities also do not map the needs of foreigners on their territory to ensure adequate availability of services, including language courses, social and legal counselling.

The main challenge for integration is a lack of knowledge of the Czech language. This problem is identified by almost all actors when evaluating the level of education of both adult and young migrants and the support of teachers. Lack of language knowledge prevents migrants who work in low-skilled positions from applying for high-skilled jobs. In research interviews, stories of refugees and migrants provide evidence about problems finding a job. Stakeholders mainly report that courses have insufficient capacity and inappropriate structure.

Existing subsidized and therefore affordable language courses cannot meet the demand and are often not available in smaller cities. There are not enough advanced or specialised courses (for technical or health professionals), which prevents educated migrants from using their skills in more specialised positions.

Young migrants who attend Czech schools have a higher chance of learning the language but also face important obstacles. Notwithstanding the importance of the education system for integration processes, until now schools and teachers have lacked both experience and support in the integration of foreigners. Schools can apply for funding from the Ministry of Education, but the application process takes place prior to the start of the school year when they do not yet know whether they will be taking students with a foreign background. Furthermore, they receive the funding too late during the school year and the filing process is complicated. All these factors contribute to the low number of applications for funding from schools. Funding from the Ministry of Education is also not available to secondary schools.

Bigger cities with a higher share of foreigners have schools that specialise in the integration of students with a foreign background, and students might concentrate here. Educational experts interviewed for the SIRIUS research point out that there is a growing number of students with a foreign background who either will not be accepted into secondary school or will not be able to graduate due to poor language knowledge.

6.7   Conclusion

The specific legal history of the Czech Republic has created a complicated and complex regulatory framework, dominated by regulatory ritualism. The dominant frame of migration policy results from the institutional design where the Ministry of Interior is a central player. Many related agendas fall within the remit of other ministries, in particular the Ministry of Labour and Social Affairs of the Ministry of Education, Youth and Sports. However, these ministries often do not perceive foreigners as their target group, which leads to shortcomings in public policies and a lack of necessary funding. Excessive centralization has led to the low engagement of local authorities, local communities and civil society (The Consortium of Non-Governmental Organisations Working with Migrants in the Czech Republic 2015).

Migration policy is driven by a vision of primarily short-term labour migration regulated according to economic needs. The services offered by public integration centres are not available everywhere and for all groups of migrants. The absence of integration services for EU citizens who face the same challenges as non-EU migrants (lack of language knowledge and poor orientation in the Czech legislation) is particularly striking. Integration services depend heavily on the availability of EU funding, and their future is therefore uncertain. These integration tools are not underpinned by a broader vision of integration, while the integration programmes provided by municipalities and schools are not universal and depend on the will of local political representation or principals, which might be influenced by the attitudes of parents and their voters.

The unwillingness of Czech political authorities to offer stronger structural solutions is linked to the general reluctance of the Czech population when it comes to migrants. We saw this erupt particularly during the period of the migrant crisis. Therefore, no major political party considers integration a priority. In the context of weak broader societal integration of foreigners, labour market integration policies have barely materialised and remain unimplemented. Due to the absence of any systematic and structural approach towards integration into the labour market, any progress in labour market integration policies will, therefore, be made in small steps, individual efforts and short-term solutions in the future. It is expected that these steps will be driven not only by the involvement of public authorities but also by other actors, primarily from the non-governmental sphere.

The regulatory ritualism that results from chaotic and unsystematic legislative work is characterized by a loss of focus on achieving goals and the outcomes themselves. This is especially visible in Czech migration policy, whose complex and unpredictable administrative system prompts migrants to use the services of problematic intermediaries. The time-consuming procedures that regulate getting work permits strengthen the illegal job market and the opaque system of subcontracting instead of protecting the domestic workforce and stabilizing the labour market. Furthermore, regulatory ritualism establishes a climate of mutual distrust among those actors involved and places obstacles to collaboration between public authorities, non-governmental organizations and the migrants themselves.

As Braithwaite (2008) notes, the defeat of ritualism requires networking between all the leading stakeholders and critics into a macro project of transforming ritualism. However, this transformation through networked governance is conditioned by acuity in grasping micro-macro linkages. To transcend ritualism means changing both how policy is formulated and how policy is implemented, establishing a dialogue and mutual learning between different levels of regulation. However, this seems a difficult task in the environment of mistrust and long-lasting conflicts among involved actors in populist times.

References

Adcock, F. (2012). The UN Special Rapporteur on the rights of indigenous peoples and New Zealand: A study in compliance ritualism. *New Zealand Yearbook of International Law, 10,* 97–120.

Baldwin, R., & Hawkins, K. (1984). Discretionary justice: Davis reconsidered. *Public Law, 1984,* 570–599.

Baršová, A., & Barša, P. (2005). *Přistěhovalectví a liberální stát.* Brno: Masarykova univerzita.

Bauerová, H. (2018). The Czech Republic and the reality of migrant integration policy in the context of European integration. *Croatian and Comparative Public Administration, 18*(3), 397–420.

Boda, Z., Szabó, G., Bartha, A., Medve-Bálint, G., & Vidra, Z. (2015). Politically driven: Mapping political and media discourses of penal populism—The Hungarian case. *East European Politics and Societies, 29*(4), 871–891.

Braithwaite, J. (2008). *Regulatory capitalism: How it works, ideas for making it work better.* Cheltenham/Northampton: Edward Elgar.

Braithwaite, V. (2009). *Defiance in taxation and governance.* Cheltenham/Northampton: Edward Elgar.

Braithwaite, J., Makkai, T., & Braithwaite, V. (2007). *Regulating aged care: Ritualism and the new pyramid.* Cheltenham/Northampton: Edward Elgar.

Čada, K., & Frantová, V. (2019). Countering Islamophobia in the Czech Republic. In I. Law, A. Easat-Daas, A. Merali, & S. Sayyid (Eds.), *Countering Islamophobia in Europe* (pp. 153–182). Cham: Palgrave Macmillan.

Čaněk, M., Qubaiová, A, Kučera, P., Voslář, V., Avramioti, I., Janků, L., Čižinský, P., & Lupačová, H. (2016). *Subcontracting and EU mobile workers in the Czech Republic: Exploitation, liability, and institutional gaps* (Labcit Country Report). https://migrationonline.cz/czech_republic_country_report.pdf. Accessed 8 Aug 2019.

Charlesworth, H. (2017). A regulatory perspective on the international human rights system. In P. Drahos (Ed.), *Regulatory theory: Foundations and application* (pp. 357–373). Canberra: Australian National University (ANU) Press.

Cicourel, A. (2005). Bureaucratic rituals in health care delivery. *Journal of Applied Linguistics and Professional Practice, 2*(3), 357–370.

Čižinský, P., Čech Valentová, E., Hradečná, P., Holíková, K., Jelínková, M., Rozumek, M., & Rozumková, P. (2014). *Foreign workers in the labour market in the Czech Republic and in selected European countries.* Association for Integration and Migration, Organization for Aid to Refugees, Multicultural Centre Prague. https://www.migrace.com/docs/141115_simizamestnanci-en-nahled.pdf. Accessed 8 Aug 2019.

Consortium of Migrants Assisting Organisations in the Czech Republic. (2015). *Migration manifesto: Suggestions to the strategy of migration policy of the Czech Republic.* http://www.migracnimanifest.cz/en/index.html. Accessed 8 Aug 2019.

Consortium of Migrants Assisting Organisations in the Czech Republic. (2018). *Právní analýza vládního návrhu novely zákona o pobytu cizinců 2018.* http://www.migracnikonsorcium.cz/wp-content/uploads/2018/10/Novela-ZPC-2018_-právn%C3%AD-analýza_FINAL.pdf. Accessed 8 Aug 2019.

Curato, N. (2016). Politics of anxiety, politics of hope: Penal populism and Duterte's rise to power. *Journal of Current Southeast Asian Affairs, 35*(3), 91–109.

Czech Chamber of Commerce. (2018). *Dlouhý: Zaměstnavatelé reálně postrádají 440 tisíc lidí.* https://www.komora.cz/press_release/dlouhy-zamestnavatele-realne-postradaji-440-tisic-lidi-ztraty-na-danich-a-odvodech-v-roce-2019-presahnou-110-miliard-korun/. Accessed 30 Oct 2019.

Czech Government. (2015). *Migration policy strategy of the Czech Republic*. https://www.mvcr.cz/migrace/soubor/migration-policy-strategy-of-the-czech-republic.aspx. Accessed 8 Aug 2019.

Czech Statistical Office. (2018a). *Data on number of foreigners*. https://www.czso.cz/csu/cizinci/number-of-foreigners-data. Accessed 31 July 2019.

Czech Statistical Office. (2018b). *Foreigners: Employment-data*. https://www.czso.cz/csu/cizinci/3-ciz_zamestnanost#rok. Accessed 31 July 2019.

Czech Statistical Office. (2019). *Zaměstnanost a nezaměstnanost podle výsledků VŠPS – 2.* čtvrtletí 2019. https://www.czso.cz/csu/czso/cri/zamestnanost-a-nezamestnanost-podle-vysledku-vsps-2-ctvrtleti-2019 (2019). Accessed 7 Aug 2019.

Czech-Moravian Confederation of Trade Unions. (2017). *Vzkaz ČMKOS budoucí vládě*. https://www.tripartita.cz/vzkaz-cmkos-budouci-vlade. Accessed 8 Aug 2019.

Drbohlav, D. (2003). Immigration and the Czech Republic (with a Special focus on the foreign labor force). *International Migration Review, 37*(1), 194–224.

European Migration Network. (2019). *Labour market integration of third-country nationals in EU member states* (Synthesis Report for the EMN Study). https://ec.europa.eu/home-affairs/sites/homeaffairs/files/00_eu_labour_market_integration_final_en.pdf. Accessed 8 Aug 2019.

Ford, J. (2016). *The risks of regulatory ritualism: Proposals for a treaty on business and human rights (April 2, 2016)*. Global Economic Governance, Working Paper 118. https://ssrn.com/abstract=3206434. Accessed 8 Aug 2019.

Heimer, C. A., & Gazley, J. L. (2012). Performing regulation: Transcending regulatory ritualism in HIV clinics. *Law & Society Review, 46*(4), 853–887.

Koldinská, K., Sheu, H. C., & Štefko, M. (2015). *Sociální integrace cizinců*. Praha: Auditorium.

Kušniráková, T. (2014). Is there an integration policy being formed in Czechia? *Identities: Global Studies in Culture and Power, 21*(6), 738–754.

Mahoney, J., & Thelen, K. (2009). *Explaining institutional change: Ambiguity, agency, and power*. Cambridge: Cambridge University Press.

Meyer, J. W., & Rowan, B. (1977). Institutionalized organizations: Formal structure as myth and ceremony. *American Journal of Sociology, 83*(2), 340–363.

Merton, R. K. (1968). *Social theory and social structure*. New York: Free Press.

Multicultural Centre Prague. (2013). *DoporuČení pro nastavení politiky v oblasti zahraniČní zaměstnanosti*. https://mkc.cz/doc/Doporuceni_pro_nastaveni_politiky_v_oblasti_zahranicni_zamestnanosti.pdf. Accessed 8 Aug 2019.

Organization for Aid to Refugees. (2016). *Aktuální problémy slučování rodin migrantů a právo na soukromý a rodinný život a připravovaná novela cizineckého zákona*. https://www.opu.cz/wp-content/uploads/2016/06/Slučován%C3%AD_rodin_cizinců.pdf. Accessed 8 Aug 2019.

Pachocka, M. (2016). Understanding the Visegrad group states' response to the migrant and refugee crises 2014+ in the European Union. *Yearbook of Polish European Studies, 19*, 101–132.

Power, M. (1997). *The audit society*. Oxford/New York: Oxford University Press.

Public Opinion Research Center. (2019). *The Czech Public views on foreign nationals*. https://cvvm.soc.cas.cz/en/press-releases/other/relations-attitudes/4904-the-czech-public-s-views-on-foreign-nationals-march-2019. Accessed 30 Oct 2019.

Rahimi, F. (2017, March 30). *Žádná přísnost není na cizince dost velká*. Deník Referendum. http://denikreferendum.cz/clanek/24956-zadna-prisnost-neni-na-cizince-dost-velka. Accessed 8 Aug 2019.

Roberts, J., Stalans, L., Indermaur, D. & Hough, M. (2003). *Penal populism and public opinion*. New York: Oxford University Press .

Samier, E. (1997). Administrative ritual and ceremony: Social aesthetics, myth and language use in the rituals of everyday organizational life. *Educational Management & Administration, 25*(4), 417–436.

Svoboda, M. (2015, November 6). *Zahraniční pracovníci nesmějí být nástrojem sociálního dumping*. Rozhovor Haló novin s předsedou Odborového svazu Stavba Stanislavem Antonivem. Haló noviny. https://www.odbory.info/obsah/5/zahranicni-pracovnici-nesmeji-byt-nastrojem-socialnihodumpi/14236. Accessed 8 Aug 2019.

Zelenka, J., & Štěpánek, N. (2018, February 26). *Cizinců pracujících v Česku načerno přibývá*. Firmy hledají zaměstnance a riskují i vysoké pokuty. Hospodářské noviny. https://archiv.ihned.cz/c1-66060730-cizincu-pracujicich-nacerno-pribyva. Accessed 8 Aug 2019.

Chapter 7
Accessing the Danish Labour Market: On the Coexistence of Legal Barriers and Enabling Factors

Liv Bjerre, Michelle Pace, and Somdeep Sen

7.1 Introduction

Denmark is often considered a "first mover" when it comes to the formulation, ratification and implementation of liberal international and national migration conventions and laws. It was the first country to sign and ratify the UN Refugee Convention which was adopted in 1951. Denmark has also been resettling refugees since 1956 and officially established a refugee resettlement program in 1979 (Olwig and Paerregaard 2011: 3). In 1983 Denmark ratified the Aliens Act, which is often considered one of the most liberal immigration laws in Europe.[1] The law specified that refugees[2] were legally entitled to family reunification, language training, financial and residential support and a work permit (Pedersen 1999; Hedetoft 2006). To an extent, these measures reflected the existence of a "general principle of welfare community inclusion" (Mouritsen and Olsen 2013: 694; see also Soysal 1994). And, to that end, the Aliens Act was an outgrowth of Denmark's long-standing effort to "cultivate a self-image of tolerance" encapsulated in a welfare state that guarantees "high levels of public provisions (healthcare, education, unemployment benefits, old-age pensions, etc.), accessible to all citizens and residents in the country" (Pace 2018: 786).

In recent years, however, Denmark – on the basis of a political discourse that insists that refugees in particular are a burden to the welfare state and their culture incompatible with Danish values – has aspired to be a different kind of "first mover"; namely, as a pioneer of some of the most restrictive asylum policies in Europe

---

[1] This, in spite of the problematic title (i.e. *Aliens* Act) of the law.

[2] As well as non-refugee migrants.

L. Bjerre · M. Pace (✉) · S. Sen
Department of Social Sciences and Business, Roskilde University, Roskilde, Denmark
e-mail: mpace@ruc.dk

© The Author(s) 2021
V. Federico, S. Baglioni (eds.), *Migrants, Refugees and Asylum Seekers'
Integration in European Labour Markets*, IMISCOE Research Series,
https://doi.org/10.1007/978-3-030-67284-3_7

(Delman 2016; Abend 2019; Khalid and Mortensen 2019; Westersø 2019; Agerhold 2016.). As we go on to demonstrate later in this chapter, the cultivation of this new image as a "bad destination" for those seeking asylum included ever-more restrictive immigration regulations, limited access to family reunification and cuts in the social and financial assistance guaranteed by the welfare state (Taylor 2015). Instinctively, one would expect that policies restricting entry into Denmark will be paired with antagonistic policies towards refugees within Denmark. To an extent, Denmark has indeed witnessed the creation of a far more hostile integration policy landscape targeting not just refugees but also economic migrants and Danish citizens with a migrant background in the aftermath of the 2015 European "refugee crisis". In this chapter we demonstrate, however, that while barriers to entering Denmark have been mirrored in some integration-related restrictive measures within Denmark, this has not been the case with regard to refugees' integration into the Danish labour market. Surprisingly perhaps, we argue that the structure and norms of the Danish labour market are such that they in fact facilitate refugees' integration in the work force and legally protect their rights.[3] To be sure, this protection, often guaranteed by key labour market stakeholders, is a way of securing the rights of Danish workers who would be adversely affected by the proliferation of an unregulated labour market where refugees are compelled to work under worse legal and economic conditions. Nevertheless, and in effect, the case of refugees' integration into the Danish labour market ends up being one where, counterintuitively, legal barriers to entering Denmark coexist alongside enabling legal guarantees of refugees' rights in the Danish labour market.

This chapter begins by describing Denmark's shift in stance, both in terms of rhetoric and policy-making, from "being a first mover" with regard to progressive migration policies to pioneering some of the most restrictive and antagonistic measures in the region and globally. Subsequently, we demonstrate that Denmark's posturing externally is not entirely reflected in the manner in which refugees encounter the Danish labour market. We elaborate that refugees' rights and privileges within the Danish workforce are guaranteed by the Danish labour market model that ensures that safe and fair working conditions are guaranteed to all workers in employment.

---

[3] It is important to note that while migrants with a humanitarian residence permit or with a residence permit on the grounds of family reunification can take up any job, non-Nordic/EU/EEA migrant workers' access to Denmark is conditional upon the existing job schemes. The current job schemes aim at attracting high-skilled labour and include among others: The Fast-track Scheme, the Pay Limit Scheme, the Positive List, schemes for researchers, employed PhDs and guest researchers and Start-up Denmark (scheme for self-employment). But while, ostensibly, the main entry routes for migrant workers are reserved for high-skilled professionals, a report from the Nordic Council of Ministers from 2010 concludes that Denmark fares very poorly in comparison to the other Nordic countries in regard to attracting high skilled workers. "An immediate explanation for this may be the tightening of the regulatory framework for access to Denmark from countries which were implemented in 2002", as stated in the report (Kornø 2010).

7.2 The Proliferation of Restrictive Measures

Claiming that Denmark, in the past, has been a front runner in the implementation of liberal migration policies is not, however, to argue that the political landscape within the country has been devoid of any criticism of the influx of foreigners. Especially with the implementation of the Aliens Act, conservative politicians considered migrants to be an invasive demographic presence that would have a detrimental impact on the economic, socio-political and cultural character of Danish society (Hvenegaard-Larsen 2002; Mouritsen and Olsen 2013; Jørgensen 2006; Nannestad 2004). This antagonistic narrative has only intensified over the years and, especially in the past decade, public intellectuals and politicians have consistently raised severe concerns regarding immigrants in general and refugees in particular becoming a burden on the Danish welfare state – not least in terms of their limited integration into the Danish labour market (The Ministry of Finance 2017). For instance, on the basis of a 2011 study conducted by the conservative Danish think-tank CEPOS that claimed that immigrants from "non-Western countries and their dependents" cost the Danish state €2 billion every year, the far-right Danish People's Party (DF) politician Pia Kjærsgaard declared that unemployed immigrants were the most significant challenge faced by the welfare state (Lehmann 2011; see also Bloch 2017). Similarly, in 2015, the Dansk Arbejdsgiverforening or the Confederation of Danish Employers' (DA) administrative director Jørn Neergaard Larsen said, "It is catastrophic that we are so bad at integrating refugees into the Danish job market. That is not acceptable for our refugees, and as a society we simply cannot afford to let this group be taken care of by public benefits" (The Local 2015; also see Andersen 2003).

Of course, any discussion of the antagonism towards migrants in the political discourse would be incomplete without recognizing the securitization of the figure of the migrant (Sen and Pace 2018; Barrett 2018, 2019; Mouritsen and Jensen 2014). In this regard, a "watershed" moment came in the aftermath of the Muhammad Cartoon Crisis and the outrage it led to among Muslim communities within and outside Denmark. When on 30th September 2005 *Jyllands Posten* published cartoons depicting the Prophet Muhammad (i.e. a practice considered blasphemous in Islam), the newspaper claimed that it was practicing its right to freedom of speech and encouraging a critical public discourse of Islam (Jyllands Posten 2006). Yet, for some commentators, the response to the cartoons was evidence of rampant religious intolerance and radicalism among (often, young) non-Western immigrants in Denmark (Ammitzbøll and Vidino 2007). Evidently, this narrative coincided with the post-9/11 global concerns regarding Islamic radicalism and terrorism and a 2007 survey showed that 42% of Danes were concerned about terrorism, criminality and (the lack of) integration of non-EU residents in Denmark (Avisen 2007; also see Ottesen 2017). This narrative was further encouraged by the so-called 2015 "refugee crisis" and related security concerns. Following the 2015 attack on the Danish synagogue DF politician Pia Kjærsgaard accused Danish Muslims "of living at a lower stage of civilization, with their own primitive and cruel customs" (The

Economist 2015). In the same vein, following the wave of terror attacks in several European countries, DF's Martin Henriksen claimed in parliament that "there is a direct correlation between refugees and terrorism" (quoted in Ritzau 2016).

Expectedly, this political discourse has encouraged the implementation of stricter immigration regulations in the last decade. And, since the beginning of the "refugee crisis", Danish authorities have engaged in a concerted campaign to portray Denmark as less attractive to asylum seekers. For example, the discretionary powers of the police were expanded to handle asylum seekers (Hvidtfeldt and Schultz--Nielsen 2017: 53). The police were given greater powers to withhold people, for instance, in order to ensure his/her presence during the asylum phase and during any appeal. A new and lower integration benefit system replaced social assistance for those who have not been in Denmark for more than seven of the last eight years (Kvist 2016). Fines for irregular stay, entry and work were raised in 2015, along with fines for aiding so called "irregular immigrants" cross the border (Hvidtfeldt and Schultz-Nielsen 2017: 52). Moreover, carrier sanctions (Schengen internal)[4] and border controls were introduced (Hvidtfeldt and Schultz-Nielsen 2017: 53). In February 2016 the right to family reunification for people with temporary protection status was restricted. Now it can only be availed after three years of residency, as opposed to the previous residency requirement of one year (Hvidtfeldt and Schultz--Nielsen 2017: 53, Kvist 2016). More stringent eligibility requirements for permanent residency were also introduced (Hvidtfeldt and Schultz-Nielsen 2017: 54). Moving on from these strict restrictions implemented to limit immigration *to* Denmark, the next section focuses on the legal guarantees of labour rights *within* the Danish labour market model.

7.3   Legal Guarantees of Labour Rights

The Danish private labour market consists of small and medium-sized enterprises (SMEs) as well as large multinational companies. The business sector is generally characterised by a high degree of individual specialisation and flexibility in terms of adapting to market changes. Denmark has a strong reputation for high quality food and design, as well as in telecommunications, IT, pharmaceuticals, electronics and biotech more recently. A majority of the population has either a vocational or a higher education. As far as the workforce is concerned, the labour market comprises more than 50% of the population – a relatively high percentage compared to other countries, partly due to the very high employment rate of women (Norrbom Vinding 2014). The overall employment rate was 78.2% in 2018 (Eurostat 2018). To be sure,

---

[4]Carrier sanctions – meaning that air carriers as well as bus, train and maritime carriers can be subject to criminal liability if they bring a foreigner without the required travel ID across external Schengen borders – have been in place since the late 1980s. What is however new is that, as of 2015, there are now carrier sanctions for bringing people across an internal Schengen border (Hvidtfeldt and Schultz-Nielsen 2017: 53).

Denmark has a long history of mass emigration, primarily to the United States (Semmingsen 1972; Larsen 1982; Hatton 1995). However, its increasingly robust economy and labour market has meant that Denmark has witnessed a greater influx of migrants and has been a net-migration country since the 1960s. Today, the foreign-born population makes up 10% of the total population. Of these, 25% have Danish citizenship, and 3.9% are born in other EU/Nordic countries. The majority of the (non-EU/Nordic) foreign-born population originates from Syria, Turkey, Iraq, Bosnia and Herzegovina, Iran, Pakistan, Afghanistan, Lebanon, Somalia and China. A smaller share of the foreign-born population (as compared to the Danish-born population) falls within the age groups <18 years and 60 + years, while a greater share falls within the working age.[5] Since 2014, more than 65,000 foreigners arrived in Denmark each year, with a peak in 2015 with more than 75,000 arrivals. The 2015 peak is mirrored in the subpopulation of immigrants who are non-EU citizens. In 2015, 38,353 non-EU citizens immigrated to Denmark compared to 29,019 in 2014 and 34,564 in 2016. This peak is primarily a result of the increase in the number of asylum seekers. The success rate (recognition rate) of applications processed in Denmark has dropped in recent years. It reached a record high of 85% in 2015, dropped to 72% in 2016 and came down to 36% in 2017, primarily reflecting the source countries of the applicants (the percentage of Syrians and Eritreans dropping, meaning that a greater share now come from other countries, who have a smaller chance of being granted refugee status) (Bendixen 2018).

Evidently, Denmark has adopted an increasingly hardline approach to its immigration policy-making and, as we have discussed earlier, the discursive construction of migrants as a burden to the Danish welfare state seems to be the key narrative driving recent immigration policies. One would then instinctively expect such restrictive immigration policies directed towards refugees to be "paired" with equally restrictive integration policies – especially with regard to refugees' integration into the Danish labour market. Yet, we would argue, labour market integration policies largely enable refugees's integration into the Danish labour market. For one thing, their enabling nature is shaped by the particular (institutional) character of the way in which integration policies in general and labour market integration policies in particular are implemented. With its three-tier system comprising the state, the region, and the municipality, the Danish governance structure leaves it to municipalities to implement integration policy – housing for refugees, integration/introduction programs, welfare benefits and finding jobs/education. All 98 municipalities in Denmark have complete discretion and independence in interpreting, managing and adapting integration policies, which further allows them to cater for the specific needs of local communities: municipalities are thus seen as best suited to address their communities' needs especially with regards to employment, education and language skills (Jørgensen 2014). The discretionary power in regard to the implementation of the law allows for diverging strategies and measures across municipalities, which might result in different outcomes. For instance, a memo from The

---

[5] See here: https://www.sirius-project.eu/sites/default/files/attachments/WP2_D2.2.pdf

Agency for International Recruitment and Integration (2017) shows significant municipal differences in the employment rate of female refugees arriving during the period 2015–2017, potentially as a consequence of differences in the administration of the integration law. These differences could also be attributed to other factors, for example, differences in the refugees' countries of origin across municipalities. Yet, despite differences in the way in which municipalities implement integration policies, a key consequence of this governance structure is that the restrictive approach undertaken with regard to Danish immigration policy does not necessarily impact the implementation of integration policies at the municipal-level, wherein the primary responsibility of municipality authorities is to enable refugees' (and non-refugee migrants') integration into the Danish labour market.

This said, the foundational character of the Danish labour market is conducive to refugees' integration into the workforce. Here we can look to the so-called September Compromise – often considered the constitution of the Danish labour market – that was signed on 5 September 1899. The agreement was seen as a national agreement for Danish industrial relations. It was signed by the Danish Employers' Confederation (DA) and the Danish Confederation of Trade Unions (LO). The intention of the agreement was to end long periods of strikes by employees and lock-outs. Considering the industrial cost of these negotiation 'tactics' the settlement was to both secure the employers' right to regulate the work environment and to establish a bargaining system that had an embargo on strikes and lockouts. Through the September Compromise employers were able to secure their right to regulate the work environment. Additionally, both parties recognized each other's right to implement work stoppages. However, work stoppages needed to be approved by three quarters of the members and sufficient notice would need to be given prior to work stoppages. The agreement resulted in a centralized bargaining system whereby negotiations would take place between the two confederations representing the employers and the unions (Jørgensen 1999). As a consequence then, in Denmark, wage and work conditions are primarily regulated by collective agreements (or individual employment contracts) and not by law. This system of labour market regulation is referred to as The Danish Labour Market Model and is characterized by the fact that "the social partners themselves determine the rules of the game on the labour market" (The Ministry of Employment 2018). The underlining assumption here is that employers and employees are organized in associations and unions that protect their interests during collective agreement negotiations. This means that pay and work conditions are agreed freely between employers and employees through the various employers' organizations and trade unions (3F 2015).

This system of labour market regulation as well as its implications for the integration of refugees is important because it is this character of the labour market that shapes the nature of their entry into the Danish labour force. For one thing, in Denmark access to the labour market is considered an important pillar for integration. Article 1 of the Integration Act explicitly stipulates that: "making newly arrived aliens self-supporting as quickly as possible through employment" is a key objective of integration efforts (Integration Act No. 1115 of 23 September 2013). To be sure, asylum seekers are not allowed to take up work during the first six months from their arrival, meaning that they have little chance of an everyday life outside the asylum centre. Refugees and family reunified persons, on the other hand, are obliged to take part in an integration program, with a clear focus on labour market participation (The Ministry of Immigration and Integration 2016: 51). This program, catering for refugees and their family members, consists of Danish education and employment-oriented offers in the form of guidance and upgrading, business practice, and employment with wage subsidies (The Ministry of Immigration and Integration 2018). The integration program is implemented in the municipalities and goes hand in hand with an integration contract that must be signed in order to receive an integration allowance. The integration contract must entail a description of the immigrant's employment and education goals together with a detailed description of the activities ensuring that the goals are met. Thus, the contract is tailored to each individual and specific goals and the identifiable means leading to employment must be described in the contract (The Ministry of Immigration and Integration 2019).

The Integration program is a one-year program, as the intention is to get refugees (and their family members) into employment within one year. It can, however, be extended with up to four additional years if employment is not achieved (The Ministry of Immigration and Integration 2016: 51). The guiding principle is that those that have been granted asylum must "work from day one" (The Ministry of Immigration and Integration 2016: 52). To this end, refugees and family reunified persons in the integration program are automatically regarded as "job-ready"; meaning that they should be enrolled in job training unless considered ineligible (due to health issues etc.) (The Ministry of Immigration and Integration 2016: 51).

In Denmark, the Assessment of Foreign Qualifications Act entitles all holders of foreign qualifications to an assessment through the central recognition agency (OECD 2017: 13). To this end, the Danish Agency for Higher Education (Styrelsen for Institutioner og Uddennalesestøtte) is able to provide qualification assessments to authorities responsible for the integration of MRAs as well as individual MRAs free of charge. (The Ministry of Immigration and Integration 2016: 58). This service is provided for the assessment of all levels of education (The Ministry of Immigration and Integration 2016: 58), and Denmark is among the relatively few countries that grants special recognition of prior learning procedures for humanitarian migrants who do not have documentary proof of their qualification (OECD 2017: 39). Even immigrants who do not formally require recognition (i.e. because they intend to work in a non-regulated profession) are encouraged to use this offer (OECD 2017: 13).

Since the Danish labour market leaves its regulation to the social partners, focus on antidiscrimination at the national level has not been strong in Denmark (Jørgensen 2014: 18). As a result of Denmark's (lack of) anti-discrimination policies, the Migrant Integration Policy Index (MIPEX) ranks Denmark number 27 out of 38 countries in the field of antidiscrimination policies, among others because Danish anti-discrimination legislation is split into several acts (Huddleston et al. 2015). Section 70 of the Danish Constitution states that nobody can be deprived of any civil or political rights on grounds of faith or origin, but there is no general prohibition against discrimination in the Danish Constitution. According to Jørgensen, this lack of a general prohibition against discrimination allows the state to promote the majority culture in specific areas, for example religion (2014: 18). The consequences of this were evident back in 2000, when a trainee was turned away from the Danish department store Magasin for turning up to work wearing a headscarf. The store management claimed that the headscarf did not comply with their rules governing employee clothing. The case was instantly taken up in the courts and the high court (Østre landret) ruled that Magasin's reason had no legal foundation and therefore constituted indirect discrimination. The young woman received compensation. The high-court decision resulted in many companies having to change their employee clothing policies. Following the ruling, employees now had the right to wear a headscarf at work (Lukowski 2010). Yet, in 2005, the Danish Supreme Court ruled in the so-called "Føtex case", where a woman had been fired for refusing to take off her headscarf at work in the department store (Supreme Court of Denmark 2005). The unanimous verdict stated that the dismissal was justified and was not a case of illegal discrimination because an employer has the right to stipulate a dress code for its employees. The ruling was significant in terms of its implications for the labour market integration of immigrants wearing a headscarf or other religious symbols as it limits not only their freedom of expression but the range of potential workplaces. Further, it provided employers with a potentially "easy tool" to dismiss employees who carry religious symbols. In 2018 Danish lawmakers also passed a law that banned the burqa and niqab. Responding to the ratification of the law, Amnesty International's Europe Director Gauri van Gulik said, "If the intention of this law was to protect women's rights, it fails abjectly. Instead, the law criminalises women for their choice of clothing and in so doing flies in the face of those freedoms Denmark purports to uphold". While only a "few Muslim women in Denmark wear full-face veils," the law would expectedly affect their ability to integrate into the Danish labour market (The Guardian 2018).

For undocumented migrants residing in Denmark without residency documentation is extremely difficult. There is a general societal belief that undocumented immigration challenges the Danish universalist welfare tradition as undocumented immigrants do not enjoy any protection, have no right to social benefits, have extremely limited access to health care, have no political rights and do not pay taxes (Trænæs and Jensen 2014: 7). In Denmark, the personal ID number (CPR) is the gateway to basically everything, from healthcare to opening a bank account, getting a Danish phone number, registering at a Danish language school or even getting a gym membership (Bahgat 2018). In this way, the Danish system can be said to work in favour of legal stay and against undocumented migration. At the same time, however, the total lack of access to Danish society without proper documents puts the undocumented population in Denmark under pressure and makes them vulnerable to exploitation and abuse as they become dependent on employers and/or alternative sources of income and assistance in a "shadow" society (Trænæs and Jensen 2014:

74). This precarity of undocumented life in Denmark may then explain the relatively few (reported) undocumented workers in the country.[6]

Overall, therefore when we look at the balance sheet of Denmark's legal barriers and enabling factors to in particular labour market integration for MRAs we have quite a mixed picture. However, we sustain that while "barriers" exist in terms of entering Denmark, the Danish labour market model facilitates refugees' integration and legally ensures the protection of their labour rights. Therefore, the Danish case study shows that legal barriers (to entering the labour market) coexist alongside enabling factors (legal guarantees) of refugees' rights.

7.4 Conclusion

Following a general election in June 2019, Denmark now has a new government made up of left-wing parties (that won an overall majority in said election). Prior to the election, Social Democrat leader Mette Frederiksen (now Denmark's prime minister) had stressed that she would continue the "broad" approach of the previous government on refugees as well as immigration, including the so-called 'paradigm shift' – referring to the then government's policy of returning refugees to their source countries once it is deemed safe to do so, rather than integrate them in Denmark: "We are still focused on repatriation and temporary asylum. When you are a refugee and come to Denmark, you can be granted our protection. But when there's peace, you must go home" (Wenane 2019). The other three parties – the Social Liberals, the Socialist People's Party and the Red-Green Alliance – had all called for a more lenient approach to refugees. The coalition agreement reflects this, with pledges to improve conditions for families of rejected asylum seekers and to move families with children from Sjælsmark deportation centre to a more humane facility.[7] Other aspects of the agreement include opening the doors for more high-skilled foreign workers.

The new Social Democratic government and its support parties also announced that refugees who lose their residence permit if conditions in their home country improve will be allowed to stay if they had a job for a minimum of 2 years and still have it. According to refugees.dk this may already be relevant for some of the 900 Somali refugees who lost their permits during the last year, and for many Syrians in the future (Bendixen 2019). The Red/Green Alliance (Enhedslisten) added that all refugees will get the same right to free education – which the 4500 Syrians with a

---

[6] The Danish Police reported only 190 cases of undocumented workers in the third quarter in 2019 (Politi 2019).

[7] A study conducted by the Danish Red Cross expressed severe concern regarding the psychological welfare of children at the deportation centre and reported that a large proportion of the children displayed significant levels of mental health issues (Red Cross 2019; Nilsson and Hergel 2019; The Local 2019).

temporary protection 7(3)-status[8] do not have today. Another announcement was made in regard to refugee families with less than 9 years stay in Denmark, receiving integration benefit: These families will now *not* be subject to the previously announced reduction in benefits (which was part of the annual finance act for 2019), and they will be receiving a special child benefit given temporarily to the poorest families with children while a commission will be looking into poverty benefits in general.

This new government is thus trying to change the course on immigration policy in a more humanitarian direction. However, we are cautiously optimistic and sustain that since historically restrictive measures have been imposed while at the same time embedded in a climate that emphasizes and guarantees workers' (social and legal) rights, we cannot be overly sure that these more recent moves go beyond symbolic politics. As we have highlighted throughout this chapter, Denmark is a clear case of how a first mover of a positive kind in terms of immigration laws and policies quickly shifted to a first mover of a highly negative and often symbolic kind – albeit with real impacts for MRAs. However, we conclude that, in spite of the highly securitized and "burden" narratives that have sought to portray MRAs in a negative light, Denmark remains overall a success story for MRAs' integration into the labour market. As 51-year-old Ghais Sangari, formerly an Afghan war refugee, but now a successful businessman with a Danish passport, puts it: "Many immigrants speak negatively about Denmark. I would rather talk about all the positive things about Danish society. I always say to my children: 'If you work hard, read and get good grades, you can do whatever you want in Denmark.' It is the most important thing" (own translation from Danish, Euroman 2019: 91).

References

3F. (2015, November 11). The Danish Labour Market Model. *3F*. https://tema.3f.dk/byg-job/english/the-danish-labour-market-model. Accessed 14 July 2019.

Abend, L. (2019, January 16). An island for 'unwanted' migrants is Denmark's latest aggressive ant-immigrant policy. *Time Magazine*. https://time.com/5504331/denmark-migrants-lindholm-island/. Accessed 12 July 2019.

Agerhold, H. (2016, July 1). Denmark uses controversial 'jewelry law' to seize assets from refugees for first time. *The Independent*. https://www.independent.co.uk/news/world/europe/denmark-jewellery-law-migrants-refugees-asylum-seekers-unhcr-united-nations-a7113056.html. Accessed 12 July 2019.

Ammitzbøll, P., & Vidino, L. (2007). After the Danish cartoon controversy. *Middle East Quarterly, 14*(1), 3–11.

Andersen, J. G. (2003). *The Danish People's Party and new cleavages in Danish politics* (working paper). Aalborg: Center for Comparative Welfare Studies, Aalborg University.

---

[8]For more information see here: http://refugees.dk/en/facts/legislation-and-definitions/more-about-art-7-3-temporary-protection-status/

Avisen.dk. (2007, May 24). *Danskerne er bange for terror og indvandrer* [Danes are afraid of terrorism and immigrants]. https://www.avisen.dk/danskerne-er-bange-for-terror-og-indvandrere_70177.aspx. Accessed 12 July 2019.

Bahgat, F. (2018, March 15). Is life in Denmark impossible without a personal registration number? *The Local.* https://www.thelocal.dk/20180315/is-life-in-denmark-impossible-without-a-personal-registration-number. Accessed 16 July 2019.

Barrett, M. (2018, December 1). Denmark to banish foreign convicted criminals to deserted island. *The Local.* https://www.thelocal.dk/20181201/denmark-to-banish-foreign-convicted-criminals-to-deserted-island. Accessed 12 July 2019.

Barrett, M. (2019, January 24). Three years after Denmark's infamous 'jewellery law' hit world headlines, not a single piece has been confiscated. *The Local.* https://www.thelocal.dk/20190124/three-years-after-denmarks-infamous-jewellery-law-hit-world-headlines-not-a-single-piece-has-been-confiscated. Accessed 12 July 2019.

Bendixen, M. C. (2018, January 29). What are the chances of being granted asylum? *Refugees Welcome.* http://refugees.dk/en/facts/numbers-and-statistics/what-are-the-chances-of-being-granted-asylum/. Accessed 12 July 2019.

Bendixen, M. C. (2019, June 30). Good news for Syrian refugees in Denmark. *Refugees Welcome.* http://refugees.dk/en/news/2019/june/good-news-for-syrian-refugees-in-denmark/. Accessed 12 July 2019.

Bloch, C. (2017, April 10). Inger Støjberg om flygtninge: "Vi har pakket dem ind i velfærd. Og vi har lullet dem i søvn, så hænderne lige så stille er sunket ned i skødet" [Inger Støjberg on refugees: "We have wrapped them [immigrants] in welfare. Lulled them to sleep and their hands have laid still on their laps"]. *Berlingske.* https://www.berlingske.dk/politik/inger-stoejberg-om-flygtninge-vi-har-pakket-dem-ind-i-velfaerd.-og-vi-har-lullet. Accessed 14 July 2019.

Delman, E. (2016, January 27). How not to welcome refugees. *Atlantic.* https://www.theatlantic.com/international/archive/2016/01/denmark-refugees-immigration-law/431520/. Accessed 12 July 2019.

Euroman. 2019. *Gennembruddet fra ghettoen* [The breakthrough from the ghetto]. April Edition, pp. 72–93.

Hatton, T. J. (1995). A model of Scandinavian emigration. *European Economic Review, 39*(3–4), 557–564.

Hedetoft, U. (2006). *Denmark: Integrating immigrants into a homogenous welfare state.* Migration Policy Institute. https://www.migrationpolicy.org/article/denmark-integrating-immigrants-homogeneous-welfare-state. Accessed 12 July 2019.

Huddleston, T., Bilgili, Ö., Joki, A.-L., & Vankova, Z. (2015). *Migrant integration policy index 2015.* CIDOB and MPG: Barcelona/Brussels.

Hvenegaard-Lassen, K. (2002). *På lige fod, samfundet, ligheden og folketingets debatter om udlændingepolitik 1973-2000* [On equal footing, the society, equality and parliamentary debates on foreign policy between 1973-2000] (PhD Dissertation). Copenhagen: University of Copenhagen.

Hvidtfeldt, C., & Schultz-Nielsen, M. L. (2017). *Flygtninge og asylansøgere i Danmark 1992–2016* [Refugees and asylum seekers in Denmark 1992–2016]. Copenhagen: Rockwool Foundation.

Jørgensen, C. (1999, August 27). September Compromise marks 100th anniversary. *Eurofund.* https://www.eurofound.europa.eu/observatories/eurwork/articles/industrial-relations/september-compromise-marks-100th-anniversary. Accessed 12 July 2019.

Jørgensen, L. (2006). *Hvad sagde vi!...om "De Andre". Den udlændingepolitiske debat i Folketinget 1961–1999* [What did we say…about "the others". The foreign policy debate in the parliament 1961–1999]. PhD dissertation. Roskilde: Roskilde University.

Jørgensen, M. B. (2014). Decentralising immigrant integration. In *Denmark's mainstreaming initiatives in employment, education, and social affairs.* Brussels: Migration Policy Institute Europe.

Jyllands, P. (2006, September 30). *Muhammed-krisen – sådan gik det til* [The Muhammad Crisis – Here is how it happened]. https://jyllands-posten.dk/indland/article4302432.ece/. Accessed 14 July 2019.

Khalid, F., & Mortensen, N. H. (2019, June 4). How anti-immigrant sentiment infected Denmark's politics. *New Statesman*. https://www.newstatesman.com/world/europe/2019/06/how-anti-immigrant-sentiment-infected-denmark-s-politics. Accessed 12 July 2019.

Kornø, H. R. (2010, June 10). Denmark loses the battle for high-skilled immigrants. *Danish Green Card Association*. https://danishgreencard.wordpress.com/2010/06/10/denmark-loses-the-battle-for-high-skilled-immigrants/. Accessed 12 July 2019.

Kvist, J. (2016). *Recent Danish migration and integration policies*. European Social Policy Network Flash Report – 2016/14. https://ec.europa.eu/social/BlobServlet?docId=15320&langId=en. Accessed 12 July 2019.

Larsen, U. M. (1982). A quantitative study of emigration from Denmark to the United States, 1870–1913. *Scandinavian Economic History Review, 30*(2), 101–128.

Lehmann, C. (2011, March 7). *Arbejdsløse indvandrere er den største velfærdsudfordring* [Unemployed immigrants are the biggest welfare challenge]. *Information*. https://www.information.dk/indland/2011/03/arbejdsloese-indvandrere-stoerste-velfaerdsudfordring, Accessed 14 July 2019.

Lukowski, S. (2010). Headscarves in Danish workplaces. *Kvinfo*, April 14. https://kvinfo.dk/headscarves-in-danish-workplaces/?lang=en. Accessed 16 July 2019.

Mouritsen, P., & Jensen, C. H. (2014). *Integration policies in Denmark* (INTERACT Research Report 2014/06). http://cadmus.eui.eu/bitstream/handle/1814/32020/INTERACT-RR-2014_06.pdf?sequence=1. Accessed 14 July 2019.

Mouritsen, P., & Olsen, T. V. (2013). Denmark between liberalism and nationalism. *Ethnic and Racial Studies, 36*(4), 691–710.

Nannestad, P. (2004). Immigration as a challenge to the Danish welfare state. *European Journal of Political Economy, 20*(3), 755–767.

Nilsson, K., & Hergel, O. (2019, April 5). Røde Kors om mistrivsel på Sjælsmark: 6 ud af 10 undersøgte børn kunne få en psykiatrisk diagnose (Red Cross on dissatisfaction at Sjælsmark: 6 out of 10 children examined could receive a psychiatric diagnosis). *Politiken*. https://politiken.dk/indland/art7127117/6-ud-af-10-unders%C3%B8gte-b%C3%B8rn-kunne-f%C3%A5-en-psykiatrisk-diagnose. Accessed 12 July 2019.

Norrbom Vinding. (2014). Setting up in Denmark. In *A brief introduction to labour and employment law in Denmark*. Copenhagen: Norrbom Vinding.

OECD. (2017). *Making integration work: Assessment and recognition of foreign qualifications*. Paris: OECD Publishing.

Olwig, K. F., & Pærregaard, K. (2011). Introduction: Strangers in the nation. In K. F. Olwig & K. Pærregaard (Eds.), *The question of integration: Immigration, exclusion and the Danish welfare state* (pp. 1–29). Newcastle upon Tyne: Cambridge Scholars Publishing.

Ottesen, K. (2017, March 15). *To ud af tre danskere vil have færre muslimske indvandrere til Danmark* [Two out of three Danes want fewer Muslim immigrants in Denmark]. *DR*. https://www.dr.dk/ligetil/indland/ud-af-tre-danskere-vil-have-faerre-muslimske-indvandrere-til-danmark. Accessed 14 July 2019.

Pace, M. (2018). Overcoming bordering practices through the arts: The case of young Syrian refugees and their Danish counterparts in Denmark. *Geopolitics, 23*(4), 781–802.

Pedersen, S. (1999). Indvandringen til Danmark [Immigration to Denmark]. In D. Coleman & E. Wadensjo (Eds.), *Indvandringen til Danmark* (pp. 1–15). Copenhagen: Spektrum.

Politi. (2019, October). Ulovligt arbejde efter udlændingelovens § 59, stk. 3 og 5. Copenhagen: Politi. https://politi.dk/-/media/mediefiler/landsdaekkende-dokumenter/statistikker/ulovligt-arbejde/2019-ulovligtarbejde3kvartal.pdf?la=da&hash=CF4FA56098C602BD088224A51DB10BE6691681A2. Accessed 26 Jan 2021.

Red Cross. (2019). *Trivsel hos børn på udrejsecenter Sjælsmark: En psykologisk undersøgelse*. Copenhagen: Red Cross. https://www.rodekors.dk/sites/rodekors.dk/files/2019-04/2019.03_Sjælsmark_V09_Final_1.pdf. Accessed 8 Nov 2019.

Ritzau. (2016, December 20). DF: Der er direkte sammenhæng mellem flygtninge og terror [DF: There is a direct connection between refugees and terror]. *Fyens.dk*. https://www.fyens.dk/

indland/DF-Der-er-direkte-sammenhaeng-mellem-flygtninge-og-terror/artikel/3108352. Accessed 14 July 2019.

Semmingsen, I. (1972). Emigration from Scandinavia. *Scandinavian Economic History Review, 20*(1), 45–60.

Sen, S., & Pace, M. (2018). The young and exiled: An introduction. In M. Pace & S. Sen (Eds.), *Syrian refugee children in the Middle East and Europe: Integrating the young and exiled* (pp. 1–7). Oxon: Routledge.

Soysal, Y. N. (1994). *Limits of citizenship: Migrants and postnational membership in Europe.* Chicago: Chicago University Press.

Supreme Court of Denmark. (2005, January 21). Fotex Case (no. U.2005.1265.H). *Religare.* http:// religaredatabase.cnrs.fr/spip.php?article116. Accessed 16 July 2019.

Taylor, A. (2015, September 7). Denmark puts ad in Lebanese newspapers: Dear refugees, don't come here. *Washington Post.* https://www.washingtonpost.com/news/worldviews/ wp/2015/09/07/denmark-places-an-advertisement-in-lebanese-newspapers-dear-refugees-dont-come-here/?utm_term=.2592cda67f5d. Accessed 12 July 2019.

The Agency for International Recruitment and Integration. (2017). *Notat vedr. kommunale forskelle i integrationsindsats* [Memo on municipal differences in integration efforts]. Copenhagen: The Agency for International Recruitment and Integration.

The Economist. (2015, February 17). *Denmark's "failed" multiculturalism.* https://www.economist.com/the-economist-explains/2015/02/17/denmarks-failed-multiculturalism. Accessed 14 July 2019.

The Guardian. (2018, May 31). *Denmark passes law banning burqa and niqab.* https://www.theguardian.com/world/2018/may/31/denmark-passes-law-banning-burqa-and-niqab. Accessed 8 Nov 2019.

The Local. (2015, March 9). *Denmark's refugee integration has "failed".* https://www.thelocal. dk/20150309/denmarks-refugee-integration-efforts-have-failed. Accessed 12 July 2019.

The Local. (2019, April 5). *Over half of children at Danish refugee centre have symptoms of mental health problems: Red Cross.* https://www.thelocal.dk/20190405/over-half-of-children-at-danish-refugee-expulsion-centre-have-symptoms-of-mental-health-problems-red-cross. Accessed 12 July 2019.

The Ministry of Employment. (2018). The Danish Labour Market. *The Ministry of Employment.* https://bm.dk/the-ministry-of-employment/the-danish-labour-market/. Accessed 14 July 2019.

The Ministry of Finance. (2017). *Økonomisk analyse: Indvandreres nettobidrag til de offentlige finanser* [Economic analysis: Immigrants' net contribution to public finances]. https://www. fm.dk/oekonomi-og-tal/oekonomisk-analyse/2017/indvandreres-nettobidrag-til-offentlige-finanser. Accessed 14 July 2019.

The Ministry of Immigration and Integration. (2016). International migration – Denmark. In *Report to OECD.* Copenhagen: The Ministry of Immigration and Integration.

The Ministry of Immigration and Integration. (2018, July 4). Integrationsprogrammet [The Integration Programme]. *The Ministry of Immigration and Integration.* http://uim.dk/arbejd-somrader/Integration/integrationsprogrammet. Accessed 14 July 2019.

The Ministry of Immigration and Integration. (2019, July 8). *Integrationskontrakt og integration-serklæring* [Integration contract and Declaration on integration]. http://uim.dk/arbejdsomrader/ Integration/integrationskontrakt-og-integrationserklaering. Accessed 16 July 2019.

Tranæs, T., & Jensen, B. (2014). *Den illegale indvandring til Europa – og til Danmark. Årsagen, omfang og betydning* [The illegal immigration to Europe – And to Denmark. Causes, extent and importance]. Copenhagen: Rockwool Fondens Forskningsenhed and Gyldendal.

Wenane, C. (2019, June 26). *Mette finally made it: Denmark to get a new Prime Minister.* http:// cphpost.dk/news/mette-made-it-denmark-has-a-new-prime-minister.html.   Accessed   12 July 2019.

Westersø, R. S. (2019, February 21). Nu er paradigmeskiltet vedtaget i Folketinget [The Paradigm Shift has now been adopted by the parliament]. *TV2.* http://nyheder.tv2.dk/politik/2019-02-21-nu-er-paradigmeskiftet-vedtaget-i-folketinget. Accessed 12 July 2019.

Chapter 8
Legal Issues Affecting Labour Market Integration of Migrants in Finland

Ilona Bontenbal and Nathan Lillie

8.1 Introduction

Finland's legal framework for migrant labour market integration aims to facilitate the official and broadly accepted policy goals of actively encouraging and supporting migrants to enter working life on terms similar to those of native born Finns. The integration legal framework sets out the basis for active labour market policies, which have been shown to be effective at reducing migrant unemployment. Despite reducing what would be an even higher unemployment rate, these policies are unable to completely overcome the various structural disadvantages of foreigners on Finnish labour markets. While Finland has a strong framework for labour rights protection in its labour laws and centrally negotiated collective agreements, anti--discrimination protection for migrants and ethnic minorities are weak. The unemployment percentages among foreign born individuals (15.8%) is significantly higher than among native born (8.4%) (OECD data from 2017).

This chapter examines the integration of migrants into the Finnish labour market from a legal perspective, asking the question: how does the Finnish legal framework facilitate and/or hinder the integration of migrants, asylum seekers and refugees into the Finnish labour market? The chapter will describe and analyse the legislative basis for the management of migration and integration, and the central labour market legislation.

The sources of law in Finland are national legislation, international law and European Union law; there is no subnational legislation. Juridical power in Finland is vested in independent courts, which are bound only by the law in force. The independence of the courts is guaranteed by the Constitution. Finland has been ranked, according to the World Economic Forum's Global Competitiveness Index, as the

I. Bontenbal (✉) · N. Lillie
University of Jyväskylä, Jyväskylä, Finland
e-mail: ilona.bontenbal@jyu.fi

© The Author(s) 2021
V. Federico, S. Baglioni (eds.), *Migrants, Refugees and Asylum Seekers'
Integration in European Labour Markets*, IMISCOE Research Series,
https://doi.org/10.1007/978-3-030-67284-3_8

country with most judicial independence in the world (The Global Competitiveness Report 2017–2018: Judicial independence). In practice this means that also regarding migration legislative issues the courts are not subject to improper influence from the other branches of government or from private or partisan interests. Finland also scores highest on the protection of fundamental rights according to the Rule of Law Index (Rule of Law Index 2018) and it is signatory to most international agreements and legal instruments relating to immigration, free movement, human rights and non-discrimination (Nykänen et al. 2012, 24). Finland has ratified all the fundamental conventions of the International Labour Organization, as well as all of the governance conventions (International Labour Organization 2018). In international comparison, there is broad public and political support for complying with international human rights norms and legal obligations. Although these norms have been questioned by the right wing populist True Finns party, whose power has increased in recent years, there have been only minor actual changes to the law. Under the conservative coalition government that was voted out in May 2019, there was an apparent tightening of *interpretation* of migration rules, which disadvantaged migrants, refugees and asylum seekers (hereinafter MRAs).

Most of Finland's migration law is newly developed. The percentage of the Finnish population which is of foreign origin has historically been small, and it continues to be quite minor compared to many other European countries. Up to until the 1980s, there were more people migrating out of Finland than migrating to Finland. A few hundred refugees from Chile and Vietnam migrated to Finland during the 1970s and in the beginning of the 1980s (Kyhä 2011, 21). The first official refugee quota was set in 1988 (Saukkonen 2013, 87). During the 1990s, the number of asylum seekers grew due to international conflicts. Finland received asylum seekers mainly from Somalia and Yugoslavia and between 1990–1994 Finland granted asylum to about 5000 individuals (Sarvimäki 2017, 3). By the end of the 1990s, c. 18,000 refugees and their family members were living in Finland (Sarvimäki 2017, 3). Whereas before the 1990s, almost half of the immigrants to Finland had been from Western countries, now greater numbers of migrants came from countries in the former Soviet Union and Asia. In 1990, c. 1.3% of the population of Finland was born abroad. Due to a steady rise in migration flows, the percentage had grown to 7.02% in 2018. (Statistics Finland – Population by country of origin 2019.) In the beginning of the twenty-first century, Finland took refugees from, among other places, Afghanistan and Iraq (Martikainen et al. 2013, 37). The number of asylum applications to Finland grew significantly and suddenly in 2015. Since 2010 asylum application numbers had been around 3200–4000 a year but in 2015 the number suddenly grew to 32,476 applications. Most applications were made by individuals of Iraqi, Albanian, Somali and Afghan nationality. The following year the number dropped to 5651 applications. (Migri – Yearly statistics by nationality; Migri – Asylum Applications 2019.)

As Fig. 8.1 illustrates, immigration flows in Finland, since the 1990s, have been growing steadily, whereas emigration flows have remained stable. In the end of 2018, there were 257,572 individuals with a foreign nationality living in Finland, which is 4.67% of the entire population (Statistics Finland – Number of individuals

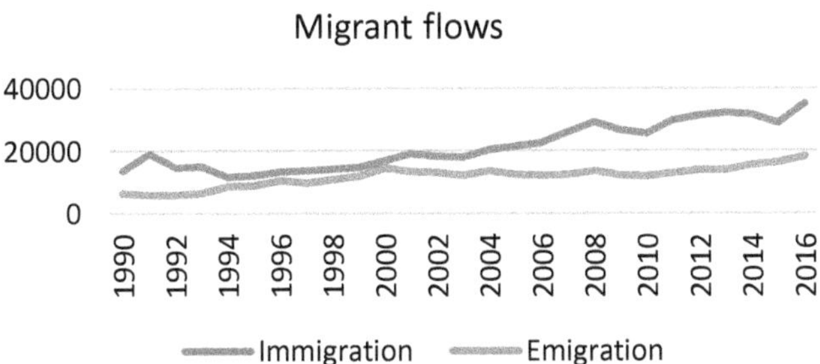

Fig. 8.1 Data from statistics Finland – Emigration and immigration flows

with foreign background 2019). The largest migrant groups by country of origin are Russians and individuals from the former Soviet Union (14,868 + 57,144), Estonians (46,206), Swedes (32,654), Iraqis (17,889), and Somalians (11,797) (Statistics Finland, 2018 – Population by country of origin 2018). The most common reason to apply for a first residence permit was on family grounds (43.6%), after which came work (31.4%), studies (22.9%) and other grounds (2%). (Migri – Statistics on Residence Permits 2018.)

8.2 Finnish Legislation on Migration

We first look at the legislative basis for the management of migration and integration in Finland, the Aliens act and the Act on the Promotion of Immigrant Integration. These two acts set out the framework for determining who can stay in Finland, on which grounds and how integration is managed. These acts fundamentally affect the opportunities that MRAs have for employment in Finland.

Migration and integration issues have in Finland been dealt with cross administratively e.g. by the Ministry of the Interior, the Ministry of Education and Culture, Ministry of Social Affairs and Health and the Ministry of Economic Affairs and Employment (Saukkonen 2013, 93). For example, the Ministry of Education and Culture is responsible for the education of migrants whereas the Ministry of Social Affairs and Health is responsible for the health care of migrants. The Act on Administration (FINLEX 434/2003) regulates the administrative procedures carried out by the authorities dealing with immigration. General legislation on administrative procedures and administrative juridical procedures apply in immigration procedures. (Nykänen et al. 2012, 21).

In Finland, the Ministry of the Interior is responsible for preparing legislation related to immigration and for steering immigration management. The Ministry is also responsible for the Finnish Immigration Service. The Ministry states its aim is *"to develop a more forward-looking migration policy and managed migration, and to make Finland a safe and open country, where everyone can find a role to play"*. (Ministry of the Interior – Migration 2018.) In 2007–2010, the Ministry of the

Interior was also in charge of coordinating the integration process in Finland. Since 2012, the main responsibility for integration has however been at the Ministry of Economic affairs and Employment. Other migration issues have remained at the Ministry of the Interior. In 2013, the Ministry published the first overall integration report of Finland (Saukkonen 2013, 94; Saukkonen 2017, 39–40.) The Finnish Immigration service has the main responsibility for carrying out decisions on immigration related issues. The office was established in 1995 (Aer 2016, 40).

In Finland, the basis for legislation related to immigration is found in the Aliens Act (FINLEX 301/2004) which constitutes the backbone of the regulation of immigration. The Aliens act contains rules on entry and stay in Finland, removal from Finland in relation to different forms of immigration, rights and obligations of foreigners in Finland, and procedures in matters of immigration. (Nykänen et al. 2012, 21.) The first Aliens act came into force in 1984. Before this, issues regarding foreigners were ordained by decrees, the last of which was given in 1958 (Aer 2016, 16). The law set in 1984 was soon found outdated and it was reformed in 1991, 1999 and 2004 (Makkonen and Koskenniemi 2013, 71; Aer 2016, 17) and 2016 (FINLEX 646/2016). During the preparations for the 2004 reform, the public discussion had started to shift towards labour migration (Aer 2016, 19). Finland joined the EU in 1995 and the Schengen agreement was introduced in 2001 (Makkonen and Koskenniemi 2013, 69). All Finnish migration policies are in accordance with the *The Common Basic Principles for Immigrant Integration Policy* set by the European Union regarding integration in 2004 (Saukkonen 2017, 17).

In 1997, the government's first migration- and refugee programme was published (Kyhä 2011, 16; FINLEX 493/1999). A general aim was set, that migrants should be effectively and flexibly integrated into Finnish society and into the labour market (Saukkonen 2017, 16). Before this, there was no official migration policy, in the sense of articulating goals and implementing government measures to achieve them (Kyhä 2011, 22). The framework for migrant integration is set out in the integration law. The first law on migrant integration came into force on May 1st 1999 (Saukkonen 2013, 92; VATT-Research Group 2014, 42; Makkonen and Koskenniemi 2013, 78). The Finnish Integration Act is similar to integration programmes introduced in other countries, such as the Temporary Assistance for Needy Families (TANF) in the US, the New Deal in the UK and the welfare-to-work policies adopted in Denmark and the Netherlands (Hämäläinen and Sarvimäki 2008, 3). The focus of the integration law in Finland has been on humanitarian migration and on the labour market integration of unemployed migrants (Makkonen and Koskenniemi 2013, 78). When the act was introduced, it brought along various reforms:

- The responsibility for supporting immigrant integration was placed with the central administration and municipalities, who were given the responsibility for coordinating existing resources at the local level (Hämäläinen and Sarvimäki 2008, 4; FINLEX 493/1999.) This also obliged all municipalities to prepare their own integration programmes and follow their execution and impact (Saukkonen 2013, 94; FINLEX 493/1999).

- The law set a new focus on the preparation of individualized integration plans. The content of these integration plans depends on the personal characteristics of the immigrant. The integration plans can include, for example, measures for acquiring language skills, career counselling, preparatory and/or vocational training, rehabilitation and/or work practice, depending on the specific needs of the migrant. The labour administration (TE-office) is responsible for preparing and implementing the integration plans of 18–64-year-old (working age) migrants, whereas municipalities take care of other age groups. (Hämäläinen and Sarvimäki 2008, 4; FINLEX 493/1999.)
- In addition, the communication between caseworkers and immigrants and the importance of training courses specifically designed for immigrants, such as language courses, increased as a result of the reform. Moreover, the importance of learning one of the local languages (Finnish or Swedish) was emphasised. Resulting from these reforms, the time spent in courses specifically designed for migrants and in language courses increased, whereas time spent in traditional activation labour-market programmes, such as job-seeking courses decreased. (Sarvimäki and Hämäläinen 2016, 480, 482–483, 498; VATT-Research Group 2014, 46; FINLEX 493/1999.)
- As part of the integration act, welfare benefits were made conditional on participation in activation measures. Refusal to participate or to follow the integration plan was made sanctionable by a reduction or withdrawal of integration benefits. (Hämäläinen and Sarvimäki 2008, 2, 4; FINLEX 493/1999.)

Only those migrants who had arrived after May 1st. 1997, and who were registered as unemployed job seekers or living in a household that received social assistance were affected by the new policies in the 1999 law (Hämäläinen and Sarvimäki 2008, 2, 4). Neither rules on the use of sanctions nor funding systems changed during this reform (Sarvimäki and Hämäläinen 2016, 483). The changes that were made in 1999 had a positive and significant effect on the integration of MRAs into the labour market. The integration plans increased participation and decreased the use of social benefits. (Hämäläinen and Sarvimäki 2008, 2, 9.) Researchers attribute the improvement to the more efficient use of existing resources, since the reform did not bring any new funds for active labour market policies (Sarvimäki and Hämäläinen 2016, 480).

The law on integration was changed several times to improve it. In 2006, migrants were also given the right to extend their integration plan by up to 2 years. In addition, the schedule for making the first integration plan was expedited so that integration plans are made sooner after arrival in Finland. (VATT-Research Group 2014, 46.)

The law on the integration of immigrants and reception of asylum seekers was reformed in 2010 and the new law (1386/2010) came into force the following year (Saukkonen 2016). During this reform, the main content of the law remained the same (Saukkonen 2013, 95; Saukkonen 2017, 16). However, the focus of the law shifted somewhat towards work and family-based migration. Due to this, more people became entitled to integration services. (Makkonen and Koskenniemi 2013, 78–79.) Before only those that were unemployed jobseekers and living on income support were included into the integration policies, whereas since 2011 all migrants were included (Eronen et al. 2014, 26). Integration services were made available to all that need them, regardless of which category of migrant the individual belonged to (Saukkonen 2013, 95). According to the renewed law, all individuals migrating to Finland have to be informed about their rights in society and in the labour market (FINLEX 1386/2010 7§).

According to Saukkonen (2013), the problem of Finnish integration has been in how to get municipalities to implement the official state policies set by the central government. This is because the controlling instruments of the government and the financial resources have been limited. (Saukkonen 2013, 94.) The integration laws in Finland however require municipalities to form local integration programmes, to be able to receive state funding to cover some of the costs related to accepting refugees (FINLEX 1386/2010 32 § & 33 §).

At the moment, the migrant integration law is being revised to meet the needs of the ongoing health, social services and regional government reform in Finland. In the future, the focus areas of the law will be on structuring the education paths and entering of MRAs into the labour market, and on family orientated integration. Special attention will also be given to the different needs of various migrant groups. Municipalities will still have the main responsibility for managing integration services. (Ministry of Economic Affairs and Employment –Briefing 5.5.2017.)

8.3   Legislation on International Protection

The management of asylum seekers has a different legislative basis than that for migrants arriving for other reasons. The right to international protection is set out in the Alien act (2004/301 87 §). An asylum seeker may enter the country even if she/he is not able to present travel documents or permission for entry, since the application for asylum is in itself a sufficient reason for entry (Nykänen 2012, 45, 58; FINLEX 2004/301 35 §). In 2011, a law on *the reception of individuals in need on international protection and on the recognition and helping of victims of human trafficking* was introduced (FINLEX 746/2011). The aim of the law is to secure protection and income for those seeking international protection, for those in need of temporary protection and to victims of human trafficking. (Martikainen et al. 2013, 75.)

A residence permit based on a successful asylum application is granted for 4 years. After this the individual has to apply for an extended residence permit. (Migri – Asylum 2018; FINLEX 2004/301.) Asylum can only be applied for in Finland, and not for example at Finnish embassies in other countries or through a letter or email. Asylum applications always need to be left personally with the police or border control. (Migri – Asylum in Finland 2018; FINLEX 2004/301 95 §.) Once the asylum application has been left, the individual is referred to a refugee centre where he/she can live and wait for the asylum interview. The refugee centres take care of needed subsistence for living and offer accommodation and guidance regarding getting legal aid. The centres also organize the necessary social and health care services as well as work and study activities and if the needed interpreter services. (Kotouttaminen.fi – Vastaanottokeskukset 2018.) The applicant can also find accommodation her/himself, for example with family or friends (FINLEX 746/2011 18 §).

The Finnish Immigration Service conducts the asylum investigation and interview. The purpose of this investigation is to establish the identity and travel route of the applicant, as well as the reason for applying for asylum and the evidence to substantiate the reason. In 2016 the asylum application process took on average 8 months (Ministry of the Interior, Usein kysytyt kysymykset turvapaikanhakijoista 2018). Once asylum is granted, the person will receive a residence permit card (Migri – Information for asylum seekers 2018). If the decision on the application is negative, the applicant can appeal the decision to the Administrative Court and if needed to the Supreme Administrative Court (Pakolaisneuvonta 2018). Once the procedure is over, the applicants who are granted asylum in Finland are placed in municipalities that have made arrangements to receive refugees (FINLEX 2010/1386, chapter 5). The local level coordination regarding receiving refugees is done by the Centres for Economic Development, Transport and the Environment (ELY Centres), who negotiate with the municipalities of their area about municipality places for refugees, living arrangements and needed services (Kotouttaminen. fi – Pakolaisten kuntaan osoittaminen 2018). Although there is effort to settle MRAs around the country, so they are not concentrated in certain areas, most MRAs still eventually end up living in growth centres (Rasinkangas 2013, 134–135). There are no legal restrictions on this, since all people in Finland are free to choose where they reside (FINLEX 731/1999 9 §). Those individuals who are not allowed to stay, can apply for assisted voluntary return (Migri – Information for asylum seekers 2018; FINLEX 2010/1386 85 §).

Quota refugees are individuals designated by UNHCR as being in need of international protection. The decision about the number of quota refugees to accept is made annually by the Parliament in connection with the approval of the state budget. The proposal is made by the Ministry of the Interior together with the Ministry of Foreign Affairs and the Ministry of Economic Affairs and Employment (FINLEX 2004/301 91 §).The UNHCR presents a group of people from which Finnish authorities choose the quota refugees that can come to Finland. The selection is done by interviewing. (Ministry of the Interior – Quota refugees 2018.) Yearly 100 places from the quota are reserved for acute cases and for those that the UNHCR has estimated to be in need of urgent resettlement. These emergency cases are chosen directly based on UNHCR documents. (Migri – Quota refugees 2018.) Since 2011, 750 quota refugees have been accepted to Finland annually. In 2014 and in 2015, the quota was however increased to 1050 refugees a year due to the situation in Syria. (Migri – Quota refugees 2018.) Quota refugees are granted residence permits and other rights on the same basis as refugees recognized in the asylum procedure (Nykänen et al. 2012, 102). Quota refugees are placed directly into municipalities, which take care of their reception and integration (Pakolaisten vastaanotto – Tietopaketti kunnille 2016).

The number of asylum applications filed in Finland greatly increased in 2014–2015, causing the Finnish government to take several measures. The first was to establish new reception centers and expand the Immigration Service's staff. (Sarvimäki 2017, 7.) Regulations for establishing reception centers are set out in *the Act on the Reception of Individuals in Need of International Protection and on the Recognition and Helping of Victims of Human Trafficking* (FINLEX 746/2011 9 § & 10 §). The government also responded to the increase in migration by publishing an action plan *"to stop uncontrolled migration"* (Finnish Government 2015). The idea was to try to make Finland a less attractive destination by changing various policies considered as *"pull factors"*. The government, for example, tightened the requirements for family reunification and reduced social benefits (Sarvimäki 2017, 7; FINLEX HE 43/2016.) Due to these changes in policy, it has among other things become more difficult for many MRAs to bring their families to Finland. One important change made in 2016 was that individuals who have been granted subsidiary protection or refugee status must show sufficient income to cover each family member's living expenses, in order to be eligible to bring their family members. The purpose of the reform was to make sure that the Finnish society does not have to pay for foreigners residing in Finland but that instead the expenses would be taken care of by the residing person or his/her family. (FINLEX HE 43/2016.) Fees were also introduced for family reunification applications in 2016 by a decision by the Ministry of the Interior (FINLEX 872/2017).

Besides making Finland seem less attractive, the government also revised integration policies. On this note, an action plan was published by the government in May 2016 (Finnish Government 2016). The action plan included measures such as improving recognition of education certificates obtained abroad, the integration of language studies into other studies and the streamlining of the starting phase of integration services. (Sarvimäki 2017, 7.)

An empirical study by *the Institute for Human Rights at Åbo Akademi University* and *the Non-Discrimination Ombudsman* on official decisions on international protection in Finland in 2015–2017, found the decisions made by the Finnish Immigration Service on international protection had become stricter during that period. The research focused on decisions made on international protection regarding 13–34-year-old Iraqi nationals. The research report notes that the tightening of decision cannot be explained by changes in the migration law but rather by stricter decision made by the Finnish Migration Service. (Saarikkomäki et al. 2018.) The tightening of decision made about asylum was much discussed in the media, and the expressed opinions of people working with migration issues seem are similar. The Migration Institute however, maintains that there has been no weakening of legal protection for migrants, in this case Iraqi migrants, or that asylum decisions are affected by political control or pressure (Interview by the chief director of the Migration Institute Jaana Vuori for the newspaper Etelä-Suomen sanomat 22.3.2018). Since the project undertaken by the Åbo Akademi and partners was only a pilot research, this issue is something that should be looked at more specifically and comprehensively. The effect of political pressure on administrative decision makings in the asylum process is something that has been discussed increasingly since the recent increase in asylum applications, not just in Finland but in other European countries as well.

8.4 Right to Stay, Residence Permits and Citizenship

According to the constitution, only Finnish nationals have the undisputed right to reside in Finland and the right of foreigners to stay in Finland is governed by legislation (Aer 2016, 24; FINLEX 2004/301). Finnish citizens and foreigners legally resident in Finland have the right to freely move within the country and to choose their place of residence. Everyone has the right to leave the country. (9 §.) When a foreigner enters Finland, he/she must have the required travel documents. What constitutes a valid travel document depends on the citizenship of the person. (Nykänen et al. 2012, 36.) The visa regulations in Finland have their background in common Schengen-area norms (Nykänen et al. 2012, 39). Visas are issued for a maximum of 90 days and they do not give the right to work in Finland (Juvonen 2013, 17). If foreigners entering the country intend to stay for longer than 90 days, they need a permit of residence. In general, the residence permit must be applied for in a country where the foreigner resides lawfully before entering Finland (Nykänen et al. 2012, 59; FINLEX 2004/301 60 §). This however is not imperative, and the first residence permit can also be applied for in Finland (FINLEX 2004/301 60 §). A residence permit needs to be applied for personally and it cannot be done by another person, such as a spouse or employer. EU-citizens as well as citizens from Iceland, Norway or Liechtenstein do not need a residence permit but only need to register their residence. (Migri – Residence permit 2018.)

The residence permit can either be temporary or permanent (FINLEX 2004/301 33 §). The first residence permit is always for a fixed-term, which is generally 1 year (Nykänen et al. 2012, 55; FINLEX 2004/301 53 §). The issuance of a residence permit must always be justified on particular grounds, such as, for example, working or studying in Finland or for international protection. Because of this, the applicants must meet the requirements for the form of permit she/he is applying for. In general, the family members of person (defined as nuclear family) who reside in Finland by virtue of a residence permit may be issued a residence permit on the basis of family ties. In this case the family must have sufficient income to cover each family member's living expenses. (Nykänen et al. 2012, 56–57, 63, 67; FINLEX 2004/301 39 §). Those individuals that have lived in Finland continuously for 4 years with a continuous residence permit may get a permanent residence permit (Migri – permanent residence permit 2018; FINLEX 2004/301 56 §). If an EU citizen resides continuously in Finland for 5 years, they receive the right to permanently stay in Finland (Makkonen and Koskenniemi 2013, 73–74; FINLEX 2004/301 161 g §). Marriage does not give an automatic right to a residence permit (Säävälä 2013, 108). The issuance of a residence permit opens up access to the Finnish social security system, since the right to social security is based on permanent residence (Aer 2016, 75; FINLEX 1993/1573). In general, the legal position of long-term residents in Finland is fairly strong. A continuous fixed-term residence permit provides its holder with a stronger legal status, including a wider range of rights and freedoms, than that provided by a temporary fixed-term residence permit. (Nykänen et al. 2012, 55, 71.) A continuous fixed-term residence permit for example provides its holder with a permanent right to work in Finland (FINLEX 2004/301 78 §). Foreigners who reside in Finland have the right to move freely in the country and to choose their place of residence (Nykänen et al. 2012, 63; FINLEX 731/1999 9 §).

Access to citizenship is a part of the integration process. The basis of Finnish citizenship is hereditary (ius sanguinis) (Aer 2016, 26; FINLEX 731/1999 5§; FINLEX 359/2003 9 §), but Finnish citizenship can also be acquired after an individual has lived in Finland for a sufficient time. Figure 8.2 illustrates the number of citizenships granted in Finland since 1990. The number has increased significantly since 1990, which can be expected since also the number of total immigration has grown steadily. The sharp increases in granted citizenships in 2004 and 2012 are explained by changes in legislation: since 2004 it became possible to maintain one's previous citizenship and thus become a dual-citizen and in 2012, the required time of living in Finland before being able to become a citizen was dropped from 6 years to 5 years (Statistics Finland – Suomen kansalaisuuden saaneet 2017). Having the host country's citizenship can facilitate integration e.g. by signalling motivation and an intention to stay (OECD 2017, 84). Other requirements are the knowledge of one of the official languages (Finnish or Swedish), integrity, means of support, established identity and fulfilled payment obligations. (FINLEX 359/2003 13 §) The application cost is c. 350–440 euro. Finland accepts multiple citizenship. (Migri–Finnish citizenship 2018; Migri – Citizenship application 2018; FINLEX 2003/359.)

Grounds for removal from Finland are laid down in section 148 of the Alien Act (2004/301 148 §). The main grounds are invalid residence permits, being found guilty of a criminal offence, or being found to be a danger to public safety or Finland's national security. In 2018, 1714 individuals were refused entry into

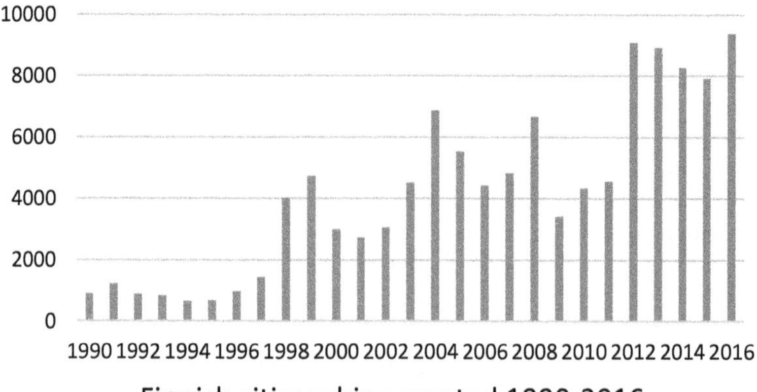

Fig. 8.2 Citizenships granted, 2016. Data from Statistics Finland

Finland and 1447 individuals were deported. Romanians, Iraqis, Russians, Estonians, and Ukrainians were the nationalities most often refused entry. The largest numbers of deportations were persons of Russian, Iraqi, Vietnamese, Somali and Ukrainian nationality. Of all the individuals deported in 2018, c. 88% were deported for unauthorized stay, whereas 12% had been found guilty of a criminal offense. According to the Immigration Service the number of deportations and refusals of entry has remained about the same in recent years. (Migri – Removal 2019.)

8.5 Permits to Work

In Finland, the Ministry of Employment and the Economy is responsible for implementing labour legislation (Ministry of the Employment and the Economy – Labour Legislation 2018). The integration of MRAs into the labour market is important considering both their individual life and the public economy of the state. By working migrants earn money to take care of themselves, and participate in funding public services through paying taxes. Employment also provides migrants with networks, social contacts and information about how the society functions. (Saukkonen 2017, 18.)

The Finnish constitution provides that everyone has the right to earn his or her livelihood by employment in the occupation or commercial activity of his or her choice. Legislation also asserts that the public authorities are responsible for labour protection, for promoting employment and for working towards guaranteeing everyone the right to work. Provisions regarding the right to receive training that promotes employability are laid down by an Act. No one shall be dismissed from employment without a lawful reason. (18 §.) Those who cannot obtain the means necessary for a dignified life have the right to receive indispensable subsistence and care. This applies if there is no subsistence from anywhere else and in practice this indispensable subsistence is channelled through income support policies. (19 § 1 mom.)

Regulation for work-based migration is set in migration law. To work in Finland, foreign citizens must first establish they have the right to work in Finland, and the employer has the responsibility to check this (2004/301 86 a §). The right to work depends on how long the individual intents to stay, what kind of work he/she is coming to perform and what country citizenship he/she has. Individuals who want to move to Finland from the European Union or the European Economic Area (EEA) are not required to apply for a permit to work (Occupational Safety and Health Administration – Foreign Employee 2018; FINLEX 2004/301 chapter 5). There are also other excepted groups such as seasonal workers and certain defined professions such as researchers, interpreters, professionals, athletes, and so on. (FINLEX 2004/301 79 §). In general, third country nationals cannot work in Finland without a valid permit to work (Aer 2016, 179).

Third Country Nationals, in general, need a residence permit, which allows them to work. Migrants who are coming specifically to work must apply for specific residence permit applications based on the type of work they plan to do. Migrants coming for dependant employment can apply for a *residence permit for an employed persons* and self-employed persons can apply for *a residence permit for self-employed persons* (FINLEX 2004/301 11 §). To be able to apply for *a residence permit for an employed person*, the migrant must comply with certain income requirements, i.e. have a confirmed job waiting and the salary must be sufficient to support the migrant for the entire time that the residence permit is valid (Migri – Working in Finland 2018). The minimum salary from gainful employment is reviewed annually. The salary of a full-time employee must at least correspond to the salary specified in the collective agreement that applies to the employment relationship. For specialists and EU Blue Card holders salary requirements are stricter. Specialists must have a salary of at least approximately 3000 euro per month and the salary of a Blue Card Holder must be at least 4732 euro per month in 2019. (Migri – Income requirement 2019.)

To get a *residence permit for a self-employed person* the migrant must register his or her business with the Trade Register, and must demonstrate having a secure means of support while in Finland. Moreover, the migrant in question must actually work in the business enterprise, and this work must be done in Finland. In practice this means that ownership in a company is not sufficient grounds for issuance of a residence permit. (Migri–EnterFinland 2018.) Even though the workers' residence permits are in principle the main category issued for employment in Finland, other types of residence permits also permit the migrant to work (Nykänen et al. 2012, 147). The adequacy of the work contract and the employer's ability to function as an employer will be checked, as well as the migrant's qualifications and his/her possibilities to earn an adequate livelihood (Kyhä 2011, 27). Families of those that have been granted a residence permit for work may usually apply for a residence permit on the basis of family ties (Migri – Working in Finland 2018).

For residence permits based on work for third country nationals, the Employment and Economic Development Offices (TE Offices) will estimate whether there is a labour market need for the type of job the migrant is filling (the "availability test") (The Central Organisation of Finnish Trade Unions, 2017; FINLEX 1218/2013 73 §). This availability test is made so that EU and European Economic Area (EEA) citizens have priority to get employed (Nykänen et al. 2012, 140). Some have noted that the availability policy tends to restrict the possibilities that enterprises have for hiring workers and slows down the process of finding suitable employers (Mäkelä 2019). Moreover, in Finland the availability consideration clause is interpreted rather strictly and it can actually be quite difficult to determine which sectors need labour and which do not (Punto 2018). The availability test is done only for manual labour jobs such as cleaning personnel, chefs, car drivers or construction workers. It does not apply to experts or professionals who receive their residence permits straight from the Finnish Immigration Service without having to go through this process. An estimation of the workforce need always uses a case-by-case approach. Individuals wanting to come from outside of EU or EEA will only receive a permit to work if it is estimated that there is a labour shortage in their field. (The Central Organisation of Finnish Trade Unions 2017.) The application of the availability test has been controversial. Since 1.6.2019 those migrant employees who have been working in Finland for at least 1 year are no longer subject to the availability test, if they want to change occupation while in Finland (Finnish Government 2019.) This change in legislation is expected to make it easier for professional workforce to change working places and it will thus improve the position of migrant workers already living in Finland. A need for this has been building up since in some sectors there are shortage of labour force. In practice, the change is expected to affect only a very limited number, only a few dozen, of migrant employees already working in Finland annually. (Ministry of Economic Affairs and Employment 2019.)

The Employment and Economic Development Offices (TE-offices) are in practice responsible for the integration of migrants into the labour market at the local level. If found useful, an initial mapping is done with individual migrants who are not part of the labour force, or who register as job seekers. Based on the initial mapping an individual integration plan is made (FINLEX 2010/1386 10 §). The integration plan is not compulsory, neither for employed nor unemployed migrants (FINLEX 2010/1386 11 §). The integration plan can include e.g. language training, internships, education, courses preparing for working life, and career counselling. (Eronen et al. 2014, 25.)

In many OECD countries, the time during asylum procedures is actively used to facilitate integration by for example offering applicants language training, skills assessment and labour market preparation (OECD 2017, 87). An asylum seeker can work in Finland 3 months after arrival if her/his travel documents are in order. This means that asylum seekers must present a valid and authenticated passport or other travel document to the authorities upon arrival. Those asylum seekers that do not have the needed travel documents can start working after 5 months has passed in Finland. (FINLEX 2004/301 79 §.) An employed asylum seeker can also apply for a residence permit based on work during the same time that the asylum application is being processed. (Ministry of the Interior – FAQ asylum seekers and employment 2018.) Asylum seekers may also take part in comprehensive education in schools and after this they may apply and accept a study place if they meet the general selection criteria (Opintopolku.fi 2018). Attending comprehensive education is not compulsory for adults. In Finland, all school-age children resident in Finland must participate in compulsory education (FINLEX 1998/628).

8.6 Regulations Regarding Working in Finland

The Finnish labour market is largely regulated by collective bargaining agreements, which are extended to all workers and employers over most economic sectors, and which set e.g. salary levels and working hours. The most important laws on labour, for individuals in an employment relationship in Finland, are the *Employment Contracts Act* (FINLEX 55/2001), *Working Hours Act* (FINLEX 605/1996) and the *Annual Holidays Act* (FINLEX 162/2005). The most central laws regarding collective labour rights on the other hand are the *Collective Agreement Act* (FINLEX

436/1946) and the *Act on Co-operation within Undertakings* (FINLEX 334/2007). The Finnish law on employment, at least in regards to its minimum requirements, applies to all work done in Finland regardless of what the nationality of the employee is. (Ministry of the Employment and the Economy – Report 2015, 5–6.) When the work is done in Finland the same laws and labour agreements apply to both Finnish and foreign employees (Finnish Institute of Occupational Health 2014, 17).

In Finland, employers' and labour organisations have a political role, particularly in issues concerning work and social security, even though they are not among the classical Parliamentary actors (Laine 2015). Trade unions are a visible presence in most work places, and many are active in recruiting and representing migrant-specific interests (Alho 2015a). About 70% of employees in Finland belong to a trade union and 95% of employees work under a collective labour agreement negotiated by a labour union (The Finnish Confederation of Professionals 2018). The right to join a union is protected legislatively (FINLEX 2001/55, Chapter 13 1 §) and employers are forbidden from discriminating against employers on the basis of union membership (FINLEX 1325/2014 8 §). In the event of unemployment, union membership entitles a worker to access that unions' unemployment insurance fund (Finnish Institute of Occupational Health 2014, 22). This means that union members receive much higher income support than non-members, if they become unemployed. The so called "Ghent system" is thus in place, in which unions have responsibility for managing unemployment insurance schemes, which are also supplemented by tax subsidies (Andersen et al. 2007, 106). There are three main central trade union confederations. These are the SAK (the Central Organisation of Finnish Trade Unions), STTK (the Finnish Confederation of Professionals) and Akava (the Confederation of Unions for Professional and Managerial Staff in Finland) (The Infopankki website –Trade Unions 2018). There is no exact information about the union membership rate of migrants in Finland. Alho (2015a) has estimated that the number of migrant members in Finnish labour unions grew 71–78% between 2006 and 2011 (Alho 2015b, pp. 13.). Furthermore, Alho estimates that for example the unionization density of migrant construction workers is somewhere between 12–14%, which is far lower than the national average in Finland (Alho 2013, pp. 144).

There are several mandatory regulations in the labour legislation that cannot be breached by a local contract, especially not in such a way that it would be harmful to the employee. *The Collective Agreement Act* (FINLEX 436/1946) regulates the rights of employers, employer associations and labour unions to negotiate binding collective agreements on behalf of all employers and workers in a sector, respectively. Collective agreements establish working time, payment for work, overtime and sickness pay, holidays, and other terms of employment (Finnish Institute of Occupational Health 2014, 22). If there is a universal collective agreement, all employers must for example comply with the minimum standards set out in that collective labour agreements. (Ministry of the Employment and the Economy–Report, 2015, 5; FINLEX 436/1946.) Each sector follows its own collective agreement and those establishments that do not have their own agreement must follow the nationally applicable and binding agreements of that sector (Ministry of the

Employment and the Economy – Report 2015, 7). There is a government board which declares collective agreements universally binding when the unions are deemed sufficiently representative of workers in that the sector (Ministry of the Employment and the Economy – Report 2015, 7–8.) According to this system about 95% of the workforce becomes covered by the collective agreements and also those individuals that do not belong to labour unions are protected (Ristikari 2012, pp. 22, 34). This also means that the collective agreements govern the working conditions of foreign workers in a similar way than those of Finnish workers. The tripartite collective bargaining system which leads to the collective agreements has in Finland been as especially important tool for labour unions (Alho 2015a, pp. 14). The tripartite decision making system is a typical feature of Nordic labour markets, and creates a tendency toward uniform pay increases within industries. Instead of negotiating wage adjustments separately in each firm, adjustments are negotiated collectively at the sectoral level. This means that all members of a particular union receive the same wage increase, in relative terms. (Andersen et al. 2007, 105, 120.)

Anti-Discrimination legislation may have an effect on the labour market position of MRAs, by establishing their nationality or ethnicity should not be considering in recruitment or deciding salaries. In practise, equality on the labour market means that only those kinds of qualities that are meaningful for conducting the work tasks should be demanded of job applicants. (Forsander 2013, 236, 238.) As with immigration law generally, norms prohibiting discrimination against migrants are a recent development in Finland.

There are now a number of laws against discrimination against MRAs in work. The law (FINLEX 1325/2014; FINLEX 2001/55 2 §) demands that employers must treat their employees equally, unless there is a reason not to do so. Reasons not to do so include, inter alia, different positions or different tasks (Ministry of the Employment and the Economy –Report, 2015, 7). Also, positive discrimination can however be a reason for treating employees differently (Ministry of the Employment and the Economy – Report 2015, 17). *The Non-Discrimination Act* (FINLEX 1325/2014), *the Act on Equality between Women and Men* (FINLEX 1329/2014) and *the Employment Contracts Act* (FINLEX 55/2001) together regulate the equality and parity of employees (Ministry of Economic Affairs and Employment – Työsopimuslaki 2017, 13). *The Non-Discrimination Act* (FINLEX 1325/2014), prohibits discrimination on the basis of age, ethnic or national origin, nationality, language, religion, conviction, opinions, health, disability, sexual orientation or any other personal quality. *The Act on Equality between Women and Men* (FINLEX 1329/2014) on the other hand prohibits discrimination on the basis of sex. According to the law (1325/2014, Chapter 2, 7 §) all employers must promote equality between women and men in work life and ensure that both sexes have the same opportunities for career progression. (Finnish Institute of Occupational Health 2014, 50.) The law also includes a discrimination prohibition and it requires that public officers must advance equality in all their actions (FINLEX 1325/2014, Chapter 2, 5 §). Discrimination has also been criminalized in the criminal law (FINLEX 39/1889). Still, enforcement seems to be poor, since discrimination is a structural feature of the Finnish labour market (Heikillä 2005). Structural factors that exclude MRAs from the labour market include the high minimum wage (de facto) and other labour costs, which demand high productivity. Employment possibilities for workers who lack the required human capital have been decreasing and in fact hardly any low paying jobs remain for unskilled or semiskilled workers in industry. The high cost of labour also hinders the expansion of the low-productivity, labour-intensive service sector. (Forsander 2004.) Moreover, MRAs are also disadvantaged as jobseekers. Liebkind et al. (2016) found that foreign applicants from a low-status ethnic minority groups, such as Polish, had significantly lower chances of being selected for a vacant position when paired with a majority Finnish applicant, or with an applicant from a high-status ethnic minority, such as Australian (Liebkind et al. 2016, pp. 417). Moreover, another study found that individuals with a foreign surname are significantly less often selected for job interviews compared to individuals with a Finnish surname (Ahmad 2019). According to results from the Eurobarometer 2015, 67% of respondents in Finland estimated that discrimination based on ethnic background is common and 66% estimated that skin-color and ethnic background may affect employment decisions. (Eurobarometer – Finland 2015).

Enforcing compliance with the labour legislation is mostly the responsibility of The Occupational Safety and Health (OSH) authorities. The Occupational Safety and Health are part of OSH Divisions of the Regional State Administrative Agencies, which come under the Ministry of Social Affairs and Health. (Ministry of the Employment and the Economy – Labour Legislation 2018.) Employers who violate the provisions of the Alien Act relating to employment can receive administrative or criminal sanctions (Nykänen et al. 2012, 151). Employers have the responsibility to check (2004/301 86 a §) that foreign employees are eligible to work. If the employer does not comply with the responsibility to check, on purpose or due to negligence, he or she may be sanctioned. In some severe cases, a foreigner working in Finland without the right to gainful employment may be fined for violation of the Aliens Act. (Nykänen et al. 2012, 153.) This however, has not been common and more often the employee faces sanctions.

8.7   Conclusions

Overall, Finnish legislation on immigration can be characterized by a rather late awakening to the requirements of democratic principles and human right concerns. It reflects modern standards and a pragmatic approach to the needs of society. (Nykänen et al. 2012, 20.) Finland is a strongly constitutional state that has law-abiding, independent and educated public officials. Issues regarding MRAs and migrant administration are discussed openly and critically. Open discussion also functions as an instrument of control since officials know that they not only must address the immediate issue, but also have to answer to civil society at large. (Pirjatanniemi 2018)

The two central acts which govern migration and integration issues in Finland are the *Aliens Act* (FINLEX 301/2004) and the *Act on the Promotion of Immigrant*

Integration (FINLEX 1386/2010). Regarding asylum procedures the *Act on the reception of individuals in need on international protection and on the recognition and helping of victims of human trafficking* (FINLEX 746/2011) is most central. In practise, these acts define e.g. who can enter the country and on which grounds, who is permitted to stay in Finland on which grounds and what kind of integration measures are taken. The legislation also defines who is responsible for which part of migration management.

The Aliens act functions as the backbone of the general regulation of immigration into Finland and the Act on the Promotion of Immigrant Integration is the backbone for migrant integration policy in Finland. Various integration measures have been tested and some have been found more effective than others, which is also reflected in the changes of the integration law. The increased number of asylum seekers coming to Finland since 2015 has not caused major changes in legislation regarding migration and integration. The interpretation of migrant legislation seems to however have somewhat tightened, reflecting public opinion.

A central cross-cutting aspect of labour market legislation regarding MRAs is that when work is done in Finland the same laws and labour agreements apply to both Finnish and foreign employees. Overall, the integration of MRAs into the Finnish labour market has not always been successful. Although there may be some aspects of the Finnish legislation (e.g. the availability tests) that may at times hinder the labour market integration of some MRAs it seems that other factors in society may have a larger role in this, such as a lack of language skills, networks, qualifications, recognition of qualification and ineffective integration procedures (Bontenbal et al. 2018). However, it seems that even though urging equality and prohibiting discrimination are taken seriously in the legislation the practical reality may not always respond to the laws in place and this may in fact hinder labour market integration.

Based on earlier research, the reforms brought about by integration legislation, in the end of the 1990s, seem to have had a positive effect on the labour market integration of MRAs. Especially the individual integration plans are of interest and could also be considered as a possible policy recommendation for other countries.

References

Aer, J. (2016). *Ulkomaalaisoikeuden perusteet*. Talentum Media Oy & Lakimiesliiton Kustannus.

Ahmad, A. (2019). When the name matters: An experimental investigation of ethnic discrimination in the Finnish labor market. *Sociological Inquiry, 2019*, 1–29.

Akava. (2011). Palkansaajakeskusjärjestöjen SAK, STTK ja Akava lausunto ulkoasiainministeriölle Suomen liittymisestä Yhdistyneiden Kansakuntien kansainväliseen yleissopimukseen siirtotyöläisten ja heidän perheenjäsentensä oikeuksista. https://www.akava.fi/uutishuone/lausunnot/lausuntoarkisto/akavan_lausunnot_2011/4.3.2011_um_yhdistyneiden_kansakuntien_kansainvalinen_yleissopimus_siirtotyolaisten_ja_heidan_perheenjasentensa_oikeuksista_suomen_liittyminen. Accessed 15 July 2018

Alho, R. (2013). Trade union responses to transnational labour mobility in the Finnish-estonian context. *Nordic Journal of Working Life Studies, 3*(3), 133–153.

Alho, R. (2015a). *Inclusion or exclusion? Trade union strategies and labor migration. Migration Studies C 27*. PhD dissertation, Institute of Migration, University of Turku, Finland.

Alho, R (2015b). Ammattiliittojen strategiat ja maahanmuutto. Talous ja yhteiskunta 4/2015.

Amnesty International. (2015). *Lukkojen takana*. https://www.amnesty.fi/lukkojen-takana/. Accessed 15 June 2018.

Andersen, T. M., Holmström, B., Honkapohja, S., Korkman, S., Söderström, H. T., & Vartiainen, J. (2007). *The Nordic model. Embracing globalization and sharing risks*. Helsinki: The Research Institute of the Finnish Economy (ETLA). Yliopistopaino.

Bontenbal, I., Pekkarinen, A-G., & Lillie, N. (2018). *Finnish integration policies as barriers and enablers to migrant labour market integration* (SIRIUS WP3 National Report).

Eronen, A., Härmälä, V., Jauhiainen, S., Karikallio, H., Karinen, R., Kosunen, A., Laamanen, J.-P., & Lahtinen, M. (2014). Maahanmuuttajien työllistyminen – Taustatekijät, työnhaku ja työvoimapalvelut. Työ- ja elinkeinoministeriö. Työ ja yrittäjyys 6/2014.

Eurobarometer. (2015). *Discrimination in the EU in 2015*. https://ec.europa.eu/COMMFrontOffice/publicopinion/index.cfm/Survey/getSurveyDetail/instruments/SPECIAL/surveyKy/2077. Accessed 2 Oct 2019.

Expat Finland. (2018). *Trade unions & employee representation*. https://www.expat-finland.com/employment/unions.html. Accessed 21 Mar 2018.

Finnish Government. (2015). *Hallituksen turvapaikkapoliittinen toimenpideohjelma 8.12.2015*. https://valtioneuvosto.fi/documents/10184/1058456/Hallituksen%2Bturvapaikkapoliittinen%2Btoimenpideohjelma%2B8.12.2015/98990892-c08e-4891-8c23-0d229f1d6099. Accessed 5 June 2019.

Finnish Government. (2016). Hallituksen kotouttamista koskeva toimintasuunnitelma: maahanmuuttajat kuntiin, koulutukseen ja työhön. TEM, OKM, YM, STM, VM. https://vnk.fi/documents/10616/1266558/Kotouttamisen-toimintasuunnitelma-030516.pdf/c600bd8f-7c5c-43b6-aba4-5aade9aafe0d. Accessed 5 June 2019.

Finnish Government. (2019). Labour market test not applied as of 1 June to the extended permits of those already working in Finland. https://valtioneuvosto.fi/artikkeli/-/asset_publisher/1410877/saatavuusharkinta-poistuu-suomessa-jo-tyoskentelevien-jatkoluvista-1-6-alkaen?_101_INSTANCE_3wyslLo1Z0ni_languageId=en_US. Accessed 5 June 2019.

Finnish Institute of Occupational Health. (2014). *Working in Finland – Information for immigrants*. https://www.ttl.fi/wp-content/uploads/2016/10/englanti_toissa_suomessa.pdf. Accessed 5 June 2019.

Forsander, A. (2004). Social capital in the context of immigration and diversity: Economic participation in the Nordic welfare states. *Journal of International Migration and Integration/Revue de l'integration et de la migration internationale, 5*(2), 207–227.

Forsander, A. (2013). Maahanmuutajien sijoittuminen työelämään. In T. Martikainen, P. Saukkonen, & M. Säävälä (Eds.), *Muuttajat - Kansainvälinen muuttoliike ja suomalainen yhteiskunta*. Helsinki: Gaudeamus Helsinki University Press.

Hämäläinen, K., & Sarvimäki, M. (2008). Moving immigrants from welfare to work – The impact of an integration program.

Heikillä, E. (2005). Mobile vulnerabilities: Perspectives on the vulnerabilities of immigrants in the Finnish labour market. *Population, Place and Space, 11*(6), 485–497.

Helsinki – Ulkomaalaistaustaiset Helsingissä. (2017). Itäisessä suurpiirissä asuu yli neljännes ulkomaalaistaustaisista ja vieraskielisistä. Published 11.8.2017. Helsingin kaupunki. Kaupunki kanslia. Kaupunkitutkimus – ja tilastot. http://ulkomaalaistaustaisethelsingissa.fi/fi/alueellinensijoittuminen. Accessed 13 Mar 2018.

Human Development Report 2016 – Finland. (2016). Human development for everyone. Briefing note for countries on the 2016 Human Development Report. http://hdr.undp.org/sites/all/themes/hdr_theme/country-notes/FIN.pdf. Accessed 3 Apr 2018.

International Labour Organization. (2018). Ratifications for Finland. http://www.ilo.org/dyn/normlex/en/f?p=1000:11200:0::NO:11200:P11200_COUNTRY_ID:102625. Accessed 26 Apr 2018.

Interview by the chief director of the Migration Institute Jaana Vuori for the newspaper Etelä-Suomen Sanomat 22.3.2018. https://www.ess.fi/uutiset/kotimaa/art2446290. Accessed 4 June 2018.

Juvonen, A.-M. (2013). Maahanmuuton juridiikka. Käytännön käsikirja. Second Edition. Edilex Libri. Edita. Helsinki

Korkeinoikeus.fi – Supreme Courts. (2018). Supreme Courts. Official webpage of Supreme Court. http://korkeinoikeus.fi/en/index.html. Accessed 7 Mar 2018.

Kotouttaminen.fi – Järjestöjen tuki. (2018). Järjestöjen monipuolinen toiminta tukee pakolaisten kotoutumista. http://kotouttaminen.fi/jarjestojen-tuki. Accessed 23 Mar 2018.

Kotouttaminen.fi – Pakolaisten kuntaan osoittaminen. (2018). Pakolaisten kuntaan osoittaminen. https://kotouttaminen.fi/pakolaisten-kuntaan-osoittaminen. Accessed 15 May 2018.

Kotouttaminen.fi – Suomen perustuslaki. (2018). Suomen perustuslaki. http://kotouttaminen.fi/perustuslaki. Accessed 5 Apr 2018.

Kotouttaminen.fi – Vastaanottokeskukset. (2018). Vastaanottokeskukset ja niiden palvelut. https://kotouttaminen.fi/vastaanottokeskukset. Accessed 15 June 2018.

Kyhä, H. (2011). Koulutetut maahanmuuttajat työmarkkinoilla. Tutkimus korkeakoulututkinnon suorittaneiden maahanmuuttajien työllistymisestä ja työurien alusta Suomessa. PhD dissertation. Turun Yliopiston julkaisuja.

Laine, J. (2015). Parliamentarism in Finland. Just about everything you need to know about the Finnish government. This if Finland –website. https://finland.fi/life-society/parliamentarism-in-finland/. Accessed 7 Mar 2018.

Liebkind, K., Larja, L., & Brylka, A. (2016). Ethnic and gender discrimination in recruitment: Experimental evidence from Finland. *Journal of Social and Political Psychology, 4*(1), 403–426.

Mäkelä, A. (2019). Interview with Lawyer representative of The Federation of Finnish Enterprises (Suomen Yrittäjät). 18 April 2019 on the phone.

Makkonen, T., & Koskenniemi, E. (2013). Muuttoliikkeen ja maahanmuuttajien aseman oikeudellinen sääntely. In T. Martikainen, P. Saukkonen, & M. Säävälä (Eds.), *Muuttajat – Kansainvälinen muuttoliike ja suomalainen yhteiskunta.* Helsinki: Gaudeamus Helsinki University Press.

Martikainen, T., Saari, M., & Korkiasaari, J. (2013). Kansainväliset muuttoliikkeet ja Suomi. In T. Martikainen, P. Saukkonen, & M. Säävälä (Eds.), *Muuttajat – Kansainvälinen muuttoliike ja suomalainen yhteiskunta.* Helsinki: Gaudeamus Helsinki University Press.

Migri – Asylum. (2018). Asylum. http://migri.fi/en/asylum. Accessed 2 May 2018.

Migri – Asylum Applications. (2019). Statistics. Decisions 1/2015 – 12/2015. http://tilastot.migri.fi/#decisions/23330/49?l=en&start=540&end=551. Accessed 29 May 2019.

Migri – Asylum in Finland. (2018). *You can only apply for asylum if you are in Finland.* Finnish Immigration Service. http://migri.fi/en/asylum-in-finland. Accessed 14 Mar 2018.

Migri – Citizenship Application. (2018). *Citizenship application.* Finnish Immigration Service. http://migri.fi/en/citizenship-application. Accessed 15 Mar 2018.

Migri – Detention. (2018). Detention. https://migri.fi/en/detention. Accessed 15 June 2018.

Migri – EnterFinland. (2018). Residence permit for an entrepreneur. https://enterfinland.fi/eServices/info/selfemployment. Accessed 5 June 2019.

Migri – Income Requirement. (2018). *Income requirement for persons who apply for a residence permit on the basis of work.* https://migri.fi/en/working-in-finland/income-requirement. Accessed 1 Oct 2019.

Migri – Information for Asylum Seekers. (2018). *Information for asylum seekers.* Finnish Immigration Service. http://migri.fi/documents/5202425/6165225/Information+for+asylum+seekers+%28en%29. Accessed 5 June 2019.

Migri – Permanent Residence Permit. (2018). *Permanent residence permit*. http://migri.fi/en/permanent-residence-permit. Accessed 6 Apr 2018.

Migri – Quota Refugees. (2018). *Asylum in Finland – Quota refugees*. http://migri.fi/en/quota-refugees. Accessed 6 Apr 2018.

Migri – Removal. (2019). Removal from the country. http://tilastot.migri.fi/#decisions/23332/52?l=en&start=576&end=587. Accessed 2 May 2018.

Migri – Residence Permit. (2018). *Oleskelupa*. Finnish Immigration Service. http://migri.fi/en/residence-permit. Accessed 15 Mar 2018.

Migri – Statistics on International Protection. (2018). *International protection*. http://tilastot.migri.fi/#decisions/23330?l=en&start=564&end=575. Accessed 2 May 2018.

Migri – Statistics on Residence Permits. (2018). *Residence permit*. http://tilastot.migri.fi/#decisions/21205?l=en&start=564&end=575. Accessed 2 May 2018.

Migri – Working in Finland. (2018). *Working in Finland*. Finnish Immigration Service. http://migri.fi/en/working-in-finland. Accessed 15 Mar 2018.

Migri – Yearly Statistics by Nationality. (2019). https://migri.fi/vanhat-tilastot. Accessed 29 May 2019.

Migri– Finnish Citizenship. (2018). *Finnish citizenship*. Finnish Immigration Service. http://migri.fi/en/finnish-citizenship. Accessed 15 Mar 2018.

Ministry of Economic Affairs and Employment. (2019). Saatavuusharkinta poistuu Suomessa jo työskentelevien jatkoluvista 1.6. alkaen. https://tem.fi/artikkeli/-/asset_publisher/saatavuusharkinta-poistuu-suomessa-jo-tyoskentelevien-jatkoluvista-1-6-alkaen. Accessed 2 Oct 2019.

Ministry of Economic Affairs and Employment – Concluding an Employment Contract. (2018). Concluding an employment contract. http://tem.fi/en/concluding-an-employment-contract. Accessed 22 Mar 2018.

Ministry of Economic Affairs and Employment – Työsopimuslaki. (2017). Työsopimuslaki Työnantajan ja työntekijän asema työsopimuslain mukaan. TEM esitteet 04/2017. https://tem.fi/documents/1410877/2918935/Ty%C3%B6sopimuslaki/079fe475-983b-453a-9bd5-d4d9205ed58f. Accessed 22 Mar 2018.

Ministry of Economic Affairs and Employment –Briefing 5.5.2017. (2017). Uusi kotoutumislaki vastaa maakunta-, sote- ja kasvupalvelu-uudistukseen. http://alueuudistus.fi/artikkeli/-/asset_publisher/1410877/uusi-kotoutumislaki-vastaa-maakunta-sote-ja-kasvupalvelu-uudistukseen. Accessed 21 Aug 2017.

Ministry of Finance – Administrative Structures. (2018). *Administrative structures*. http://vm.fi/en/administrative-structures. Accessed 5 Apr 2018.

Ministry of Social Affairs and Health. (2018). *Mediation in criminal and civil cases*. https://goo.gl/qcg1Qz. Accessed 21 Mar 2018.

Ministry of the Employment and the Economy – Labour Legislation. (2018). http://tem.fi/en/labour-legislation. Accessed 22 Mar 2018.

Ministry of the Employment and the Economy – Report. (2015). *Suomen työlainsäädäntö ja työelämän suhteet*. https://tem.fi/documents/1410877/2918774/Suomen+työlainsäädäntö+ja+työelämän+suhteet/66681b2a-b817-4f79-8482-9f26091f7602. Accessed 19 Mar 2018.

Ministry of the Interior – FAQ Asylum Seekers and Employment. (2018). *Frequently asked questions about applying for a residence permit based on employment*. http://intermin.fi/en/areas-of-expertise/migration/refugees-and-asylum-seekers/faq-asylum-seekers-and-employment. Accessed 14 Mar 2018.

Ministry of the Interior – Migration. (2018). *Areas of expertise: Migration*. http://intermin.fi/en/areas-of-expertise/migration. Accessed 5 Apr 2018.

Ministry of the Interior – Quota Refugees. (2018). *The resettlement of quota refugees is one way of helping people in severe distress*. https://intermin.fi/en/areas-of-expertise/migration/refugees-and-asylum-seekers/quota-refugees. Accessed 15 June 2018.

Ministry of the Interior, Usein kysytyt kysymykset turvapaikanhakijoista. (2018). *Kuinka kauan turvapaikkapäätöksen tekeminen kestää?* https://intermin.fi/maahanmuutto/turvapaikanhakijat-ja-pakolaiset/ukk. Accessed 15 June 2018.

Nykänen, E., Pirjatanniemi, E., Sorainen, O., & Staffans, I. (2012). *Migration law in Finland* (2nd ed.). Alphen aan den Rijn: Wolters Kluwer – Law & Business.

Occupational Safety and Health Administration – Foreign Employee. (2018). http://www.tyosuojelu.fi/web/en/employment-relationship/foreign-employee. Accessed 8 May 2018.

Occupational Safety and Health Administration – Rights and Responsibilities at Work. (2016). *Rights and responsibilities at work.* http://www.tyosuojelu.fi/web/en/employment-relationship/rights-and-responsibilities-at-work. Accessed 20 Mar 2018.

OECD. (2017). *International migration outlook 2017.* Paris: OECD Publishing. Published on June 29, 2017. http://www.oecd.org/migration/international-migration-outlook-1999124x.htm. Accessed 6 Apr 2018.

OECD Data. (2017). *Native born unemployment & Foreign born unemployment.* https://data.oecd.org/migration/native-born-unemployment.htm#indicator-chart. Accessed 1 Oct 2019.

Oikeus.fi – Administrative Courts. (2018). Administrative courts. Official information webpage of judicial administration. https://oikeus.fi/tuomioistuimet/hallintooikeudet/en/index.html. Accessed 7 Mar 2018.

Oikeus.fi – Courts of Appeal. (2018). Courts of appeal. Official information webpage of judicial administration. https://oikeus.fi/tuomioistuimet/hovioikeudet/en/index.html. Accessed 7 Mar 2018.

Oikeus.fi – District Courts. (2018). District courts. Official information webpage of judicial administration. https://oikeus.fi/tuomioistuimet/en/index.html. Accessed 7 Mar 2018.

Oikeus.fi – Finnish Courts. (2018). Finnish courts. Official information webpage of judicial administration. https://oikeus.fi/tuomioistuimet/en/index.html. Accessed 7 Mar 2018.

Opintopolku.fi. (2018). Maahanmuuttajien koulutus. https://opintopolku.fi/wp/valintojen-tuki/maahanmuuttajien-koulutus/. Accessed 22 Mar 2018.

Pakolaisneuvonta. (2018). Kansainvälinen suojelu. http://www.pakolaisneuvonta.fi/asiantuntijajarjesto/tietoa-pakolais-ja-ulkomaalaisoikeudesta/kansainvalinen-suojelu/. Accessed 14 Mar 2018.

Pakolaisten vastaanotto – Tietopaketti kunnille. (2016). Pakolaisten vastaanotto – Tietopaketti kunnille. Ministry of Economic Affairs and Employment. Published online 17 June 2016. http://kotouttaminen.fi/documents/3464316/4355252/pakolaisten_vastaanotto_-_tietopaketti_kunnille.pdf/1dca2c9d-03f2-4244-9cee-4fa909977567/pakolaisten_vastaanotto_-_tietopaketti_kunnille.pdf.pdf. Accessed 14 Mar 2018.

Punto, V. (2018). Interview with lawyer specialized in residence permits and citizenship issues, Law firm Punto. 4 May 2019 on the phone.

Rasinkangas, J. (2013). Maahanmuuttajien asuminen ja alueellinen sijoittuminen. In T. Martikainen, P. Saukkonen, & M. Säävälä (Eds.), *Muuttajat – Kansainvälinen muuttoliike ja suomalainen yhteiskunta.* Helsinki: Gaudeamus Helsinki University Press.

Ristikari, T. (2012). *Finnish trade unions and immigrant labour.* Institute of migration, Migration studies C22. PhD dissertation. University of Tampere.

Rule of Law Index. (2018). *World justice project.* http://data.worldjusticeproject.org/#table. Accessed 13 Mar 2018.

Saarikkomäki, E., Oljakka, N., Vanto, J., Pirjatanniemi, E., Lavapuro, J., & Alvesalo-Kuusi, A. (2018). Kansainvälistä suojelua koskevat päätökset Maahanmuuttovirastossa 2015–2017. Pilottitutkimus 18–34-vuotiaita Irakin kansalaisia koskevista myönteisistä ja kielteisistä päätöksistä. Oikeustieteellisen tiedekunnan tutkimusraportteja ja katsauksia 1/2018.

Säävälä, M. (2013). Maahanmuutto perheilmiönä. In T. Martikainen, P. Saukkonen, & M. Säävälä (Eds.), *Muuttajat – Kansainvälinen muuttoliike ja suomalainen yhteiskunta.* Helsinki: Gaudeamus Helsinki University Press.

Sarvimäki, M. (2017). Labor market integration of refugees in Finland. VATT Government Institute for Economic Research. Research Reports 185. Helsinki 2017.

Sarvimäki, M., & Hämäläinen, K. (2016). Integrating immigrants: The impact of restructuring active labor market programs. *Journal of Labor Economics, 34*(2), 479–508.

Saukkonen, P. (2013). Maahanmuutto- ja kotouttamispolitiikka. In T. Martikainen, P. Saukkonen, & M. Säävälä (Eds.), *Muuttajat – Kansainvälinen muuttoliike ja suomalainen yhteiskunta.* Helsinki: Gaudeamus Helsinki University Press.

Saukkonen, P. (2016). Mitä on kotoutuminen? Kvartti verkkolehti 4/2016. Published 08.12.2016. https://www.kvartti.fi/fi/artikkelit/mita-kotoutuminen%20. Accessed 6 Apr 2018.

Saukkonen, P. (2017). Kotoutumisen seurantajärjestelmän kehittäminen Helsingin kaupungilla. Tutkimuskatsauksia 2017:2. City of Helsinki, Executive Office, Urban Research and Statistics.

Statistics Finland – Citizenships Granted. (2016). Citizenships granted according to country of previous citizenship 1990–2016. http://pxnet2.stat.fi/PXWeb/pxweb/en/Maahanmuuttajat_ja_kotoutuminen/Maahanmuuttajat_ja_kotoutuminen__Maahanmuuttajat_ja_kotoutu-minen/070_kansal_saaneet.px/?rxid=c97ea740-49e0-4c8f-a31a-a1f79c20a83f. Accessed 28 May 2018.

Statistics Finland – Emigration and Immigration Flows. (2017). *Immigration and emigration by country of exit/entry, sex and citizenship 1990–2016.* http://pxnet2.stat.fi/PXWeb/pxweb/en/Maahanmuuttajat_ja_kotoutuminen/Maahanmuuttajat_ja_kotoutuminen__Maahanmuuttajat_ja_kotoutuminen/050_muutto_kansalaisuus.px/?rxid=20134ff0-de11-49d2-aafe-7d8fcbb7770e. Accessed 2 May 2018.

Statistics Finland – Immigrants in Population. (2017). *Immigrants in the population.* https://www.stat.fi/tup/maahanmuutto/maahanmuuttajat-vaestossa.html. Accessed 13 Mar 2018.

Statistics Finland – Kaupungistuminen. (2017). Kaupungistuminen haastaa asuntotuotannon. Published 31.5.2018. https://www.stat.fi/uutinen/kaupungistuminen-haastaa-asuntotuotannon. Accessed 13 Mar 2018.

Statistics Finland – Migrant Flows by Country of Origin. (2018). Immigration and emigration by country of exit/entry, sex and citizenship 1990–2016 Statistic Finland's PX-Web-database. http://pxnet2.stat.fi/PXWeb/pxweb/en/Maahanmuuttajat_ja_kotoutuminen/Maahanmuuttajat_ja_kotoutuminen__Maahanmuuttajat_ja_kotoutuminen/050_muutto_kansalaisuus.px/?rxid=e0ae4efb-6aa6-431a-9cc0-f4adf51b0f58. Accessed 30 Feb 2018.

Statistics Finland – Number of Individuals with Foreign Background. (2019). Numbers and shares of persons with immigrant background by area 1990–2016. Statistic Finland's PX-Web-database. http://pxnet2.stat.fi/PXWeb/pxweb/fi/Maahanmuuttajat_ja_kotoutuminen/Maahanmuuttajat_ja_kotoutuminen__Maahanmuuttajat_ja_kotoutuminen/010_kansalaisuus.px/. Accessed 29 May 2019.

Statistics Finland – Population. (2018). Population structure, 31 December. https://www.tilastokeskus.fi/tup/suoluk/suoluk_vaesto_en.html. Accessed 3 Apr 2018.

Statistics Finland – Population by Country of Origin. (2019). Population according to country of birth, age and sex 1990–2017. Statistic Finland's PX-Web-database. http://pxnet2.stat.fi/PXWeb/pxweb/fi/Maahanmuuttajat_ja_kotoutuminen/Maahanmuuttajat_ja_kotoutuminen__Maahanmuuttajat_ja_kotoutuminen/020_syntymamaa.px/. Accessed 29 May 2019.

Statistics Finland – Suomen kansalaisuuden saaneet. (2017). Suomen kansalaisuuden saaneet. https://www.stat.fi/tup/maahanmuutto/suomen-kansalaisuuden-saaneet.html. Accessed 1 Oct 2019.

Statistics Finland – Työttömyysaste. (2018). Helmikuun työttömyysaste 8,6 prosenttia. Työvoimatutkimus. Published 20.3.2018. https://tilastokeskus.fi/til/tyti/2018/02/tyti_2018_02_2018-03-20_tie_001_fi.html. Accessed 3 Apr 2018.

Statists Finland –Population by Nationality. (2018). Population according to citizenship, age and sex 1990–2017. Statistic Finland's PX-Web-database. http://pxnet2.stat.fi/PXWeb/pxweb/en/Maahanmuuttajat_ja_kotoutuminen/Maahanmuuttajat_ja_kotoutuminen__Maahanmuuttajat_ja_kotoutuminen/010_kansalaisuus.px/?rxid=ed947348-2706-4328-b70f-d095ca9accf4. Accessed 2 May 2018.

TE-Office. (2018). *Työntekijän oikeudet ja velvollisuudet.* http://toimistot.te-palvelut.fi/-/tyontekijan-oikeudet-ja-velvollisuudet. Accessed 20 Mar 2018.

The Central Organisation of Finnish Trade Unions. (2017). *Kymmenen faktaa ulkomaisen työvoiman saatavuusharkinnasta*.   https://www.sak.fi/aineistot/uutiset/kymmenen-faktaa-ulkomaisen-tyovoiman-saatavuusharkinnasta. Accessed 21 Mar 2019.

The Constitution of Finland. (1999). The constitution of Finland 11 June 1999. Unofficial translation. Ministry of Justice. https://www.finlex.fi/fi/laki/kaannokset/1999/en19990731_20111112.pdf. Accessed 5 Apr 2018.

The Employment Office. (2018). *Developing your vocational skills*. http://www.tepalvelut.fi/te/en/jobseekers/support_finding_job/integration_services_for_immigrants/developing_your_vocational_skills/index.html. Accessed 23 Mar 2018.

The Finnish Confederation of Professionals. (2018). *Ammattiliitto*. https://tyoelamaan.fi/tukea-tyoelamassa/ammattiliitto/. Accessed 21 Mar 2018.

The Global Competitiveness Report 2017–2018: Judicial independence (2018). *World economic forum*. http://reports.weforum.org/global-competitiveness-index-2017-2018/competitiveness-rankings/#series=EOSQ144. Accessed 13 Mar 2018.

The Infopankki website – Employee's rights and obligations. (2018). Employee's rights and obligations. The Infopankki website is published by the City of Helsinki. https://www.infopankki.fi/en/living-in-finland/work-and-enterprise/employee-s-rights-and-obligations. Accessed 20 Mar 2018.

The Infopankki website – Trade Unions. (2018). Trade Unions. The Infopankki website is published by the City of Helsinki. https://www.infopankki.fi/en/living-in-finland/work-and-enterprise/employee-s-rights-and-obligations/trade-unions. Accessed 20 Mar 2018.

The National Conciliator's Office. (2018). *Työriitojen sovittelu*. http://valtakunnansovittelija.fi/tyoriitojen-sovittelu. Accessed 21 Mar 2018.

Valtioneuvoston periaatepäätös 28.4.2016. (2016). Valtioneuvoston periaatepäätös harmaan talouden ja talousrikollisuuden torjunnan strategiaksi 2016–2020. http://intermin.fi/documents/1410869/3723676/VN+periaatep%C3%A4%C3%A4t%C3%B6s+harmaan+talouden+torjunta/4c2e9795-9d6f-4fe4-9be7-b96dedd48635. Accessed 22 Mar 2018.

VATT – Research Group. (2014). *Maahanmuuttajien integroituminen Suomeen* (Publication 67). Helsinki: Government Institute for Economic Research.

Chapter 9
Between Reception, Legal Stay and Integration in a Changing Migration Landscape in Greece

Christos Bagavos, Nikos Kourachanis, Konstantina Lagoudakou, and Katerina Xatzigiannakou

9.1 Introduction

Greece, historically considered a typical emigration country, experienced two significant periods of outward migration: the first took place in the early twentieth century (1900–1920), while the second extended from the end of World War II to the first half of the 1970s (Bagavos 2015; Hassiotis 1993; Lazaretou 2016). The United States was by far the main destination country over the first period, whereas in the second period the largest majority of emigrants moved to the Federal Republic of Germany. Between 1900 and 1920, around 400,000 people emigrated abroad; during 1955–1975 the figure was almost 1.2 million (Bagavos 2015). From 2009 onward, a third emigration period occurred as a result of the economic downturn (Labrianidis and Pratsinakis 2016). Estimates for the entire 2009–2017 period indicate that emigration, including both national and foreign populations, accounts for around 850,000 persons (EL.STAT. 2019a).

As for immigration, the 1990s mark a turning point in the history of Greek migration since the country had by this period received a significant number of immigrants. Although the second half of the 1970s and the whole of the 1980s can be considered as the starting period of migration inflows to Greece, the last decade of the twentieth century is marked by unprecedented immigration waves of foreigners coming mainly from the Balkans and to a lesser extent from Asian countries (Cavounidis 2015). Moreover, from 2014 onward, subsequent to the refugee crisis, a substantial number of arrivals, estimated at around 1.2 million third-country nationals and almost 850,000 in the year 2015 alone (UNHCR 2019), was recorded. Consequently, the foreign population increased from 167,000 to more than 800,000 between 1991 and 2018 (Bagavos 2015; EL.STAT. 2019b) and the share of

C. Bagavos (✉) · N. Kourachanis · K. Lagoudakou · K. Xatzigiannakou
Department of Social Policy, Panteion University of Social and Political Sciences, Athens, Greece

© The Author(s) 2021
V. Federico, S. Baglioni (eds.), *Migrants, Refugees and Asylum Seekers' Integration in European Labour Markets*, IMISCOE Research Series,
https://doi.org/10.1007/978-3-030-67284-3_9

foreigners to the total population went from 1.6% to 7.6% (from 1% to 5.6% for third-country nationals). Inevitably, immigration, either in terms of transit or of settled immigrants, has become a major policy issue and has mobilized the national authorities, international bodies as well as formal and informal civil society organizations. In addition, the shifting immigration landscape in Greece has led to the changing composition of migrants and of migrants' needs; immigrants from the period before 2014, who are quite well integrated in Greek society, coexist with refugees and asylum seekers for whom reception conditions have been the main concern.

Changes in the immigration landscape were coupled with adverse economic conditions from 2009 onwards. Unemployment rose sharply and GDP fell significantly. Unemployment rates increased from 7.8% in 2008 to 24.9% in 2015 and reached 23.6% in 2016. Long-term unemployment rates as a percentage of total unemployment rose from 47.0% in 2008 to 73.4% in 2014, reaching 71.8% in 2016. In addition, GDP decreased by around 28% between 2008 and 2016. In this context along with austerity measures the labor market has undergone a number of major changes, among them the stifling control over the shaping of the labor law. Thus, despite the end of the economic tutelage of Greece by the International Monetary Fund (IMF) and the EU in August 2018, the situation in the Greek labor market, after several years of austerity, is still one of deregulation. This gloomy economic and labor market environment did not favor the integration of MRAs into the labor market. With widespread unemployment, the prospect of developing targeted employment policies for MRAs seems impractical, since employment policies are mainly oriented towards the fight against overall unemployment. At the same time, economic hardship has particularly affected those sectors where MRAs are mainly employed, such as construction, retail and personal and domestic services.

The chapter deals with the main legislative developments in migration and the integration of MRAs into the labor market over recent years. It seeks to highlight the significant differences between migrants and refugees in terms of the legal framework put in place by the public authorities to effectively manage the migration phenomenon and the integration of MRAs into the labor market. The chapter stresses that changes in the immigration landscape, along with adverse economic conditions, have led to further efforts by the public authorities for the effective management of refugee flows and reducing the risks of irregular stay for a significant number of migrants. These efforts, however, underestimate the importance of issues relating to the integration of MRAs into the labor market. The paper is structured as follows: Section 9.2 presents the legislative framework on migration and asylum, while Sect. 9.3 deals with legislation on the integration of migrants, asylum seekers and refugees into the Greek labor market. The main concluding remarks are included in Sect. 9.4.[1]

---

[1]As this chapter was being finalised a new law was adopted (the International Protection Act L 4636/2019) which establishes a 6-month employment ban for asylum seekers to occur from 1.1.2020.

9.2 The Legislative Framework in the Fields of Migration and Asylum

9.2.1 Developments in the Legislative Framework of Migration

The Immigration and Social Integration Code (Law 4251/2014) voted in by Parliament in April 2014 is the most significant development in managing migration over the recent period. The modifications introduced aim to simplify procedures, revise terms for access to the labor market, encourage investment by third-country nationals, modify terms and conditions for granting long-term residence permits, and to ensure the legal stay of the second generation of third-country migrants.

One of the most relevant aspects of the Code is that it seeks to simplify and better manage the procedures for residence permits, with the aim of reducing the risks of irregularity for a significant number of migrants, in particular within the context of the persistent economic recession (Greek Parliament 2014; Kapsalis 2018a; The Greek Ombudsman 2013). The promotion of the legal stay of migrants is reflected in various provisions, such as the increase in the length of the validity of the initial permits and the renewed residence permits, from 1 to 2 years and from 2 to 3 years respectively, and the issuing of a document, in practice a temporary permit to stay which is valid for 12 months and that certifies that a third-country national has submitted a complete application for the issuing or renewal of a permit to stay (Triandafyllidou 2015).

The Code also promotes the status of long-term residence for third-country nationals who have lived in Greece for a long period, enabling the holder to move to and work in all EU countries, a right not granted to holders of the 10-year residence permit. In addition, a second-generation residence status has been adopted (Article 108), which grants a 5-year residence permit that can be renewed simply by presenting the previous residence permit to adult third-country nationals born in Greece or those who have successfully completed six Greek school grades in Greece before their 21st birthday, and who are legally resident in Greece.

The Code's provisions, further strengthened by Law 4332/2015, also offer a 2-year residence permit and access to the labor market to third-country nationals on the basis of exceptional grounds (The Greek Ombudsman 2015). This permit is granted if the interested third-country national has procured a visa issued by a Greek consular authority at least 3 years before submission of the application, or a permanent residence permit even if it had expired in the previous 10 years, or that he or she can prove by way of dated documents the actual fact of his or her residence in the country for at least seven instead of 10 consecutive years, as foreseen by the Code. In the above cases, the third-country national must prove that he or she has long-lasting ties[2] with the country unless he or she had a residence permit for Greece for at least 5 years in the decade prior to the application (Spirou 2017).

---

[2] Factors considered as proof of strong ties with the country are: very good Greek-language skills; attendance of a Greek primary or secondary school by the applicant or his or her children; duration

Another important aspect is that the Migration Code and Law 4332/2015 regulate the entry and residence of seasonal[3] migrants in order to work in agriculture and the fisheries industry (EMN 2015; Triandafyllidou 2015). On the basis of a simplified entry procedure, permits are provided to third-country nationals for seasonal residence and work and several guarantees are foreseen as regards social rights (for more details see Sect. 9.3.2).

Further provisions were introduced by Joint Ministerial Decision 30651/2014 and Law 4332/2015, which regulate the reasons and procedures for granting a 2-year residence permit on humanitarian grounds to several categories of third-country nationals, such as victims of trafficking, crime and domestic violence, or those who work in inappropriate working conditions, or suffer from serious health problems or follow an approved mental health treatment programme. Those provisions are also applied to victims of violations of Article 3 of the European Convention for the Prevention of Torture and Inhuman or Degrading Treatment or Punishment, Article 3 of the Convention for the Protection of Human Rights and Fundamental Freedoms or Article 3 of the New York Convention against Torture and Other Cruel, Inhuman or Degrading Treatment etc., that is to people who have suffered "inhuman or degrading treatments or punishments" (Council of Europe 1950).

This legislative framework, implemented in the context of a long-standing economic recession, led to a simplification of the procedure and extending the legal residence of third-county nationals (Triandafyllidou and Gemi 2018). In this respect, there is no doubt that the legislation has contributed to regularizing the stay of a significant number of irregular migrants even on humanitarian or exceptional grounds. Nevertheless, developments in the legal and institutional aspects of migration issues mainly reflect the efforts to manage existing migration rather than to provide a perspective for facilitating and sustaining future legal labor migration.

9.2.2 Migrants, Refugees and the EU-Turkey Statement

The EU-Turkey Statement provides the main framework for the management of refugee flows over the last 4 years in Greece. The 2015 refugee crisis in Europe led to the involvement of the European Union through the identification of measures aiming to better manage refugee flows. At the beginning of 2016, the Member States recognized the need for further measures to manage issues emanating from the refugee crisis, which led to the EU-Turkey Statement.

Of course, the issues covered by the EU-Turkey Statement and its importance in controlling the number of arrivals, the protection of a migrant's fundamental rights and compliance with international standards have been widely discussed over the

---

of residence, primarily legally, in Greece; social security contributions; fulfilment of tax obligations; and blood relations with a Greek national or expatriate.

[3] Seasonal work refers to activity performed in Greece for up to 3 months in total within a 12-month period, in a field related to provisional and seasonal employment.

recent period. The basic content of the Statement is that all people irregularly arriving in the Greek islands will be transferred back to Turkey. For each Syrian returning to Turkey from the Greek islands, another Syrian will be relocated from Turkey to the EU (the 'One for One' procedure). In addition, the agreement includes a commitment for the EU to cooperate with Turkey in order to facilitate the provision of reception services to refugees returned to Turkey, and to establish so-called 'safe areas' inside Syria.

The statement has been criticized as being legally problematic, impractical to implement, and in contravention of refugee law (Amnesty International 2017; Kourachanis 2018). The statement, without being a convention of the Union with a third country, from a legal aspect introduces a host of derogations from the EU regulatory framework (The Greek Ombudsman 2017). It is also seen as unclear on how individual needs for international protection would be fairly assessed during the mass expulsions (Amnesty International 2017). Indeed, Turkey has ratified the 1951 Refugee Convention, but only by applying a geographical limitation whereby only Europeans can be granted refugee status in the country, making the EU's recognition of Turkey as a safe third country rather problematic (Spyropoulou and Christopoulos 2016). At the same time, the scope for establishing 'safe areas', in the current situation, seems to be unrealistic.

Although the EU-Turkey Statement is not related in a direct way to issues of asylum seekers' integration into the labor market, many scholars comment that it provides a preparatory stage for their deployment in low-status sectors (Kourachanis 2018; Xypolytas 2017). The unfavorable living conditions of asylum seekers in hotspots and camps risks making them willing to take up any job and any employment relationship and hence being more vulnerable to exploitation.

9.2.3 Developments in the Legislative Framework of Asylum

Changes in the legislation on asylum over the recent period were undertaken in the context of the refugee crisis and Greece's international legislative commitments. These changes mainly concern four distinct developments: (a) the increase in (sea) refugee flows; (b) the closure of the so-called Balkan route in March 2016; (c) the EU-Turkey Statement of March 2016;[4] and (d) the transposition into Greek law of EU Directive (2013/32/EU) on common procedures for granting and withdrawing international protection. Those developments resulted in new asylum legislation, in particular Law 4375/2016, adopted in April 2016 and amended in June 2016 (Law 4399/2016, Article 86). This law aimed to implement the aforementioned EU-Turkey Statement and the recast Asylum Procedures Directive (AIDA 2017; Greek Parliament 2016).

---

[4] The EU-Turkey Statement contains actions to address the refugee and migration crisis, including the return of all persons irregularly entering Greece after 20 March 2016 to Turkey.

Through various provisions, the new asylum legislation reforms reception and asylum procedures, introduces a special regime applicable at border areas, regulates the backlog of cases (in particular those of the 'old regime'[5]), restructures the Appeals Committees and regulates matters relating to beneficiaries of international protection. A main aspect of the implementation of the new legislation is the different asylum procedures for those applicants who arrive in Greece after 20 March 2016 compared to those who were relocated to the mainland and had reached the country before this date (Koulocheris 2017; GCR 2016).

Developments in the legislative framework of asylum over the recent period, as reflected in particular in Law 4375/2016, in response to the EU-Turkey Statement, resulted in a clear division between reception and asylum procedures for those entering the country before and after 20 March 2016 and consequently for those staying on the mainland or on the islands. Thus, the Greek administration faced a double challenge (The Greek Ombudsman 2017): (a) to enable people who were transferring to and living in temporary accommodation facilities on mainland Greece to access the asylum process; and (b) to rapidly evaluate the asylum applications of those who crossed the sea borders after 20 March and were being held in the hotspots for readmission to Turkey.

The Administration addressed the first challenge in a quite satisfactory way since, by April 2017 over 27,000 1-year legal certificates for residence in the country had been granted through the pre-registration procedure. In contrast, the fast-track border procedure has not operated adequately. One of the reasons for this was the limited number of national and EASO staff, which was not sufficient to tackle the number of applications they received (AIDA 2017; The Greek Ombudsman 2017). Another reason is the lack of coordination and insufficient distribution of competencies between public agencies, services, international organizations, NGOs and local authorities (Koulocheris 2017). Furthermore, the fast-track border procedure has predominantly taken the form of an admissibility procedure to examine whether applications may be dismissed (AIDA 2017), and asylum seekers have been practically excluded from relocation. Moreover, due to the priority of nationality for the submission and evaluation of the asylum applications, the asylum procedure has been severely delayed for non-prioritized nationalities. Consequently, the hotspots were overcrowded, reception conditions deteriorated in terms of sanitation and hygiene, and access to health care was limited, in particular for vulnerable groups (ECRE et al. 2016; NCHR 2017). There is no doubt that reducing the risk of the Reception and Identification Centres being transformed into permanent detention centers remains a major challenge.

---

[5] Asylum procedure governed by Presidential Decree 114/2010, applicable to claims lodged before 7 June 2013 (AIDA 2017).

9.3   The Legislative Framework on the Integration of Migrants, Asylum Seekers and Refugees into the Greek Labour Market

9.3.1   Migration and the Labour Market in the Context of the Economic Recession

The Greek labor market has undergone a number of major changes in recent years due to the economic crisis and fiscal adjustment programs. The emergence of economic hardship and austerity policies led to rising unemployment and steadily falling GDP. In addition, the institutional protection framework for the labor market is not regulated. The main changes since 2010 are based on five key axes: first, the decline in the role of full employment and the expansion of flexible industrial relations, which favor sectoral rather than collective agreements between social partners. Secondly, the weakening of collective agreements and the shrinkage of wages. Thirdly, the spread of flexible working hours, fully adapted to the needs of markets. Fourth, the gradual liberalization of the institutional framework of redundancies. Fifth, the convergence of working conditions in the public and private sectors, leading to significant cuts in the employment protection of civil servants (Kouzis 2016).

At the same time, issuing residence permits has often been an obstacle to integrating migrants into the labor market. Greek migration policy and the subsequent access of migrants to the labor market was for a long time connected to the issuing of two permits, a work permit and a residence permit, particularly since the work permit was a prerequisite for the residence permit required for the purposes of working (Kapsalis 2018b). In addition, migration law aimed mainly to regularize illegal migration rather than promoting legal migration for employment purposes. Practically, the only two options for legal migration (that are often interconnected), that of recall/*metaklissis*[6] and seasonal work are almost exclusively connected to the agricultural sector and their effectiveness is questionable (Triandafyllidou 2014). The ineffective application of these schemes results from the fact that, given the flexibility of labor needs in those sectors where migrants are employed, employers frequently demand changes to the needs they have for a workforce. It also seems that no substantive procedures for a dialogue between the various actors involved in the planning process have been put in place.

The interconnection between the economic recession, subsequent changes in the labor market and those legislative initiatives that aim to offer illegal migrants the opportunity to gain a legal status have led to the following paradox: there is a trend towards the greater convergence of the labor relations of Greek workers with those of MRAs than in the past. However, this trend is not necessarily due to any improvement in the working conditions of foreign workers. On the contrary, it is the

---

[6]A procedure that enables a non-EU national to enter and reside in Greece in order to provide paid work to a specific employer, in a specific field of employment.

shrinking of labor rights and deregulation of the labor market that have exacerbated the working conditions of Greek citizens. As a result, there is a kind of convergence of common labor law with migration law, in a downward spiral (Kapsalis 2018a). As Kapsalis (2018a) states, it is of particular interest that in Greece, before the economic crisis, a migrant labor law with residual labor protection features was established, while during the Great Recession a corresponding residual labor protection framework was applied to native workers. Therefore, the labor protection both for native workers and MRAs has become a race to the bottom.

9.3.2 The National Legislation on Migrant Access to the Greek Labor Market

Since the beginning of the 1990s and the transformation of Greece from a sending to a receiving migration country, migration laws have clearly connected the stay of immigrants to their employment status and financial resources. In reality, the basic requirements for the legal residence of immigrants in Greece were, and remained so to a lesser extent, structured around the existence of a job, the filing of a formal employment contract, the compulsory presentation of a minimum number of social security (insurance) stamps[7] per year and the obligation to have an annual minimum income.

As mentioned above, the method of *metaklissis*, first introduced by Law 1975/1991, remains one of the main paths for legal immigration in Greece, despite the fact that its previous application in the main sectors in which migrants are employed (construction, catering, small factories and retail services) proved rather unrealistic (Triandafyllidou 2014). In this procedure, there is a pre-approval of the entry of a foreign worker for a specific employer and for a specific type of work. Individual employment contracts are then concluded, with state control being exerted at all stages of their implementation. In the last quarter of each second year, the maximum number of dependent jobs allocated to Non-EU nationals per region and occupation is determined by the regional authorities. The same decision may provide for an increase in the maximum number of positions by up to 10% in order to cover unforeseen and emergency needs.

Given the difficulties for an effective application of the *metaklissis* scheme, in particular during the period of the economic recession, national legislation aimed at reducing the risk of increasing irregularity among migrants by increasing the validity of residence permits and reducing financial and duration of employment requirements for their renewal. In this respect, one of the most significant innovations of the 2014 Code (Law 4251/2014) was the abolition of the obligation to produce a written employment contract as a condition for renewal of a residence permit for the

---

[7] The completion of a minimum number of insurance stamps, through minimum working days per year, is a prerequisite for the renewal of a residence permit for employment purposes.

purposes of paid employment. Thus, the reduced number of insurance stamps, the fulfilment of tax obligations and the existence of a valid health booklet are now the main requirements for the renewal of the residence permit related to employment. It is worth noting that, with the adoption of a Joint Ministerial Decision (51738/2014), the number of stamps needed for the renewal of legal residence becomes equal to the number of stamps required for the renewal of health insurance (50 stamps). These developments entail moving from a framework of work-centric immigration legislation to a framework geared towards maintaining legal residence due to the long-standing social ties immigrants may have developed (Kapsalis 2018a). This shift was due to the high unemployment rates, which meant that immigrants were unable to complete the minimum number of stamps per year and consequently, large groups of immigrant populations who have lived in the country for years would return, after many years, once again to an illegal residence status.

It is also worth noting that the Code regulates the situation of migrant investors wishing to settle in Greece. Thus, Article 16 states that Non-EU nationals are permitted to enter and stay in Greece in order to make an investment that will have a positive impact on national growth and the economy. A prerequisite for allowing them to enter and reside in Greece is a motion from the Department of Intragroup Services and Direct Investments to the Ministry for Development and Competitiveness, which means that immigrants with a high financial standing (250,000 euros or more) have the opportunity to pursue professional activities in Greece as they are granted a 5-year residence permit.

In 2015 a new law sought improvements to issues related to the participation of migrants in the labor market. More than the amendments of the Code of Greek Citizenship and the Migration Code, the new Law (4332/2015) aimed at incorporating two EU directives into national legislation. Directive 2011/98/EU concerned the single application procedure for a single permit to stay and to work, already introduced by previous national legislation (Law 3386/2005), to be issued to Non-EU nationals, and a common set of rights for third-country workers legally residing in a Member State. It also incorporates Directive 2014/36/EU on the conditions of entry and residence of Non-EU nationals for seasonal work. The most relevant provisions of Law 4332/2015 are related to the equal treatment of migrant workers, holders of a single permit, and of seasonal workers with EU nationals. Thus (in Articles 21A and B), both categories of Non-EU workers are entitled to equal treatment with EU nationals as regards the terms of employment (including minimum working age, working conditions, working hours and leave and holidays), the right to strike and take industrial action, education and vocational training, as well as the recognition of diplomas, certificates and other professional qualifications.

In 2016 the Greek state issued the special Circular 27430/2016, which gives access to the labor market to those immigrants who find themselves in a situation between illegality and legality, known as 'para-legality' (Kapsalis 2018b). This intermediate category includes irregular immigrants whose order to leave the country was postponed for humanitarian reasons and so they were granted a special certificate to remain in the country for 6 months, without the right to access social integration programs, and which is renewable for 6 months. The status of 'para-legality' offers limited access to the labor market in specific sectors (such as agriculture, animal husbandry and domestic work) and geographical destinations (mainly rural areas).

9.3.3 National Legislation for the Participation of Asylum Seekers and Refugees in the Greek Labor Market

Aside from migrants, national legislation aims to regularize access to the labor market for the beneficiaries of international protection and asylum seekers (along with holders of a residence permit for humanitarian reasons).

In particular, refugee legislation is based on the Geneva Convention (1951) and mainly on Articles 17, 18, 19 and 24, which refer to the social rights of recognized refugees to social security and employment. In Greek legislation those rights are currently extended to persons who have been granted residence on subsidiary protection grounds. A relevant special regulation for the access to the labor market of the two groups of beneficiaries of international protection is contained in Presidential Decree 141/2013. This Presidential Decree aims to incorporate Directive 2011/95/EU into domestic law. Article 27 of the Presidential Decree (incorporating Article 26 of the Community Directive) provides that beneficiaries of international protection are permitted to engage in employed or self-employed activity, in accordance with the provisions of Presidential Decree 189/1998 (A 140). This means that the beneficiaries of international protection must hold a permit to work, in the case of a salaried activity, or prove the existence of the necessary capital in the case of an independent economic activity.

Although Presidential Decree 141/2013 does not contain anything new regarding the preconditions for the access of the beneficiaries of international protection to the labor market, it provides clear improvements for other relevant issues. In particular, articles 27–31 foresee that persons who have been recognized as refugees or beneficiaries of subsidiary protection can participate in employment-related adult education programs, vocational training, including training courses for upgrading skills, workplace practice and counselling by employment services with the same conditions applicable to Greek citizens. These articles also allow these groups to utilize the available procedures for the recognition of diplomas, certificates and other formal qualifications as well as be assessed according to the same conditions as Greek citizens as regards the social security system, working conditions and health care. Nonetheless, despite the institutionalization of access to these benefits, policies and services for delivering these provisions have not yet been developed as public policies but take more the form of specific activities undertaken by NGOs (see Sect. 9.3.4).

The access of beneficiaries of international protection to the labor market was further facilitated by Law 4375/2016. This Law, which governs the current legislation on access to employment, is an adaptation of Greek Legislation to the provisions of Directive 2013/32/EU. The most important change brought about by the law is the abolition of the requirement for the possession of a permit to work as a condition for participation in the labor market (Ministerial Circular 17131/313/12-04-2016). Thus, beneficiaries of international protection and their families have the right to employment under the same conditions as nationals. The only condition for their participation in the labor market is the possession of the required residence permits. The Law also contains similar provisions (Article 69) as those of Presidential Decree 141/2013 on the same work conditions and access to services for beneficiaries of international protection and EU nationals. In practical terms, the labor rights and obligations of beneficiaries of international protection are defined by the same legal regime as for Greek workers. This arrangement concerns both the individuals themselves and the members of their families (Marouda and Sarandi 2017).

As for asylum seekers, Law 4375/2016 also facilitates their access to the labor market. As mentioned, the law abolishes the requirement for the possession of a permit in order to work, a provision foreseen by Presidential Decree 189/1998. Thus, according to article 71, asylum seekers have access to salaried employment and to the provision of services or work if they are in possession of the 'international protection applicant card' or 'asylum seeker's card'. In practical terms, there is no time restriction from the moment that an application is submitted to when the applicant can access the labor market. A last important point is that, as regards free access to public health services and medical treatment for uninsured citizens and the vulnerable population (Joint Ministerial Decision 25132/4-4-2016), asylum seekers now have access to health services on the same terms as nationals.

Despite the formulation of an institutional framework that gives asylum seekers and beneficiaries of international protection access to the Greek labor market, the reality is that these people remain mostly in the camps, with only a minority living in housing structures (Niemann and Zaun 2017; The Greek Ombudsman 2017; Kourachanis 2018). Their integration into the Greek labor market is thus extremely difficult in practice. The development of mechanisms[8] to diagnose labor market needs that are compatible with their professional skills and the formulation of coherent employment policies arc key challenges for their integration into Greek society (Karandinos 2016; Koulocheris 2017). Applying such mechanisms to channel MRAs into the gaps found in the labor market may in the future be a viable solution for their integration into the labor market.

---

[8]The Labor Market Needs Diagnosis Mechanism was set up by the Ministry of Labor, Social Solidarity in 2016, following the Action Plan adopted by the European Commission in 2015. It offers an extensive business network of stakeholders and social partners as well as a dedicated Information System. The National Institute of Labor and Human Resources (EIHRD) is responsible for presenting results, coordinating the network and managing the Information System.

9.3.4 Further Involvement of NGOs in Issues Related to the Integration of Refugees and Asylum Seekers into the Labor Market

The 2015 refugee crisis marked a kind of turning point in the role of Civil Society Organizations (CSOs) as service provider for refugees and asylum seekers in Greece (Bagavos et al. 2019). First, the institutional involvement of NGOs is foreseen by recent asylum legislation (Law 4375/2016). In particular, if a Regional Asylum Office, Reception and Identification Centre, Temporary Reception Structure or Temporary Accommodation Structure has problems in operating smoothly, the processing of some tasks can be entrusted for a set period of time to civil society actors that meet the appropriate standards of quality and safety and have received the necessary permission. Exceptions to this option include those tasks that involve the exercise of public authority, such as the issuance of administrative acts, the examination of applications for international protection, the conduct of interviews and providing applicants with travel or identity documents.

Second, CSOs and NGOs in particular have undertaken a large spectrum of activities related to humanitarian aid, human rights, human trafficking, legal and administrative assistance, advocacy work, accommodation and housing, dissemination and information, socio-economic integration and culture. In practice, CSOs especially are attempting to manage the governmental gap of a migration policy designed with the integration of MRAs in mind. In this context NGOs in particular have been overseeing a majority of services, such as the provision of language courses, skills development training, and employability programs which aim to help integrate refugees and asylum seekers into the labor market. The focus is mainly on job searching techniques and curriculum vitae improvements rather than actually finding job positions for the persons concerned.

Empirical findings based on the opinions of refugees and asylum seekers themselves (Bagavos et al. 2019) seem to indicate that although CSOs have made an extremely significant contribution to humanitarian aid, legal and administrative assistance, the protection of human rights and the dissemination of information, they did not appear to be as successful in meeting refugees' and asylum seekers needs' in terms of their integration into the labor market. This was for a variety of reasons, such as: there were no expected results from the services provided; the actions did not have a follow-up; fragmented funding meant that services were provided for a limited period of time; or because CSOs and NGOs in particular were being asked to fill the gap created by the inability of public actors, supported by the public administration, to provide a clear integration policy. It is also probably related to the fact that, in some cases, refugees and asylum seekers perceive CSOs and NGOs as employment services providers that therefore have expectations that ultimately are not met.

It is, however, worth noting that although NGOs are key actors in the provision of employability services, public authorities have recently attempted to take a much more active role in this area. The trend towards the greater involvement of public authorities in the socio-economic integration of MRAs is reflected in the skills recognition activities. In that respect, perhaps the most typical example is the European Qualifications Passport for Refugees,[9] which assesses refugees' education level, work experience and language proficiency in the absence of full documentation, by using a tested methodology and a structured interview. This was started in 2017 as a pilot project under the responsibility of the Council of Europe and involves several national and international actors, in particular the Greek Ministry of Education, Research and Religious Affairs. At the same time, the initiative of the Athens Coordination Centre for Migrants and Refugee[10] Issues, where someone can attend job counseling sessions as well as other services, such as Greek and English language courses, must be seen as a sign of the further involvement of the public authorities in the social integration of MRAs.

9.3.5 Anti-discrimination Legislation and Legal Instruments to Fight Informal Employment and the Exploitation of Workers

The fight against discrimination is another dimension that can facilitate MRAs' access to the labor market. This is foreseen in Law 4443/2016 (Article 14), which aims to promote the principle of equal treatment and anti-discrimination: (a) on grounds of race, color, national or ethnic origin and generations; (b) religious or other beliefs, disability or chronic illness, age, or social status, sexual orientation, gender identity or gender in the field of employment and work; and (c) on the exercise of workers' rights in the context of the free movement of labor.

Under the 2016 law, the principle of equal treatment concerns: (a) conditions of access to employment and in the area of employment in general; (b) access to all types and levels of vocational guidance, apprenticeship, vocational training, retraining and vocational retraining, including the acquisition of practical professional experience; (c) working and employment conditions, in particular with regard to remuneration, dismissal, health and safety at work and, in the event of unemployment, reintegration and rehabilitation, as well as re-employment; and (d) membership of and participation in a workers' or employers' trade union or in any professional organization.

Over the recent period, the Greek state was more actively involved in the fight against undeclared work, an issue of significant importance for the country's labor market (ILO 2016; The Greek Ombudsman 2016). Specifically, according to the unpublished report regarding the plan 'Artemis', the percentage of undeclared work

---

[9] https://blog.refugee.info/european-qualifications-passport/

[10] https://www.accmr.gr/en/

decreased from 19.2% in 2014 to 9% in 2018.[11] The introduction of the method of payment and the retention of insurance contributions on the basis of the *ergossimo* was introduced, as a measure against undeclared work, for the first time in Greek legislation with Law 3863/2010. This is a kind of a special pay cheque for workers doing non-fixed or casual work (a form of employment in which the worker is not entitled to the regular provision of work) with one or more employers. The *ergossimo* does not focus on businesses or individual employers, but on workers, in particular those in specific disciplines, occupations or jobs (such as domestic workers, construction workers and agricultural workers). Consequently, it is a means of combating undeclared work, in particular tax evasion, and it is as such that it has been classified in the Greek legal order. It mainly concerns providers of services to households, such as domestic workers, (Kapsalis 2015). Several modifying interventions for the measure regarding were made in the following years. These amendments are mainly related to procedures for extending the measure of *ergossimo* to other sectors of employment as well as the procedures for monitoring its implementation. It is also worth noting that Article 2 of Law 4225/2014 attempts to include *ergossimo* in the labor inspections carried out by IKA (Social Insurance Institute). A large proportion of recipients who were targeted by this measure were immigrants, both domestic and farm workers. This is a positive measure that can lead to a greater reduction of undeclared work.

Lastly, in 2012, the Greek state incorporated EU Directive 2009/52/EU with Law 4052/2012. This Directive imposes minimum standards for the sanctions and measures against employers who illegally employ third-country nationals. The aim is to combat illegal immigration by preventing the illegal employment of migrants without residence permits in the Member States of the European Union. In Greek law this is reflected in Article 79 of the relevant law, which explicitly mentions the ban on the employment of illegally resident third-country nationals and in Article 80 which details the obligations of employers. These provisions set the framework for the application of labor protection measures.

9.4 Conclusion

There can be no doubt that migration remains one of the most significant socio-economic issues for Europe – and Greece in particular. After the transformation of Greece from a sending to a receiving country, which resulted in the entry of a large number of economic migrants, the recent refugee crisis has modified the features of the migrant population. At the same time, contextual factors and changes in the economic environment over time have had a significant impact on the framing and implementation of policies on the legal status of MRAs, i.e. the first step towards

---

[11] Indicatively see https://www.efsyn.gr/oikonomia/elliniki-oikonomia/183580_meiosi-tis-adilotis-ergasias-sto-894-2018

their socio-economic integration into the host society. Indeed, the legal stay of migrants and the availability of reception facilities for refugees and asylum seekers have been two significant issues as regards implementation of the policy. In this respect, immigration policy has undoubtedly contributed to simplifying and better managing the procedures for residence permits by reducing the risks of irregularity for a significant number of migrants. This is in the context of the persistent economic recession. In reality, since 2014, there has been a shift in Greek immigration law, which now aims to reduce the employment requirements that immigrants must fulfil for their residence permits to be renewed. There is no doubt that removing those requirements, in the context of a significant increase in unemployment, has enabled their further integration into the labor market.

Nevertheless, despite the great efforts made, both policies and public administration fail to fully address the challenges presented for the effective reception of refugees, which is a determinant preliminary stage for their future integration into the labor market. Developments in the legislative framework have led to a clear division between reception and asylum procedures for those entering the country before and after 20 March 2016 – the cut-off date established by the EU-Turkey Statement – and consequently for those staying on the mainland or on the islands. Although the government addressed the challenge of enabling people who were transferring to and living in temporary accommodation facilities on mainland Greece to access the asylum process in a fairly satisfactory way by accelerating the procedure for issuing decisions on claims for international protection, it failed to provide means to rapidly evaluate the asylum applications of those who crossed the sea borders after 20 March and were being held in the hotspots for readmission to Turkey. Consequently, the hotspots were overcrowded and reception conditions were poor in sanitation and hygiene, while access to health care was limited. In such a context, the hope for integration into the labor market sounds fanciful.

The economic downturn and subsequent austerity measures were and remain important barriers for the integration of MRAs into the labor market. High unemployment rates among the overall population make targeted job creation for MRAs even more daunting since priority is given mainly to the fight against overall unemployment. Additionally, because of the economic downturn and decreasing household incomes, migrants' reduced employment in sectors such as construction, retail, cleaning, private care and domestic services has resulted in a challenging and unfavorable environment for the participation of MRAs in the labor market. In reality, given that third-country nationals are mostly low-skilled workers who are employed in low-skilled jobs, they remain extremely vulnerable to unfavorable economic conditions. This environment is likely to be more gloomy for refugees and asylum seekers than for migrants who are in a better position to secure a long legal stay, given the existence of informal ethnic networks among them, their knowledge of the Greek language and familiarization with the State administration. In other words, the factors enabling their integration into the labor market. Consequently, it is likely that MRAs' integration into the labor market will be further connected to an ethnic dimension; for example, migrant groups such Albanians and Pakistanis entering Greece in the first period of its transformation from a sending to a receiving country, are more likely to be better integrated in the labor market than the recent refugee streams from Afghanistan and Syria.

In practice, the framing and implementation of policies fail to deal with the barriers in place, such as the inability to transfer skills and credentials to a European context, the precarious legal status, limited education and language skills and limited work experience that immigrants are most of the time confronted with when they seek stable jobs in the European receiving countries. Those barriers are even more significant in Greece which is characterized by the polarization and fragmentation of policies aiming to facilitate the access of MRAs into the labor market and the limited involvement of the Public Employment Services in the labor market integration of MRAs. Barriers are also related to the features of the Greek labor market itself. Third-country nationals, particularly those who have resided in Greece for only a short time, are mostly pushed into the underground economy and undeclared work, an issue relevant in the context of adverse economic conditions. Despite the intensification of labor inspections, there has been no sign of improvement up to now (2020), mainly because of the non-systematic application of those inspections as well as common views among many people, who very often consider undeclared employment as something legitimate. Thus, migrants are trapped in low wage and low-skilled occupations, very often in the informal sector with no labor rights, without social insurance and with limited opportunities for any improvement in their socio-economic status. Although sectors such as catering, tourism and agriculture, which have experienced continuous growth in recent years, offer increasing opportunities to migrants for entering the labor market, those sectors are characterized by flexibility, irregularity, discrimination and undeclared work.

In addition, given the persistent economic recession in Greece and the lack of job search assistance programmes, the integration of MRAs, in particular refugees and asylum seekers, is hindered by the fact that they most likely desire relocation to another European country and are unwilling to be fully integrated into the labor market of a country which is seen more as a transit than a settlement country. It is worth noting that, according to empirical findings on the aspirations of young Syrian refugees, 74% of them intended to remain in the UK, compared to just 12% and 39% in Greece and Lebanon respectively (Karyotis et al. 2018). In addition, three out of four young Syrians in Greece aimed to reach another European country whereas the same ambition was expressed only by 13% and less than 2% of those living in Lebanon and the UK respectively. There is no doubt that this aspect acts as an important barrier for access and integration into the labor market of the newly-arrived refugees and asylum seekers in Greece.

The limited role played by the public authorities as a provider of services such as language courses, employability services and skills development training must be seen as significant barriers for the integration of MRAs into the labor market. Although NGOs have significantly contributed in these areas, public authorities have still not implemented many monitoring and validation processes, such as validation of the level of language knowledge or validation of skills. In general, despite the recent trend for the further involvement of the public authorities in the integration of MRAs into the labor market, the current increase in refugee flows risks diverting the attention of public actors to issues relating to the reception rather than to the integration of MRAs.

It is evident that the integration of refugees and asylum seekers will be a significant issue in the years to come. The management of the increased refugee flows of the last 5 years is being performed within a more protected humanitarian framework, while the labor integration of asylum seekers and refugees is still governed by a residual framework. To date, targeted employment policies have still not been designed. The consequence of this situation for asylum seekers and refugees may be the resumption of the labor integration paths followed by immigrants in the 1990s and 2000s, when there were high rates of undeclared work and any form of unfavorable employment was accepted in order to survive.

References

AIDA (Asylum Information Database). (2017). *Country Report: Greece-2016 update*. http://www.asylumineurope.org/reports/country/greece

AIDA (Asylum Information Database). (2019). *Country Report: Greece-2018 update*. http://www.asylumineurope.org/reports/country/greece

AIRE (Advice on Individual Rights in Europe), ECRE (European Council on Refugees and Exiles). (2016). *With Greece. Recommendations for refugee protection. Report on Greece*. http://www.asylumineurope.org/sites/default/files/resources/with_greece.pdf

Amnesty International. (2017). *Greece: A blueprint for despair. Human rights impact of the EU-Turkey deal*. https://www.amnesty.org/download/Documents/EUR2556642017ENGLISH.PDF

Bagavos, C. (2015). Chapter 11: International migration: The transformation of Greece from sending to receiving country. In A. Tragaki, C. Bagavos, & D. Ntounas (Eds.), *On demography and population changes*. e-book. https://repository.kallipos.gr/handle/11419/4670 (in Greek).

Bagavos, C., Xatzigiannakou, K., & Kourachanis, N. (2019). *Civil society barriers and enablers – Report on Greece*. Report prepared for the SIRIUS research. https://www.sirius-project.eu/

Cavounidis, J. (2015). *The changing face of emigration: Harnessing the potential of the new Greek diaspora*. Report prepared for the Migration Policy Institute. https://www.migrationpolicy.org/research/changing-face-emigration-harnessing-potential-new-greek-diaspora

Council of Europe. (1950). *Convention for the protection of human rights and fundamental freedoms as amended by protocols No. 11 and No. 14* (European Treaty Series – No. 5). https://rm.coe.int/1680063765

ECRE (European Council on Refugees and Exiles). (2016). Successful completion of pre-registration of asylum seekers in Greece – More needed to meet long term concerns. *News*. https://www.ecre.org/successful-completion-of-pre-registration-in-greece-more-needed-to-meet-long-term-concerns/

ECRE (European Council on Refugees and Exiles), GCR (Greek Council for Refugees), et al. (2016). *The implementation of the hotspots in Italy and Greece – A study*. https://www.ecre.org/wp-content/uploads/2016/12/HOTSPOTS-Report-5.12.2016.pdf

EL.STAT. (Hellenic Statistical Authority). (2019a). *Estimations of emigrants by age group and sex*. http://www.statistics.gr/el/statistics/-/publication/SPO15/-. Accessed 21 June 2019.

EL.STAT. (Hellenic Statistical Authority). (2019b). *Population estimates by age group, sex and broad group of citizenship*. http://www.statistics.gr/el/statistics/-/publication/SPO18/-. Accessed 21 June 2019.

EMN (European Migration Network). (2015). *Annual policy report 2015 – Annual report 2015 on Asylum and migration – Part 2*. https://ec.europa.eu/home-affairs/sites/homeaffairs/files/what-we-do/networks/european_migration_network/reports/docs/annual-policy/annual-policy-12a_greece_apr_part2_english.pdf

European Commission. (2017). *Seventh report on the Progress made in the implementation of the EU-Turkey*. Report from the Commission to the European Parliament and the Council. Brussels, 6.9.2017, COM(2017) 470 final. https://ec.europa.eu/neighbourhood-enlargement/sites/near/files/20170906_seventh_report_on_the_progress_in_the_implementation_of_the_eu-turkey_statement_en.pdf

GCR (Greek Council for Refugees). (2016). *Remarks by the Greek Council on Refugees on Law 4375/2016*. http://www.gcr.gr/index.php/el/news/press-releases-announcements/item/551-oi-paratiriseis-tou-esp-epi-tou-nomou-4375-2016. (in Greek).

Greek Parliament. (2014). *Explanatory report on the draft law on Ratification of immigration and social integration code*. http://www.parliament.gr/UserFiles/2f026f42-950c-4efc-b950-340c4fb76a24/k-koinent-eis.pdf. (in Greek).

Greek Parliament. (2016). *Explanatory report to Law 4375/2016*. http://goo.gl/RGbrKD. (in Greek).

Hassiotis, I. K. (1993). *Historical overview of the Greek diaspora*. Thessaloniki: Vanias. (in Greek).

ILO (International Labour Organization). (2016). *Diagnostic report on undeclared work in Greece*. Geneva: International Labour Organization. http://www.ilo.org/wcmsp5/groups/public/%2D%2D-ed_emp/documents/projectdocumentation/wcms_531548.pdf

Kapsalis, A. (2015). *Undeclared work in Greece. Assessment of modern anti-fighting measures, stay of immigrants stay of immigrants*. Athens: Labour Institute of GSEE (Greek General Confederation of Labour), Study No 43. https://www.inegsee.gr/wp-content/uploads/2015/06/Meleti-43-INE.pdf. (in Greek).

Kapsalis, A. (2018a). *Migrant workers in Greece. Industrial relations and migration policy in times of memorandums*. Athens: Topos. (in Greek).

Kapsalis, A. (2018b). The development of Greek migration policy and the invention of "Para-legality" in labour relations of immigrants. *Koinoniki Politiki/Social Policy, 9,* 67–87.

Karandinos, D. (2016). *Labour market integration of asylum seekers and refugees-Greece*. Report submitted to the Directorate of Employment, Social Affairs and Inclusion of the European Commission. http://ec.europa.eu/social/search.jsp?pager.offset=20&langId=en&searchType=&mode=advancedSubmit&order=&mainCat=0&subCat=0&year=0&country=0&city=0&advSearchKey=Labour%20market%20integration%20of%20asylum%20seekers%20and%20refugees

Karyotis, G., Colburn, B., Doyle, L., Hermannsson, K., Mulvey, G., & Skleparis, D. (2018). *Building a new life in Britain: The skills, experiences and aspirations of young Syrian refugees* (Building Futures Policy Report No 1). Glasgow: Policy Scotland. http://www.RefugeePolitics.net and www.PolicyScotland.gla.ac.uk.

Koulocheris, S. (2017). *Integration of refugees in Greece, Hungary and Italy. Annex 1: Country case study Greece*. Report prepared for the European Parliament's Committee on Employment and Social Affairs. http://www.europarl.europa.eu/RegData/etudes/STUD/2017/614194/IPOL_STU%282017%29614194%28ANN01%29_EN.pdf

Kourachanis, N. (2018). Asylum seekers, hotspot approach and anti-social policy responses in Greece (2015–2017). *Journal of International Migration and Integration*. https://doi.org/10.1007/s12134-018-0592-y.

Kouzis, I. (2016). Crisis and memorandums deconstruct the employment. *Koinoniki Politiki/Social Policy, 6,* 7–20. (in Greek).

Labrianidis, L., & Pratsinakis, M. (2016). *Greece's new emigration at times of crisis* (GreeSE Paper no. 99). Hellenic Observatory on Greece and Southeast Europe, LSE. http://eprints.lse.ac.uk/66811/1/GreeSE-No.99.pdf

Lazaretou, S. (2016). Fleeing of human capital: Recent trends in migration of Greeks over the years of the crisis. *Bank of Greece, Bulletin of Economics, 43,* 33–58. (in Greek). http://www.bankofgreece.gr/BogEkdoseis/oikodelt201607.pdf.

Marouda, M. N., & Sarandi, V. (2017). *Refugee law. Interpretation, charts, patterns*. Athens: Nomiki Vivliothiki. (in Greek).

Ministry for Migration Policy. (2018). *National Register of Greek and Foreign Non-Governmental Organizations (NGOs) dealing with international protection, migration and social integration issues*. https://mko.ypes.gr/home_in_mitroo_report

Ministry of Interior and Administrative Reform, UNHCR and ESPO. (2016a). What is pre-registration? *Information Poster*. http://asylo.gov.gr/wp-content/uploads/2016/06/W001-2-What-is-Pre-Registration-Poster.pdf

Ministry of Interior and Administrative Reform, UNHCR and ESPO. (2016b). *End of large scale pre-registration on mainland Greece Joint Press Release*. http://asylo.gov.gr/en/wp-content/uploads/2016/08/EN-01.08.2016-Press-Release-end-pre-registration.pdf

Ministry of Migration Policy. (2018a). *2 Years since the Common Statement between European Union and Turkey, March 2016–March 2018*. http://asylo.gov.gr/en/wp-content/uploads/2018/03/EU-Turkey-Common-Statement-2-years_EN.pdf

Ministry of Migration Policy. (2018b). *The work of the asylum service in 2017*. Press Release 25.01.2018. http://asylo.gov.gr/en/wp-content/uploads/2018/01/Press-Release-25.1.2018.pdf

NCHR (National Commission for Human Rights). (2017). *Annual report 2016*. http://www.nchr.gr/images/ekthesi2016.pdf

Niemann, A., & Zaun, N. (2017). EU refugee policies and politics in times of crisis: Theoretical and empirical perspectives. *Journal of Common Market Studies, 56*(1), 3–22.

Spirou, C. (2017). *Exceptional reasons: Restoring legality and the notion of ties with the country*. Problems in the correct application of Law 4251/2014 and Law 4332/2015. Paper presented at the 7th legal conference of Association of Trainees and New Lawyers "Modern Issues of Immigration Law: Immigration – Citizenship – Refugee", Patras, 10–12 November 2017. http://www.eanda.gr/sites/default/files/%20%CE%A7%CE%A1%CE%97%CE%A3%CE%A4%CE%9F%CE%A5%20%CE%A3%CE%A0%CE%A5%CE%A1%CE%9F%CE%A5.pdf

Spyropoulou, A., & Christopoulos, D. (2016). *Refugees: "will we make it"? A management account and recommendations for a way out*. Athens: Papazisi. (in Greek).

The Greek Ombudsman. (2013). *Comments on the Draft Law on Ratification of immigration and social integration code*. https://www.synigoros.gr/resources/paratiriseissxedionomou.pdf. (in Greek).

The Greek Ombudsman. (2015). *Annual report*. http://docplayer.gr/38967035-Synigoros-toy-politi-etisia-ekthesi.html. (in Greek).

The Greek Ombudsman. (2016). *Combating discrimination-Special report*. https://www.synigoros.gr/resources/docs/ee2016-14-diakriseis.pdf. (in Greek).

The Greek Ombudsman. (2017). *Migration flows and refugee protection Administrative challenges and human rights issues*. https://www.synigoros.gr/?i=human-rights.en.recentinterventions.434107

Triandafyllidou, A. (2014). *Migration in Greece: Recent developments in 2014*. Report prepared for the OECD Network of International Migration Experts. http://www.eliamep.gr/wp-content/uploads/2014/10/Migration-in-Greece-Recent-Developments-2014_2.pdf

Triandafyllidou, A. (2015). *Migration in Greece: Recent developments in 2015*. Report prepared for the OECD Network of International Migration Experts. http://www.eliamep.gr/wp-content/uploads/2014/10/2015.pdf

Triandafyllidou, A., & Gemi, E. (2018). *Migration in Greece: Recent developments in 2018*. Report prepared for the OECD Network of International Migration Experts. https://www.eliamep.gr/wp-content/uploads/2017/11/Greece-report-for-OECD_Triandafyllidou-Gemi_Nov2018.pdf

UNHCR (United Nations High Commissioner for Refugees). (2019). *Mediterranean situation – Operational portal refugee situations*. Accessed 21 June 2019.

Xypolytas, N. (2017). Preparation, allocation, habituation: The holistic approach to migrant exclusion. *Social Cohesion and Development, 12*(1), 57–71.

Chapter 10
The Labour Market Needs Them, But We Don't Want Them to Stay for Good: The Conundrum of Migrants, Refugees and Asylum Seekers' Integration in Italy

William Chiaromonte and Veronica Federico

10.1 Discussing Migration in a Challenging Economic and Political Landscape

Over the past 5 years, migration flows have become crucial to alleviate but not completely counter-balance the overall negative demographic balance in Italy. In 2019, according to the National Institute of Statistics (ISTAT), the resident population totalled 60,391,000, while the foreign resident population counted 5,234,000 individuals, representing 8.7% of the total population. In 2018, nationals have decreased 3.3%, whereas the foreign resident population has increased 17.4%. Moreover, Eurostat confirms that while the Italian population is on average elderly, the foreign population is quite young (the average age is under 34), which means a strong net contribution to the available workforce.

Much has changed in the demography of the country over the last three decades. At the beginning of the 1990s, the foreign population totalled less than one million. In 2019 it is five times more, representing a rise of 405%. From a country of emigration, with the Italian diaspora present in almost every country in the world, Italy has become a country of immigration. This transformation has been relatively abrupt; social, cultural, political, economic and legal categories have struggled to keep pace with the demography. There are critical consequences to this underlying and problematic lack of syntony, which leads to a constant mismatch between (i) social and

---

This study is the product of common research and long discussions on problems and perspectives of MRA's integration in the complex and fragmented Italian labour market. Nonetheless, W. Chiaromonte is mainly responsible for Sects. 10.3 and 10.5, V. Federico for Sects. 10.1, 10.2, 10.4 and 10.6.

W. Chiaromonte · V. Federico (✉)
Department of Legal Sciences, University of Florence, Firenze, Italy
e-mail: william.chiaromonte@unifi.it; veronica.federico@unifi.it

© The Author(s) 2021
V. Federico, S. Baglioni (eds.), *Migrants, Refugees and Asylum Seekers' Integration in European Labour Markets*, IMISCOE Research Series,
https://doi.org/10.1007/978-3-030-67284-3_10

economic needs and the legal and administrative instruments to address them; (ii) new cultural perspectives and the public discourse and media frames that should represent and voice those perspectives; (iii) migration numbers and political discourses about them. This chapter discusses how such disparities also permeate the field of labour market integration.

A brief recap of the data on migration and the Italian labour market helps to contextualise the discussion: among the foreign population resident in Italy, EU migrants represent a little more than 30%. The most numerous non-EU nationalities resident in Italy come from Morocco, Albania, China, Ukraine and the Philippines. Over the last decade, the general trend of the legal reason for acquiring the residence permit has been shifting. Residence permits issued for reasons of work represented almost 50% of the total permits released in 2011, but they have decreased consistently every year, under pressure *inter alia* of the economic crisis. In 2019 (last available data), rates dropped to little more than 6%. On the contrary, residence permits for asylum or humanitarian reasons have significantly increased, peaking in 2017 (more than 28%) and beginning to decrease in 2018 (26.7%). Nonetheless, the main channel for obtaining the resience permit is represented by family reunification, which consistently represents between 40% and 45% of permits granted between 2011 and 2017, and reaches more than 50% in 2018.

These data suggest the migration challenge currently faced by Italy is not necessarily a stand-alone state of affairs. The growing presence of foreign populations is more related to a slow process of stabilisation of the migratory phenomena over the recent two decades, rather than current international conflicts or crises. It should therefore be managed in such terms.

Similar to other European countries, migration trends and developments have been influenced by the geographical, economic, political and sociocultural peculiarities of the Italian context in many regards. The geographical position of the Italian peninsula in close proximity to north African coasts plays a significant role. The relevance of the Italian geographical element juxtaposes with some peculiar economic traits. In particular, research emphasizes the link between immigration and the extended informal sector of the country and those of other southern European states (Testaì 2015; Ambrosini 2013). However, the formal sector, with its unmet labour demand, also contributes to attracting foreign workers. Thus, it is not a coincidence that the majority of foreign workers are concentrated in the highly-industrialized and developed northern regions, while only a small quota, mainly seasonal workers, reside in the less-developed and more agriculture-dependant southern regions. Interestingly, foreign workers' participation in Italian economic life remained high even after the economic crisis of 2008. Indeed, it has been shown (Ambrosini and Panichella 2016; Sciarra and Chiaromonte 2014) that the crisis had a lower impact on foreigners' employment rate compared to the employment rate of nationals, except for the sector of manufacturing and construction – even though it should be noted that the crisis enhanced the structural problems of the Italian labour market, such as segmentation, disparities and pay gaps. Moreover, it is important to point out that: "foreign workers are strongly labour-oriented, so that the phenomenon of the so-called 'disheartenment', that is giving up the search for employment, is very uncommon. In fact, unemployed foreigners can be constrained to accept the first job they find, under the pressure to maintain themselves and their families and/or renovate the residence permit" (Italian Ministry of Labour 2017: 41).

It is against this background that the Italian political discourse began to focus on immigration from the early 1990s, when the number of non-EU newcomers to the country started to increase, which is quite late in comparison with other European countries. Nonetheless, the Italian political discourse caught up with the overall European political trend: it was influenced by significant anti-immigrant narratives, particularly during the pre-electoral periods (Korkut et al. 2013). Under the slogan "Italians First" and the creation of a dangerous equation between immigrants and criminals, echoed by the mainstream media, demands to close borders and progressively reduce migrants' rights have permeated the political arena. Consequently, the politicization of migration featured in all recent national (2008, 2013 and 2018) and European (2009, 2014 and 2019) elections (Cavallaro et al. 2018).

Overall, the increasingly strident political discourse, together with the negative media representation of migration, have contributed to a deterioration of the Italian attitude toward migrants (Diamanti 2016). Furthermore, scapegoating the "other" for threatening Italian cultural identity, along with Italian social welfare, security and economic stability, has found a fertile terrain in the limited sense of nationhood and belonging that traditionally characterise Italian citizens (Triandafyllidou and Ambrosini 2011). Further, the economic crisis has exacerbated competition for resources, so that "Italians First" slogans have made sense for a growing number of voters (Cavallaro et al. 2018).

Despite this opposing trend, the labour market does need foreign workers and entire economic sectors are heavily dependant on foreign workforce; foreigners also fill societal gaps, first and foremost in the care of children, the elderly and people with disabilities. Moreover, the practical management of migration displays examples of openness and solidarity. Indeed, the migration crisis has shed new light on the long-standing tradition of volunteerism in Italy, fed by a curious interplay between the Catholic Church, trade unions and others secular associations of the left matrix (Ambrosini 2018).

The chapter goes on to discusses the Italian legal framework governing foreign workers' integration into the labour market, workers' rights and guarantees, the enforcement of a complex web of norms and regulations, and finally how the implementation of the legal framework is in tension with the basic principles that ground the Italian legal system.

10.2 Labour, Workers' Rights and the Constitution: The Basic Principles

Historically, Italy has been primarily a country of emigration; this is reflected in the Italian Constitution of 1948, which recognizes the freedom to emigrate (art. 35(4)) and proclaims the freedom to "leave the territory of the Republic and return to it except for obligations defined by law" (art. 16(2)). At the same time, only few and generic provisions have been devoted to the right of asylum and the legal status of foreigners,[1] and little is stated concerning foreigners' rights. This constitutional gap has been filled over the years by ordinary legislation and the Courts' intervention.

If the Constitution is concise on foreigners' rights, it is more vocal on the value of labour, labour relations and workers' rights. In fact, the constitutional enforcement of the right to work has strongly influenced labour law and its developments (Gaeta 2014) by providing the institutional foundations and reference values of the Italian social market economy, where economic efficiency and social cohesion should coexist. Social rights, recognized in the Constitution alongside civil and political rights, play a fundamental role in enforcing labour-related rights. Social rights are concerned with protection against the material conditions of deprivation that might prevent the individual from meeting his/her fundamental needs. To be fully enforced, social rights require either the provision of public services, delivered by the state or any other public authority (e.g. the right to education, art. 34 Const.), or the regulation of contractual relationships, as is the case with employment relationships (e.g. the right to a decent wage, art. 36 Const.).

The fundamental principles concerning labour laid down in the Constitution are basically all found in the first articles of the Charter. Art. 1.1 affirms that the Republic

---

[1] Art. 10 states that "(2) legal regulation of the status of foreigners conforms to international rules and treaties; [and] (3) foreigners who are, in their own country, denied the actual exercise of the democratic freedoms guaranteed by the Italian constitution, are entitled to the right to asylum under those conditions provided by law." Other pivotal constitutional provisions, nonetheless, contribute enhancing the national standards of foreigners' rights. In particular, art. 117, through which the EU legislation and international treaties signed by Italy acquire "constitutional relevance"; the "personalist principle" of art. 2, according to which "the Republic recognizes and guarantees the inviolable human rights, be it as an individual or in social groups expressing their personality, and it ensures the performance of the unalterable duty to political, economic, and social solidarity", and the equality clause of art. 3 that forbids unfair discrimination and entrenches substantial equality. And indeed, international conventions and jurisprudence (especially the European Convention on Human Rights (ECHR) and the principle of non-discrimination proclaimed by art. 14 ECHR), equality and the personalist principle have been frequently invoked by the Italian Constitutional Court to secure and extend the fundamental rights of foreigners (Corsi 2014, 2018; Carrozza 2016; Biondi Dal Monte 2013; Chiaromonte 2008). In particular, in several decisions the Constitutional Court affirmed that limiting the access to social benefits aimed to satisfy human basic needs only to foreigners with an EC residence permit for long-residents entails an "unreasonable discrimination" between Italian citizens and foreigners regularly residing in Italy. See, amongst the others, the decision of the Constitutional Court No. 187/2010, in which the Court also makes explicit reference to the decisions of the European Court of Human Rights Gaygusuz v. Austria 16.9.96 and Niedzwieck v. Germania 25.10.05

is "founded on labour", recognizing the historical value of labour as a cornerstone of the state, together with the democratic principle ("sovereignty belongs to the people", art. 1.2 Const). Art.s 2 and 3 recognise and guarantee "inviolable human rights, be it as an individual or in social groups expressing their personality", and equality in its broad meaning of formal and substantial equality. Art. 4.1 recognises the right to work for all citizens, establishing the duty of the state to promote conditions enforcing the right to work and to pursue policies aiming to achieve full employment. The Constitution commits the state to ensuring its citizens the right to work primarily through the promotion of full employment; thus, with regard to access to work, citizens take priority over foreigners. The guarantee of the foreigner's rights, here, is therefore limited by the privileged status of the citizen.[2] Art. 4 provides the legal basis for restrictions on the entry of foreign workers in order to protect Italian nationals and the regular functioning of the domestic labour market. The Constitutional Court – which in fact has occasionally intervened on this topic – has supported this reasoning, assuming that it is reasonable to subordinate foreigners' access to employment to the prior recognition of the unavailability of national workforce (decision No. 144/1970 e 54/1979).

Even though the Constitutional Court has often ruled that, despite art. 3 making reference to citizens only, when the respect of fundamental rights is at stake the principle of equality also applies to foreigners,[3] the Court's argument is more complex than a simple equalization between citizens and foreigners. It instead ascertains the difference between citizens and foreigners: while citizens have an "original" relation with the state, foreigners have a non-original and often temporary relationship. Hence, the different legal status of foreigners may justify a different legal treatment (decision No. 104/1969) with regard to security, public health, public order, international treaties and national policy on migration (decision No. 62/1994), but not with regard to the protection of inviolable rights (decision No. 249/2010) since they belong "to individuals not as members of a political community but as human beings as such".[4]

Following the same reasoning, a Constitutional Court's consolidated case-law maintained foreigners' full entitlement to social rights, such as the right to health and healthcare services (decision No. 269/2010) and to "essential social benefits", such as invalidity benefits for mobility, blindness and deafness regardless of the length of the foreigner's residence. In particular, the Court clarified that specific social benefits that constitute "a remedy to satisfy the primary needs for the protection of the human person", have to be considered "fundamental rights because they represent a guarantee for the person's survival".[5] The same argument, coupled with

---

[2] Here, reference is made to foreigner's access to employment in the private sector, since access to employment in the public sector is regulated by specific provisions, which however do not fall within the scope of this study.

[3] See the following decisions of the Constitutional Court: No. 120/67; No. 104/1969; No. 46/1997.

[4] Among the others see Constitutional Court, decision No. 105/2001, No. 249/2010.

[5] Constitutional Court, decision No. 187/2010. See also Constitutional Court No. 329/2011; No. 40/2013, No. 22/2015 and No. 230/2015.

the anti-discrimination principle, permitted the Court to extend some guarantees and (social) rights to undocumented migrants as well.

Alongside these fundamental principles, Title III of the Constitution devotes few articles to economic relations, establishing a rather conspicuous corpus of constitutional principles that labour law and labour policies must respect and enforce. These principles are crucial for the definition of foreign workforce rights and entitlements. First, citizens' priority over foreign workers when it comes to accessing work may be at odds with the provisions of art. 35, according to which the Republic "protects labour in all its forms" without any limitation. This means that, once the foreigner is authorised to work in Italy, the protection of labour "in all its forms" – including precarious or unstable employment – applies regardless of the nationality of the workers, as the Constitutional Court has emphasised (decision No. 454/1998). Therefore, Italian and foreign workers enjoy full equality of treatment (see art. 2.3, of the Consolidated Law on Immigration, Legislative Decree No. 286/1998). The principle of equal treatment has a very wide scope, covering the internal aspects of the employment activity and relationship, as well as all the additional advantages resulting from his/her employment status. Furthermore, art. 35 states that the Republic "provides for the training and professional enhancement of workers", and "encourages international treaties and institutions aiming to assert and regulate labour rights". Moreover – as already mentioned – art.35.4 recognises the freedom to emigrate and ensures the protection of Italian workers abroad.

Art. 36 affirms the worker's right to a fair remuneration that should be sufficient to ensure him/her and his/her families a free and honourable existence. As a further guarantee, the maximum daily working hours and rest days must be established by law, and workers "cannot waive [the] right [to a weekly day of rest and to annual paid holidays]". Special conditions require special attention, and that is why art. 37 guarantees working women in both formal and substantial terms: "women are entitled to equal rights and, for comparable jobs, equal pay as men. Working conditions must allow women to fulfil their essential family duties and ensure an adequate protection of mothers and children". The article also covers minors, whose minimal age for paid labour shall be defined by the law. Moreover, art. 38, while guaranteeing workers the right to social security, commits the state to providing social assistance to those unable to work and without the necessary means of subsistence, as well as providing education and vocational training to people with disabilities.

Finally, art. 39 establishes trade union freedom and the right to collective bargaining; art. 40, ensures the right to strike; art. 41 guarantees the freedom of private economic enterprise, but envisages the limit of the common good and of safety, liberty and human dignity; and art. 46 recognises the right of workers to collaborate in the management of companies.

What emerges from this brief overview is a complete but coherent system of binding norms that on the one hand recognizes the value of labour in its multiple dimensions (the funding element of the Republic, the means of self and family subsistence, but also the instrument of social integration, of self-promotion and locus "where human personality is expressed" (art. 2 Const.)), and on the other hand sets the standards for human dignity in a prime place in the workplace. Unfortunately, however, this system does not guarantee *per se* "labour rights" oriented laws and policies, and even less so when laws and policies target foreigners, as discussed in the next section.

10.3   Entering the Country and Becoming a Worker: A Difficult Path

The integration of MRAs into labour market is connected to the progressive tightening of immigration regulation over the last three decades (Colucci 2018, 140 ss.).

Since the 2002 "Bossi-Fini" Law (Law No. 189 of 2002), any new law and regulation in the field of immigration has contributed to the narrowing of access to the country, and making foreigners' legal status increasingly precarious and fragile (see the most recent acts: the "security package" – Law No. 94/2009, Law No. 125/2009 and Law No. 217/2010-; the "Minniti decrees" – Law No. 46/2017 and Law No. 48/2017-; and finally the "Salvini decrees" – Law No. 132/2018 and Law No. 77/2019, as modified by Law No. 173/2020). This has not been without consequences for their integration into labour market.

If we consider employment conditions alone, in principle no subordinate employment contract (as regulated by art. 2094 of the Civil Code) can violate the "golden rule" of the non-derogation *in pejus* of the law and of collective agreements. Nonetheless, since the 1990s – and particularly following the severe global recession triggered by the 2007 financial crisis – the rate of flexibility allowed in the labour market has grown considerably. This has resulted in a (partial) liberalisation of the labour market, the increasing use of non-standard typologies of contract and, in the attempt to mitigate the impact of growing unemployment, in a simultaneous weakening of the protection traditionally provided to workers. The main and most recent expressions of this trend are embodied in the so-called "Fornero reform" (Law No. 92/2012) and in the so-called "Jobs Act", a composite "package" of Legislative Decrees adopted in 2015.

With particular reference to the condition of foreign workers, we recall that Italian labour law is based on the principle of equal treatment between regular foreign workers and national workers, as well as workers of other EU Member States. The protection of work "in all its forms and practices" (art. 35 Const.) operates regardless of the nationality of the worker, as noted previously. According to the Consolidated Law on Immigration, the foreigner who holds a work permit has the right to receive the very same remuneration, social security and assistance as any Italian worker. On the contrary, undocumented foreigners willing to work can only resort to the shadow economy and the black market. Unfortunately, undocumented stays inevitably lead to irregular work (Calafà 2017), even though some forms of protection also exist in the black market, especially with reference to the remuneration and contributory position of the worker (Chiaromonte 2018, 348 ss.).

As mentioned, the employment contract involving a foreign worker does not have significant peculiarities. Non-discrimination with respect to other workers is particularly guaranteed (see art. 43, par. 2, letter *e*, Legislative Decree No. 286/1998 and Legislative Decree No. 215/2003), contrary to the access of foreign workers to the national labour market, which has always been subject to specific regulation.

The system of foreign workers' entry to the country is based on the idea of planning incoming migration flows according to national labour market needs through specific legislation (the *Decreto flussi*) that should determine quotas for regular entry each year (Sciarra and Chiaromonte 2014; Chiaromonte 2016). The Consolidated Law articulates migration policy into two levels. The first level – the cornerstone of Italian migration policy – is represented by a three-year plan (art. 3, para. 1–3), aiming in particular to define the general criteria for the subsequent annual determination of the entry flows and integration measures. The second level consists of the so-called *Decreto flussi*, or "flows decree" (art. 3, para. 4), which should be issued each year and establishes the exact annual quotas for work purposes.

However, the provisions of the Consolidated Law that regulate the 3-year plan have gone unheeded (the last plan refers to the period 2004–2006). In other words, the sole instrument for determining migration policy and regulating foreign workers' access to the labour market has been the *Decreto flussi*, a measure conceived to operationalise a mid-term plan, though not to strategically intervene in such a delicate and crucial field as migration. And indeed, it has been issued annually exclusively to allow the entry of seasonal workers, while the same frequency has not been respected for non-seasonal workers and for self-employment. Moreover, rather than determining quotas for new arrivals, the *Decreto flussi* has become the instrument to annually regularise the position of undocumented migrants already in Italy (the latest regularization, linked to the Covid-19 health emergency, was laid down by Law Decree No. 34/2020).

In addition, recent years have seen a dramatic reduction of the working permits issued annually: from 250,000 permits issued in the frame of the 2007 *Decreto flussi* to 30,850 in 2020. The reduction is complemented with a similarly dramatic increase in international protection applications, which indicates a distorted use of international protection regimes by migrants whose migration may not primarily be determined by humanitarian reasons (Chiaromonte 2019, 335 ss.).

Indeed, entering Italy as a foreign worker is not easy: the process of issuing visas, residence and work permits is long and complex. The employer who intends to hire an alien worker, either permanently or on a fixed-term basis,[6] must apply[7] to

---

[6] Noticeably, unless the foreign worker has a permit to stay for other reasons compatible with the transformation into a work permit, it is not possible to directly hire undocumented migrants already in Italy, so what happens for them is to set up the whole proceeding as if they were first entering the country.

[7] It is a nominal application, and the employers has to prove also the accommodation facilities and has to commit to pay for the worker's return ticket in his/her country of origin.

the special office for immigration (the so-called *Sportello Unico*) at the Police Headquarters once they have ensured there are no available workers in Italy.

The work permit should be issued in 60 days, provided it does not exceed the annual quota. The work permit being granted, the Consulate of the foreigner's residence or origin country issues an entry visa, and the worker has 8 days from her/his arrival in Italy to sign the *residence agreement for work reasons* at the *Sportello Unico*. Only after this procedure is completed does the Police Headquarters issue the residence permit for work purposes. The duration of the "residence agreement" cannot exceed 9 months for one or more seasonal jobs, 1 year for a fixed-term employment contract, and 2 years for a permanent employment contract.

In the event the worker loses his/her job for whatever reason, he/she can register as unemployed to the employment centre for a period that cannot exceed the duration of the residence permit (art. 22, para. 11, Consolidated Law). The Law does not provide for the possibility of obtaining a residence permit to actively look for a job; moreover, the complex and lengthy proceedings make it difficult for both job seekers and companies to meet their needs of finding a job on the one hand, and ensuring stable workforce on the other.

Beneficiaries of international protection are recognised by unlimited access to the national labour market. On the contrary, asylum applicants are allowed to work only from the sixtieth day from the submission of the application for international protection, if the application has not been processed yet and the delay is not due to the applicant. In any case, the residence permit thus granted cannot be converted into a residence permit for work reasons (art. 22, Legislative Decree No. 142/2015).

Neither European nor Italian Laws envisage the possibility of working for people in repatriation centres or those awaiting a decision of repatriation. Moreover, no specific incentives are provided to access the labour market for: asylum seekers, international protection applicants, refugees and legal economic migrants (without a long-term residence permit). This represents a critical aspect of the Law here, since the conditions for work placement are often disadvantageous due to language barriers, low levels of education, traumatic experiences related to separation from family and country of origin, the cultural gap, and, for asylum seekers and international protection applicants, their transitional legal status. For beneficiaries of international protection and for asylum seekers and international protection applicants, the employment rate 1 year after arrival in an EU country is very low (around 8%).[8] On average, between 5 and 6 years are necessary for integration into the labour market of more than half of the refugees and individuals entitled to international protection. However, data for Italy (which does not monitor this phenomenon) are missing.

Furthermore, so far in Italy there has been a lack of specific investment into integration and inclusion programmes, while the relationship between the state and asylum seekers has mainly conformed to welfare assistance types of dynamics.

---

[8] EU Parliament, Directorate General for Internal Policies (2016:22).

10.4 Working to Integrate: Easy to Say, Hard to Do

Over the past 20 years, public debate about foreigners has been dominated by the insistence that foreign workers are welcome in Italy, as long as they contribute to the wellbeing of the host society and its economy (Ambrosini 2001). Yet, as a matter of fact, the barriers to accessing the labour market remain considerable, and, from a legal perspective, pertain to two different clusters of reasons: a narrow recognition of rights, and the weakness of measures to develop MRAs' capabilities.

First and foremost, the right to work is not universally recognized for all those living in Italy. Entering the country as a worker is difficult, as discussed; obtaining the right to work once in the country for other reasons may also be very hard. Asylum seekers are allowed to work after 60 days from their asylum application, but if they need to receive accommodation facilities, their annual income should not exceed approximately 6000 euro. This forces people to make hard choices, often pushing them to resort to the black or grey labour market. The rigidity of their legal status is a second barrier that blocks full benefit of the right to work. The margin of manoeuvre foreign workers have depends heavily on their entry channel and the legal status they have been allocated: "Each legal status is subject to a number of conditions, which need to be fulfilled in order to obtain a specific set of rights. Conditions to be fulfilled and rights guaranteed vary a lot from one legal status to another. With more than 40 different foreigners' legal statuses, the landscape becomes pretty heterogeneous and labyrinthine" (Federico and Pannia 2019).

Second, while language knowledge is a potent enabler, it becomes a barrier when no learning services are available. Following the Law No. 132/2018, a new tender specification scheme (*Capitolato*) was adopted by the Ministry of Interior. Under the new *Capitolato*, only few basic services are provided in CAS (centre for extraordinary reception for asylum seekers), excluding language courses; there are few public language learning facilities for seasonal workers, either. The large majority of language courses are provided by third sector entities, some of which have become proper informal education institutions. Yet, the presence of civil society associations is not homogeneous throughout the country, which entails a highly differenciated offer of opportunities that depends on geography rather than needs.

Third, the problem of recognizing professional qualifications should be noted. Qualifications and training acquired in the country of origin are not easy to officialy recognise in Italy, since long and complicated procedures are generally required. Moreover, applicants and beneficiaries of international protection often do not have certificates issued by their country of origin, meaning they cannot apply for jobs appropriate to their education level (Favilli 2015, 726). This opens the door to another possible enabler to labour market integration that may become a barrier: accessing education and vocational training. Access to schooling and academy is granted to all MRAs, except to undocumented migrants, even though the children of undocumented families are allowed to enter the schooling system. Yet, temporary economic migrants are not allowed to enroll in tertiary education unless they have been in Italy for at least 1 year and obtained a diploma in the country. The same applies to vocational training, with a sole, major problem: likewise language learning opportunities, the new tender specification scheme for CAS provided for by

Law No. 132/2018 excludes training services. This means that, *de facto*, organising vocational training within the reception centers has become extremely difficult and should be done at zero cost, which is unrealistic and undermines integration into labour market. Furthermore, the Law No. 132/2018 excluded asylum seekers from the right to be enrolled on the civil registry. This *de facto,* once again, prevented asylum seekers from accessing a number of social services provided by local municipalities, such as training. The provision has been expunged by the Constitutional Court in a recent decision in July 2020 (No. 186/2020) for the intrinsic inconsistency with the purpose of the law itself, therefore asylum seekers can be enrolled again, and benefit from the related services.

Finally, a full enforcement of the right to work entails the recognition and concrete enactment of a number of social rights as ancillary provision connected to the recognition of the worker, the worker's family and dignity. Housing is one such social right. Art. 40(6) of the Consolidation Law and art. 29 of Legislative Decree No. 251/2007 guarantee refugees the right to access public housing, but public houses are much less than required, therefore, in practice, a widespread recourse to informal settlements is reported amongst refugees. The same applies to long-term economic migrants. Foreigners unable to provide for their housing and subsistence needs have the right to be accommodated in public housing at the same conditions as destitute nationals. However, in the long term, housing is subjected to limitations. In fact, the Consolidated Law on Immigration stipulates that only foreigners holding a EU long-term residence permit or foreign workers with a permit to stay no less than 2 years can have access to public housing accommodation and housing support measures (art. 40 of the Consolidated Law on Immigration). Under the Law No. 132/2018, asylum seekers, who previously could enter the SPRAR system, can only be accommodated in centres of extraordinary reception (CAS) activated by the Prefectures, quite often large facilities, far from workplaces. A new Decree Law No. 13/2020 has readmitted asylum seekers in the SPRAR system (which has been renamed while maintaining the same organising principles), but with a non-priority admission scheme. No access to public housing and housing measures is granted to seasonal workers.

No unemployment benefits are recognised for seasonal foreign workers, and even though asylum seekers formally are recognised, the requirement of 2 years of contributions *de facto* reduces their opportunities to effectively enjoy this right. All other categories of MRA are entitled to the same treatment as Italian citizens. The case of unemployment benefits clarifies a crucial point underlying our discourse: from a legal perspective, much depends on the foreign worker's legal status, which may become a barrier that blocks their right to work being recognised and enforced, or it may become one of the most potent enablers to their labour market integration.

10.5   They Should Work as Nationals Do, But This Is Not Always the Case

In a joint paper of December 2016, the OECD, ILO, the World Bank and the IMF observe that "effective labour market integration is a key factor to enhance the benefits of migration – for both origin and destination countries, but also for the migrants themselves. Migrant workers are best protected where the fundamental principles and rights at work are effectively enforced" (OECD, ILO, the World Bank and IMF 2016). What is interesting in this otherwise self-evident statement is the qualification attributed to labor maket integration. There is consensus among scholars, stakeholders and policy-makers that to unleash the potential of MRAs, labour market integration should be "effective", which means allowing foreigners, regardless their status (except from the regularity of their stay), to work as nationals do. In Italy, this entails three dimensions: anti-discrimination measures, contrasting undeclared work and accessing welfare benefits.

10.5.1   Anti-discrimination Measures

Italian labour law has no overarching equal treatment provision covering all aspects of employment conditions, but there are specific norms applying to peculiar aspects. Compared to equality, non-discrimination has a narrower and more focused scope, since it only prohibits differences in treatment – between workers and groups of workers – determined by grounds specifically listed by the law. Therefore, diversified treatments in the workplace become discriminatory and illegal only when they are against one of the listed grounds (Barbera and Guariso 2019). Yet, non--discrimination is strongly enforced at the European level (art. 10 TFEU and art. 21, para. 1, Charter of Fundamental Rights of the European Union) and the EU Court of Justice has stated that European anti-discrimination rules shall prevail over any eventual breach entrenched in domestic legislation.

Gender (Legislative Decree No. 198/2006), political opinions and trade union activity (art. 15, Law No. 300/1970), race and ethnic origins (Legislative Decree No. 215/2003), linguistic group and nationality (art. 2, para. 3 and art. 43, para. 2, lett. *e*, Consolidated Law on Immigration), religion,[9] personal beliefs, disability, age and sexual orientation (Legislative Decree No. 216/2003) are all listed grounds.

Discrimination may be direct or indirect, individual or collective, but not every difference in treatment constitutes discrimination: "In compliance with the principles of proportionality and reasonableness, [...] differences in treatment based on characteristics related to race or ethnic origin do not constitute discrimination [...] if, by reason of the nature of the working activity or the context in which the latter is carried out, such characteristics constitute an essential and decisive requirement for the pursuit of that working activity" (art. 3, para. 3, Legislative Decree No. 215/2003). Furthermore, differences in treatment which – though indirectly discriminatory – are objectively justified by "legitimate aims pursued through appropriate and necessary means" are considered as legitimate (art. 3, para. 4, Legislative

---

[9] With regard to this point, on the sensitive question of whether it constitutes religious discrimination to prohibit an employee from wearing the Islamic headscarf at work see CJEU, 14 March 2017, C-157/15, *Achbita*; CJEU, 14 March 2017, C-188/15, *Bougnaoui*.

Decree No. 215/2003). The same applies to religion or belief, disability, age or sexual orientation (art. 3, para. 3 and 5, Legislative Decree No. 215/2003).[10]

A special form of judicial protection is provided in legal cases entailing discrimination (art. 28, Legislative Decree No. 150/2011). This takes the form of the partial reversal of the burden of proof, so that if the worker allegedly discriminated against provides the Court with evidence suitable for establishing – in "precise and consistent" (for discriminations on the grounds of race or ethnic origin) or in "serious, precise and consistent" (for discrimination on the grounds of religion, personal beliefs, etc.) terms – the existence of discriminatory acts, pacts or behaviours, it is up to the defendant employer to prove there has not be any discrimination.

Ordinary judges and the Constitutional Court have only very occasionally intervened in the principle of equal treatment, they have rarely condemned discriminatory treatment of foreigners in the private sector, not because of the judiciary's reluctance but rather because few cases have reached the courts. The most common cases involving discrimination against foreigners brought to the attention of the judges have not been directly concerned with working conditions, but rather with the ban on access to public services, the guarantee of the right to group identity (e.g. the right to speak one's own language) and of the neutrality of the public sphere.[11] Moreover, most of the decisions involve disputes with the public administration, the so-called "institutional discriminations". This points to the difficulty of intercepting discriminations between individuals (even discrimination at work, for which the prohibition of discrimination has traditionally arisen), where the individual's contractual freedom competes with the principle of equality.

10.5.2 *Contrasting Undeclared Work and* **Caporalato**

Art. 22, para. 12 of the Consolidated Law on Immigration imposes criminal sanctions[12] on the employer "who employs foreign workers without a residence permit […], or whose permit has expired and whose renewal, has not been requested by

---

[10] The parallel with discrimination on the grounds of race and ethnic origin continues with the fact that those differences in treatment that, although indirectly discriminatory, are objectively justified by "legitimate aims pursued through appropriate and necessary means" (art. 3, para. 6, Legislative Decree No. 216/2003) are in any case considered legitimate.

[11] See e.g. the rulings available at the ASGI (*Associazione per gli Studi Giuridici sull'Immigrazione* (https://www.asgi.it/banca-dati/) database, and Guariso (2012).

[12] The penalties consist of prison sentences of between 1 and 6 years, and a fine of 5000 euro for each worker employed. In cases of particular exploitation of the worker, art. 12, para. 5 of the Consolidated Law also provides for the most serious crime of facilitation of the illegal permanence of the foreigner for the purpose of unjustified profit. The sanctions have been strengthened by the Legislative Decree No. 109/2012, which has transposed Directive 2009/52/EC. The decree provides that the above mentioned penalties are increased by one third or more when the number of employees exceeds three, when they are minors under the working age, or when they are exposed to situations of serious danger, taking into account the characteristics of the services to be provided

law, or has been revoked or cancelled". Legislative Decree No. 109/2012 provides for the extension of criminal liability to legal persons who are responsible for facilitation of illegal immigration (art. 12, Consolidated Law on Immigration).

Moreover, art. 22, para. 5 *bis* of the Consolidated Law on Immigration authorises the *Sportello Unico* for immigration to refuse the authorization to work to any employer who in the last 5 years has been convicted for facilitating illegal immigration or emigration, or for crimes related to the recruitment of persons for the purpose of (the exploitation of) prostitution or of minors.

The employer must pay the irregular foreign worker the full wages and social contributions provided for lawful employment for a minimum period of 3 months, unless the employer or the employee prove otherwise (art. 3, Legislative Decree No. 109/2012). However, due to the undesirable consequences, it is very unlikely for the worker to receive what is due before his/her removal, since the emergence of the unlawful presence of the undocumented worker entails her/his voluntary or forced removal, in accordance with the provisions of the Returns Directive (2008/115/EC).

Yet, in the event of severe labour exploitation, charging files against the employer and collaborating with the prosecuting authority grants the undocumented worker a 6-month residence permit, renewable for 1 year or till completion of the criminal proceedings (art. 22, para. 12 *quater* and *quinquies*). The provision of a residence permit to the foreigner who is victim of labour exploitation is certainly an important novelty in the Italian legal system, especially in light of her/his subsequent integration into the (regular) labour market. However, Legislative Decree No. 109/2012 has narrowed the typology of "serious labour exploitation".

With regard to the additional administrative and financial sanctions provided by Directive 2009/52/EC against employers who have employed an irregular labour force, no implementation measures are found in the Legislative Decree No. 109/2012. However, precisely these sanctions could potentially play a fundamental deterrent role, since the consequences for employers would be very serious and particularly from an economic point of view. Moreover, Legislative Decree No. 109/2012 does not provide any specific measure against subcontracting, a common phenomenon of the exploitation of undocumented labour.

Concerning the phenomenon of *caporalato*, Law No. 199/2016, amending art. 603 *bis* of the Penal Code, introduced new provisions aimed to contrast the widespread and serious phenomenon of illegally recruiting labour through exploiting the worker's condition of need, a phenomenon particularly rooted in the agricultural sector and, more generally, in the agri-food production chain (D'Onghia and de Martino 2018; Chiaromonte 2018; Fanizza and Omizzolo 2018).

The *caporalato*, which "succeeds" in keeping foreign labour in Italy that would otherwise be expelled, and intercepts the incoming flows attracting new labour force, often involves undocumented migrants, who are further particularly vulnerable. Since reporting to public authorities would lead to those workers'

---

and the working conditions (art. 22, para. 12 *bis*). Together with the conviction, the judge also applies the accessory administrative sanction, consisting of the payment of the average repatriation cost of the illegally employed foreign worker (art. 22, para. 12 *ter*).

expulsion – except for the already mentioned very few cases for which the law provides for the possibility of issuing a residence permit – they tend not to criticize their situation of exploitation, confirming the well-known difficulties of access to justice for foreigners (especially the undocumented) also with reference to the most serious cases of labour exploitation (the number of complaints is strongly conditioned by their undocumented status, sanctioned by criminal law, of the worker victim of serious exploitation). Therefore, they accept working and living in situations of particular degradation, as well as precarious health conditions, often with limited access to drinking water, basic medical care and decent housing.

The most relevant innovation of the Law No. 199/2016 consists in the identification (art. 603 *bis*, para. 1) of two distinct criminal conducts: (1) the *caporale*, who recruits workers (often, but not necessarily, undocumented migrants) for third parties in conditions of exploitation, and taking advantage of their state of need (in this case the crime is that of illegal intermediation and exploitation of labour); and (2) the employer, who hires or employs workers, even without the intermediation of the *caporale*, subjecting them to conditions of exploitation and taking advantage of their state of need (in this case the illegal intermediation can only potentially occur).

Two elements characterize the criminal conduct of both the *caporale* and the employer: on the one hand, the exploitation of labour: para. 2 of art. 603 *bis* identifies the "legal indices of exploitation", most of which refer to the conduct of the employer only, which are grouped into four categories: remuneration, working hours, safety and hygiene at work, and the general working conditions, which means a systematic violation of the "hard core" labour law conditions. On the other hand, is the exploitation of the state of need of the workers. At stake here is the breach of the fundamental value of the human dignity of the worker. Unless the fact constitutes a more serious crime, the *caporale* or employer is punished with imprisonment from 1 to 6 years, and with a fine from 500 to 1000 euros for each employed worker. Moreover, imprisonment from 5 to 8 years and a fine from 1000 to 2000 euros for each employed worker is given when the acts are committed with violence or threat.

10.5.3   Access to Welfare Benefits

Despite the long and rich catalogue of national and supranational regulations enforcing the principle of equal treatment between Italian and EU citizens and extra-EU nationals concerning access to welfare benefits, the most recent legislation has introduced the condition of residence. This means that welfare benefits may be reserved for those who can prove they have resided for a certain period in a given region or in the country. This kind of condition, while not directly discriminatory, can generate indirect prejudice to foreigners' interests (Chiaromonte and Guariso 2019).

The same rationale has inspired anti-poverty measures. The basic income established by Law No. 26 of 2019, for example, targets poor Italians, EU citizens and third country nationals with a long-time residence permit, that can prove having spent in Italy at least 10 years and the last two continuously.

The Constitutional Court does not have a unilateral position on the subject. The Court has often adopted the distinction between services directed to meet the fundamental rights and basic needs of the individual, that cannot be conditioned by any long-term residence requirement, and services that, on the other hand, do not address basic needs and can be restricted, but restrictions and conditions should not be arbitrary and unreasonable, as is the case for restrictions based on the public spending reduction (*inter alia*, judgments n. 187/2010, 329/2011, 40/2013, 222/2013, 168/2014, 22/2015, 230/2015).

When services exceed the notion of essential needs, the Court takes into exam, case by case, the existence of a reasonable correlation between the service and the residence requirement. Usually, the Court has considered in breach of the Constitution the requirement of qualified residence when it concerns foreigners exclusively, who are requested by the law to prove the regularity of their permanence in the country to benefit from a given service (*inter alia*, decisions No. 61/2011, 2/2013, 4/2013, 133/2013, 172/2013, 106/2018, 107/2018, 166/2018). When the residence requirement concerns both nationals and foreigners, in some cases the Courts has qualified the condition as indirect discrimination, especially if it has an unequal impact on foreigners (decisions No. 168/2014, 172/2013, 107/2018). In other cases the residence condition has been judged as in line with the constitutional principles (*inter alia*, decisions No. 222/2013, 141/2014, 50/2019).

10.6 Concluding Considerations

After decades of emigration, Italy has become the gateway to the European Union but also a country of destination for growing numbers of people in search of protection and better opportunities for themselves and their families. Contrary to the narrative of "the invasion" of Italy, the numbers of the foreign resident population results are in line with the European context, and data reveal that the growing presence of foreigners is not exclusively related to current international conflicts or crisis but also to a slow process of stabilisation of the migratory phenomenon seen over the last two decades. Decision-making and law-making, nonetheless, mainly respond to the "invasion" narrative as opposed to real data, so that the enforced new measures continue to be dedicated more to combating irregular immigration (and to the regularisation of undocumented migrants) and to guaranteeing public security, than to the integration of MRAs into Italian society.

Work is certainly among the most effective instruments for ensuring the effective integration of foreigners into the social fabric of the host country, but the labour market of foreigners has some peculiar characteristics. First, the complementarity with the labour market of Italians, which means that Italian workers can often afford to avoid certain occupations traditionally are considered unattractive (the so-called *ddd, dirty, dangerous and demeaning jobs*), and migrants undertake such unskilled jobs. Moreover, this suggests that the ideological rhetoric – dominant in the public debate on immigration – according to which migrants "steal jobs" is misleading (Allievi and Dalla Zuanna 2016: 12; Fondazione Leone Moressa 2017: 71).[13] Second, the Italian labour market (for both nationals and foreigners) is segmented into regular and undeclared (or non-regular) work. The vastness of the phenomenon of foreigners' undeclared work certainly depends on a number of factors, many of which are of an extra-legal nature. However, the legal framework has its own responsibilities, with the Consolidated Law on Immigration that not only fails preventing and fighting the phenomenon, but in some cases tends to favour it (Sciarra and Chiaromonte 2014: 124–127).

Even though the Italian legal framework is in line with both EU legislation and the core labour standards recognized by the eight fundamental ILO Conventions, it remains disorganized and fragmented. Fundamental social rights are not always granted at the same conditions of Italian citizens, while some social welfare allowances can only be obtained through the intervention of the courts. Standards of care and assistance for asylum seekers and refugees vary considerably between the different centres of accommodation, so that the enjoyment of basic rights becomes "a matter of luck" (Oxfam 2017). As a result, harsh living conditions in overcrowded and self-organized settlements, illegal labour and exploitation represent a frequent outcome of the absence of efficient services supporting access to housing, employment, and more broadly to integration (Council of Europe, Commissioner for Human Rights 2011; UN Human Rights Council 2014).

Obstacles that hinder the full integration of foreigners into the Italian labour market take precendence over enablers, especially when foreign workers do not have a residence permit for work reasons but are instead beneficiaries of international and humanitarian protection. Since access to work for beneficiaries of international and humanitarian protection is still very complicated, there is a strong risk that the progressive reduction in the number of permits granted for work reasons and the simultaneous increase in the number of those granted for humanitarian reasons will slow down the process of integration through work. Moreover, the fact that it is generally possible to legally enter the country for work reasons only after having already found a job and not to look for a job, makes the already difficult process of integration even more complicated. Furthermore, particularly long and complicated administrative recruitment procedures would require a comprehensive review of the legislation to become instruments of social and economic integration and not of marginalization. The recently enacted measures to fight against labour exploitation and *caporalato* could be considered a valid contribution to the enhancement of workers' rights and dignity and a Italian best practice. Unfortunately, the law has not found full enforcement and it does not seem that the Italian legislator is currently devoting proper attention to this flaw in the original legislation.

---

[13] It is estimated that more than two thirds of foreigners work in unskilled professions, and only 6.7% in skilled professions. This is accompanied by the fact that they are often overeducated with respect to the working activities they carry out (37.4% foreigners are overeducated compared to 22.2% of Italians) (Centro Studi e Ricerche IDOS, 2017)

The Italian labour market needs foreign workers and entire sectors heavily rely on foreing workforce; Italians are reluctant to accept that foreign workers should stay for good, and the legal framework mirrors these contradictory visions.

References

Allievi, S., & Dalla Zuanna, G. (2016). *Tutto quello che non vi hanno mai detto sull'immigrazione.* Roma-Bari: Laterza.

Ambrosini, M. (2001). *La fatica di integrarsi: immigrati e lavoro in Italia.* Bologna: Il Mulino.

Ambrosini, M. (2013). Immigration in Italy: Between economic acceptance and political rejection. *Journal of International Migration and Integration, 14*(1), 175–194.

Ambrosini, M. (2018). *Irregular immigration in Southern Europe: Actors, dynamics and governance.* London: Springer.

Ambrosini, M., & Panichella, N. (2016). Immigrazione, occupazione e crisi economica in Italia. *Quaderni di Sociologia, 72*, 115–134.

Barbera, M., & Guariso, A. (2019). *La tutela antidiscriminatoria. Fonti, strumenti, interpreti.* Torino: Giappichelli.

Biondi Dal Monte, F. (2013). *Dai diritti sociali alla cittadinanza. La condizione giuridica dello straniero tra ordinamento italiano e prospettive sovranazionali.* Torino: Giappichelli.

Calafà, L. (2017). Lavoro irregolare (degli stranieri) e sanzioni. Il caso italiano. *Lavoro e diritto, 31*(1), 67–90.

Carrozza, P. (2016). Diritti degli stranieri e politiche regionali e locali. In C. Panzera, A. Rauti, C. Salazar, & A. Spadaro (Eds.), *Metamorfosi della cittadinanza e diritti degli stranieri.* Napoli: Editoriale Scientifica. 57 ff.

Cavallaro, M., Diamanti, G., & Pregliasco, L. (2018). *Una nuova Italia: Dalla comunicazione ai risultati, un'analisi delle elezioni del 4 marzo.* Roma: LIT EDIZIONI.

Centro Studi e Ricerche IDOS. (2017). *Dossier statistico immigrazione 2017.* Roma: IDOS.

Chiaromonte, W. (2008). Le prestazioni di assistenza sociale per i cittadini non comunitari ed il principio di non discriminazione. Una rassegna critica della giurisprudenza nazionale ed europea. *Giornale Diritto del Lavoro e di Relazioni Industriali, 1*, 101–145.

Chiaromonte, W. (2016). The Italian regulation on labour migration and the impact and possible impact of three EU directives on labour migration: Towards a human rights-based approach? In R. Blanpain, F. Hendrickx, & P. H. Olsson (Eds.), *National effects of the implementation of EU directives on labour migration from third countries.* Alphen aan den Rijn: Kluwer Law International. 117 ff.

Chiaromonte, W. (2018). «Cercavamo braccia, sono arrivati uomini». Il lavoro dei migranti in agricoltura fra sfruttamento ed istanze di tutela, *Giornale di diritto del lavoro e di relazioni industriali, 158*, 321–356.

Chiaromonte, W. (2019). Ideologia e tecnica della disciplina sovranista dell'immigrazione. Protezione internazionale, accoglienza e lavoro dopo il "decreto Salvini". *Giornale di diritto del lavoro e di relazioni industriali, 162*, 321–354.

Chiaromonte, W., & Guariso, A. (2019). Discriminazioni e welfare. In M. Barbera & A. Guariso (Eds.), *La tutela antidiscriminatoria. Fonti, strumenti, interpreti.* Torino: Giappichelli. 329 ff.

Colucci, M. (2018). *Storia dell'immigrazione straniera in Italia. Dal 1945 ai giorni nostri.* Roma: Carocci.

Corsi, C. (2014). Stranieri, diritti sociali e principio di eguaglianza nella giurisprudenza della Corte Costituzionale. *Federalismi, 3/2014*, 1–30.

Corsi, C. (2018). Peripezie di un cammino verso l'integrazione giuridica degli stranieri. Alcuni elementi sintomatici. *Associazione Italiana Costituzionalisti, Osservatorio costituzionale, 1*.

Council of Europe. (2011). *Report of the Commissioner for Human Rights*. Available at: https://www.coe.int/it/web/commissioner

D'Onghia, M., & de Martino, C. (2018). *Gli strumenti giuslavoristici di contrasto allo sfruttamento del lavoro in agricoltura nella legge n. 199 del 2016: ancora timide risposte a un fenomeno molto più complesso*, Working Paper CSDLE "Massimo D'Antona", 352/2018.

Diamanti, I. (2016). L'invasione mediale degli immigrati senza volto. *IV Rapporto Carta di Roma*, 9–13.

Direzione generale dell'immigrazione e delle politiche di integrazione – Ministero del lavoro e delle politiche sociali (2017). *Settimo rapporto annuale. Gli stranieri nel mercato del lavoro in Italia*. Roma.

EU Parliament, Directorate General for Internal Policies. (2016). *Labour Market Integration of Refugees: Strategies and Good Practices*. Available at: https://www.europarl.europa.eu/RegData/etudes/STUD/2016/578956/IPOL_STU%282016%29578956_EN.pdf

Fanizza, F., & Omizzolo, M. (2018). *Caporalato. An authentic agromafia*. Milano: Mimesis.

Favilli, C. (2015). *Reciproca fiducia, mutuo riconoscimento e libertà di circolazione di rifugiati e richiedenti protezione internazionale nell'Unione europea. Rivista di diritto internazionale, 98*(3), 701–747.

Federico, V., & Pannia, P. (2019). Migrants' legal statuses in contemporary Italy. First attempts of conceptualization. *Percorsi Costituzionali, 1*(18), 17–36.

Fondazione Leone Moressa. (2017). *Rapporto annuale sull'economia dell'immigrazione. La dimensione internazionale delle migrazioni*. Bologna: Il Mulino.

Gaeta, L. (2014). *Prima di tutto il lavoro. La costruzione di un diritto all'Assemblea Costituente*. Roma: Ediesse.

Guariso, A. (2012). Senza distinzioni. Quattro anni di contrasto alle discriminazioni istituzionali nel Nord Italia. *Quaderni di Apn, 2*, 1–25.

Korkut, U., et al. (2013). *The discourses and politics of migration in Europe*. London: Springer.

OECD, ILO, the World Bank and IMF. (2016). *Towards a Framework for Fair and Effective Integration of Migrants into the Labour Market*. Available at: https://www.ilo.org/wcmsp5/groups/public/%2D%2D-europe/%2D%2D-ro-geneva/%2D%2D-ilo-berlin/documents/genericdocument/wcms_556988.pdf

Oxfam. (2017). *La lotteria dell'accoglienza. Il Sistema dell'emergenza permanente*. Available at: https://www.oxfamitalia.org/wp-content/uploads/2017/11/La-Lotteria-Italia-dellaccoglienza_Report-Oxfam_8_11_2017_Final.pdf

Sciarra, S., & Chiaromonte, W. (2014). Migration status in labour and social security law. Between inclusion and exclusion in Italy. In C. Costello & M. Freedland (Eds.), *Migrants at work. Immigration and vulnerability in labour law*. Oxford: Oxford University Press. 121 ff.

Testaì, P. (2015). "From the (e)migrant to the (im)migrant": The Italian nation-state and its migration rhetoric and history. *Transnational Social Review, 5*, 24–38.

Triandafyllidou, A., & Ambrosini, M. (2011). Irregular immigration control in Italy and Greece: Strong fencing and weak gate-keeping serving the labour market. *European Journal of Migration and Law, 13*, 251–273.

UN Human Rights Council. (2014). *Report by the Special Rapporteur on the human rights of migrants, Addendum: Follow-up mission to Italy*, 2–6 December 2014. Available at: http://www.refworld.org/docid/5576e8404.html

Chapter 11
'Fortress' Switzerland? Challenges to Integrating Migrants, Refugees and Asylum-Seekers

Maria M. Mexi, Paula Moreno Russi, and Eva Fernández Guzman

11.1 Introduction: Setting the Scene

Migration historically plays an important role in the Swiss economy; foreign population recruitment has contributed to both past and recent economic growth in the country and today Switzerland is recognised as a country of immigration. The end of 2018 saw 2,081,169 legally resident foreign nationals in Switzerland, 1.3% more than 2017 (SEM Migration Report 2018). More than one third of the Swiss population has an immigrant background (is an immigrant or has at least one immigrant parent), while over one quarter of the population over 15-years-old living permanently in the country was born abroad (FSO 2018).

The country has driven active economic recruitment policies, opening doors to foreign labour forces when needed while retaining quite restrictive integration and naturalization policies (Ruedin et al. 2015). In this chapter, we argue that understanding how enablers and barriers to the labour market integration of migrants, refugees and asylum-seekers (MRAs) are shaped in relation to those historical, economic and political dimensions that drive evolution of migration and asylum policy is crucial if we want to grasp Switzerland's selective regime of migration and mobility.

Foreign nationals' access to Swiss territory over the last 50 years has been mostly based on economic interests. Yet today, third country nationals who migrate to Switzerland for family reunification, education or asylum application reasons represent an important part of the immigrating population. In this context, adapting legislation to ensure MRAs integrate better into the labour market is a challenge for the Swiss authorities. Political discussions about the implementation of art. 121a Cst. on the control of immigration adopted by the popular vote on 9 February 2014 and

M. M. Mexi (✉) · P. Moreno Russi · E. F. Guzman
University of Geneva, Geneva, Switzerland
e-mail: maria.mexi@unige.ch

V. Federico, S. Baglioni (eds.), *Migrants, Refugees and Asylum Seekers'
Integration in European Labour Markets*, IMISCOE Research Series,
https://doi.org/10.1007/978-3-030-67284-3_11

the implementation of this constitutional article are, together with other legislative changes, a tipping point that shows that integration issues acquired more prominence as an important objective of immigration policy at the federal level (Graf and Mahon 2018).

As observed in other European countries, awareness of the economic and social costs of non-integration has led Swiss policy-makers to promote integration as both an *individual duty* (conditional on the requirements and individual responsibilities of a foreign person) as well as a significant *priority* for policy stakeholders at federal, cantonal, and communal levels. This *pragmatic* yet in some cases *restrictive* approach to integration has indeed evolved over time. It has also been strengthened by the divisive debates around foreigners that surrounded the 2014 initiative against mass immigration (discussed later).

Against this background, the chapter aims to identify and critically analyse the socio-economic and political structure of Switzerland to provide a timely analysis of the evolving legal and policy framework that regulates the integration of MRAs into the Swiss labour market and society. The first part of the chapter sets the scene by presenting information about the constitutional principles that govern labour, immigration and asylum. The second part examines the relevant legislative and institutional framework in the fields of migration and asylum and captures how this framework and the Swiss approach to integration has evolved and adapted over the last decade. The third part *contextualizes* the relevant legislative and institutional framework that regulates labour market access for MRAs in Switzerland, drawing attention to historical, economic and political dimensions. The concluding part of the chapter summarizes the main findings of the analysis and outlines key aspects that (still) play an *obstructing role* for the integration of MRAs. We consequently problematize some impacts of direct democratic instruments on MRAs' rights and welfare, raising questions about whether the '*Fortress*' as a 'public metaphor' for restrictive and exclusionary migration and asylum policy resonates with Switzerland's current institutional and socio-historical trajectory.

11.2 Constitutional, Regulatory and Policy Framework on Labour, Migration and Asylum

11.2.1 Constitutional Principles and Provisions

Provisions on labour are entrenched in the Swiss Constitution. In particular, art.110 Cst. on employment gives the Confederation the power to legislate on employee protection, relations between employer and employee and the employment services. The article also stands provisions on the scope of application of collective labour agreements. The confederation has legislative powers over unemployment insurance and social security (art. 114 para.1 Cst.) as well as civil law, which includes legislation on employment contracts (art. 122 para.1 Cst.). Regarding fundamental rights in the labour area, the Constitution sets out *free choice of occupation, free access to an economic activity* (art. 27 para. 2 Cst.) and *freedom of association* (art. 23 and 28 Cst.) as fundamental rights. Free choice of occupation as a fundamental right (art. 27 Cst) is reserved for persons admitted without restriction in the Swiss labour market or those who are entitled to a residence permit (SCHR 2015a, b, c). The Constitution further sets out social objectives such as the objective that all persons capable of work should be able to practise an occupation under equitable conditions to assure their maintenance, and whereby children can receive appropriate education. Those objectives bind the Swiss lawmaker but cannot be directly invoked before the courts as subjective rights (art. 41 Cst.) (2007, ILO national labour law, Swiss profile) (International Labour Organization 2017).

Concurrently with these general principles on employment, the main constitutional principles on migration and asylum are those laid down in two articles under section 9 of the Swiss Constitution: *Residence and Permanent Settlement of Foreign Nationals*, art. 121 Cst. on legislation on foreign nationals and asylum and art. 121a Cst. Moreover, Art. 25 Cst. refers to migration and asylum introducing the principle of non-refoulement, adopted from the 1951 *Convention Relating to the Status of Refugees*, as a fundamental right. Art. 121 Cst. sets up the Confederation as the authority in charge of legislation on entry to and exit from Switzerland, the residence and permanent settlement of foreign nationals and granting asylum. The article also details the possibility of expelling foreign nationals from Switzerland *if they pose a risk to the security of the country* and it defines the offences for which the legal binding conviction of the foreigner may lead to the expulsion of the foreign national.

Crucially, and more recently, art. 121a Cst., in force since February 2014 after the acceptance of the initiative against mass immigration,[1] sets out the main principles controlling immigration. This must be effected autonomously by defining annual limits and a quota of residence permits delivered to foreign nationals coming to the country for gainful employment. As explained in more detail below, when defining the quotas of permits for gainful employment, two major principles need to be taken into consideration: Switzerland's *general economic interest* and *labour priority to Swiss citizens*.[2]

---

[1] The initiative against mass immigration, launched by the right wing party (SPV), was voted by the Swiss people on 14 February 2014. The vote led to the adoption of a new article of the Swiss Constitution on migration control. This article contained transitional provisions that gave 3 years to legislators to adapt the legislation on migration. Art. 121a Cst. provides full power and autonomy to the Swiss State to control immigration flux and policies. The article introduces a limit on the number of residence permits granted to foreign nationals using annual quotas (Boillet 2016). Art. 121 a para 3 Cst. lists the criteria to be taken into account when setting the quota: quotas and a ceiling must be defined in light of Switzerland's general economic interests and they must prioritize Swiss citizens. The criteria for granting residence permits are primarily: the application from an employer, the ability to integrate, and the adequate and independent means of subsistence of the foreign applicant. Additionally, Art. 121a para. 4 Cst. stipulates that no international agreements that breach this article may be concluded.

[2] In accordance with the principle of the national preference of Art.121a para. 3 Cst.

Apart from the chapter dedicated to foreign nationals, the Swiss Constitution also refers to migration and asylum in its fundamental principles, *by stressing the protection against expulsion, extradition and deportation* as a fundamental right. Art. 25 para 2 Cst. bans the deportation or extradition of refugees to a state in which they will be persecuted. Art. 25 para 3. Cst. mentions that no person may be deported to a state in which they face the threat of torture or any other form of cruel or inhumane treatment or punishment. The Asylum Act (AsylA, 26 June 1998) provides criteria to be met in order to be granted asylum and rules the request. It also provides, amongst others, the right to reside in Switzerland (art. 2, para 2, AsylA). As described by Fernández and Abbiate (2018, p. 451):

> The Lasi [AsylA] is tightly linked to the Letr [FNA] which specify the particular status of persons admitted temporarily into Switzerland (Art. 80a para 6, Art. 86, para 2, Art. 88, Art. 126a), the measures about the right to family reunification (Art. 3, para 2, Art. 47) and the departure from the country (Art. 76). (…) Contrary to the Member States of the European Union which are subject to European regulations concerning asylum, Switzerland's peculiar status makes the country not subject to most European directives concerning asylum. In this regard, Switzerland is not subject to either the Directive 2013/33 "Procedures", or the Directive 2011/95 "Qualification". This however does not mean that the country adopts a completely different legal framework.

In practice, after filing the asylum application and initial questioning, the State Secretariat for Migration (SEM) determines whether the substance of the application can be verified. In cases where it cannot be verified, the authority rejects the application by refusing it without a formal procedure or by issuing a decision of NEM (non-consideration),[3] which dismisses the application. If Switzerland is responsible for the examination of the asylum application, the SEM starts the procedure. After completion of the procedure, the SEM determines whether the asylum seeker meets the criteria in first place for refugee status and in second place, if he or she can be granted asylum. Accordingly, the SEM can render four types of decisions in addition to the NEM decision (refugeecouncil.ch 2018). After the complete examination procedure, the SEM can:

1. Grant asylum (decision in favour of granting asylum) (B permit)
2. Temporary admission as a refugee (decision against granting asylum although the person is recognised as refugee under international law, with suspension of the enforcement of the removal order) (F permit with refugee status)
3. Temporary admission (decision against granting asylum with suspension of the enforcement of the removal order) (F permit)

---

[3] The SEM can decide a 'non-consideration' (NEM) if the persons can return or continue: (1) to a safe third country under Article 6*a* para. 2 let. b AsylA in which he or she was previously resident; (2) to a third country that is responsible under an international agreement for conducting the asylum and removal procedures; (3) to the country of previous residence if possible; (4) to a third country for which he or she holds a visa and in which he or she can seek protection; (5) to a third country in which persons with whom he or she has a close relationship or dependants live; (6) to the their native country or country of origin under Article 31 *AsylA (article on recognition of asylum and removal decisions made in* the Dublin Regulation (Regulation 604/2013*).

4. Rejection (decision against granting asylum with removal order) (no legal status)

According to the AsylA, asylum may be granted to persons recognized as refugees under international law if there are no exclusion motivations (art. 49 AsylA). Those exclusion motivations are the unworthiness of the refugee status (art. 53 AsylA) and subjective post-flight grounds (art. 54 AsylA). Individuals granted asylum are entitled to receive a residence permit (B permit), which is delivered by their canton of residence.

In cases where asylum is denied, the SEM determines a removal order or an alternative measure that refers to articles 83 and 84 FNA. If the removal order execution is not permitted, not reasonable or not possible, the individual is admitted temporarily. In each case, the foreigner obtains a permit F, valid for 12 months, extendable if there are no motivations that could stop the temporary admission (art. 41 para 2 FNA).

More precisely, removal is not permitted (art. 83 para. 3 FNA) if it contravenes Switzerland's obligations under international law. It is not reasonable (art. 83 para. 4 FNA) when the removal would seriously endanger the foreigner's life, and it is not possible (art. 83 para. 2 FNA) when technical reasons prevent removal (no means of transportation, no travel documents issued from the native country, etc.). In that sense, a temporary admission is seen as an 'alternative measure' to removal. In cases where asylum is denied under the AsylA but there is a recognition of the refugee status under international law, the removal is postponed and the individual is provisionally admitted as a refugee and receives a permit F with the refugee mention. The AsylA provides for procedural guarantees and the "status" of 'temporary admittance' similar to the EU status on 'subsidiary protection'.

Since 2010, asylum legislation began a restructuration process that is still ongoing and which was not driven by the so-called 2014 Refugee Crisis. Since this period, urgent measures entered into force on 29 September 2012. Amongst those measures are: the abolition of the possibility of submitting an asylum application abroad (art. 19 and 20 AsylA), and the abolition of desertion or refusal to perform military service as asylum motivations (art. 3 para. 3 AsylA). Additional modifications entered into force stated that the removal of citizens from countries considered as safe is usually reasonable (art. 83 para. 5 FNA) and that persons subject to a legally binding removal decision for which a departure deadline has been fixed are excluded from receiving social assistance (art. 82 para. 1 AsylA). More recently, in June 2016, Swiss voters approved an amendment proposal, the main objective is to accelerate the procedures and shorten the time-limit for appeals. Amongst the new disposals of the amendment, we find: the gathering of all the persons playing a role in the asylum process in registration and procedure centres, managed by the federal authorities, the separation between applications to be processed as accelerated procedures and extended procedures with respective timelimits for the duration of the process and the granting of free legal representation (ODAE Romand 2017). However, the complete reform will enter into force by the end of 2019, but the accelerated procedure has already been tested in Zurich since 2014.

11.2.2 Legal and Policy Framework Governing the Labour Market Integration of MRAs

Switzerland's immigration policy is embodied in the Foreign Nationals Act (FNA),[4] approved by the Swiss electorate on 24 September 2006 and in force since 1 January 2008. However, persons who fall under the Swiss-EU Bilateral Agreement on the Free Movement of Persons (AFMP) face different legal treatment compared to third country nationals. The AFMP applies to citizens of EU-28/EFTA Member States and their family members, as well as to posted workers (regardless of their citizenship) of a legal entity based in an EU-28/EFTA Member State (SEM Migration Report 2018). Nationals from third countries (also called third state nationals) are subject to the FNA. This 'two circles' model of the Swiss foreign law distinguishes between the liberal European internal migration (first circle) and migration from outside Europe/EFTA (second circle) (SCHR 2015a). In practical terms, regardless of nationality or the motivations that influence their decisions to enter Switzerland, foreign nationals are subject to the ordinary regime regulated by the FNA. Two special regimes complete the ordinary regime, translated by two exceptions: AFMP and Asylum regimes. Nationals from EU/EFTA member states are subject to the AFMP, whereas persons seeking protection against persecution fall under the special asylum regime regulated by the Asylum Act (AsylA), the Geneva Convention of 1951 and the Dublin regulation (Amarelle and Nguyen 2017). In practice, the FNA is only applied where the AFMP or Asylum legislation do not contain relevant provisions that could be applied in cases where the FNA lays down more favourable provisions (Art. 2 FNA and Amarelle and Nguyen 2017).

To settle in Switzerland, people from third countries must meet very specific criteria (SEM 2017). These criteria differ and correspond to an administrative criteria allocated to immigration reasons. The Swiss foreigners legislation admits:

– Selected persons coming for gainful employment, which implies the person settles in Switzerland because she/he has been previously hired and she/he meets the various relatively strict criteria mentioned in the law. Among the range of criteria and factors assessed are the level of specialization and qualification as well as the ability to integrate into Swiss society. Furthermore, the precedence principle must be respected.[5]

---

[4] Now known as: Federal Act on Foreign Nationals (FNIA) since January 2019.

[5] For a foreign national to be granted a permit with gainful employment, a set of requirements must be fulfilled. A principle of priority (precedence), which states that employers must prove that they have not been able to recruit a suitable employee from the priority categories considered together as the 'internal workforce', must be respected (art. 21 FNA). Moreover, salary and employment conditions customary for the location, profession and sector must be satisfied (art. 22 FNA) and personal qualifications are thoroughly examined (art. 23 FNA). Art. 23 FNA provides that short-term stays and residence permits for work purposes may only be granted to cadre, specialist and other qualified employees with a degree from a university or institution of higher education and several years of experience. Additional criteria as professional and social adaptability, language skills and age are examined to ensure the professional and social integration of the applicant (art.

- People who do not come for gainful employment but for other specific reasons such as rentiers, for medical treatment or to study[6] must have sufficient funds to support themselves.
- Persons who come for family reunification reasons to join a Swiss or a foreign national with a residence permit. The right to admission by family reunification depends on very specific criteria such as independence from social assistance. The integration dimension is also required and has been reinforced in the Federal Act on Foreign Nationals and Integration (FNIA).

Third-country nationals willing to immigrate to Switzerland for gainful employment face several barriers before being admitted into the territory and having access to the Swiss labour market. They need to have found a job beforehand in order to receive a residence permit. According to the economic interest principle, the Federal Council has the power to limit the number of first-time short stay and residence permits for work purposes (art. 20 FNA). Concretely, in order to regulate the admission of third-country citizens, the Swiss government publishes, at the beginning of each year, the maximum quantity of permits that can be allocated to third-country nationals. Different quotas are allocated to cantons according to their size and needs, while another set of quota (package of permits) is kept at the federal level as a reserve for cantons that have exhausted their quota (Sandoz 2016b, p. 41).

The legislative framework that organises MRAs' labour, access to territory and integration has faced major changes in recent years. In September 2016, two projects were led the Swiss Parliament to decide on the amendment of the Foreign Nationals Act (FNA). The first concerned the implementation of the aforementioned Art. 121a of the Swiss Constitution on immigration control, resulting from the initiative from February 2014 against mass immigration. The article in the FNA that implements art. 121a Cst. places refugees and temporarily admitted persons in the category of a 'native workforce' that ought, from a legal point of view, to be considered as having priority access to the labour market.

The second project focused on provisions to improve the integration of foreigners and to strengthen the application of the already well-established principle of 'promoting and requiring' in the field of integration. The amendments came into force in several waves between June 2018 and January 2019. According to the amendments, the foreigner's level of integration is assessed when renewing his or her residence permit and when applying for a more long term residency permit (Art. 34 para.4 and 5 FNIA Art.42, para.3 FNIA). The amendments legally define four

---

23 FNA). Furthermore, foreign nationals must have suitable accommodation to be admitted (art. 24 FNA).

[6] Art. 27–29 of the FNA: Foreign nationals may be admitted for education purposes if there is confirmation from an educational establishment that the person is eligible for education or training, if suitable accommodation is available, if the person has the required financial means and if the foreign national fulfils the personal and educational requirements for the planned education or training course. Retired persons must have reached the minimum age set by the Federal Council, special relations to the country and have required financial means. In case of medical treatment, persons must also have the required financial means and a guarantee of their return.

criteria: respect for public safety and order, respect for constitutional values, language skills and participation in economic life or educational training (art. 58a FNIA). Language requirements to obtain and renew residency permits are specified and reinforced according to the status of the permit and the rights related to the permit status.

Long term residence permits (C) can now be withdrawn and replaced by other residence permits[7] if the conditions for integration are not met. In these cases, the person whose permit has been downgraded will have to wait 5 years before applying again for a long term residence permit. Also, the changes introduced for family reunification requirements demand: the spouses of holders of a residence or long term residence permit to provide proof of an A1 level orally, or to prove their enrolment in a language course. In addition, the cantons can now conclude integration agreements and set specific objectives for people who do not meet the integration criteria (Stanic 2018). Information concerning the reception of social assistance or unemployment allowance may be taken into account in assessing the level of integration and the payment of supplementary benefits may constitute a criterion for revoking the residence permit of a person without gainful employment or become an obstacle to family reunification. If the use of social assistance was already a reason for revoking the residence permit and sometimes even the long term residence permit, according to the new amendments, the long term residence permits of persons who make long-term and substantial use of social assistance may also be revoked even if they have resided in the country legally and without interruption for more than 15 years. Previously, persons residing in the country for more than 15 years without interruption were protected against this provision. It is important to note that most of the amended provisions do not apply to EU and EFTA nationals, as their stay is regulated by the Agreement on the Free Movement of Persons (AFMP), which does not impose any integration requirements (ibid). With the amendments to the foreigners legislation, Switzerland has introduced a gradual integration model, according to the following principle: the higher the legal status under the law on foreigners, the higher the requirements for integration (Kurt 2017c).

Regarding access for refugees and provisionally admitted persons, the work permit that employers used to have to apply for was replaced by a simple registration procedure that also extended their geographical work mobility within the country. The 10% tax this population had to pay on its income from gainful employment was abolished. In the event of recourse to social assistance, participation in integration programmes has been made compulsory, under penalty of reduction of benefits.

---

[7] Other country nationals may be granted different types of permit: These include the short stay permit (1 year permit, named 'L' permit), residence permit (more than 1 year but limited to a certain number of years and renewable, named 'B' permit) and the permanent residence permit (unlimited period and newly legal criterion for Swiss citizenship, named 'C' permit). A fourth type of permit is granted for employment in a border zone as a 'cross-border commuter permit' (art. 35 FNA).

11.2.3 Integration as an Individual Duty and a Policy Priority

To better understand the legal framework for the labour market integration of migrants and foreign nationals linked to the asylum domain, it is important to analyse the concept of integration from the point of view of Swiss law. The integration of the foreign population was already (from 2008) one of the fundamental objectives of the FNA, and was ruled by the specific ordinance on the integration of foreigners (OIE; RS 142 205). Principles of integration were given by article 4 FNA. Chapter 8 of the FNA with art. 53–58 FNA gives more focused provisions on integration, specifically on encouraging integration (art. 53 FNA) and the consideration of integration in the case of decisions, e.g. in the cases of admission or permit granting, where integration is seen as a duty (art. 54 FNA). More specifically, *the co-existence of the Swiss and foreign resident population on the basis of the values stated in the Federal Constitution as mutual respect and tolerance, which are the aims of integration. In addition to foreigners' obligation to participate in the economic, social and cultural life of the Swiss society* (art. 4 FNA).

Integration was already crucial in the FNA, where it was emphasized as a requirement and an *individual duty* of the foreign person. Moreover, in the FNIA the strong connection between work and residence permits is further stressed and a model of gradual integration is introduced, as longer-term residence permits and renewals become linked to progressively stricter integration requirements (Kurt 2017c). Obtaining, extending and being able to keep the various residence permits and family reunification becomes thus possible only if the assessment from the authorities shows that the person meets the conditions for integration.[8] Additionally, if a foreign person relies on social assistance, an aspect also assessed, may even lead to downgrading or revocation of a permit (Art.62 para 1 let.e, Art. 63 para 1 let. C and Art 63 para2 FNIA).

Next to being promoted as an individual duty, integration is also emphasized as a *policy priority* that needs to be promoted by authorities at the Confederation, cantons and communal levels (see e.g. specific provisions in art. 53FNA). Art.53 para 3. FNA sets goals of professional advancement and encouragement of foreign population as a major task fulfill by the Confederation, cantons and communes, creating favourable regulatory conditions of equal opportunities for the foreign population. Additionally, in the case of integration, national and local authorities are called to cooperate with social partners, non-governmental organisations and expatriate' organisations (art.53 para 5 FNA). Among the new elements introduced with the FNIA, we find: the protection against discrimination toward foreign population, the avoidance of underuse of the foreign population potential, the support to basic skills development and registration of unemployed refugees and temporarily admitted

---

[8] Criteria to assess integration are listed in Art. 58a FNIA. Those include *respect for public safety, security and order; respect for the values of the Federal Constitution; language skills; and participation in working life or efforts to acquire education.*

persons in public employment agencies. The article also includes provisions for special needs of women, children and adolescents.

The operationalization of the FNIA (art. 54) points to existing ordinary structures at federal, cantonal and municipal level as first instances through which integration must be achieved (these structures are in charge of education and training programs, employment and labour issues, social security, health, among others). The task of ordinary structures in the promotion of integration was previously stated in the former OIE, yet is now enshrined in the foreigners' act. In cases where gaps exist in ordinary structures or where offers are not accessible, the FNIA provides for a specific integration promotion that can be set at federal, municipal or cantonal level (art. 55 FNIA). In addition, Article 55a. FNIA requires cantons to immediately provide for special integration measures for foreigners with relevant needs hampering their integration (as lack of education and basic labour skills). Finally, the law also clearly specifies the distribution of competences between local and national administrations as well as financial contributions from the Confederation to other administrative levels (art. 58 FNIA).

According to the Swiss Law, immigrants' social and labour integration is a duty of the ordinary structures, also called 'established frameworks', such as the employment offices, welfare or education services. The Swiss state develops integration through the ordinary structures in accordance with their legal mandates and their existing offers and services. However, ordinary structures conceived for the needs of the local population can often not accommodate specific categories of migrants because those migrants do not meet the entry criteria (e.g. level of knowledge of the local language, lack of basic skills, years in the canton as a taxpayer, etc.) and/or the services offered do not suit specific migrants' needs. Therefore, the Law foresees for a specific provision on the promotion of integration of immigrants, which provides special support to foreigners to develop the required conditions to access existing ordinary structures. The specific provision on the promotion of integration of immigrants was a guiding principle of the former FNA, the new FNIA includes now a specific provision on this matter (art. 55 FNIA). Since 2014, Cantonal Integration Programs (CIPs) have been the policy instrument, which strategically focus on the planning and implementation of the specific provision on the promotion of immigrants' integration in collaboration with ordinary structures. Those programs are the result of a joint strategy agreed in 2011 between the Cantons and the Confederation. Each Canton established its own Cantonal Integration Program (CIP I 2014–2017 & CIP II 2018–2021) with the purpose of strengthening: *social cohesion, mutual respect, tolerance, participation, and equality of opportunities* for foreigners living in Switzerland. The programmes aim to strengthen the existing measures, reduce disparities between cantons, to fill gaps while allowing leeway to take local factors into account, and letting the cantons set their own implementation priorities.

Additionally, to further boost integration efforts regarding migrants from the asylum framework, the Confederation and the cantons established recently a joint nationwide integration agenda, the 'Swiss Integration Agenda', advanced in spring 2018 and implemented from 2019 provides for binding measures and strengthens individual support and case management for refugees and temporarily admitted persons. Additionally, it increases the lump sum paid by the Confederation to the Cantons to fund integration measures from 6000 to 18,000 Swiss francs per refugee or temporarily admitted person. As explained in SEM's Migration Report (2018, p. 38), the Integration Agenda foresees certain clearly measurable targets that the Confederation and the cantons should abide with:

> All recognised refugees and temporarily admitted persons have basic knowledge of one national language after three years. 80% of children from the asylum system can communicate in the language of their place of residence before they start school. Two-thirds of recognised refugees and temporarily admitted persons aged between 16 and 25 are enrolled in a vocational education and training course within five years. Half of adult refugees and temporarily admitted persons are integrated in the labour market within seven years. All recognised refugees and temporarily admitted persons are within a few years familiar with the Swiss way of life and have contact with the local community. Regular reviews are needed to ensure that these targets are being met and to evaluate the impact that integration measures have had. The decision was therefore taken to develop a monitoring system; its introduction is scheduled for mid-2020.

Future assessments of the implementation of the Integration Agenda will be crucial to assess if and how the Swiss recent approach to integration has indeed functioned as an *enabler* to MRAs' labour market integration – and under what cantonal specificities and conditions. 'Promoting' and 'requiring' are the two keywords of Swiss integration policy from recent years, stating the requirements and individual responsibilities of a foreign person with regard to integration and the policy priorities involving inter alia promotion of equal opportunities (Kurt 2017b).

That said, it is relevant to consider that in practice within a context of Federalism, several acts and law provisions are loosely defined at the federal level: the cantons have a degree of flexibility and discretionality while applying the legal mandates. This is especially the case for decisions on admissions for family reunification, permit extensions and decisions involving integration as a requirement (in decisions for granting unlimited residence permits). For instance, one of the criteria for granting a residence permit to a spouse or child is having suitable housing. Criteria to assess if the foreign citizen has suitable housing can differ according to the cantons (e.g. number of bedrooms). On the one hand, this flexibility allows the cantons to adapt the provisions to its situation and needs. On the other hand, those discretionary margin lead to unequal treatment of migrants according to the cantons (Wichmann et al. 2011). Until 2018, no official definition of integration was provided by the Swiss legislation. When determining the degree of integration of foreign nationals living in Switzerland for permit decisions, the practice shows that cantonal authorities have taken their decisions based on respect for legal order and the values of the Constitution, knowledge of local language and willingness to participate in economic activities and education as well as knowledge of the 'Swiss way of life' as mentioned by the Citizenship Act. According to Wichmann et al. (2011), cantonal interpretation and practices diverge from 'inclusive' practices that have low requirements with many exceptions to 'exclusive' practices with a high requirement and a low number of exceptions. Cantonal differences, give rise to unequal treatment, as in the case for asylum seekers, who, depending on the canton, can easily access the labour market, while in others, the exercise of a gainful activity is subject to certain restrictions. Additionally, several cantons allow asylum seekers to access language courses at an early application stage, while in others they have to wait for a positive decision on their case.

Moreover, according to the law, the integration of foreigners must first be carried out through ordinary structures and since these structures operate differently in each canton, these are additional enablers of social inequalities across cantons.

To sum up, the latest findings of a study of the Swiss Forum for Migration and Population Studies by Probst et al. (2019) into cantonal discretionary powers in migration policy distinguishes two approaches for cantonal practices to tackle integration provisions. The first are restrictive practices, whereby integration is based on individual will and responsibility; this supposes high barriers to immigrants' rights and privileges, translated into limited offers of support and conditional offers of incentives. The second comprise inclusive practices, which are enablers for immigrants' access to rights, to extensive offers of support and intensive encouragement of individual capacities, resulting in opportunity-based support and facilitated labour market access. According to the study, preferences are related to contextual factors such as political orientations, demographic factors, economic conditions and the administrative cultures of the cantons. Additionally, services in charge of integration vary according to institutional cultures and the provision of services distribution and responsibility across local structures (e.g. service for immigrant population are in some cases responsibility of the population office, while in others of the security or social affairs office). Therefore the importance and the role of ordinary structures in promoting integration also varies from one canton to another, which is due as well to the lack of presence of some of these specific structures at the local levels (Probst et al. 2019).

11.3 Contextualizing Immigration: Historical, Economic and Political Dimensions

11.3.1 Seven Phases and Major Evolutions

Historical contextualization is crucial for understanding how the recent approach to integration put forward by Swiss policy-makers and legislators has evolved and crystalized. According to Etienne Piguet (2017), the country's history of immigration can be divided into six major phases. Following Piguet's logic, we could see a seventh phase starting with the 2014 initiative against mass immigration. Piguet's first phase, from 1948 to 1962, can be seen as an open period. The labour shortage faced by the country after the Second World War drives the Government to engage in labour recruitments agreements, first with Italy, then with Spain. The beginning of this 'Open Door' period is also the starting point of the 'Gastarbeiter' immigration regime (ibid, p. 19). Delivering seasonal and one-year renewable permits, the government sees immigration as *temporary* without the possibility of long-term residence and makes sure the situation remains temporary.

From 1963 to 1973, increasing xenophobia within the Swiss population, housing shortage and the country's struggle to deliver public goods and services, drive the country to attempt to decrease immigration. The country implements successive measures to limit labour migration and attempt to control the risks of 'foreign over-population' without real results (ibid). As an example of a limitation measure, with the 'simple ceiling' that has been introduced in 1963, permits were awarded only to workers in companies with less than 2% increase in overall employment compared to December 1962. However, foreign workers came to replace high numbers of Swiss workers that changed their job to pass from the secondary to tertiary sector in that period, limiting the expected results of the simple ceiling. A new attempt was made with the introduction of the 'double ceiling' in 1965, asking companies to reduce 5% of the level of their foreign workforce and not to increase their total number of foreign workers. The measure, however, had negative effects, hindering the development of small enterprises. Finally, the concept of a global ceiling, which is still in force today,[9] was introduced in 1970, with the definition of new annual quotas every year on the basis of the departures.

The first oil shock marked the start of the third phase, which led to a decrease in the total foreign population. From 1973, tens of thousands of foreigners left the country after losing their jobs. The precarious situation of immigrants raised awareness on the living and social conditions of the seasonal workers, and led the Government in 1978 to propose measures to facilitate foreigners' social integration, seeking to create a more enabling environment, by addressing a number of issues pertaining, for instance, to a person's access to local language courses or family reunification as well as the status of seasonal workers. However, the relevant proposals for legal revisions were submitted to a popular referendum in 1982 and they were rejected by a very narrow majority (50.4%).

From around 1985 to 1992, the fourth phase represents the second wave of large-scale immigration. With an improving economy, the need for a workforce pushes the authorities to implement a flexible quota system. Almost 50,000 new permits are issued every year between 1985 and 1995 and more than 130,000 seasonal workers enter the country during the same period (Piguet 2013). This new wave of immigration is primarily comprised of citizens from Yugoslavia and Portugal. The fifth phase begins in the early 1990s. If immigration to Switzerland in the 1970s was largely characterised by workers who entered the country through the quotas system, the 1980s saw a gradual change with immigration comprised of people who entered the country not for work, but for family reunification, education, retirement and asylum, amongst other reasons. Immigrants' countries of origin diversify as well, and an increasing number of migrants come from countries other than the

---

[9] "Quotas have continually been used since the 70's but the categories of foreigners subject to this quota system have change over time and the system as undergone numerous modifications" (Sandoz 2016b, p.40).

historically traditional sending states (Piguet 2013; D'Amato 2008). Therefore, since the beginning of the 1990s the increase and diversification of immigrants journeys and the country's fear of being isolated in the middle of Europe while the continent increasingly embraces the free movement of persons, forces Switzerland to question its migration policy.

In 2002, the beginning of the progressively implementation of the AFMP signed with the European Union and approved by the voters in 2000 marked one of the *turning points of the renewed six phase policy*. This agreement provides freedom of mobility for EU and EFTA citizens to access the Swiss labour market. In 2008, the implementation of FNA completes the renewal of the immigration policy in regards to third countries nationals (Piguet 2013; D'Amato 2008). The new act *limits with exceptions*, the third countries nationals immigration to highly skilled workers by implementing the quota system, which allowed an immigration control adapted to the needs of the Swiss economy (Piguet 2017).

We can now advance a seventh phase, a new turning point on the politization of immigration issues and more restrictive immigration policies, which coincided with the 2014 right-wing 'initiative against mass immigration', supported by 50.3% of Swiss voters, and that requests the *re-establishment of quotas for all categories of foreigners*, including European citizens. This places the government in a delicate position, as reintroducing quotas would not be compatible with the principles of the Free Movement of Persons (Sandoz 2016a, b). As a result of the approved initiative, art. 21a FNA introduces measures aimed at supporting the 'native' workforce (or domestic employees) and more precisely the unemployed people registered in Regional Employment Office. The Federal Council, the Swiss executive power, established a list of professions or sectors by an unemployment rate only the sectors touched with a unemployment rate over the 5% are subject to these measure. In practice, when an employer wants to publish a job offer, she/he has first to check if the required profile/position is included in the list. If this is the case, she/he must follow a particular procedure: the employer must announce the job vacancy to the Regional Employment Office. During five working days, the employer cannot publish this job offer on other platforms. After 3 days, the Regional Employment Office has to communicate the relevant application files to the employer. The latter has to convene interviews or tests of professional ability with the applicants who fit the required profile. Finally, if the employer hires a candidate or, on the contrary, if not satisfied, she/he has to inform the Regional Employment Office. This measure aims at fostering the workforce available in Switzerland in areas affected by high rates of unemployment by giving priority to job seekers registered in Regional Employment Offices.

Interestingly, according to Boillet and Maiani (2016) the text of the initiative (art. 121a Cst.) is a clear and direct discrimination principle towards immigrants because it *explicitly* states the *national preference*. The transposition from the constitutional art. 121a Cst. to the art. 21a FNA transforms direct discrimination into indirect discrimination. In the case of nationality, a direct discrimination is to enact a different treatment between nationals and foreigners (as did art. 121a Cst.); an indirect discrimination introduces seemingly neutral criteria but from which consequences are similar to a direct discrimination principle. In that respect, the place of residence is considered as indirectly discriminatory (Boillet and Maiani 2016). Therefore, legally speaking, the art. 21a FNA is not compatible with the principle of equal employment opportunity (article 7 let. a AFMP) or with the principle of equal treatment (art. 9, annex 1 AFMP) (ibid). In other words, the required registration in a Regional Employment Office is more easily fulfilled by Swiss nationals and it clearly disadvantages foreign nationals who are looking for a job in Switzerland. Nevertheless, as art. 21a FNA has included temporarily admitted persons and refugees in the category of internal workforce (as mentioned above), the article should facilitate labour market integration for those two categories of persons (Graf and Mahon 2018). Although the example of the art. 21a FNA – among other changes in the legislation – does not seem to resolve conflicts with the AFMP act, it is indeed *less extreme* in comparison with art.121a Cst. Art. 21a FNA could be considered a 'light version' of the national preference principle.

The applicability in practice of Art 21a FNA is complex. Legally, for a person to be registered in a regional employment office, he or she must fulfill criteria that demonstrate his or her employability. The assessment of this employability differs from case to case and canton to canton. While the light implementation does not yet seem to have a direct positive impact on the integration of refugees and temporary migrants into the labour market. The implementation of the initiative against mass immigration was partially transformed to accompanying legal and policy measures to strengthen support for the integration of refugees and temporary, reserving as a reminder of the availability of resources and labour potential of some groups of immigrants in the territory (Graf and Mahon 2018).

Additionally, further parliamentary discussions on attempts to control immigration from the European Union still polarize public opinion. The new initiative of the SVP ('limitation initiative', August 2018), currently under examination by parliament and on which the people may be called upon to vote, calls for a constitutional amendment to renegotiate the end of the AFMP and enact a prohibition on establishing of new treaties that would grant a regime of free movement of persons to foreign people. The Federal Council and the National Council have already recommended the rejection of this initiative. The reasons given are the desire to preserve the agreements with the EU, which would be threatened by a breach of the AFMP, and the desire to preserve the country's economic interest.

11.3.2 Politics Matters No Less Than Economics

Over recent decades, most Swiss immigration policies and regulatory frameworks have been largely driven by economic considerations. As Klöti et al. (2007, p. 622) note, Switzerland is a country "which has successfully implemented guest worker initiatives with active economic recruitment policies alongside restrictive integration and naturalisation policies." Concurrently, economic considerations have often provoked hostile public opinion and a general political climate that finds against both immigration and asylum-seekers, as suggested by the results of a number of direct democratic votes. Other than the 2014 initiative against mass immigration, these include the ban on new Islamic minarets accepted by 58% of Swiss citizens, and the popular initiative of 2010 asking for the expulsion of foreign criminals, which was accepted by 53% of Swiss voters. In this regard, to better understand the migration landscape in Switzerland, it is important to keep in mind the country's political 'infrastructure'. The direct democracy component of the Swiss political system allows citizens' initiatives to request revisions of the Federal Constitution based on 100,000 citizens signatures gathered over an 18-month period (art. 138 and 139 Cst.) Any constitutional amendment proposed by parliament has to be approved by a majority of the people and the cantons. Laws that have been passed by parliament can be challenged through an optional legislative referendum. In this case, citizens have to gather by 50,000 signatures against the law within 100 days after it has been passed. After the Second World War, referenda and initiatives became more frequent and the latter became a tool to promote political innovation *against the will of the political elite*, in particularly to limit migration flux (Linder 2010).

In a country characterised by 'solid' political stability, recent changes and the move to the right signal the salience of immigration issues. As of 2018, the Federal Council includes representatives from the Liberal Party (FDP), the Swiss Social Democratic Party (SP), the Swiss People's Party (SVP), and the Swiss Christian Democratic Party (CVP). Considerable gains made by the SVP (right-wing conservative party), which has its roots in the farming community, have marked the country polarization on immigration issues over the last two decades. Between 1995 and 2015, the SVP won additional 36 parliamentary seats, while the FDP lost 12 and the CVP 10. In this political context, migration has become a matter of *heightened political dispute*. On the one hand, populist parties have pledged more restrictive policies and promoted controversial initiatives such as the 2014 popular initiative against mass immigration (Ruedin and D'Amato 2015). Yet, as shown by the Integration Agenda and implementation of the constitutional article resulting from the initiative against mass immigration, the Swiss federal and cantonal authorities have made concrete efforts to promote a more pragmatic approach to fostering immigrants' integration, considering the social tensions and additional costs of the non-inclusion of the MRAs into the labour market.

11.4 Conclusion: 'Fortress' Switzerland?

Our review of the legal and policy framework governing immigration sheds light on the crucial role of integration, not only when discussing the potential of professional integration but also as a condition in cases of granting residence permits or extensions.

Overall, different amendments and revisions of the foreigners and asylum legislation reflect the willingness of the authorities to foster the integration of certain groups of immigrants into the labour market. This is represented by adapting the laws and policies concerning those migrants who are likely to stay and who entail a cost to society in case of unemployment. Through the amendment process, some administrative barriers that have been removed or simplified may in fact facilitate labour market integration. These include, for instance, the abolishment of the 10% special tax that working asylum-seekers and temporary admitted foreigners without asylum recognition were required to pay, and the replacement of the employer's request by a simple announcement. Despite positive signs, though, new barriers relating to certain administrative barriers have been raised. A clear example of these new barriers concerns immigrants who rely on social assistance as they seek to gain a foothold in the labour market. Indeed, as previously mentioned, according to new FNIA provisions, dependency on social assistance is sometimes a ground for the non-renewal of residence permits; also, the fear of seeking support may result in greater insecurity and become an important obstacle to a foreign person's entry and sustainable integration into the labour market (Mexi et al 2019).

At the same time, the *fluid character of certain statuses*, such as those illustrated in the most extreme form by the "temporary admission status" (permit F), remains an important obstacle to integration (ODAE Romand 2015; Matthey 2015), despite reactions from various actors and political forces that have proposed to introduce changes. According to Matthey (2015), half of the foreigners with temporary admission end up staying in Switzerland more than 7 years, including the stay before the grant of the permit F. Though its name suggests that the person is staying temporarily in the country, migrants with permit 'F' usually stay many years in Switzerland. Stigmatization and lack of information about this status are significant obstacles, as potential employers may be afraid to hire people they perceive as not being able to stay in the territory in the long term. Moreover, permit 'F' restricts freedom of movement since the foreigner is constrained to stay in the canton where she/he was granted the temporary admission. Low mobility makes it difficult to find a job. Moreover, with the recent amendments of the immigration legislation, the type of security bestowed upon a foreign person by other types of permits, such as the long-term residence permit, has been weakened. This has become more intense with the introduction of the gradual integration model in the FNIA, which allows for the possibility to have the status of a foreigner downgraded if integration is deemed insufficient (Kurt 2017c).

Depending on the type of permit, *geographical and professional mobility* can be either allowed or not allowed. This impacts on the professional integration of foreign nationals. Since permits are linked to the cantons, third-country nationals with short stay permits wanting to change their canton of residence must request a new permit from the new canton (art. 37 FNA). This can be seen as *barrier* when looking for new work positions in other cantons. Foreign nationals who have been granted a short stay permit with gainful employment can take advantage of professional mobility only under certain conditions. In those cases, since permits are linked to employment, beneficiaries might be afraid of being dismissed.

The *recognition of qualifications* also continues to be an obstacle to overcome, as shown by the over-qualification rates. Skills acquired in third-countries are often considered as being of lower standard. This makes granting an equivalence diploma more difficult. Additionally, for persons under the asylum framework who had to flee their countries, it is often difficult to obtain documents that certify their diploma or past professional experience (Sandoz 2016a). As stated by the Federal Commission for Migration-FCM, besides the diploma and professional certificates, informal skills also need to be considered. It is, therefore, important to validate and assess practical skills to complete the current system of diploma recognition (Release FCM 2016).

On another – very important – note, even though the legal framework for the promotion of integration has significantly evolved, certain groups of the population are *not* entitled to benefit from integration programs from their first day in Switzerland. Art.4 para. 2 FNA specifies that integration is aimed only at "foreign nationals who are lawful residents in Switzerland for the longer term". This provision excludes, therefore, asylum-seekers and irregular migrants. This is the case even though the stability of the protection rate shows that significant numbers of asylum seekers are likely to stay in Switzerland (Kurt 2017a, b). The harsh realities of asylum-seeking have been particularly documented in *The Fortress* (*La Forteresse*) – a 2008 documentary film showing how men, women and children, running from war, persecution and economic crises, are held in processing centers under conditions that closely resemble detention while they wait for the Swiss authorities to decide to grant them – or not – refugee status. While the documentary subtly problematizes the moral aspects of Switzerland's asylum policy, a recent empirical study by Hainmüeller et al. (2016) provides evidence for the fact that longer waiting times for asylum status determination delay refugees' subsequent economic integration. The authors suggest psychological distress as the primary explanation for their results.

Additionally, the federalist nature of the Swiss state does not make the task of integrating foreigners any easier. As we have seen, cantons have a relevant margin of manoeuvre which leads to the unequal treatment of immigrants groups within the territory (Manatschal 2014). Initiatives at the federal level, such as the CIPs, are paving the way for immigration policy harmonisation. Policies such as the Integration Agenda and the amendments to the FNIA should also help to reduce differences across cantons in some areas of integration. However, the implementation of laws and policies still depends heavily on the diversity of the cantons' political positioning and institutional systems in which ordinary structures are embedded. That said, differences between cantons can also be seen as opportunities. As stated by the *Laboratory Democracies* metaphor in Brandeis's decentralised democracies,[10] the different practices can serve as a laboratory, cantons and communes have the opportunity to learn from the experiences of others (Cattacin 1996), even if the exact transposition of policies is not necessarily realistic given the structural and organisational differences between the administrative levels.

---

[10] Refer to *New State Ice Co. v. Liebmann*, 285 U.S. Supreme Court 262 (1932).

Generally, as pointed out by the Federal Commission of Migration - FCM and the civil society, integration should be considered as a "dynamic and reciprocal process that requires the involvement of the foreign population and its hosting society. Thus, the whole society should be responsible for the foreign nationals' integration and this cannot be reduced to a simple measuring instrument" (OSAR 2018, p. 4). This assertion develops a perspective that is undoubtedly critical: over the years, the increase in the number of migrants in Switzerland has had a significant impact on public policy making and has given rise to several direct democratic votes (Sciarini 2017). Yet, ultimately, according to the Migration-Mobility Indicators from the NCCR, there has been a significant *restrictive effect* of referendums and popular initiatives on migrants' rights (Arrighi 2017).[11] Direct democratic instruments have, therefore, provided important disabling barriers to migrant integration as they have not effectively managed to challenge 'Fortress' actualities and exclusionary trajectories of boundary construction in the host labour market and society.

References

Amarelle, C., & Nguyen, M. S. (2017). *Code annoté en droit des migrations, Volume II: loi sur les étrangers*. Berne: Stämpfli Éditions SA.

Arrighi, J.-T. (2017). *Dataset on migration referendums and initiatives in Switzerland*. Neuchâtel: NCCR – On the Move.

Boillet, V. (2016). Initiative 'Contre l'immigration de masse': analyse du vote sous l'angle de la démocratie directe. *Revue de Droit Suisse, 135*, 105–133.

Boillet, V., & Maiani, F. (2016). La 'préférence Suisse light' et sa compatibilité avec l'Accord sur la libre circulation des personnes. *Annuaire Du Droit de La Migration*, 61–78.

Cattacin, S. (1996). Die transformation des Schweizer sozialstaates. Überlegungen zu seiner entwicklungslogik. *Swiss Political Science Review, 2*(1), 1–14.

D'Amato, G. (2008). Une revue historique et sociologique des migrations en Suisse. In D. Efionayi-Mäder, A. Monsutti, G. Perroulaz, et C. Schümperli Younossian (Dir.), *Annuaire suisse de politique de développement: Migration et développement; un mariage arrangé* (Vol. 27 (2), pp. 169–187). Gènève: Institut de hautes études internationales et du développement.

Federal Commission for Migration, FCM. (2016). *Economie et travail en point de mire – Prise de Position*, 19 Décembre.

Federal Council, Admission provisoire et personnes à protéger. (2016). *Analyse et possibilités d'action – Rapport*, 12 Octobre.

Fernández, G. G. E., & Abbiate, T. (2018). Switzerland: Vulnerable groups and multiple solidarities in a composite state: Law and public policies in the European Union. In V. Federico & C. Lahusen (Eds.), *Solidarity as a public virtue? Law and public policies in the European Union* (pp. 421–468). Baden-Baden: NOMOS.

FSO (Federal Statistic Office). (2018). *Enquête Suisse de la population active (ESPA)*.

Graf, A.-L., & Mahon, P. (2018, août). Article 121a de la Constitution et accès au marché du travail. *Jusletter*, 1–26.

Hainmüeller, J., Hangartner, D., & Duncan, L. (2016). When lives are put on hold: Lengthy asylum processes decrease employment among refugees. *Science Advances, 2*(8), e1600432.

---

[11] For more information please also refer here: https://indicators.nccr-onthemove.ch/did-federal-referendums-and-initiatives-affect-immigrants-rights/

International Labour Organization. (2017). *National labour law profile: The Swiss Confederation*. http://www.ilo.org/ifpdial/information-resources/national-labourlaw-profiles/ WCMS_158921/lang%2D%2Den/index.htm

Klöti, U., Knoepfel, P., & Kriesi, H. (Eds.). (2007). *Handbook of Swiss politics*. Zurich: NZZ publications.

Kurt, S. (2017a). *Fast-tracking full citizenship in the context of the Swiss integration stage model. NCCR on the move* (Working Paper n°15).

Kurt, S. (2017b). *A modest start: Integration policies in the field of asylum* (NCCR On The Move, Highlights n°2).

Kurt, S. (2017c). Nouvelles exigences en matière d'intégration des étrangers. In plaidoyer 04/2017 du 3 juillet 2017c, 20–24.

Linder, W. (2010). *Swiss democracy, possible solutions to conflict in multicultural societies* (Vol. 3). Basingstoke: Palgrave Macmillan.

Manatschal, A. (2014). Swiss immigration federalism. In S. Baglay & N. Delphine (Eds.), *Immigration regulation in Federal States* (pp. 179–198). Dordrecht: Springer.

Matthey, F. (2015, January 29). 'Admission provisoire': entre admission et exclusion, entre provisoire et indéfini. *Newsletter CSDH*, pp. 1–9.

Mexi, M., Moreno Russi, P., & Fischbach, A. (2019). Policy barriers and enablers of MRAAs' integration to the labour market, Switzerland /Research report. In I. Bontenbal & N. Lillie (Eds.), *Policy Barriers and Enablers* (WP3 Report). SIRIUS Project. https://www.sirius-project.eu/ publications/wp-reports-results. Accessed 15 Nov 2019.

NCCR On the move: Migration mobility indicators. (n.d.). https://indicators.nccronthemove.ch. Accessed 21 Sept 2019.

ODAE Romand. (2017). *Révision de la loi de l'asile*. https://odae-romand.ch/revision-lasi/. Accessed 12 July 2019.

ODAE Romand. (2015). *Permis F: Admission provisoire ou exclusion durable?* Genève. https:// odae-romand.ch/wp/wpcontent/uploads/2010/08/Rapport_Permis_F_admission_provisoire. pdf. Accessed 15 Nov 2019.

OSAR – Organisation Suisse d'Aide aux Réfugiés. (2018). Position relative à la modification de l'OASA, et révision totale de l'ordonnance sur l'intégration des étrangers (OIE). https://www. refugeecouncil.ch/assets/asylrecht/stellungnahmen/180309-osar-prisede-position-oasa-oie. pdf. Accessed 18 Aug 2019.

Piguet, E. (2013). *L'immigration en Suisse. Soixante ans d'entrouverture*. Lausanne: Presses polytechniques et universitaires romandes.

Piguet, E. (2017). Immigration et diversité: la Suisse a-t-elle un secret? La Suisse, une autre vision de l'Europe. *Questions Internationales, 87*, 91–104.

Probst, J., D'Amato, G., Dunning, S., Efionayi-Mäder, D., Fehlmann, J., Perret, A., Ruedin, D., & Sille, I. (2019). SFM Studies #73 Marges de manœuvre cantonales en mutation -Politique migratoire en Suisse.

Refugeecouncil.ch. (2018). *Asylum process*. https://www.refugeecouncil.ch/asylum-law/asylum-procedure.html. Accessed 5 Dec 2019.

Ruedin, D., & D'Amato, G. (2015). Politicisation of immigration in Switzerland: The importance of direct democracy. In W. Van Der Brug, G. D'Amato, & D. Ruedin (Eds.), *The politicisation of migration* (pp. 140–158). Routledge: Abingdon.

Ruedin, D., Alberti, C., & D'Amato, G. (2015). Immigration and integration policy in Switzerland, 1848 to 2014. *Swiss Political Science Review, 0*, 1–18.

Sandoz, L. (2016a). L'interminable chemin vers une place de travail. Experiences. https://www. osar.ch/des-faits-plutot-que-des-mythes/articles-2016/linterminablechemin-vers-une-place-de-travail.html. Accessed 10 Nov 2019.

Sandoz, L. (2016b). The symbolic value of quotas in the Swiss immigration system. NCCR on the Move, highlights # 1 November. https://nccr-onthemove.ch/highlights1/highlights-1-5/. Accessed 10 Nov 2019.

SCHR, Swiss Centre of Expertise in Human Rights. (2015a). *Manuel de droit Suisse des Migrations*. SA Berne: Stämpfli Éditions.

SCHR, Swiss Centre of Expertise in Human Rights. (2015b). L'accès à la justice en cas de discriminations. Synthèse.

SCHR, Swiss Centre of Expertise in Human Rights. (2015c). L'accès à la justice en cas de discrimination. Partie 6. Racisme – Analyse juridique.

Sciarini, P. (2017). Direct democracy in Switzerland: The growing tension between domestic and foreign politics. In R. Saskia, Y. Welp, & L. Whitehead (Eds.), *Let the people rule?: Direct democracy in the twenty-first century*. London: ECPR Press.

Stanic, P. (2018). Révision sur la loi fédérale sur les étrangers: les dispositions concernant l'intégration entrent en vigueur au 1er janvier 2019. Artias Website: http://www.artias.ch/artias_veille/revision-sur-la-loi-federale-sur-les-etrangers-les-dispositions-concernant-lintegration-entrent-en-vigueur-au-1er-janvier-2019/. Accessed 23 Sept 2019.

State Secretariat for Migration – SEM. (2017). Modification de l'ordonnance relative à l'admission, au séjour et à l'exercice d'une acivité lucrative. Rapport explicatif.

State Secretariat for Migration – SEM. (2018). *Migration report 2018*. SFBL. Bern: Federal Publications.

Wichmann, N., Hernann, M., D'Amato, G., Efionayi-Mader, D., Fibbi, R., Menet, J., & Ruedin, D. (2011). *Les marges de manœuvre au sein du fédéralisme: la politique de migration dans les cantons*. Berne: Commission fédérale pour les questions de migration CFM.

Chapter 12
Regulating Fortress Britain: Migrants, Refugees and Asylum Applicants in the British Labour Market

Francesca Calò, Simone Baglioni, Tom Montgomery, and Olga Biosca

12.1 Introduction: From a Multicultural Society to the Fortress Britain

Any analysis of the legal framework concerning the integration of migrants, refugees and asylum seekers should not be isolated from the socio-economic, political and cultural context of a country. The UK has for some time been portrayed as a multicultural liberal society with some studies showing that the integration of migrants in Britain compares relatively favourably with other countries across various measures of social and political integration (Koopmans 2010; Wright and Bloemraad 2012). The emphasis from the mid-1960s until the beginning of the 2000s has been placed on the 'multicultural' society or 'ethnic pluralism', with different groups co-existing but retaining their independent cultural identities (although placing the blame for racial problems on the minority populations) (Ager and Strang 2008). However, over recent years (according to some scholars from 2000 onwards – see for example Joppke 2004) there has been a significant shift in UK public discourses regarding nationhood, prompted initially by race riots in Northern England,[1]

---

[1] For information and details about the race riots and the policy recommendations see Cantle Report (2001).

F. Calò
Department of Public Leadership and Social Enterprise, Faculty of Business and Law, The Open University, Milton Keynes, UK

S. Baglioni (✉)
Department of Economics and Management, University of Parma, Parma, Italy
e-mail: simone.baglioni@unipr.it

T. Montgomery · O. Biosca
Yunus Centre for Social Business and Health, Glasgow Caledonian University, Glasgow, UK

© The Author(s) 2021
V. Federico, S. Baglioni (eds.), *Migrants, Refugees and Asylum Seekers' Integration in European Labour Markets*, IMISCOE Research Series,
https://doi.org/10.1007/978-3-030-67284-3_12

then by concerns over Muslim extremism fostering terrorist threats and exacerbated by the economic crisis and the rise of populist xenophobia alongside anti-migration narratives (Ager and Strang 2008; Geddes and Scholten 2016). From being a multicultural liberal society, which has witnessed a steady growth in immigration, the more recent policies of the UK Government have cultivated a "hostile environment for illegal migrants" (Theresa May speech, 10th October 2013[2]) where nationhood and assimilation processes became central to policies and political narratives (at least at the national level). To understand why Britain changed from a multicultural society to a hostile one, it is important to explore briefly the recent history of migration.

During an earlier wave of migration, in 1948, the British Government adopted legislation (in the form of the British Nationality Act 1948) ensuring that the UK and Colonies received the status of a British subject and was thus entitled to legal, social and political rights. Colonial migrant labour was used to feed the post-war boom while being employed in the growing industrial and public sectors (Geddes and Scholten 2016; Hansen 2003). After 15 years of colonial migration, moves towards greater restriction emerged in the political agenda as a result of an increasing tension within civil society, the rise of a more populist Conservative Party and the lack of public support for the Labour Party in opposing the introduction of more restrictive legislation. Between 1962 and 1970, citizens of Commonwealth countries that had previously been welcomed as British citizens, became subject to immigration controls and strict regulations were applied in particular to family migration. Over time, these changes were reinforced by further legislation through the British Nationality Act 1981 that steadily reduced the rights of Commonwealth citizens.[3]

More recently, from the mid-1990s up until the present day, large scale net migration, the freedom of movement that comes with EU membership (in particular the enlargement from 2004 onwards) and the rise of populist and anti-immigration movements in the political arena (such as UKIP) fuelling concerns in society about immigration were some of the forces that have shaped the contemporary context of migration in the UK (Geddes and Scholten 2016). As net migration increased EU citizens became an important part of this second wave of migrants. European migration was also accompanied by an incremental increase of non-EU net migration, although non-EU migration had always been based upon stricter and controlling policies that incentivised mainly the arrival of high skilled workers, students and people from former colonies with an ancestral connection to the UK.

During the 2000s, issues of asylum became a central focus of migration debates and the scale of the problem of people being forced to flee their home countries is illustrated by the fact that in 2014 there were more refugees globally than any time

---

[2]Theresa May speech accessible at: https://www.theguardian.com/politics/2013/oct/10/immigration-bill-theresa-may-hostile-environment

[3]The British Nationality Act of 1981 abolished the 1948 definition of British citizenship and replaced it with three categories: British citizenship, citizenship of British dependent territories and British Overseas citizenship. Of these, only British citizenship provides the right to live in the UK. From 1981 all foreign nationals have had to apply for naturalisation to become British citizens.

since the Second World War (Geddes and Scholten 2016). Strict controls and a hostile environment (as will be fully explored later in this chapter) towards asylum applications were implemented by the British Government since the 2000s and asylum applications, as well as the numbers of those in the end granted leave to remain consequently remained low in comparison with other countries such as for example Germany, Italy and France (Blinder 2017; Eurostat 2018). Policies focused upon controlling borders remain in place to the present day and issues relating to migration have become a permanent fixture of contemporary political campaigns in the UK, from parliamentary elections to referenda.

A fourth phase of the UK migration history can be traced from 2015 onwards. The election of a new Conservative government with a clear commitment to renegotiate the relationship between the UK and the European Union, the rise of populist political movements and the austerity measures that followed the economic crisis in 2008 have, alongside aspects of the campaign to leave the European Union, contributed to the development of a dominant narrative in UK policymaking that emphasises the securing of borders and a more restrictive disposition towards migration more generally (Montgomery et al. 2018; Wallace 2018). Against this background, tighter restrictions in terms of the rights of Non-EU citizens have been implemented in more recent legislation such as the Immigration Acts of 2014 and 2016, encompassing stricter controls in terms of asylum applications, complemented by the opt-out from the European Union refugee relocation schemes and part of the Reception Conditions Directive.[4]

This changing context is part of a long-term process where anti-migrant and anti-refugee discourses, legislations, and policies have dominated policymaking and the media. For example, anti-migration narratives were placed at the centre of Leave campaign in the 2016 EU referendum (Cummings 2017) and they have also been one of the most frequent arguments advanced by the Conservative party in modern elections (see the Conservative Manifesto 2010 and 2015[5] as well as the 2005 campaign led by Michael Howard). Policies and legislation prioritising the control of immigration instead of integration have been favoured, espousing narratives about the negative effect of migration on public services and on the reduction of wages:

> In the last decade or so, we have seen record levels of long-term net migration in the UK, and that sheer volume has given rise to public concern about pressure on public services [...] as well as placing downward pressure on wages for people on the lowest incomes. The public must have confidence in our ability to control migration. (Department for Exiting the European Union 2017)

Fresh legislation such as the Immigration Act 2014 and 2016, the opt-out from the EU relocation scheme of Syrian refugees and the recent cases involving the deportation of citizens who were part of the Windrush generation[6] are some of the examples

---

[4] https://ec.europa.eu/home-affairs/what-we-do/policies/asylum/reception-conditions_en

[5] Parties policy positions and party policies manifesto are available at: https://manifesto-project.wzb.eu/

[6] The Windrush generation refers to immigrants who were invited to the UK between 1948 and 1971 from Caribbean countries. In 2018, these immigrants who had arrived as children on their parents' passports and they never formally became British citizens have been denied services, lost their jobs and faced deportations, raising what it has been called the Windrush generation scandal.

of the environment that has been created in recent years. The negative frame of the debates about migration has also been reflected and reinforced by the way in which the media portrays refugees and migrants. This hostile environment has been mirrored by political uncertainty following the results of the 2015 and the recent 2017 elections. In a landscape of political tumult, marked by reductions in public spending and cuts to welfare, alongside processes of labour market flexibility, increasing levels of inequality have impacted upon the everyday lives of people in the UK, making the context for promoting and implementing integration and inclusion even more challenging.

12.2   Evolution and Main Stages of Migration and Asylum Law

Legislation concerning the integration of migrants, refugees and asylum seekers into the labour market has always been intertwined with legislation concerning the accessibility of migrants, refugees and asylum seekers to enter the country. In post-war Britain a key piece of legislation relating to migration was developed in 1948 and it constitutes a milestone in migration law. The 1948 British Nationality Act formally gave all subjects of the Crown including British colonies the right to settle in Britain. Citizens from colonies and the Commonwealth countries were enabled to cement their status as British citizens and access the same formal legal, social and political rights as other subjects of the Crown. This relatively open migration regime lasted until 1962, when consequent to an increasing number of race riots and the rise of right-wing populism, the ruling Conservative Party introduced a new Act *(the Commonwealth Immigration Act),* restricting the flow of immigration (Geddes and Scholten 2016). The Act distinguished between citizens of the UK and its colonies and citizens of independent Commonwealth countries. The latter became subject to immigration and employment control through the establishment of work vouchers (a type of visa) which reduced the overall numbers of migrants. In addition, only a few of these vouchers were granted to women, setting a precedent (that is still evident today) of preventing women to enjoy the right to family reunification. In 1968 a second Commonwealth Immigration Bill was introduced, again diminishing the rights of people to enter the UK, particularly those British citizens of Indian descent facing persecution in Kenya and Uganda. New immigration controls based upon the 'patriality' rule were then established. This restrictive legislative framework reached its peak in 1971, with the Immigration Act (1971) which distinguished between citizens of the UK and its colonies that had the right to indefinitely being settled in the UK (patrial rule) and those who instead had to apply for work permits to be granted, (definite) right to remain. More modifications regarding the categories of citizens were established in the British Nationality Act (1981). Three typologies of citizens were defined by this legislation, implying the prioritisation of the "white commonwealth": British citizens, British dependent territories citizens and British overseas citizens. New implications for the colonial citizens were then implemented, amending the status of post-colonial peoples from citizens to migrants.

During the 1980s the issue of migration received less attention from policymakers while it returned to the spotlight from the 1990s onwards. When the New Labour Government (1997–2001) came to power, a more liberal approach to migration was promoted (Hansen 2003; Wright 2017). In 2001, the High Skilled Migrant Programme (renamed the Tier 1 visa) was introduced which established the first points-based system to regulate access to the country. It allowed people entry in relation to factors such as their level of education and earnings, without imposing an upper limit on their numbers. Moreover, work permit (later renamed Tier 2 visa) regulations were loosened to be more responsive to the needs of employers. A key decision of the New Labour period was allowing uncontrolled access to Britain for citizens of the ten member states that joined the European Union in 2004. The UK was one of only three countries that decided not to impose transitional controls on migration from the new EU member states (Wright 2017).

However, in the latter period of the New Labour government, the rhetoric reflected a less open disposition towards migration and marked a return to restrictive policies and legislation. As part of this shift, a five-tier system for labour migration was imposed on Non-EU citizens: Highly skilled migrants (Tier 1), medium skilled migrants (Tier 2), Low skilled and temporary employment visa (Tier 3 – never opened), students (Tier 4) and youth mobility (Tier 5). These more restrictive policies would be continued following the election of the Conservative-led Coalition Government in 2010. Quotas on the numbers of Non-EU arrivals entering the UK (and visas granted to them) were established and a more hostile environment was constructed. The exemplification of this "hostile environment" and legislation were the 2014 and 2016 Immigration Acts. The 2014 Act aimed at facilitating the removal of people without leave to remain, overhauling the appeals process (although following *R (on the application of Kiarie) (Appellant) v Secretary of State for the Home Department (Respondent) [2017] UKSC 42* this part of the Act was dismissed), limiting the access to services such as the National Health System (NHS) and housing to people without the leave to remain and tightening controls on immigration status (Wallace 2018). More restrictive changes were included in the Immigration Act 2016, in which penalties (fines and imprisonment) for employers who hire irregular migrants and landlords who rent premises to irregular migrants were established and everyday necessities such as access to a bank account were revoked for irregular migrants.

A parallel but slightly divergent evolution in asylum law can also be distinguished. Until the 1990s the UK had no specific asylum legislation. The right to claim asylum is based upon international law and governments are obliged to provide protection to people who meet the criteria for asylum. The UK is a signatory to these international laws and has long since integrated them into UK legislation. Three pieces of international law can be used to support an asylum application in the UK: the 1951 Geneva Convention relating to the status of refugees, the 1950 European Convention on Human rights (ECHR) and the European Union Asylum Qualification Directive (2003/9/EC) which lays down minimum standards for the reception of asylum seekers. Excluding the integration of these laws, in the UK, from the 1990s onwards policies and legislation were implemented aiming at curbing the numbers of asylum seekers and at making life more difficult for those who arrived. While a more open although "managed" migration was promoted between 1997 and 2005 (as described above), measures concerning asylum were mainly aimed at reducing the number of applicants (Mayblin 2016). Measures pertained to three different areas: increasing the control of external borders, the reduction of welfare entitlements and denying access to labour markets and speeding up the legal process (Geddes and Scholten 2016). The presumption that underpinned this legislation (enacted both by Labour and Conservative Governments) was that many asylum seekers were not genuine (and were instead "bogus") and thus were undeserving of welfare state support or should not be allowed access to labour markets at least until they were verified as "genuine" (Geddes 2003).

Although the Asylum and Immigration Appeals Act of 1993 integrated the United Nations Convention 1951 definition of asylum claims, it also constituted the first act that reduced the benefit entitlements of asylum applicants, introduced tighter controls on the application process and involved the detention of asylum seekers. The Asylum and Immigration Act of 1996 extended penalties associated with being an irregular migrant and removed access to welfare benefits for "in-country" applicants as opposed to applying at the port of entry and, in 1999, support for asylum seekers (£35 per week using mainly vouchers) was implemented. A no-choice dispersal system across the UK for destitute asylum applicants was enacted to lessen the burden on the London and South East regions. Through the Nationality, Immigration and Asylum Act of 2002 an asylum architecture was created to regulate induction, accommodation and removals including the National Asylum Support Service (NASS) (now the UK Visas and Immigration – UKVI) which assumed responsibility for arrivals, housing and economic support provision (Meer et al. 2018). In 2002, the right to access labour markets for asylum applicants was also removed and to this day it is extremely difficult for asylum seekers to be integrated into the job market (Mayblin 2016). Furthermore, the indefinite leave to remain (the right to stay in the country indefinitely) for refugees was modified into a 5-years leave to remain status with a reassessment of the situation in the country of origin taking place at the end of that period (Bloch 2008). After 2010, the Conservative-led Governments maintained an emphasis on restricting asylum. The focus on speeding up the asylum process and the consequent lack of appropriate time to seek and obtain legal assistance led the British High Court to find the fast-track system unlawful because of an unacceptable risk of unfairness for asylum seekers who have lived through specific trauma. In another example of ever restrictive access, the UK Government also opted out of the EU relocation schemes for Syrian refugees in order to reduce the number of people that the UK would receive (Geddes and Scholten 2016). This brief overview of the main stages of migration and asylum law reveals that UK Governments from the 1990s onwards aimed first at "managing" migration and afterwards focused upon "controlling" migration, imposing a mix of increased border control and reduced internal rights which have contributed to the emergence of the legislative and institutional frameworks of today.

To understand the complex rules that regulate contemporary immigration to the UK, it is useful to provide a brief overview of the right to enter and to have leave to remain in the country for each category of migrants (Non-EU migrants, asylum seekers and refugees that are part of relocation schemes). Each of these categories of migrants must adhere to different regulations and procedures.

12.2.1   Non-EU Arrivals

Non-EU migrants have the right to enter the country (for a period longer than 6 months) if they have a valid entry clearance based upon a visa. A visa has to be released in the country of origin and this can be issued under different schemes which will be fully discussed later in this chapter. The visa can eventually be renewed in the UK based upon valid documentation. After spending a specific continuous period lawfully in the country (from 5 to 10 years depending on the schemes), providing specific documentation, undertaking language and culture tests and presenting specific characteristics (such as not being an illegal entrant), Non-EU migrants can apply for the indefinite leave to remain. Afterwards, they are eligible to apply for British citizenship.

12.2.2   Asylum Seekers and Refugees Status

Very different regulations are applied to asylum seekers in the UK. For someone to claim asylum in the UK, they are required to present themselves to the offices of the UK Border Agency immediately upon their arrival into the country (claiming UK asylum from outside the UK is not legally possible). A person may apply for asylum in relation to the 1951 Convention through fear of persecution in their own country or may instead make a "human rights claim" under the 1950 ECHR, indeed an asylum seeker may make a human rights claim as part of a refugee claim. In terms of human rights, an asylum seeker may make a claim in accordance with Article 3 of the ECHR which protects individuals from torture, inhumane and degrading treatment or in accordance with Article 8 of the ECHR which protects the person's right to a personal and family life. Following a pivotal court case (Regina (Razgar) v Secretary of State for the Home Department 2004) those seeking asylum according to their right to a personal and family life have their claims heard in relation to the "Razgar Test" which aims to balance the rights of the person seeking asylum with the right of the state to effectively control its borders. The Razgar test includes a five-stage test comprehensive of the following issues:

1. Does the [refusal] amount to an interference by a public authority with the exercise of the applicant's right to respect for his private or (as the case may be) family life?
2. If so, will such interference have consequences of such gravity as potentially to engage the operation of article 8?

3. If so, is such interference in accordance with the law?
4. If so, is such interference necessary in a democratic society in the interests of national security, public safety or the economic well-being of the country, for the prevention of disorder or crime, for the protection of health or morals, or for the protection of the rights and freedoms of others?
5. If so, is such interference proportionate to the legitimate public end sought to be achieved?

Once a person makes a claim for asylum they are required to undergo a "screening interview" which involves providing basic information including why the person is seeking asylum and their route of travel to the UK (to assess whether the persons' claim for asylum is the responsibility of another country under the Dublin regulations[7]). At the screening interview, a triage process is implemented. According to the Asylum operating model (2013), the purpose of 'triage' is to identify 'types' of cases and assess them based on the length of time it is likely to take to decide the claim and to finally resolve the case. The triage establishes if the case can be considered an expedited case or not. Expedited cases cover detained fast-track cases and cases where a person will be sent to a European country through which they passed en route to the UK to have the case decided there ('third country cases'). In a non-expedited case, three characteristics will determine the type of cases: the length of time a claim; the likelihood that the claim will be granted; and, thirdly, if refused, the speed at which removal can take place. If asylum applicants are considered destitute, they are eligible for accommodation inside the UK dispersal scheme and a payment of £37.65 per week to cover their essential living needs (ELN).

If an asylum application is accepted, there are two successful forms of asylum, one being "refugee status", the other "humanitarian protection", in both situations the person is awarded limited leave to remain (lasting 5 years), following which they can apply for indefinite leave to remain in the UK and consequently British citizenship. Once asylum seekers have gained leave to remain, they are obliged to leave their accommodation – if provided inside the dispersal scheme – within 28 days and register for administrated welfare support on the same basis as British citizens. For those whose applications are refused, some applicants may have the opportunity to appeal this decision which involves taking their case through a process of tribunal and in those cases where there are challenges as to how the law has been applied, to higher courts, including the UK Supreme Court and the European Court of Human Rights.

---

[7] An overview of the screening interview is available in the policy guidance "Asylum Screening and routing" published by the Home Office in 2018: https://assets.publishing.service.gov.uk/government/uploads/system/uploads/attachment_data/file/700624/screening-and-routing-v1.0ext.pdf

12.2.3   Refugees Under Relocation Schemes

Four resettlement schemes fully funded by the UK's Official Development Assistance (ODA) budget were provided by the UK government in the period 2014 to 2016: the Syrian Vulnerable Persons Resettlement Scheme (VPRS), the Gateway Protection Resettlement programme, the Mandate Scheme and the Vulnerable Children Resettlement Scheme from the Middle East and North Africa (MENA). People who can apply to these schemes are identified by the United Nations and brought directly to the UK (Home Office 2017b). The VPRS is a joint scheme between the Home Office, the Department for International Development and the Ministry of Housing, Communities and Local Government aiming at relocating 20,000 exclusively Syrian persons by 2020. The UK sets the criteria and then UNCHR identifies and submits potential cases (Mulvey 2015). The Home Office screens the potential cases and afterwards, a full medical assessment is conducted by the International Organisation of Migration (IOM). Full details of cases are sent to the local authority and after eligibility to enter the UK has been granted, visas and leave to remain for 5 years are issued under humanitarian protection (Home Office 2017b). At the time of writing, 10,538 people have been involved in the VPRS. A similar process has been established in the Gateway Protection Resettlement programme co-funded by the European Union, which aims at offering a legal route for up to 750 refugees to settle in the UK each year and for the Vulnerable Children Resettlement Scheme which aims at supporting vulnerable and refugee children at risk and their families. Up to February 2018, 539 people have been resettled with the MENA scheme. Finally, the Mandate Scheme is applicable to refugees that have been recognised as such by the UNHCR (from applications in their country of origin or in the country where they were recognised as refugees). Although Mandate Scheme refugees have no entitlement to asylum in the UK, the UK Border Agency accepts that in determining the asylum claim of a Mandate Scheme refugee the decision maker must give mandate status due weight and take it into account when assessing credibility and determining the risk on return.

12.3   Legislation Concerning Migrants, Refugees and Asylum Seekers Integration into Labour Market

The right to work is a restricted privilege to which migrants are granted unequal access in relation to citizens and in relation to each other. Some migrants are able to obtain visas to work in the UK relatively easily, while for others working is prohibited (Mayblin 2016). The next section will outline the different legal statuses and the rights to work in the UK depending on the legal status of migration.

12.3.1   *Non-EU Arrivals*

The Non-EU migrants (excepted asylum seekers and refugees) can apply to various visas to access the labour market in the UK. Three different visa tiers have been established and are currently operating: Tier 1, Tier 2 and Tier 5. Non-EU migrants can apply before arriving to the UK for Tier 1 visas if they are willing to open a business activity (with investment of at least £50,000), they represent an exceptional talent or promise in the field of science, humanities, engineering, medicine, digital technology or the arts (endorsement has to be granted by the Home Office), they aim to invest at least £2 million in the UK or if they are graduate entrepreneurs with an endorsed idea from the Department of International Trade or from a UK Higher Education institution. Until 2015, high skilled migrants achieving a high score in the points-based system[8] were also entitled to apply to Tier 1. However, the programme has since been closed and only extensions are considered. A Tier 2 visa can be requested if a non-EU migrant has received a skilled job offer by one of the recognised and licenced sponsors. Sponsors must offer a salary higher than £30,000 or a job that is included in the shortage occupation list.[9] The Tier 2 visa also includes migrants who are involved in intra-company mobility, are ministers of religion or are an elite sportsperson. Non-EU migrants can apply for the Tier 5 visa if they are willing to volunteer in a charity, they have been sponsored to work as a sportsperson or creative worker, they are aiming to participate in a work exchange programme for a short time, they are employed under international law (e.g. working for a foreign government) or they are working for a religious order. The Tier 5 visa also offers the possibility for young people between 18 and 30 years of age from specific countries[10] to spend a period up to 2 years in the UK (Youth Mobility Scheme).

Although eligibility rules are very different across the different schemes, all non-EU migrants must have a valid clearance for entry under these routes. The majority of the visas request a specific endorsement from a public sector organisation (e.g. the Home Office) or a sponsorship from a list of licensed companies. When an endorsement or the sponsorship is not requested, a high level of skills is necessary, an amount of investment is requested (such as for Tier 1) or there are restrictions concerning the eligible countries (such as for the Youth Mobility Scheme). These regulations clearly increase the barriers to access the UK labour market for non-EU migrants. Most non-EU migrants who are subject to immigration control are also unable to access "public funds" (such as jobseekers' allowance or tax credits), although they can use public services like the NHS and education. Finally, through the Immigration Act 2014 and 2016, an NHS surcharge (Immigration Health

---

[8] In order to be eligible for a visa in any of the five tiers the applicant must pass a points-based assessment. In work visa applications, points are generally awarded according to the applicant's ability, experience and age.

[9] The Shortage Occupation List revised in July 2019 is available at: https://www.gov.uk/guidance/immigration-rules/immigration-rules-appendix-k-shortage-occupation-list

[10] Australia, Canada, Japan, Monaco, New Zealand, Hong Kong, Republic of Korea, Taiwan.

Surcharge) to cover the entire period of the visa has been introduced in the immigration application for all non-EU migrants.

12.3.2 Asylum Seekers

A completely different system and right to work has been established concerning asylum seekers. Asylum policy has been identified as institutionally exclusionist, given that the restriction of rights demarcates asylum seekers as "other" and undeserving (Bakker et al. 2016). According to the Immigration Act of 1999, asylum seekers are explicitly excluded from the labour market. Up until 2002, asylum seekers could request permission to work after 5 months of awaiting their application, but in 2002 this period was extended to 12 months. Moreover, the pending period should not be a consequence of mistakes made by the asylum seeker in the application ("fault of the claimant") (Home Office 2017a). This is in contradiction with the Reception Conditions Directive (COM[2011] 320 final) published in 2011 which only allows a labour market restriction for 6 months (Bales 2013). However, the UK government, as explored in the case law section, rejected the 2011 Reception Conditions Directive. After the 12-month period lapses, asylum seekers can only apply for jobs specified under Tier 2 of the Shortage Occupation list. The Tier 2 restriction was justified by the UK Government due to the legislation on labour market access for Non-EU migrants (explored above). It is therefore very difficult for asylum applicants to comply with the Tier 2 shortage occupation lists and this clearly affects their opportunities for integration, and consequently has an impact on their health and connectedness (particularly of women) (Mayblin 2016; Mulvey 2015). In addition, asylum seekers are also precluded from self-employment and starting a business according to Immigration Rules part 11B (Reception Conditions for Non-EU Asylum Applicants).

Exclusion from employment makes the asylum seekers fully dependent on the state for their means of their existence (Bales 2013). In addition, they are also immediately excluded from the provision of mainstream benefits (such as for example Child Benefit, Disability Living Allowance). Only in those cases where the asylum applicant is considered to be destitute or is likely to become destitute with the next 14 days (section 95 of Asylum Act 1999), do they receive support from the Home Office. Payments to meet essential living needs (equivalent to £37.75 per week) and/or accommodation on a no-choice basis are provided. There is a somewhat different situation for refused asylum seekers: they are generally not entitled to any help, and their accommodation and public welfare support is removed. However, if they demonstrate that they are taking action to leave the country or they can demonstrate that they cannot return to their home due to the situation in their country of origin they could receive basic shelter and a lower level of support.

12.3.3 Refugees

Migrants granted refugee or humanitarian protection statuses (including refugees who are resettled as part of the VPRS) are entitled to work without any restrictions (both as an employee or self-employed) and thus have the same right to work as British citizens. However, the definite leave to remain for 5 years has been identified as a barrier to labour-market access due to the uncertainty surrounding the long-term future of a refugee in employment (Bloch 2008; Stewart and Mulvey 2014). Refugees are eligible for mainstream benefits such as the most recent Universal Credit reform.[11] However, new refugees could face a period without any income due to the specific timeframe of the welfare benefit and the gap with the transition period of 28 days (APPG 2017). Newly recognised refugees are able to apply for an interest-free integration loan to negotiate this period where there is a risk of destitution. The Home Office is responsible for accepting the request while the Department for Work and Pensions is responsible for the payment and the recovery of the loan. Different experiences in terms of welfare entitlement are faced by refugees that are part of the Vulnerable Persons Resettlement Scheme. They, in fact, receive a pre-departure cultural orientation and they are immediately provided with accommodation, a welcome pack, an allowance and support for health and education services.

Table 12.1 summarises the rights to residence, work and welfare access that the different migrants are entitled to.

12.3.4 Constitutional Milestones Case-Law on MRA Access to Labour and Labour Markets

Constitutional milestones in case-law on MRA access to labour markets have been particularly significant in the field of asylum because of the differences in their right to work in comparison with refugees, migrants and citizens (Bales 2013).

Asylum seekers are explicitly excluded from the UK labour market until their claim has been pending for 12 months or until they have been granted refugee status. This restriction contradicts Article 15 (1) of the amended EU Reception Conditions Directive published in June 2011 in which asylum seekers can access labour markets after 6 months. The UK Government, in fact, decided to opt out from the EU Directive amendment. Moreover, after a 12-month period, asylum seekers are limited to applying for jobs specified under Tier 2 of the Shortage Occupation List. This decision was introduced in September 2010 following the case of *ZO (Somalia) and others: (Respondents) v Secretary of State for the Home Department (2010) UKSC 36*.[12] The Supreme Court decided that restricting employment to

---

[11] Universal credit is a social security benefit introduced in 2013 to replace six different benefits and tax credits.

[12] Accessible at: https://www.supremecourt.uk/cases/docs/uksc-2009-0151-judgment.pdf

Table 12.1 Rights entitlement for migrants

Definition/status	Right to residence	Right to work	Welfare rights
Asylum seeker: a person who has applied for asylum and whose application has not yet been decided	Yes, whilst their application is considered	No (curtailed since 2002). Can apply for permission to work after 1 year if the delay of initial claim is not their fault – Only Tier 2 shortage list	Basic accommodation and public welfare support. Must be destitute and willing to accept no-choice dispersal policy
Humanitarian protection: a person whose case does not fit the refugee criteria but who is given permission to enter or remain in the UK because they need protection from harm by others	Yes Granted for 5 years in first instance	Yes	Access to welfare rights on the same base of UK citizens. They need to wait 3 years to access financial support for universities.
Refugee: a person who has received a positive decision on their asylum claim	Yes Granted 5 years temporary leave to remain (since 2005)	Yes	Access to welfare rights on the same base of UK citizens.
Refused asylum seeker: a person whose asylum claim has been refused	No Expected to return to their country of origin	No	Not generally entitled to support. Accommodation and Public Welfare support removed. Basic shelter and support may be available for some hard cases
Non-EU migrant: a person who came to the UK for work and study under a visa programme	Yes. Granted for the time of the Visa	Depending on the Visa (Tier for work)	Education and NHS (NHS Surcharge)

Adapted from Dwyer et al. (2016)

refused asylum seekers, who had made further applications on their claim, was against the Reception Conditions Directive. This decision would have allowed asylum seekers access to the UK labour market after 12 months from their application or appeals. Therefore, the Coalition Government decided to impose the Tier 2 restriction Shortage Occupation List as the only employment possibilities available to asylum seekers. The list includes only very specific high skilled occupations such as for example classical ballet dancers who meet the standard required by internationally recognised United Kingdom ballet companies, physical scientists, engineers or doctors. It is thus evidently challenging for asylum seekers to access the UK labour market once the 12 month period lapses (Mayblin 2016).

According to Section 95 of the Immigration and Asylum Act 1999, asylum seekers are not only excluded from the labour market, but they are also unable to access national welfare benefits. They are provided with cash/vouchers support and/or accommodation if they are considered destitute. According to Randall (2015) destitution has been defined in two different ways. The Home Office under Section 95 of Immigration and Asylum Act 1999 defines destitution as lacking access to adequate accommodation or the inability to meet essential living needs (ELN). Other research instead has defined destitution as lacking shelter, food, heating, lighting, clothing and basic toiletries or having an income level so low that it is not possible to access minimum material necessities. Until *R (Refugee Action) v Secretary of State for the Home Department [2014] EWHC 1033* the definition of essential living needs was not clear (Bales 2015). Consequent to the decision of the Secretary of State in 2013 of freezing the income support to asylum seekers (equivalent at that time to £36.62 per week for a single person), Refugee Action – a charity organisation in England and Wales – sought judicial review of the decision. The judge responded that the rate was not enough to guarantee an adequate standard of living as stipulated by the European Reception Conditions Directive and it did not include items such as household goods, nappies and non-prescription medical goods considered to be essential (Bales 2015). However, after reconsideration by the Secretary of State, the decision was to maintain the same cash support (the rate was increased at the beginning of 2018 from £36.95 to £37.75 according to the Asylum Support Amendment Regulations 2018 No.30). Although the judgement of this case is limited to the confines of this decision, the restrictions on which the asylum support system is built were questioned. The lack of an adequate rate of support for essential living needs affects the integration of asylum seekers, often inducing them to live in poverty and can often increase their risk of exposure to forced and irregular employment.

The third case, and the most recent, dealt with what has become known as the *'deport first, appeal later'* provision, an amendment to the 2002 Nationality, Immigration and Asylum Act, which came into force as part of the Immigration Act 2014. The power to remove a person from the UK pending his/her deportation appeal, where such removal would not be unlawful, was thus established. The provision specifies that the grounds upon which such power may be exercised is that removing the person to the country or territory to which the Home Office proposes to remove them would not cause them to face *'serious irreversible harm.' In the case of R (on the application of Kiarie) (Appellant) v Secretary of State for the Home Department (Respondent) [2017] UKSC 42*, the Supreme Court in March 2018 found this section unlawful. The Court's principal concerns highlighted the barriers for deportees to secure, fund, and instruct legal representatives from abroad, the ability to obtain expert evidence where relevant, and, crucially, the ability of the individual to give effective oral evidence. Therefore "deport first, appeal later" was considered to be a breach of the procedural requirements of Article 8 of the European Convention on Human Rights, that is, the right to an appeal against a decision affecting an individual's right to respect for their private and family life. Thus, asylum seekers as well as refugees and migrants who are awaiting the response of the

Home Office concerning their appeals, are allowed to stay in the country whilst their appeal is being processed.

12.3.5 Anti-discriminatory Legislation

Another piece of legislation which deals with the integration of migrants, refugees and asylum seekers into the labour market concerns anti-discriminatory and anti-exploitation laws (explored in the next paragraph). The UK race relations model has historically been influenced by managing diversity through racial equality, non-discrimination acts and limiting numbers (Scholten et al. 2017). The first attempts to deal with the potential for racial conflict and to tackle racial discrimination can be traced back to the 1960s and 1970s. Three Race Relations Acts (1965, 1968, 1976) were enacted, aiming at banning discrimination on the basis of race, colour or ethnic origin through legal sanctions. Regulatory agencies were also established to promote greater equality of opportunity and access to employment, education and public facilities. However, according to several studies, these goals remained unfilled (Schuster and Solomos 2004).

Only after the election of the Labour government in 1997, were race relations modified, through the 2000 Race Relations (Amendment Act) which enforced on public authorities a new duty to promote racial equality. However, officials from the Home Office that make decisions on immigration cases were excluded. The persistent underemployment of minority ethnic groups resulted in the formation of the Ethnic Minority Employment Task Force in 2003. In 2007 the Equality and Human Rights Commission (EHRC) had taken on the responsibilities of the Commission for Racial Equality and the 2010 Equality Act superseded the four Race Relations Acts, combining everything into a broader framework (Geddes and Scholten 2016). The Equality Act 2010 sets out nine protected characteristics which are: age; disability; gender reassignment; marriage or civil partnership (in employment only); pregnancy and maternity; race; religion or belief; sex; and sexual orientation. The 2010 Act encompasses the protections previously provided by legislation including the Equal Pay Act 1970, the Race Relations Act 1976 and the Disability Discrimination Act 1995. Finally, included in the 2010 Act was a "public sector equality duty" which harmonised some of the existing duties not to discriminate based upon race, disability and gender in public sector organisation. However, criticisms of the Equality Act highlighted that including race alongside other categories has watered down the protection of minorities in terms of discrimination in the labour market.

12.3.6 Anti-exploitation Legislation

Irregular migrants and asylum seekers that face a limited access to benefits and a restriction to the rights to work are often involved in irregular and informal sectors of employment (Dwyer et al. 2016). However, also refugees and regular migrants could be exposed to severe exploitative labour because of the high barriers they face in finding employment (Dwyer et al. 2016). Since 1996, it has been possible to prosecute UK employers for hiring irregular immigrants. Sanctions were further strengthened in 2004 and 2008, up to the arrival of the Immigration Act of 2016 which again increased penalties. Today, those employers who have "reasonable cause to believe" that an employee has no right to work as a consequence of their immigration status can face up to 5 years in prison and an unlimited fine. Although some of the measures are directed at employers, they are likely to affect workers who may become more exploited through employers seeking to manage risks by lowering wages and/or increasing working hours (Dwyer et al. 2016). Unauthorised workers themselves, who became criminalised for the new offence of "illegal working" would also face deportation without appeal if they did not have the right to remain in the UK. The UK, then, is characterised by a strong degree of state intervention to maintain formal labour markets. This legislation, more than tackling informal employment, seems to increase the barriers to access labour markets and indirectly affect the conditions of employment. This also confirms that a major focus, in fact, has been placed on border enforcement and the reduction of irregular migrants instead of improving working conditions. Trade unions and community organisations have thus asserted some role in campaigning and promoting better working conditions for migrants and ethnic minorities. For example, the Living Wage campaign in London is a key case example of unions and community organisations working together to improve working conditions for a mainly migrant group of workers.

12.4 Integration in the UK Labour Market: Institutional Challenges

The lack of a national strategy for the integration of migrants, refugees and asylum seekers is one of the main institutional challenges and barriers that can be identified in the UK context (MacIver 2016). Integration has, in fact, remained notably absent from policy, at least since 2010 (Meer et al. 2018). Refugees are the only category for which the UK Government has introduced an integration strategy in 2000 (*Equal Citizens*) that aimed at supporting refugee access to jobs, benefits, accommodation, health, education and language classes (Mulvey 2015). In addition, initial policies were aimed at supporting the involvement of third sector organisations in service provision (Cheung and Phillimore 2017). A second refugee integration strategy was developed in 2005, firstly through the Strategic Upgrade of National Refugee

Integration Service (SUNRISE) and then via the Refugee Integration and Employment Service (RIES). These two programmes aimed at enabling integration through the signposting to mainstream services across key social policy areas. Both programmes were operated by the Refugee Councils and local authorities and they helped to assist refugees to recognise their own skills and experience, improving their ability to access employment services (Bloch 2008). However, after the General Election in 2010 and due to the austerity measures that followed, the integration programmes were closed, placing the responsibility of integration fully in the hands of local government and communities (Bales 2013). While a range of government departments have been under pressure to reduce their budgets, migrants, refugees and particularly asylum seekers were targeted as a relatively easy area for austerity measures. Asylum seekers are unable to vote, unable to work and are often portrayed negatively in the media (Darling 2016; Sales 2002). Thus, instead of focusing on integration policies, the major focus of the UK Government has been on increasing barriers at entry, investing in removals and creating an inhospitable and difficult environment for all migrants. In recent years the policy emphasis shifted from separate and specific immigrant integration policies to the broader social inclusion and mobilities priorities (van Breugel and Scholten 2017).

A dark picture comes out also from the potential enablers of integration into labour market. The UK Government identifies language learning and education as key facilitators of the integration of MRA (Meer et al. 2018). Acquisition of language has been identified as central to obtain employment, increase social connectedness and achieve positive health and well-being (Bakker et al. 2016). However, despite the focus of the UK Government on English-language abilities in its policies, funds to provide courses have been reduced. Asylum seekers were excluded from free access to English courses in England (Mulvey 2015) and restrictions on the provision of courses for refugees were also established. According to Court (2017), between 2008 and 2015, there was a 50% funding reduction of English as a Second or Other Language (ESOL) classes. Increasing waiting lists and a lack of provision in the local community were among some of the effects of this funding reduction. Although a £10 million funding scheme has been announced in 2016 for providing free English classes, these courses are only accessible to Syrian refugees who arrived through the VPR Scheme (MacIver 2016). For the other refugees there are no specific funding streams except those that are dedicated to any other individuals who meet the eligibility criteria. As described above, education is one of the areas devolved to subnational constituent nations of the UK. Thus, the level of access to education differs across these nations. In Scotland, for example, education policies have worked alongside Scottish Government integration approaches to provide access for both refugees and asylum seekers to education (Meer et al. 2018). All children and young people from different backgrounds including asylum seekers and refugees have universal access to compulsory education in Scotland. For those over the age of 16, fees for attending college and studying full or part-time course are waived. In addition, ESOL classes are offered to all migrants independently from their legal status and programmes to integrate local communities and migrants through English language courses have been provided.

Concerning education, the UK exercised its right under Protocol 21 not to opt-in to the Qualification Directive (Directive 2011/95/EU). Thus, the UK does not apply the Directives with respect to procedures for the recognition of qualifications, in particular, the equal treatment between refugees and nationals and access to schemes for the assessment and validation of prior learning. The UK has a National Recognition Information Centre (NARIC) who is responsible for providing information and advice on the skills and qualifications of all migrants and it provides international qualifications conversion. Support for university access is fragmented and dependent upon the legal status of the migrant. For example, refugees have the same access to University as British students (with the same fees as home students) and scholarships alongside loans are often offered. Migrants that arrive with the aim of studying in the UK have to pay a higher level of fees than home students and do not have access to the same levels of financial support (APPG 2017).

Some vocational programmes of work placement and job intermediation initiatives have also been implemented. Examples of this are the Phoenix Mentoring Project or the Bridges Programmes which arrange short-term placement and mentoring activities. The Phoenix Mentoring project in Newcastle aims at supporting young asylum seekers and refugees between 16 and 25 years old in a process of learning and development based upon a one-to-one mentor support programme. The Bridges Programmes based in Scotland aims at providing employability support to migrants, refugees and asylum seekers, investing in further education, short work placement programs (not paid placement) and vocational training. However, the risk of losing Job Seekers Allowance during the work placement programmes has been identified as a disincentive for participation in vocational schemes (MacIver 2016) and the entry criteria ascribed by the professional standards required in the UK, the difficult process of re-qualifications and examinations have been identified as barriers to access the labour market in these sectors (Piętka-Nykaza 2015). Some training schemes have been developed to incentivise refugees to be self-employed and run their own businesses. The Refugees into Business scheme, for example, supported applicants in each of the steps necessary to set up a small enterprise. However, the lack of a national strategy and policies in terms of educational access and training, multiplies the risk of creating a fragmented and project-based response to integration issues, a response that risks being insufficient to address the complex and multifaceted path of inclusion.

Scotland

Migration is one of the policy fields where the divergence between Westminster and Holyrood (Scottish Parliament) is evident (Mulvey 2015). Outside of the borders issues and the naturalisation process, most policies that could affect integration processes, such as health, education, some aspects of welfare and housing are devolved. Recently, a narrative of a dynamic two-way integration process and engagement was promoted in the New Scots 2014–2017 strategy and an integration infrastructure based upon this dynamic two-way process was advocated by the Scottish Government (Meer et al. 2018). In fact, the recent New Scots Refugee integration 2018–2022 strategy defined clearly the integration path detailing the responsibility both on the displaced and the settled population in different fields such as employability, welfare, housing, education, health and social connections. A specific Race Equality Framework for Scotland was also enacted in 2016 to promote race equality and tackle racism and very recently a campaign about the integration of migrants (#WeAreScotland) has been launched.

Concerning asylum applicants, the Scottish Government decided to focus on integration from the moment asylum seekers arrive in Scotland and not only when refugee status has been granted. This means that while rights to work and to access mainstream benefits are still restricted for asylum seekers (due to the Westminster immigration rules above explored), education, healthcare, and free English courses are instead available not only to refugees but also to asylum applicants and rejected asylum seekers. However, for some services the jurisdiction remains contentious (Meer et al. 2018), for example, in the housing sector, while the Home Office is responsible for the dispersal accommodation, the standards of housing are regulated by the Scottish Government.

Multi-agency networks that include several different stakeholders have been established in Scotland and in particular in Glasgow to promote services aimed at integrating MRA (Meer et al. 2018). For example, the Holistic Integration Service has been provided at regional level through a partnership of non-profit organisations and educational organisations and is aimed at supporting people that have recently been granted the refugee status, facilitating finding accommodation, applying for welfare benefits and accessing the labour market (see Strang et al. 2018 for more information). Two specific programmes were also promoted at a regional level to support integration into employment: the Refugees into Teaching in Scotland programme implemented between 2004 and 2011 and the New Refugee Doctors Project from 2016, subsequent to the UK wide Refugee Doctors scheme. Another initiative, the Bridges programme (non profit organisation) was also established from 2002 aiming to connect employers and migrants, refugees and asylum seekers, to introduce people to the labour market. These are just some of the examples of the programmes sustained in Scotland which are useful to highlight the different approach that has been endorsed. However, a fragmented approach with diverse initiatives and projects promoted by different organisations has been also identified as a barrier to long-term integration, with the risking of simply moving people from one project to another without a long-term outcome (Meer et al. 2018).

Wales

Tensions between the levels of governance involved in migration policy can be evidenced also in the Welsh case. Although the Welsh government is not responsible for UK migration policies, as in the case of Scotland it is responsible for several devolved competencies such as housing, social services, education and healthcare. Contrary to Scotland, Wales has not yet developed an integration strategy, but it has published a specific approach towards migrants, refugees and asylum seekers in several pieces of legislation, such as the Well-Being of Future Generations (Wales) Act 2015, the Social Services and Well-Being (Wales) Act 2014, or in policies plans such as the Community Cohesion and Refugee and Asylum seeker Delivery plan (Spencer and Sanders 2016). The Social Services and Well-Being (Wales) Act established that people who do not have leave to remain in the UK are not excluded from the provisions of services. In the Community Cohesion Delivery Plan 2016–2017, a specific outcome on raising awareness on migration has been promoted, while key actions to increase the availability of information for migrants and the communities where they live have been undertaken. The specific plan concerning refugees and asylum seekers details collaborative actions in sectors such as housing, social care, education and employment. Concerning employment, programmes aiming at increasing the skills and opportunities for MRAs have been promoted in collaboration with non-profit organisations and educational institutions.

12.5   Conclusion

Our analysis of the UK context presents a very challenging environment for the integration of migrants, refugees and asylum seekers. The legislation of previous decades has been mainly based on increasing border control and decreasing entitlements to migrants, asylum seekers and refugees. Scarce attention has been placed upon strategies of integration and inclusion, based upon the idea (dismissed by several studies) that employment will constitute a pull factor in terms of migration and that the presence of migrants, in a period of economic crisis, affects the displacement of national workers. The main legislation has emphasised control of borders and have systematised a hostile environment towards migration, involving employers, landlords, banks, universities and even the NHS in controlling the presence of irregular migrants. This hostile environment has seen its peak in the Spring of 2018, in which the former Home Secretary has been forced to resign after the scandal of Windrush generation deportation and admitting to there being targets for the removal of irregular migrants.

This lack of integration policies in the UK has been highly criticised by the UNHCR. Diversity has been mainly managed through racial equality and non-discrimination acts. But this does not seem enough to stimulate a process of integration and inclusion, which has been defined as a complex multidimensional path that affects different policy areas. The cross-cutting nature of policymaking in the field of integration has also generated tensions between the national and subnational level of government. Scotland and Wales, in fact, have promoted a different narrative and they have promoted integration strategies (Scotland) or specific delivery plans (Wales) in their devolved responsibilities, which not only include migrants and refugees but also asylum seekers and failed asylum applicants. Although local authorities and third sector organisations have a fundamental role in trying to address issues of integration, they have been affected by the austerity measures and their funds have been depleted in recent years. This alongside a lack of strategic coordination has generated a fragmented approach that risks undermining the aim of facilitating long-term inclusion.

Migrants, refugees and particularly asylum seekers represent a relatively easy target for austerity measures due to the increasingly negative narrative promoted by policy-makers and the UK media. Asylum seekers are the main targets of such policies. The prohibition of working, the lack of access to mainstream benefits and the freezing of support implemented in the last 20 years of legislation have deeply affected the lives of people that are waiting for their asylum claim to be processed. Increasing poverty and health inequalities among migrants with different legal statuses and between citizens and migrants have been increasing. Some of the rhetoric distinguishing between those who are deserving and undeserving in terms of welfare appears to lead us to question if there is now a tangible dividing line between the valorisation of high skilled immigrants who invest or work in jobs with occupational shortages compared to those with low skills or those who seek asylum. This division most probably will not improve with the results of the Brexit referendum. The risk of opting out from the European directives that have invested in promoting an adequate standard of living and the fair reception of migrants and refugees and in improving workers' rights will certainly have an impact on migrants in the UK.

However, rather than conclude that as a consequence of social, cultural and institutional change, the only future is a hostile environment for migrants, asylum seekers and refugees alongside a lack of integration, we argue that there is space to promote positive processes of integration. Through understanding the barriers and enablers that could facilitate or hinder inclusion into labour markets, it would hopefully be possible to counteract the hostile environment of today. However, the only way to test this idea thoroughly is to undertake a more in-depth analysis into what constrains or hinders integration processes into employment at macro (policies), meso (civil society and social partners) and micro (individuals) levels. This is our intention in the future stages of our research agenda.

References

Ager, A., & Strang, A. (2008). Understanding integration: A conceptual framework. *Journal of Refugee Studies, 21*(2), 166–191. https://doi.org/10.1093/jrs/fen016.

APPG. (2017). *Refugees welcome? The experience of new refugees in the UK*. All Party Parliamentary Group on Refugees.

Bakker, L., Cheung, S. Y., & Phillimore, J. (2016). The asylum-integration paradox: Comparing asylum support systems and refugee integration in The Netherlands and the UK. *International Migration, 54*(4), 118–132. https://doi.org/10.1111/imig.12251.

Bales, K. (2013). Universal credit: Not so universal? Deconstructing the impact of the asylum support system. *Journal of Social Welfare and Family Law, 35*(4), 427–443. https://doi.org/10.108 0/09649069.2013.851168.

Bales, K. (2015). The 'essential living needs' of asylum seekers: Lessons learned from R (Refugee Action) v Secretary of State for the Home Department [2014] EWHC 1033. *Journal of Social Welfare and Family Law, 37*(2), 247–249. https://doi.org/10.1080/09649069.2015.1028159.

Blinder, S. (2017). *Migration to the UK: Asylum* (Migration Observatory Briefing). Oxford: COMPAS, University of Oxford.

Bloch, A. (2008). Refugees in the UK labour market: The conflict between economic integration and policy-led labour market restriction. *Journal of Social Policy, 37*(1), 21–36.

Cantle, T. (2001). *Community cohesion: A report of the Independent Review Team*. London: Home Office. Retrieved from http://tedcantle.co.uk/pdf/communitycohesion%20cantlereport.pdf.

Cheung, S. Y., & Phillimore, J. (2017). Gender and refugee integration: A quantitative analysis of integration and social policy outcomes. *Journal of Social Policy, 46*(2), 211–230. https://doi.org/10.1017/S0047279416000775.

Court, J. (2017). 'I feel integrated when I help myself': ESOL learners' views and experiences of language learning and integration. *Language and Intercultural Communication, 17*(4), 396–421.

Cummings, D. (2017, January 9). Dominic Cummings: How the Brexit referendum was won. *The Spectator*. Retrieved from https://blogs.spectator.co.uk/2017/01/dominic-cummings-brexit-referendum-won/

Darling, J. (2016). Asylum in austere times: Instability, privatization and experimentation within the UK asylum dispersal system. *Journal of Refugee Studies, 29*(4), 483–505. https://doi.org/10.1093/jrs/few038.

Department for Exiting the European Union. (2017). *The United Kingdom's exit from and new partnership with the European Union White Paper* (Policy Paper). London: Department for Exiting the European Union. Retrieved from https://www.gov.uk/government/publications/the-united-kingdoms-exit-from-and-new-partnership-with-the-european-union-white-paper.

Dwyer, P., Hodkinson, S., Lewis, H., & Waite, L. (2016). Socio-legal status and experiences of forced labour among asylum seekers and refugees in the UK. *Journal of International and Comparative Social Policy, 32*(3), 182–198. https://doi.org/10.1080/21699763.2016.1175961.

Eurostat. (2018). *Asylum quarterly report*. Retrieved from http://ec.europa.eu/eurostat/statistics-explained/index.php/Asylum_quarterly_report#Further_Eurostat_information

Geddes, A. (2003). Migration and the welfare state in Europe. *The Political Quarterly, 74*(s1), 150–162. https://doi.org/10.1111/j.1467-923X.2003.00587.x.

Geddes, A., & Scholten, P. (2016). Britain: The unexpected Europeanisation of immigration. In *The politics of migration and immigration in Europe*. Los Angeles: Sage.

Hansen, R. (2003). Migration to Europe since 1945: Its history and its lessons. *The Political Quarterly, 74*(s1), 25–38. https://doi.org/10.1111/j.1467-923X.2003.00579.x.

Home Office. (2017a). *Permission to work and volunteering for asylum seekers* (Guidance Report No. 7). London: Home Office.

Home Office. (2017b). *Syrian vulnerable resettlement scheme (VPRS) guidance for local authorities and partners*. London: Home Office.

Joppke, C. (2004). The retreat of multiculturalism in the liberal state: Theory and policy1. *The British Journal of Sociology, 55*(2), 237–257. https://doi.org/10.1111/j.1468-4446.2004.00017.x.

Koopmans, R. (2010). Trade-offs between equality and difference: Immigrant integration, multiculturalism and the welfare state in cross-national perspective. *Journal of Ethnic and Migration Studies, 36*(1), 1–26. https://doi.org/10.1080/13691830903250881.

MacIver, A. (2016). *From refugees to workers. Mapping labour-market integration support measures for asylum seekers and refugees in EU Member States – The United Kingdom case study* (Research Report No. Volume II-Literature Review and Country Case Studies). BertelsmannStiftung.

Mayblin, L. (2016). Complexity reduction and policy consensus: Asylum seekers, the right to work, and the 'pull factor' thesis in the UK context. *The British Journal of Politics and International Relations, 18*(4), 812–828. https://doi.org/10.1177/1369148116656986.

Meer, N., Peace, T., & Hill, E. (2018). *The governance and local integration of migrants and Europe's refugees: the UK, Scotland and Glasgow* (Research Report No. WP2). University of Glasgow.

Montgomery, T., Calo, F., & Baglioni, S. (2018). *Claims making and the construction of the refugee crisis in Brexit Britain* (Research Report). Glasgow: TransSOL Project.

Mulvey, G. (2015). Refugee integration policy: The effects of UK policy-making on refugees in Scotland. *Journal of Social Policy, 44*(2), 357–375. https://doi.org/10.1017/S004727941500001X.

ONS. (2017). *Migration levels: What do you know about your area?* Retrieved from https://www.ons.gov.uk/peoplepopulationandcommunity/populationandmigration/internationalmigration/articles/migrationlevelswhatdoyouknowaboutyourarea/2017-08-24

ONS. (2018). *Long-term international migration estimates methodology*. London: Office for National Statistics. Retrieved from https://www.ons.gov.uk/peoplepopulationandcommunity/populationandmigration/internationalmigration/methodologies/longterminternationalmigrationestimatesmethodology.

Piętka-Nykaza, E. (2015). 'I want to do anything which is decent and relates to my profession': Refugee doctors' and teachers' strategies of re-entering their professions in the UK. *Journal of Refugee Studies, 28*(4), 523–543. https://doi.org/10.1093/jrs/fev008.

Sales, R. (2002). The deserving and the undeserving? Refugees, asylum seekers and welfare in Britain. *Critical Social Policy, 22*(3), 456–478.

Scholten, P., Collett, E., & Petrovic, M. (2017). Mainstreaming migrant integration? A critical analysis of a new trend in integration governance. *International Review of Administrative Sciences, 83*(2), 283–302. https://doi.org/10.1177/0020852315612902.

Schuster, L., & Solomos, J. (2004). Race, immigration and asylum – New labour's agenda and its consequences. *Ethnicities, 4*(2), 267–300.

Spencer, S., & Sanders, S. (2016). *Developing a strategic approach to integration in Wales* (Research Report). Oxford: COMPAS, University of Oxford and Welsh Refugee Council.

Stewart, E., & Mulvey, G. (2014). Seeking safety beyond refuge: The impact of immigration and citizenship policy upon refugees in the UK. *Journal of Ethnic and Migration Studies, 40*(7), 1023–1039. https://doi.org/10.1080/1369183X.2013.836960.

Strang, A. B., Baillot, H., & Mignard, E. (2018). 'I want to participate.' Transition experiences of new refugees in Glasgow. *Journal of Ethnic and Migration Studies, 44*(2), 197–214. https://doi.org/10.1080/1369183X.2017.1341717.

van Breugel, I., & Scholten, P. (2017). Mainstreaming in response to superdiversity? The governance of migration-related diversity in France, the UK and the Netherlands. *Policy and Politics, 45*(4), 511–526. https://doi.org/10.1332/030557317X14849132401769.

Wallace, T. (2018). Policy-driven evidence: Evaluating the UK government's approach to immigration policy making. *Critical Social Policy, 38*(2), 283–301. https://doi.org/10.1177/0261018317726251.

Wright, C. F. (2017). Employer organizations and labour immigration policy in Australia and the United Kingdom: The power of political salience and social institutional legacies. *British Journal of Industrial Relations, 55*(2), 347–371. https://doi.org/10.1111/bjir.12216.

Wright, M., & Bloemraad, I. (2012). Is there a trade-off between multiculturalism and socio-political integration? Policy regimes and immigrant incorporation in comparative perspective. *Perspectives on Politics, 10*(1), 77–95.

Ingram Content Group UK Ltd.
Milton Keynes UK
UKHW020807180623
423483UK00016B/556